THE
BORDERS
OF
"EUROPE"

THE BORDERS OF "EUROPE"

Autonomy of Migration, Tactics of Bordering

NICHOLAS DE GENOVA, EDITOR

Duke University Press · Durham and London · 2017

Library of Congress Cataloging-in-Publication Data
Names: De Genova, Nicholas, editor.
Title: The borders of "Europe" : autonomy of migration, tactics of bordering /
Nicholas De Genova, editor.
Description: Durham : Duke University Press, 2017. | Includes bibliographical
references and index. | Description based on print version record and
CIP data provided by publisher; resource not viewed.
Identifiers: LCCN 2017007582 (print) | LCCN 2017014618 (ebook)
ISBN 9780822372660 (e-book)
ISBN 9780822368885 (hardcover : alk. paper)
ISBN 9780822369165 (pbk. : alk. paper)
Subjects: LCSH: Europe—Emigration and immigration. | Europe—Boundaries. |
Border security—Europe. | Refugees—Europe.
Classification: LCC JV7590 (ebook) | LCC JV7590 .B675 2017 (print) | DDC 325.4—dc23
LC record available at https://lccn.loc.gov/2017007582

Cover art: Refugees next to the fence on the Macedonian side of the border as they wait to go back to Greece near Gevgelija, a town in southern Macedonia, Wednesday, March 2, 2016. AP Photo/Visar Kryeziu

A special note of gratitude is owed to Kristofer Chan and Alejandro Coca Castro for their care and persistence in the preparation of the customized maps included throughout this volume (with the exception of the map reconstructing the chain of events of the "left-to-die boat" case in chapter 3, which was produced by the authors, Charles Heller and Lorenzo Pezzani, with SITU Research).

CONTENTS

ACKNOWLEDGMENTS

In his "Reflections on Exile," Edward Said notes that there is "a particular sense of achievement in acting as if one were at home wherever one happens to be." During my years of exile in London, I inhabited the peculiar hybrid condition of being both a relatively privileged labor migrant (professional, academic) and a virtual political refugee. Despite the sometimes bitter alienation that characterizes any exile, I enjoyed the rare and precious gift of contemplating my predicament in Europe—and indeed, the predicament of "Europe"—simultaneously from multiple angles of vision. To a great extent, this was made possible by the intellectual companionship and political camaraderie afforded by the contributors to this volume, whom I have known as my students, colleagues, or both. I have learned much about the borders of "Europe" through their fine research and scholarship, which has been a source of constant stimulation and inspiration. Together, albeit in our discrepant ways, we have become dedicated to asking what I have come to call the European Question. While I scrutinized their "home" from the critical perspective of the exiled "outsider," they afforded me the hospitality that made it possible to feel something of both the gratifying comfort as well as the intense disquiet of being both "within and against" a place. In short, in their various ways, the contributors to this book afforded me a kind of "home" in exile, for which I am profoundly grateful. As Said notes, however, an exile understands deeply that a home is always provisional, and that its borders and boundaries, which may provide familiarity and security, can also become prisons. Thus, confronted with my eligibility for permanent residence in Britain, I opted instead to leave. I am therefore gratified to have had the opportunity to showcase in this volume the work of a cohort of junior scholars who are confronting and challenging precisely how the borders of "Europe" (home, more or less, for nearly all of them) operate as cruel mechanisms of confinement and subjugation. This exploration of the borders of "Europe" is a testament to the journey we have made together.

—NICHOLAS DE GENOVA
Chicago, January 2017

The Borders of "Europe" and
the European Question

NICHOLAS DE GENOVA

Today everything is immigration.
—DONALD TUSK, President of the European Council, September 3, 2015

We cannot point to a place, state or continent called Europe which readily reveals its
borders, edges or divisions to an impartial observer. On the contrary . . . debates about
the frontiers of Europe are unavoidably political interventions which interject elements
of fixture into the fluid and ambiguous space that is Europe.
—WILLIAM WALTERS, "Europe's Borders," 487

The representation of Europe's borders is, of course, symbolic. But the signs and symbols
have a history.
—TALAL ASAD, "Muslims and European Identity," 220

European Deathscape

This book has arisen in the midst of what has been ubiquitously and virtually
unanimously declared in mass-mediated public discourse and the dominant
political debate to be a "crisis" of migration in Europe.

The first intimations of a European crisis arose amid the unsightly accumulation of dead black and brown bodies awash on the halcyon shores of the
Mediterranean Sea. When a ship transporting as many as 850 migrants and
refugees capsized on April 19, 2015, all but 28 of the vessel's passengers were sent to
their deaths in what appears to have been the worst border-crossing shipwreck

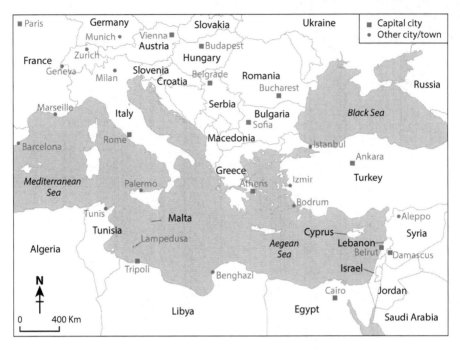

MAP INTRO.1. Central and Eastern Mediterranean

in the Mediterranean on record. This single event instantly established the prospect that 2015 would earn the dubious distinction of the most deadly year to date for would-be asylum-seekers striving to reach Europe's borders. Subsequently, unnumbered capsized "migrant boats" and incidents of mass death turned that grim likelihood into gruesome fact. These human catastrophes at sea have indisputably transformed the maritime borders of Europe into a macabre deathscape (cf. Andersson 2012; De Genova 2015c; Heller et al. 2012; IOM 2014; Jansen et al. 2015; Pezzani and Heller 2013; Rygiel 2014; Stierl 2016; see also Heller and Pezzani, this volume).[1] During the ensuing months, the accumulating momentum of a gathering storm of human mobility over both sea and land served to fix in place a newfound dominant common sense about a "migrant crisis." Then, on September 2, 2015, social media (followed by mass news media) briefly became captivated by haunting photographs featuring the corpse of a drowned Syrian boy, soon identified as Aylan Kurdi, washed ashore in Turkey after a failed attempt to reach the Greek island of Kos left at least 12 people dead. Abruptly, the desensitizing and rather cynical rhetoric of a mi-

MAP INTRO.2. The Aegean Sea, featuring Greek islands

grant crisis began to recede in favor of appeals for compassion in the face of tragedy, accompanied by a reinvigorated (if ephemeral) language of "refugee crisis" (New Keywords Collective 2016).

The putative crisis surrounding the influx of migrants and refugees in Europe—and the border spectacle that it generates (De Genova 2002, 2013a)—has long been nowhere more extravagantly put on display than in the Mediterranean Sea. Alongside the proliferation of migrant deaths in transit in border zones across the planet, the Mediterranean has incontestably earned the disgraceful distinction of being the veritable epicenter of such lethal border crossings.[2] Indeed, for several years now, the European Union (EU) has actively converted the Mediterranean into a mass grave (see Heller and Pezzani, this volume). The singularity or momentousness of the April 19, 2015, shipwreck was in fact only apparent, therefore, because it came as merely the most ghastly and most publicized in a long and unrelenting list of comparable episodes that have utterly banalized such human disasters, and which continued during the ensuing months. The toll of migrants and refugees who perished in transit to Europe during 2016 predictably exceeded the number of lives lost in 2015, but with considerably less publicity. Indeed, prior to the record-high death tolls of 2015 and 2016, untold tens of thousands of ordinarily nameless refugees, migrants, and their children had already been consigned to horrific, unnatural, premature deaths by shipwreck and drowning, often following protracted ordeals of hunger, thirst, exposure, and abandonment on the high seas.[3] Prospective migrant shipwrecks have perhaps been abated intermittently and inconsistently during one or another period of heightened search-and-rescue operations by the various enforcers of the borders of Europe (see Andersson; Garelli and Tazzioli, this volume), but it is likewise probable that countless potential incidents of mass migrant and refugee deaths at sea have been circumvented by the sheer versatility of migratory movements that have sought alternate routes over land in the aftermath of such human tragedies. Hence, following the April shipwreck, although there continued to be a record-high volume of migration across the central Mediterranean for months, there was also increasing evidence of a massive reorientation of migratory movement to land routes through the Balkans.[4]

Of course, the option of illegalized travel by land routes is also treacherous: hunger, thirst, exposure, abandonment, and the related lethal risks are not the exclusive travails of illegalized maritime journeys (Andersson 2014b; Ataç et al. 2015; Lecadet 2013a; Tazzioli 2013; see also Garelli and Tazzioli; Lecadet; Soto Bermant; Stierl, this volume). On August 27, 2015, for instance, Austrian police discovered an abandoned meat truck on the highway at Nickelsdorf near the Hungarian border, in which 71 mainly Syrian and Iraqi migrants and refugees' bodies were decomposing in a sealed refrigeration compartment. Hundreds if not thousands of migrants and refugees have died of asphyxiation after extended periods of overcrowded transit by road or rail in sealed, unventilated shipping containers and other means of clandestine (illegalized) transport over land, while others have merely met their doom after dangling precariously from the bottoms of moving trains and trucks. In addition, migrants must navigate the sometimes deadly violence of European border enforcement authorities, as well as their "non-European" counterparts to whom they frequently outsource the most aggressive sorts of border policing, and also other European police forces routinely engaged in the everyday work of superintending migrant precarity (Andersson 2014a, 2014b; see also Andersson; Soto Bermant; and Stierl, this volume).[5] Indeed, another form of border casualty arises from the lack of access to critical health care during extended periods of migrant transit, or the callous disregard for migrants' and refugees' medical needs during detention or deportation (Flynn and Cannon 2010).[6] Furthermore, any consideration of the diffuse violence of these extended border zones must not neglect to consider the less systematic but no less systemic physical attacks of far-right anti-immigrant racists (Ataç et al. 2015; De Genova 2015d; see also Stierl, this volume).

What presents itself as a "crisis" of territorially defined state powers over transnational, cross-border human mobility—in short, what is fundamentally a moment of governmental impasse on the European scale—has been mobilized and strategically deployed as "crisis" or "emergency" for the reconfiguration of tactics and techniques of border policing and immigration and asylum law enforcement (New Keywords Collective 2016). This has been pronouncedly true in Europe, but these sociopolitical processes and struggles resonate far beyond the borders of Europe. In this regard, it is instructive to briefly reflect upon the conceptual framework that informs this volume. For it is the sheer incorrigibility of migrant and refugee subjectivities and their mobility projects—the autonomy of migration—that has instigated a crisis on the scale of Europe as such.[7]

The mass movements of refugees and migrants in Europe and beyond signify different and disparate problems from the varied and opposed perspectives at play. Sovereign power is manifested through the complex and contradictory formations of diverse European authorities and jurisdictions—notably including not only the supranational state formation of the EU and the various nation-states involved, whether EU members or not (across and beyond "Europe"), as well as an array of nonstate actors, from private capitalist enterprises to "smuggling" networks to humanitarian agencies—arrayed in what we may consider to be a heterogeneous and contradictory border regime (Hess 2010; Tsianos and Karakayali 2010) or assemblage (Mezzadra and Neilson 2013). From the standpoints of this plurality of contenders for sovereign power, the "crisis" customarily appears to be a problem defined principally in terms of (border) "control" and (migration and asylum) "management." This putative crisis therefore summons the ever-reinvigorated and convulsive recalibration of strategies for border policing and immigration and asylum law enforcement, and thus always resolves itself into a dispute over the most effective and efficient tactics of bordering. Yet it is not difficult to see that these strategies and tactics, even when they are anticipatory and presumably regulatory—whether they are intended to preempt or, alternately, to facilitate or even proactively channel one or another formation of border crossing—are always themselves embedded within larger reaction formations.

Border patrols and the diverse efforts of state powers aimed at border control have everywhere arisen as reaction formations. They are responses to a prior fact— the mass mobility of human beings on the move, the manifest expression of the freedom of movement of the human species, on a global scale. Consequently, the heterogeneous tactics of bordering respond to all the unpredictable and intractable dimensions of the elementary subjectivity and autonomy of migration. Thus, these two key figures—the autonomy of migration and the tactics of bordering—are central to and mutually constitutive of the agonistic, if not antagonistic, drama that repeatedly manifests itself as the pervasive crisis of what is finally an effectively global border regime. Even to designate this elementary and elemental fact and primacy of human mobility as "migration," however, is already to risk colluding in the naturalization of the borders that serve to produce the spatial difference between one or another state formation's putative inside and outside, constructing the very profoundly consequential difference between the presumably proper subjects of a state's authority and those mobile human beings variously branded as "aliens," "foreigners," and indeed "migrants." Here, it is important to underscore that such human mobility has come to be pervasively construed as migration only to the extent that it is understood to involve the crossing (or transgression) of one or another sort of state-imposed border. If there were no borders, there would be no migration— only mobility (De Genova 2013b). Nonetheless, such borders themselves have only acquired their contemporary significance and materiality—indeed, their productivity—as the effect of histories of reactive tactics on the part of state powers in response to these human movements and their double-faced, double-voiced politics of mobility and presence (De Genova 2009, 2010d). Yet the movement of people around the world, and hence across these border zones, came first. The multifarious attempts to manage or control this autonomous mobility have always come as a response. Confronting the statist perspective of a global regime of borders, the basic human freedom of movement thus could only ever seem to be perfectly incorrigible (De Genova 2010d). What presents itself as the autonomy of migration, therefore, is finally but a particular manifestation of a more elementary and elemental exercise of the human freedom of movement (De Genova 2010b).

A Question of "Crisis"

Regardless of the specific sites and forms of bordering, migrants' and refugees' lives have been mercilessly sacrificed—usually with callous disregard, occasionally with sanctimonious hypocrisy—in the interests of instituting a "new" Europe encircled by ever-increasingly militarized and securitized borders. Hence, following the reports of the April 19, 2015, shipwreck, as has happened repeatedly, so many times before and since, European authorities were immediately catapulted into a political frenzy to redress this "tragedy of epic proportions."[8] Predictably, however, despite the obligatory pronouncements of exalted humanitarian ideals, the ensuing discourse was compulsively preoccupied with "illegal" migration[9] and the "criminal" predations of "smugglers" and "traffickers" as pretexts for renewed and expanded tactics of militarized interdiction, including proposals to bomb the coasts of Libya from which many maritime border crossers depart, or even to deploy ground troops (Traynor 2015a; cf. Garelli and Tazzioli 2017). Whereas Maltese Prime Minister Joseph Muscat suggested that history would judge Europe and "the global community" in ways comparable to the outcry following the disregard of past genocides for being blind to these beleaguered migrant and refugee movements "of epic proportions," Italian Prime Minister Matteo Renzi resorted rather more strategically to a discourse that likened migration across the Mediterranean (now equated with human trafficking) to slavery,[10] denouncing it as "a plague in our continent" (BBC News 2015). In other words, the invocation of tragedy was cynically conscripted to supply the pretext for reinforcing and exacerbating precisely the material and practical conditions of possibility for the escalation in migrant deaths—namely, the fortification of various forms of border policing that inevitably serve to channel illegalized human mobility into ever more perilous pathways and modes of passage. That is to say, if migrant smuggling is to be genuinely likened to slave-trading (and indeed, if it is to be sincerely decried as "a plague"), it is precisely the European authorities who have the power to completely (and more or less immediately) eliminate it—by reversing the very border enforcement that makes it an utter necessity.

Even to the extent that part of the official debate turns on the question of various formulations of a kind of military humanitarianism (Garelli and Tazzioli 2017; Pallister-Wilkins 2015; Tazzioli 2014, 2015a; Vaughan-Williams 2015; cf. Agier 2006, 2011; Walters 2011a; Williams 2015; see also Andersson; Garelli and Tazzioli; Heller and Pezzani, this volume), whereby European authorities may be charged with expanded responsibilities for the "rescue" of so-called migrant boats in distress on the high seas, every ostensible rescue comes to be haunted for the illegalized border crossers by the ambiguous prospect of apprehension and indefinite detention, with deportation as a defining horizon. Indeed, the commonplace deployment of the term *asylum-seeker* inherently invokes the specter of the allegedly bogus refugee seeking undue benefits or the presumably undeserving (merely "economic") migrant opportunistically claiming asylum. Indeed, here we may recognize that these people on the move across state borders are not in fact considered to be the genuine bearers of any presumptive (purportedly universal) "human right" to asylum, but rather are always under suspicion of deception and subterfuge, produced as the inherently dubious claimants to various forms of institutionalized international protection (Griffiths 2012; see also Garelli and Tazzioli; Lecadet; Scheel, this volume). Similarly, the pervasive depiction of refugees as (mere) migrants has been a crucial discursive maneuver in the spectacle of Europe's border crisis. Little surprise, then, that begrudging gestures of belated magnanimity toward those who are ultimately granted the status of bona fide refugees by European authorities have been coupled with promises of expedited expulsion for those who may eventually be deemed to be only "migrants"—unwelcome, presumably "irregular" and hence undesirable, illegalized, and deportable all (Ataç et al. 2015; see also Lecadet; Picozza, this volume).[11]

Mass media news coverage has vacillated remarkably between depictions of a European "refugee crisis" and the implicitly more derisive label "migrant crisis." Ambivalence and equivocation around the very labels by which various forms of human mobility are presumed to be knowable are telling signals of the ambiguities and contradictions that bedevil such terminological categories as governmental contrivances (Garelli and Tazzioli 2013a; Tazzioli 2013, 2014; see also Garelli and Tazzioli; Osseiran; Picozza, this volume). It is telling that literally every article related to these topics published by BBC News, to choose one prominent example, is accompanied with a kind of disclaimer: "A note on terminology: The BBC uses the term migrant to refer to all people on the move who have yet to complete the legal process of claiming asylum. This group includes people fleeing war-torn countries such as Syria, who are likely to be granted refugee status, as well as people who are seeking jobs and better lives, who governments are likely to rule are economic migrants." In short, in this example and many others, an epistemic crisis related to migration and refugee movements is deflected and displaced: the vexed question of how to most appropriately characterize people on the move across nation-state borders is deferred to a presumed eventual decision on the part of the proper governmental authorities, the ostensible experts, who purport to manage Europe's border regime by sorting and ranking distinct mobilities—in this case, assessing asylum claims and adjudicating the matter of who may be deemed to qualify as a legitimate and credible refugee (see Garelli and Tazzioli, this volume). Accordingly, until such a day of reckoning, all refugees may be reduced to the presumed status of mere migrants. Again, we are reminded that the very term *asylum-seeker* is always already predicated upon a basic suspicion of all people who petition for asylum within a European asylum system that has routinely and systematically disqualified and rejected the great majority of applicants, and thereby ratifies anew the processes by which their mobilities have been illegalized (De Genova 2013a, 2016a, 2016b; see also Lecadet; Scheel, this volume). Here, indeed, we may appreciate that borders are not simply spatial technologies but also operate in ways that are fundamentally dedicated to the *temporal* processing of distinct mobilities, ultimately consigning various categories of mobile people to one or another protracted trajectory of indeterminate and contingent subjection to the governmentalities of migration (see Osseiran; Picozza, this volume).

The ongoing crisis of European borders, therefore, corresponds above all to a permanent epistemic instability within the governance of transnational human mobility, which itself relies on the exercise of a power over classifying, naming, and partitioning migrants/refugees, and the more general multiplication of subtle nuances and contradictions among the categories that regiment mobility. Indeed, such a proliferation arises as an inescapable effect of the multifarious reasons and entangled predicaments that motivate or compel people to move across state borders, or alternately find themselves stranded en route, temporarily but indefinitely stuck someplace along the way on their migratory itineraries (Andersson 2014b; Collyer 2007, 2010; Dowd 2008; Lecadet 2013a; Tazzioli 2013; see also Garelli and Tazzioli; Lecadet; Osseiran; Picozza; Stierl, this volume). Simply put, refugees never cease to also have aspirations and, against the dominant tendency to figure them as pure victims (and thus as the passive objects of others' compassion, pity, or protection), they remain *subjects* who make more or less calculated strategic and tactical choices about how to reconfigure their lives and advance their life projects despite the dispossession and dislocation of their refugee condition (see Garelli and Tazzioli; Osseiran; Picozza; Stierl, this volume). And likewise, migrants are often in flight (or fleeing) from various social or political conditions that they have come to deem intolerable, thereby actively escaping or deserting forms of everyday deprivation, persecution, or (structural) violence that may be no less pernicious for their mundanity (Mezzadra 2001, 2004; see also Lecadet, this volume). Hence, the labels migrant and refugee commonly remain suspended in a state of tension and ambiguity, and may only be sorted into neat and clean distinctions or separated by hermetically sealed partitions through more or less heavy-handed governmental interventions.

In the face of the resultant proliferation of alternating and seemingly interchangeable discourses of migrant or refugee crisis, the primary question that must be asked, repeatedly, is: *Whose crisis?* The naming of this crisis as such thus operates precisely as a device for the authorization of exceptional or emergency governmental measures toward the ends of enhanced and expanded border enforcement and immigration policing. The spectacle of Europe's migrant crisis is largely equated, consequently, with a crisis of *control* over the ostensible borders of Europe (New Keywords Collective 2016). One such

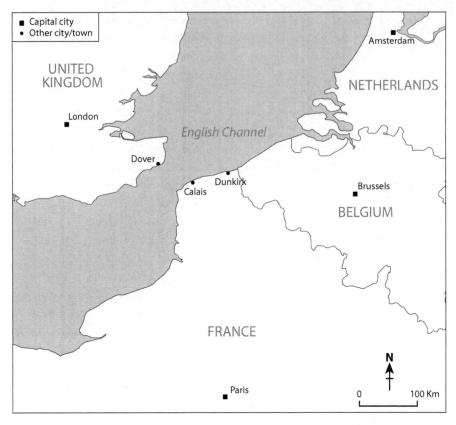

MAP INTRO.3. Calais (France)

European border, configured at the port of Calais in France (near the entrance to the Channel Tunnel connecting Britain to the continent), has long been a site where migrants and refugees have regrouped their energies during more or less protracted periods of deceleration in the makeshift camps notoriously known as "the Jungle" (Millner 2011; Reinisch 2015; Rigby and Schlembach 2013; Rygiel 2011; Tazzioli 2015b; see also Picozza, this volume).[12] Following militant strike action by French port and ferry workers at the end of July 2015, several hundred migrants and refugees (perhaps as many as a few thousand) charged the Eurotunnel barriers in an effort to board trucks and trains heading into Britain, provoking massive traffic delays. French authorities deployed riot police, and the British constructed a new razor-wire fence. Confronting this "Calais crisis," British Prime Minister David Cameron reacted with promises of deportations and alarmist calls for more aggressive border policing to stop the migrant "swarm," accompanied by the clamor of British tabloid newspapers calling for the authorities to "send in the army" (Elgot and Taylor 2015).

Remarkably, by August, September, and October 2015, literally from week to week and even day to day, the apparent front line of European border struggles was repeatedly dislocated from one country to another, oftentimes further and further removed from any imagined outer periphery or frontier of Europe, in a dramatic dialectic of contestation between diverse migrant and refugee autonomies and a feckless heterogeneity of tactics of bordering. These ostensible frontline dramas of the borders of Europe had moved decidedly inward, from the shores of Italy, Malta, and Greece (or Greece and Bulgaria's land borders with Turkey) to Macedonia, Serbia, and Hungary, then further still into Austria and Germany, and then back again to Croatia and Slovenia. Eventually, by November, Germany, Austria, the Czech Republic, Slovakia, the Netherlands, Belgium, France, Italy, Spain, and Sweden had all begun to reintroduce temporary border controls, and pronouncements became commonplace asserting that the Schengen agreement—widely considered to be one of the paramount achievements of European integration—was effectively dead.[13]

Notably, brutal border spectacles of "exclusion" have often exposed their own obscene dynamics of subordinate (illegalized) migrant "inclusion" (De Genova 2013a; cf. 2002:439, 2008; see also Soto Bermant, this volume). The various deployments of military troops or riot police against migrants and refugees, the construction of razor-wire barricades, and assaults against migrant and refugee families with tear gas, stun grenades, rubber truncheons, and eventually live ammunition[14] have been intermittently alternated with the outright facilitation or the de facto ferrying of these same migrant movements through the provision of bus caravans and trains to expedite transit onward. Hence, state tactics of bordering have been abundantly shown to be convulsive reaction formations, responding always to the primacy of the sheer autonomy of migration. This was perhaps nowhere more dramatically manifest than in the self-mobilization on September 4, 2015, of refugees and migrants who had been encamped in Budapest's Keleti railway station. Hungarian riot police had begun to deny migrants access to trains by which they aspired to travel on to Austria and Germany, and had attempted to forcibly evacuate some of them. Following various skirmishes with the riot police in the makeshift refugee camp in the train station, and then a devious rerouting of trains by the authorities toward "transit" (detention) camps outside the city, at least 1,000 migrants and refugees chanting "Freedom!" indignantly coalesced into an ad-hoc protest march (quickly designated the March of Hope) and, following the determined leadership of a one-legged man, defiantly proceeded onto a six-lane highway leading out of the country. This action promptly culminated in the Hungarian state authorities' capitulation and compliance, albeit cynical and self-serving, with the urgency of the refugees' determination to freely move forward on their chosen itineraries. The march was provided a police escort and then buses that would transport the unruly refugees and migrants further along on their journeys toward the next border. Likewise, Austria and Germany promptly confirmed that their borders were open (Hartocollis 2015; see also Kasparek and Speer 2015). Just the day before, Hungary's right-wing Prime Minister Viktor Orbán had proclaimed that Europe's putative magnanimity toward refugees and migrants was "madness," and argued that his attempts to close the border with Serbia with a razor-wire fence were a matter of defending Europe's "Christian roots" against a Muslim menace (Traynor 2015b). Orbán has repeatedly declared baldly that Hungary does not welcome the prospect of granting residence to refugees, and Muslim refugees in particular. Earlier in the summer, Hungary had already announced its refusal to honor the Dublin Regulation (by which other European signatory states could deport refugees to Hungary if they had originally registered there as asylum claimants). In short, much like Italy, Malta, Greece, and Bulgaria previously, Hungary—now as a frontline defender of the borders of the EU—had come to actively resist the imperative that it do the proverbial dirty work of insulating the wealthiest EU member states from migrants and refugees seeking ultimately to resettle where they would have better prospects (see Osseiran; Picozza, this volume).

Such junior partners in the fragmented and externalized bordering of "Europe"—including EU member states (such as Hungary), non-EU European states (such as several Balkan countries), and "non-European" states subcontracted to preempt migratory movements before they ever reach European territory (from Turkey through North Africa, and even several sub-Saharan African countries)—have been poignantly depicted as "wardens of the European border regime" (Ataç et al. 2015; cf. Andersson 2014a, 2014b; see also Andersson; Lecadet; Soto Bermant, this volume).[15] Indeed, as in the case of Hungary, the more aggressive tactics in Europe's extended border zones have sometimes served to proactively and cynically redirect human mobilities onward toward other borders within other states' jurisdictions (see Andersson; Heller and Pezzani; Lecadet; Soto Bermant, this volume). Yet, during much of what Bernd Kasparek and Marc Speer have called Europe's "long summer of migration" (2015), "It was as if the transit countries had made an unspoken pact: move along, there's nothing to see here." Then, in September, Hungary instituted emergency legislation in the border zone that threatened all border crossers with up to three years' imprisonment—in flagrant disregard of any and all petitions for asylum—in an extravagant gesture of renewed commitment to its assigned role in enforcing the borders of Europe. "Paradoxically," as Kasparek and Speer underscore, "Hungary is now being pilloried for its callous attempts at maintaining the rules of the European border and migration regime, while Germany, regardless of its role as architect and driving force of that very regime, wins worldwide acclaim for its humanitarian stance."[16] Indeed, after having initially opened their borders to the mass movement of refugees and migrants, Austria and Germany were later prompted to reinstitute their own border controls in the face of the sheer volume and velocity of human mobility through Hungary, in order to better manage the crisis. Most importantly, despite their more draconian proclivities, Hungarian authorities opted to do nothing in the face of the refugees' defiant march through Budapest except assist them on their way toward the border with Austria. Thus the example of Hungary is merely the most dramatic instance of a recurrent vacillation between vicious violence and begrudging complicity on the part of state actors seeking to reinstitute Europe's borders in the face of the veritable intractability of migrant and refugee movements. The crisis of border control and migration management may therefore be seen to be a crisis of sovereignty that is repeatedly instigated, first and foremost, by diverse manifestations of the autonomous subjectivity of human mobility itself.

The Cross-Contamination of "Crisis"

Precisely when the discourses of migrant/refugee crisis seemed to have reached an unsustainable crescendo, the grisly spectacle of "terrorism" in Paris on November 13, 2015, supplied the catalytic event that could conjure anew the well-worn specter of "Muslim extremism." Ornamented with a (fake) Syrian passport fortuitously deposited in the vicinity of one of the bombings, the horrific bloodbath in the heart of urbane Europe was quickly conscripted to allege that the seemingly uncontrollable refugee influx was somehow providing cover for a nefarious ambush by the putative enemies of "civilization" itself, and therefore that the refugee (or migrant) crisis truly represented a security threat, after all.[17] Notably, within a few hours of the events in Paris—and within days of having been branded a "lawless slum" that presented the risk of an "infiltration" of "guerrilla warfare"—the migrant and refugee camps at Calais were subjected to what appeared to be an arson attack (Campbell 2015). Thereafter, in the ensuing days, amid the predictable (indeed, obligatory) speculations about a hydra-headed phantasm of "foreign fighters" and "homegrown extremists" traveling unhindered between combat zones in Syria and Western European countries,

France—long among the most stalwart advocates of European integration—stridently called for an unprecedented securitization of the external borders of the EU's Schengen zone of free mobility. Within a week of the events, amid police raids against Muslim "suspects" across multiple countries, and various calls for mass internment, deportations, and the electronic monitoring of such alleged suspects, EU interior and justice ministers convened an emergency meeting and vowed to institute significantly tighter external border controls and expanded surveillance over human mobility, citizen and noncitizen alike. The urgent push to create new "hotspot" migrant and refugee reception and processing facilities (i.e., detention camps) at sites of illegalized border crossing (Garelli and Tazzioli 2016a; Sciurba 2016), likewise, came now to be reimagined as a matter of perimeter defense against terrorist infiltration, refigured as vital strategic sites for "culling terrorist wolves from refugee sheep" (Lyman 2015). Despite the fact that all of the alleged culprits identified were in fact (racialized minority) Europeans, therefore, the spectacle of terror nevertheless served quite effectively as a virtually unquestionable pretext for dramatically reinvigorated border enforcement.

With various aspects of the Paris attacks associated in one way or another with the Muslim-identified (predominantly Moroccan and Turkish) migrant neighborhoods in the Brussels suburb of Molenbeek, where some of Belgium's most impoverished racialized "minority" communities live in close proximity to some of its most affluent white ones, *The Guardian* newspaper proclaimed Molenbeek's "unique place in European jihadism," and nominated the borough "Europe's jihadi central." In the days following the Paris attacks, and referring to the prominence of Molenbeek in European counterterrorist policing efforts, Belgian Prime Minister Charles Michel proclaimed, "Now we'll have to get repressive" (Traynor 2015c). Four months later, a few days after the arrest in Molenbeek of the prime suspect in the Paris attacks, three bombings in Brussels on March 22, 2016, including one in the Molenbeek metro station, reanimated anew the twin spectacles of terror and security. Once again, despite the manifest absence of migrants or refugees in these events, the specter of Europe's homegrown (disaffected, "second-generation," racialized minority) "Muslim extremist" citizens—routinely racialized as being "of migrant background"—has served to reconfirm the pernicious affiliation between migrant and refugee noncitizens with the threat of a corrosive and inimical pathology festering within the bosom of Europe.

Following the violent events in Paris that served to reenergize the securitarian figuration of "the Muslim"—as a condensation of religious fundamentalism, fanaticism, radicalization, and terrorism—as Europe's premier Other, the abrupt outbreak in January 2016 of a moral panic over multiple sexual assaults during the New Year's Eve festivities in Köln/Cologne promptly delivered up yet another instantiation of the ostensible Muslim Problem. Allegedly perpetrated by unruly mobs of young men, casually characterized as being "of North African or Middle Eastern appearance," the Cologne events reinvigorated the racialization of "Muslim" identity. In the face of these offenses, the racialization of "Muslims"/"Arabs" (eagerly depicted as including asylum-seekers) could now be represented in terms of unsavory cultural differences that had to be excoriated and criminalized as transparently inimical to "European" norms of civility and moral decency. Revealingly, the eminent philosopher and cultural critic—and avowed ("leftist") Eurocentric—Slavoj Žižek seized upon the refugee crisis as an occasion to unabashedly celebrate Europe, demanding: "Isn't the very fact that millions want to go to Europe proof that people still see something in Europe?" (2016b). Confronting the Cologne events, then, Žižek unsurprisingly adopted the condescending moralistic standpoint of European (white) supremacism: "Immigrant refugees," as he designated them, "are well aware that what they are doing is foreign to our predominant culture, but they are doing it precisely to wound our sensitivities. The task is to change this stance of envy and revengeful aggressiveness. . . . They have to be educated (by others and by themselves) into their freedom" (2016a). Making his commitment to a culturalist Europeanism still more explicit and emphatic, Žižek goes further: "Europe needs to be open to refugees, but we have to be clear they are in our culture. Certain ethical limits . . . are non-negotiable. We should be more assertive toward our values. . . . Europe means something noble—human rights, welfare state, social programs for the poor. All of this is embodied in enlightenment of the European legacy" (2016b). Elsewhere, discussing the wider question of the refugee "crisis," and exuding his characteristic flair for unapologetic authoritarianism, Žižek likewise contends:

> Europe should organize itself and impose clear rules and regulations. State control of the stream of refugees should be enforced through a vast administrative network encompassing all of the European Union. . . . Refugees should be reassured of their safety, but it should also be made clear to them that they have to accept the area of living allocated to them by European authorities, plus they have to respect the laws and social norms of European states. . . . Yes, such a set of rules privileges the Western European way of life, but it is a price for European hospitality. These rules should be clearly stated and enforced, by repressive measures (against

foreign fundamentalists as well as against our own anti-immigrant racists) if necessary. (2015)[18]

Decrying the self-righteous and condescending liberal multiculturalist tendency to engage in the "humanitarian idealization of refugees" (2016c) or to objectify refugees as mere victims, notably, Žižek's insistence upon a recognition of the agency and subjectivity of the migrant/refugee Other thus becomes the occasion for projecting the migrant/refugee's subjectivity as an unsavory and misguided one: "not just escaping from their war-torn homelands; they are also possessed by a certain dream," while nonetheless "offering themselves to become cheap precarious workforce, in many cases at the expense of local workers, who react to this threat by joining anti-immigrant political parties" (2015). Consequently, he suggests, refugees must be held to account for their own "responsibility in the crisis" (2016b).

Deemed to be dangerously deficient in terms of "European values," presumptively newly arrived, culturally alien, unassimilated (and by implication, unassimilable) Muslim/Arab asylum-seekers were now refigured, in the aftermath of the Cologne events, as probable sexual predators and potential rapists, suspected of dangerous and violent types of putatively cultural tendencies toward flagrant misogyny and "uncivilized" forms of deviancy and perversity. Thus, a menace previously fashioned as the rather more rarefied threat of terrorism could now be dramatically expanded to encompass virtually all Muslim men as potential criminals. Predictably, this anti-Muslim moral panic was laced with racial hysteria: images proliferated in the mass media in Germany of white women's bodies stained or otherwise graphically violated by black or brown hands. Even the iconic innocent—Aylan Kurdi, the three-year old Syrian boy found dead on the shores of the Aegean Sea—was now, just a few months later, callously denigrated in a cartoon published by the notoriously anti-Muslim French satirical magazine *Charlie Hebdo*. Under the titular heading "Migrants," the drawing depicts two lascivious pig-like (or ape-like) men with lolling tongues and outstretched groping hands, chasing two women. An insert at the top the cartoon duplicates the famous image of Kurdi, laying face-down on the beach, drowned. The top of the page poses the purportedly comical riddle: "What would little Aylan have become if he had grown up?" The answer appears at the bottom of the page: "Ass fondler in Germany." Plainly, the cynical and derisive insinuation was that even this helpless and harmless victim, by sheer dint of the barbaric moral deficiencies of his despised Muslim heritage, could only have inevitably become a vicious perpetrator, one more predatory miscreant, like all the rest of the Muslim migrant men alleged to have perpetrated the sexual assaults in Cologne. Thus, the figure of the refugee—so recently fashioned as an object of European compassion, pity, and protection—was refashioned with astounding speed, first as the potential terrorist who surreptitiously infiltrates the space of Europe, and then as the potential criminal/rapist who corrodes the social and moral fabric of Europe from within.

Most significantly, the controversy around the Cologne events immediately authorized public debates over how recently arrived refugees and migrants could be expeditiously rendered deportable and promptly expelled. The rather selective logic of antiterrorist suspicion that has been mobilized for the purposes of more stringent (external) border enforcement, once confronted within the European interior with the palpable presence of recent arrivals of "Muslim" refugees and migrants, was promptly repurposed as a considerably more expansive problem of internal law enforcement, emphatically conjoined to arguments for new powers to unceremoniously deport allegedly criminal asylum-seekers. Thus, nebulous and spectral affiliations are invoked to encompass refugees, ("illegal") migrants, smugglers, sexual deviants, religious fundamentalists, criminals, homegrown and international terrorists, and "foreign fighters" along an inchoate continuum of suspicion and contempt: the "fake" asylum-seeker therefore reappears now not only as the actual (duplicitous) economic migrant, but also as the (deviant) rapist whose culture or morals are simply inimical to the "European" way of life, or as the (devious) terrorist who conceals himself among the genuine refugees in order to wreak havoc on Europe. Above all, migrant and refugee mobilities and subjectivities have instigated for European authorities an epistemic and governmental dilemma regarding an amorphous mob composed simultaneously of people "in need of protection," shadowed by the specter of predators or enemies against whom Europe itself must be protected. Hence, the "emergency" associated with the uncontrolled arrival of migrants and refugees quickly became not only a matter of border enforcement but also of mundane policing, and signaled an incipient crisis not only of the borders of Europe but also of the entire fabric of the European social order.

A Question of "Europe"

The profound source of the intractable crisis of migration in Europe is the veritable struggle over the borders of Europe—migrants' and refugees' struggles to realize their heterogeneous migratory projects by exercising their elementary freedom of movement, thereby appropriating mobility, transgressing the border regime, and thus making spatial claims, as well as the struggle of European state powers to subdue and discipline the autonomy of migration (cf. Ataç et al. 2015; Garelli and Tazzioli 2013a, 2013b; Kasparek and Speer 2015; Pezzani and Heller 2013; Rigo 2011; Tazzioli 2015b; see also Gambino; Lecadet; Picozza; Scheel; Soto Bermant, this volume). Notably, the European border crisis has been commonly depicted in depoliticizing language as a humanitarian crisis with its root causes always attributed to troubles elsewhere, usually in desperate and chaotic places ostensibly "outside" of Europe. These putative elsewheres, beyond the borders of Europe, are systematically represented as historically sanitized, which is to say, shorn of their deeply European (post)colonial histories as well as disarticulated from the European political and economic interests implicated in producing and sustaining their fractured presents.

The refugees and migrants whose mobilities may be productively understood to appropriate the space of Europe (cf. De Genova 2016a, 2016b; Garelli et al. 2013; Garelli and Tazzioli 2013a; Mezzadra 2006; Tazzioli 2015b) nevertheless most commonly originate from places across Africa, the Middle East, and Asia that were formerly the outright or de facto colonies of European masters. In effect, migrants arriving in Europe today, much as has been true for several decades, originate from places that were effectively mass-scale prison labor camps where their forebears contributed to collectively producing the greater part of the material basis for the prosperity, power, and prestige of Europe, historically. In other words, virtually all migrations and refugee movements that today seek their futures in Europe have been deeply shaped by an indisputably European (colonial) past. Furthermore, particularly for those who flee the devastation of war and military occupation or civil war—from Afghanistan or Iraq to Syria, Libya, Somalia, or Mali (to name but a few)—the expansive human consequences of what Derek Gregory (2004) has incisively called the U.S.-dominated, global "colonial present" (cf. De Genova 2010a) are likewise inextricable from their entrenched and enduring European "post"-colonial entanglements. Consequently, with the imposition, enforcement, and continuous reconfiguration of a European border over the last decades, a brave new Europe has, in effect, been busily redrawing the colonial boundary between a European space largely reserved "for Europeans only" and the postcolonial harvest of centuries of European exploitation and subjugation (De Genova 2010c, 2016a, 2016b; cf. van Houtum 2010; van Houtum and Pijpers 2007; see also Soto Bermant, this volume). Thus, it is a new Europe, fortified by very old and morbid cruelties.

The spatialized partitioning of Europe from its putative outside notably begins within Europe itself, where the borders of Europe and the boundaries of European-ness have repeatedly been reinstituted in the uneasy borderlands that extend eastward (see Dzenovska, this volume). The legacies of the Cold

1	Netherlands
2	Switzerland
3	Czech Rep.
4	Slovakia
5	Hungary
6	Slovenia
7	Croatia
8	Serbia
9	Macedonia

MAP INTRO.4. Europe Provincialized

War have ensured that some regions of "the East" of Europe have been and largely remain a crucial reserve of migrant labor, both within and across the borders of EU citizenship and mobility (Dzenovska 2013a, 2014). This is particularly pertinent with regard to the Balkans, as Europe extends eastward toward Turkey as the perhaps most enduring Orientalized frontier (Mastnak 2003). It is, of course, not incidental that it is precisely the southeastern European countries that previously found themselves within the realm of the Ottoman Empire, where many Europeans themselves are Muslim, that the borders of Europe become riddled with ambiguity, whereby cultural essentialisms can be readily converted into effectively racialized ones. In this manner, European-ness comes to encompass a variegated and contradictory nexus of racialized formations of whiteness that extend toward a series of "off-white" or "not-quite-white" borderland identities. Hence, the recent prominence of "the Balkan route" for migrant and refugee movements has been haunted by the awkward fact that several European countries which emerged from the genocidal dissolution of Yugoslavia have yet to be (re)admitted into the self-anointed circle of genuine and proper European-ness. Moreover, while there have been intimations that some of these illegalized mobile subjects (particularly Syrians) may ultimately be recognized to be credible and worthy recipients of the status of "refugees,"[19] there are concurrent and insistent assurances that speedy deportation will be the rightful fate of others who may be rejected as mere "migrants." Predictably, the great majority of sub-Saharan Africans are counted among the asylum-seekers preemptively deemed to be immediately eligible for rejection, but notably included among these are also those originating in the Balkan countries themselves. Here, importantly, in addition to the duplicitous insinuation that the devastating effects of the internecine violence of the Yugoslavian civil wars can now be assumed to be simply over and done, and consequently the reductive presumption that human mobilities from the Balkan region are purely economic in motivation, we must also be alert to the systematic deployment of "Balkan" and other "Eastern European" regional or national-origin categorizations for the elision and euphemization of the specificity of Roma (Gypsy) mobilities, in particular (Fox 2012; Fox et al. 2012; Grill 2012a, 2012b). As one of the foundational and constitutive internal racial alterities of Europe, the Roma are now reconstructed anew as a mobile (racialized, criminalized) menace to the stability and integrity of (Western) European "civilization," whose flight from protracted poverty and entrenched marginalization must not even conceivably be apprehensible as the mobility of refugees fleeing institutionalized persecution and structural violence within Europe (Fekete 2014; Hepworth 2012, 2014, 2015; Riedner et al. 2016; Sigona and Trehan 2009; van Baar 2011a, 2011b, 2015; Yildiz and De Genova n.d.).

Consequently, the crisis of European borders is eminently political, in manifold ways. Most importantly, these struggles expose the fact that the borders of Europe are never reducible to anything resembling immutable, integral, internally consistent, or objective boundaries corresponding to any self-evident "natural" fact of physical geography. Nor can these European borders be apprehensible as simply the outward projections of a stable and coherent center, whereby the sociopolitical, cultural, or civilizational identity, and spatial integrity of Europe may be presupposed in contradistinction with a variety of alterities beyond or outside the ostensible limits demarcated by those boundaries. Instead,

Europe's borders, like all borders, are the materializations of sociopolitical relations that mediate the continuous production of the distinction between the putative inside and outside, and likewise mediate the diverse mobilities that are orchestrated and regimented through the production of that spatial divide (De Genova 2013b). Thus, with respect to the abundant inequalities of human mobility, the borders of Europe are simultaneously entangled with a global (postcolonial) politics of race that redraws the proverbial color line and refortifies European-ness as a racial formation of whiteness (De Genova 2016a, 2016b; see also Dzenovska; Soto Bermant; Stierl, this volume), and a comparably global (neoliberal) politics of transnational labor mobility and capitalist labor subordination that produces such spatialized (and racialized) differences, above all, to capitalize upon them (see Gambino, this volume).

For many illegalized asylum-seekers, braving the horrors of the European border regime comes only after fleeing from all manner of atrocities, persecution, and misery in their countries of origin and, commonly, also in numerous other countries of "transit," crossed en route to Europe, which have been materially and practically incorporated to various extents into the externalized policing of the frontiers of Europe (Andersson 2014a, 2014b; see Andersson; Garelli and Tazzioli; Lecadet; Osseiran; Stierl, this volume). For most of these same refugees, as well as many others who migrate in the quest to make a better life for themselves and their loved ones, the vicious severities of this extended and expansive European borderzone present a fierce endurance test, a preliminary apprenticeship in what promises to be a more or less protracted career of migrant "illegality," precarious labor, and deportability (De Genova 2015c; cf. 2002; see Gambino; Garelli and Tazzioli; Lecadet; Picozza; Stierl, this volume). Whether these mobile subjects come to be governed as refugees or migrants, however, their needs, desires, and aspirations always supersede this death-defying obstacle course—albeit, at times, at the cost of their lives. Little surprise, then, that one mode of critical response to the European border regime's ultimate responsibility for the April 2015 shipwreck was to invoke an analogy with the premier slogan of contemporary African American civil rights struggles in the United States—Black Lives Matter—by insisting that Migrant Lives Matter. Here we are reminded that in the European context, the very figure of migration is always already racialized, even as dominant discourses of migration in Europe systematically disavow and dissimulate race as such (Balibar 1991a, 1991b, 1991c, 1992, 1999b; De Genova 2010c, 2016a, 2016b, 2016c; Goldberg 2006, 2009:151–98; see also Dzenovska; Gambino; Scheel; Soto Bermant; Stierl, this volume). Furthermore, given that the horrendous risk of migrant death systematically generated by the European border regime is disproportionately inflicted upon migrants and refugees from sub-Saharan Africa, the poignant question of whether Black Lives Matter in Europe presents itself ever more urgently. Haunted as Europe's borders are by this appalling proliferation of almost exclusively non-European/nonwhite migrant and refugee deaths and other forms of structural violence and generalized suffering, anyone interested in questions of borders and migration, on the one hand, or questions of race and racism, on the other, today must readily recognize that these questions present themselves in a particularly acute way in the European context.

Conversely, but similarly, anyone concerned with the question of Europe today cannot avoid eventually confronting the urgent and anxious problem of the borders of Europe, and therefore must inevitably come to recognize that the question of Europe itself has become inextricable from the question of migration (Ataç et al. 2015; Balibar 1991a, 1991b, 1991c, 1993a, 1993b, 1999a, 2004; De Genova 2016a, 2016b; Karakayali and Rigo 2010; Mezzadra 2006, 2010a, 2010b; Rigo 2011; Tazzioli 2015b; Walters 2004, 2009; see also Dzenovska; Soto Bermant, this volume). These questions regarding migration in Europe and the putative borders of Europe, however, cannot be reduced to subsidiary or derivative concerns for a field of inquiry presumed to be more expansive and encompassing, which might be called European studies. It is quite simply no longer credible, or indeed even plausible, to sustain the pretense of any self-satisfied, self-referential scholarship in European studies that complacently disregards or derisively marginalizes the questions of migration and borders. Rather than a discrete and parochial subset for a field that takes Europe to be a greater totality, predictably and presumptuously imagined to be of more universal significance, a genuinely critical examination of borders and migration in Europe unsettles and destabilizes "Europe" as an object of knowledge, and instigates a confrontation with the problem of Europe itself.

The uneven geopolitics of policing the borders of Europe and the heterogeneous tactics of various nation-states for managing the ostensible crisis, as we have seen, have riddled the project of EU-ropean integration and border harmonization with its own irreconcilable contradictions. The referendum in the United Kingdom on June 23, 2016, in which a majority of British voters demanded a formal exit from the European Union, following a prolonged political campaign of anti-immigrant hostility and heightened anxiety over border control, has been merely the most dramatic index of the fractures threatening the viability of the EU in the wake of the migration and border "crisis." Following the so-called Brexit vote, various far-right political movements across Europe chiefly dedicated to reactionary populist hostility toward migrants and anti-Muslim racism were predictably enthused that they might successfully capitalize on the British example. On the other hand, the spontaneous mobilization of EU citizens' solidarity campaigns under the banner of "Refugees Welcome"—and most poignantly, the collective organization of automotive caravans to openly provide material and practical assistance to refugees and migrants in the completion their cross-border journeys, particularly from Hungary into Austria and Germany, in flagrant defiance of legal prohibitions that would construe such acts of compassion and solidarity as the alleged trafficking or smuggling of "illegal" migrants, and hence as criminal offenses—have only served to amplify and telescope the fracture between these European citizens' transnational solidarity with migrants' and refugees' struggles and the sovereign power of European states (cf. Ataç et al. 2015; Doppler 2015; Kasparek and Speer 2015; Stierl 2015). In other words, political movements on both the right and left, anti-immigrant nativists as well as movements in solidarity with migrants and refugees, help to underscore a fracture between the presumptive sovereignty of state powers and the communities otherwise figured as the polities from which such claims to sovereign power are purported to be democratically derived (De Genova 2015b). Thus, the larger conflictive processes of bordering Europe have generated a still larger political crisis for the institutional politico-juridical formation of the European Union, for EU-ropean citizenship, and for European democracy more generally.

The struggles of migration and borders reanimate race and postcoloniality as central to adequately addressing the most fundamental problems of what "Europe" is supposed to be, and who may be counted as "European"—which together I enfold as the European Question (De Genova 2016a, 2016b). Much as the borders of Europe have been instituted and are constantly being policed for the sake of stabilizing and purportedly protecting the space of Europe— first and foremost, and above all, as a preserve for the presumable birthright entitlements of "Europeans"—the unrelenting struggle over the autonomous mobility of "non-Europeans" across those symbolic and material boundaries continuously instigates a restaging of the borders of Europe as sites of their own subversion, and concomitantly as the scene for the spectral undoing of Europe itself. The borders of Europe therefore present a premier site for the enactment and disputation of the very question of and about Europe. This book therefore situates the borders of Europe not at the margins but rather at the very center of contemporary questions and debates about Europe. And here, behind the debates over the borders of Europe, the still more fundamental point bears emphatic reiteration: The question of Europe itself has become inextricable from the question of migration, which itself is systematically pressed to serve as a proxy for an ever-deferred confrontation with the European Question as a problem of race and postcoloniality.

Finally, beyond these relatively parochial questions of Europe and European studies, this book is centrally concerned with the autonomous dynamics of human mobility on a global scale and the formations of state power and sovereignty that react to the exercise of an elementary freedom of movement through diverse tactics and techniques of bordering. To the extent that the European Union entails a transnational and partially supranational juridical and political formation, with an extraordinarily variegated and graduated spectrum of differential (and never perfectly harmonized) arrangements that regulate and modulate its internal and external relations, a high degree of instability and mobility is always already implied by the very existence of the borders that may now be characterized as European (see Andersson; Heller and Pezzani; Picozza; Soto Bermant, this volume). And with regard to "unwanted" refugees or "undesirable" illegalized migrants, these European borders have been externalized and virtualized to extraordinary and unprecedented degrees (see Lecadet, this volume). Hence, scholarship in migration and border studies only neglects a rigorous and critical examination of these processes and struggles in the contemporary European context at the risk of failing to apprehend what is indisputably a remarkable site of unprecedented experimentation and improvisation, a transnational and intercontinental laboratory for the regimentation and subordination of human powers and freedoms in relation to the space of the planet. In this respect, this volume contributes to the much wider critical literature on the themes of migration, refugee movements, and border struggles—from the U.S.–Mexico border, and its externalization and extension through the length of Mexico and across the geography of Central America, at least as far as Colombia and Ecuador; to the maritime border enforcement tactics of Australia's "Pacific Solution" and its extension across variegated maritime borderscapes from the Indian subcontinent through Southeast Asia and into the South Pacific; to the complex migration regimes of Saudi Arabia and the Arab/Persian Gulf and their reach into India and the Philippines; to the simultaneous militarized barricading of both the exterior borders and the interior (colonial) frontiers of Israel, to name only the most obvious comparative examples. Thus, *The Borders of "Europe"* (re)situates the seemingly parochial or particularistic matter of Europe and its border and migration crisis within a global frame, profoundly interconnected to the ongoing reconfigurations of an effectively planetary regime dedicated to the neoliberal and postcolonial government of human mobility, and the border struggles that are ever increasingly manifest across the world.

Contributions to This Volume

This volume showcases original research on the borders of "Europe" by some of the most promising junior scholars working in this dynamic field of critical inquiry today. Their work exudes the greatest promise of genuine interdisciplinarity, deftly bridging the political and social sciences, integrating critical analyses of law, policy, and politics with fine-grained ethnographic insights into the everyday experiences and perspectives arising from the lived encounters between the autonomy and subjectivity of migration with the tactics and technologies of bordering.

In the opening chapter, Stephan Scheel provides an indispensable contextualization of the ways that the ostensible "crisis" of the borders of Europe supplies a spectacle of border enforcement that systematically diverts critical scrutiny away from the actual production of migrant "illegality" in the laws and policies that govern transnational mobility into the European Union. This chapter reminds us of the well-established fact that the vast majority of illegalized migrants within the European Union do *not* enter by crossing state borders clandestinely or in unseaworthy boats, but rather do so in a perfectly "legal" manner with a Schengen visa to a European destination, only later to become "illegal" once the visa has expired. Thus, Scheel demonstrates how the Schengen visa regime facilitates migratory access to the space of Europe even as it effectively forecloses such forms of "legitimate" mobility for the great majority of humanity. This less visible (less spectacularized) mode of illegalized migration has tended to receive rather scant attention, however. This chapter therefore focuses on the introduction of the EU's Visa Information System (VIS) and the consequent development of a vast biometric database that has foreclosed some of the practices by which migrants could previously successfully appropriate mobility to Europe through access to a Schengen visa. Approaching the Schengen visa regime from the perspective of mobility and the autonomy of migration, Scheel examines how migrants succeed in appropriating the Schengen visa in the context of biometric border controls. From the standpoint of visa applicants, Scheel argues, the Schengen visa regime constitutes an unpredictable regime of institutionalized distrust that renders mobility to Europe a scarce resource by setting unreasonable or unrealistic requirements for a visa that seldom correspond to local circumstances in the places where prospective travelers/migrants submit their visa applications. Hence, in addition to and apart from the dangerous modes of clandestine border crossing that forgo any hope of "legal" arrival in Europe, the Schengen visa regime indeed emerges as a vast machine of migrant illegalization that provokes precisely the "illegal" practices of appropriation of visas that it is presumably meant to fore-stall. Illustrated through the example of the provision of manipulated support-ing documents, this chapter formulates a conceptual outline of six defining features that migrant practices of mobility appropriation share, irrespective of their diverse forms. Apart from demonstrating that moments of migrant autonomy persist within biometric border regimes, Scheel thus promotes the concept of appropriation as an alternative framework for theorizing migrants' capacities to subvert border controls.

Moving from the comparatively obscure but prosaic practices of biometric bordering enacted through visa controls, Ruben Andersson directs our attention to a seeming paradox that defines the European Union's responses to "irregu-lar" migration and refugee flows across its southern frontiers—that the often draconian practices of border control are conjoined with humanitarian man-dates, such that the apparatuses of migrant capture and "rescue" become deeply entangled. While Italy's navy "rescued" and effectively ferried tens of thousands of migrants intercepted on unseaworthy boats in 2014, Spain added razor wire to the border fences surrounding its North African enclave in Melilla and al-lowed violent "push-backs" into Morocco. Foregrounding these governmental ambivalences, this chapter situates humanitarian and liberal measures firmly within the context of a larger assemblage of migration controls that now reaches far beyond the Euro-African frontier. Whereas the ostensible divide between liberal/humanitarian and securitarian approaches to bordering appears to be substantial, Andersson examines how these are in fact deeply enmeshed within Europe's larger response to unauthorized border crossings. It becomes clear, for instance, that border fences and mass deployments of policing at land borders have pushed migrants and refugees toward more risky maritime crossings—and thus directly into the hands of Europe's humanitarian apparatus. At sea, meanwhile, European security forces have used humanitarian justifications for intercepting boats along African coasts (including boats that were not in dis-tress), yet this co-optation of humanitarianism has in turn been co-opted by migrants themselves, who subsequently came to actively seek rescue. Through such interactions, moreover, Andersson demonstrates how an industry has grown up around migratory routes in which care and control functions both clash and sometimes merge with each other, making any attempt at dismantling the border machinery or implementing alternative approaches increasingly difficult and implausible.

In the third chapter, Charles Heller and Lorenzo Pezzani focus on the specific contradictions and complexities raised for tactics of bordering imple-mented across the Mediterranean Sea. Considering how the liquid expanse of the sea has traditionally represented a challenge for governance, whereby the impossibility of drawing fixed and stable boundaries in ever-changing waters has inspired notions of the seas as a space of absolute freedom and uninhibited flow, this chapter demonstrates in contrast how the Mediterranean is increasingly subjected to elaborate forms of surveillance and documentation for purposes of governance. A complex sensing apparatus is fundamental to a form of governance that combines the division of maritime spaces and the control of movement, and that instrumentalizes the partial, overlapping, and "elastic" nature of maritime jurisdictions and international law. It is under these conditions that the EU migration regime operates, selectively expanding sovereign rights through patrols on the high seas but also retracting them in tactical retreats from responsibility, as in numerous instances of nonassistance to migrants at sea. Through the policies and the conditions of maritime governance organized by the EU, the authors argue, the sea is turned into a deadly liquid and converted into the direct and immediate cause of death for untold thousands of migrants and refugees. However, Heller and Pezzani also contend that by using the Mediterranean's remote sensing apparatus against the grain and spatializing violations and abuses by border authorities at sea, it is possible to challenge the regimes of governance and visibility imposed on this contested geography.

Crossing the Mediterranean to its North African shore, Laia Soto Bermant considers the constitution of Europe as a political, economic, and cultural project from the point of view of one of its most controversial borderlands: the Spanish enclave of Melilla. A 12-km^2 enclave located in northeastern Morocco, Melilla has been under Spanish sovereignty since the late fifteenth century. In the early 1990s, when Spain joined the Schengen area, Melilla became one of Europe's southernmost borderlands. Since then, Melilla—as a "European" outpost in Africa—has played a crucial role as a buffer zone between the two continents, operating as a first line of defense against migratory flows into "Europe." This chapter explores Melilla's "border experiments" as a paradigmatic example of the conflicting forces at play in the global move toward border securitization. First, Soto Bermant examines how the enclave has been physically reconfigured over the past two decades in the interests of enhanced "security," and demonstrates how, behind the image of Melilla as a European bastion under siege, there lies a complex system of selective permeability designed to facilitate informal trade flows while nonetheless obstructing migration flows. Further, in the effort to critically problematize the question of "Europe" itself, the chapter explores the discursive activities of place construction that legitimize this system, and considers how "Europe," as an idea and as a political space, has been incorporated into these local narratives.

Moving from the frontiers of Europe into the amorphous and expansive spaces of expulsion where deported migrants must regroup their energies, Clara Lecadet offers a perspective on the European deportation regime from the vantage point of the politicization of expelled migrants in Africa, starting from the middle of the 1990s with the creation of the Malian Expelled Migrants Association in Bamako. Lecadet analyzes the ways in which deportees organized themselves to take collective action, and the spread of a critique of the communitization of European expulsion policies through various forms of political action. The politicization of expellees in fact produced claims directed at the deporting states from beyond their territorial boundaries, with regard to the reception, rights, and citizenship of forcibly "returned" migrants. The chapter likewise examines the inherent contradictions in the claims-making of these political movements as they fluctuated between emancipatory and instrumentalized tactics and strategies within the wider context of a global approach to the implementation of "return" measures promoted by European authorities and international agencies.

From an analogous space in the borderlands of Europe, in their chapter, Glenda Garelli and Martina Tazzioli look at the restructuring of the tactics of bordering along the lines of humanitarian rationalities through the lens of the refugee camp at Choucha, in Tunisia, at the border with Libya. The humanitarian camp had originally been established to provide refugees from Libya's civil war with shelter while their asylum claims were considered. Many who had originally been labor migrants to Libya (mainly from sub-Saharan African countries) found themselves stranded at Choucha, following the camp's official closure by the authorities of the United Nations. Effectively abandoned after having been deemed to be mere "migrants," these refugees enacted various strategies: some remained at Choucha and persisted in their efforts to claim resettlement; some fled to Tunis to seek informal employment, now as irregularized migrants in Tunisia; others left for Europe on "migrant boats." The authors map how these different paths encountered, displaced, and rearticulated humanitarian technologies for migration management, focusing in particular on the refusal by some to take to the sea, on the one hand, and the encounters between others with the Italian Navy's "military and humanitarian" mission Mare Nostrum in the Mediterranean, on the other. Far from being a homogeneous political technology, Garelli and Tazzioli contend, the humanitarian regime emerges as a fragmented mechanism wherein disparate regimes of visibility, temporal borders, tactics of border enforcement, and forms of capture intersect in the production of vulnerability for displaced people.

The next chapter, by Souad Osseiran, examines the predicament of Syrians in Istanbul who inhabit the ambiguous and ambivalent condition that she characterizes as "migrants/refugees," who commonly migrate to Istanbul with the aim of continuing on to "Europe." While in Istanbul, they dedicate much of their time and energies to arranging their ensuing journeys. Part of their preparations entails discussing the various possibilities of migration and the particularities of distinct versions of "Europe," specifically the various EU member states to which or through which they might prospectively travel. This chapter explores the ways in which Syrian migrants/refugees exchange stories in Istanbul about "Europe" and contemplate the peculiarities of the uneven space of the EU. Drawing on ethnographic data gathered in Istanbul from mid-2012 through the end of 2013, Osseiran argues that through the exchange of such narratives about various migratory routes and the divergent encounters with migratory and asylum regimes that these routes imply, Syrian migrants/refugees develop a discrepant understanding of "Europe" and the space of the EU beyond official political boundaries or the constructions of the EU's juridical or legislative bodies. In their stories, notably depicting various European destinations as spaces of greater or lesser temporariness or potential permanence, Syrian migrants/refugees blur borders and boundaries, and elaborate an alternative perspective on "Europe."

Moving from the Turkish zone of migrant "transit" to Greece, on the "European" side of the border, Maurice Stierl recounts his encounters with an extended Syrian family seeking to escape the Greek/EU-ropean borderscape of Athens. Renarrating the struggles of Jaser and his relatives to overcome their migrant predicament in Greece and move onward toward Western European countries highlights not only the effects of diffuse and violent forms of border governance but also the refugees' endurance and resistance in a climate of fear and unwantedness. It is through these encounters in (arrested) transit that this chapter engages with conceptualizations of the autonomy of migration, which tend to depict migration as a social force with "excessive potentialities." Revisiting Michel Foucault's short reflection on the "Lives of Infamous Men," questions of excess, anonymity, im/perceptibility, and autonomy are addressed to (discourses on) contemporary migration movements. The author points out that contemporary EU border governance can be understood as being excessively violent in its own right, often enacting horrific border spectacles that come to be inscribed in both the minds and bodies of border crossers as fear, trauma, and depression, even long after having arrived at their desired destinations. Beginning with such "border entanglements," Stierl argues, enables a closer exploration of the ways in which human creativity and excess are manifested as well as violated in (attempted) enactments of cross-border movement.

In her chapter, Fiorenza Picozza endeavors to deconstruct the categories through which migrant identities are conventionally read, analyzing the socio-legal production of migrant "illegality" and "refugee"-ness within the context of the Dublin Regulation—the EU's common framework for asylum. The analysis draws upon ethnographic fieldwork in Rome and London, focusing on the trans-European mobility of Afghan "Dubliners" and on how they subjectively experience the Dublin regime at simultaneously legal, social, and existential levels. Dubliners, the chapter demonstrates, seem to be "stuck in transit," constantly moving from one EU country to another, and sometimes spending up to ten years struggling to settle. In spite of the limitations imposed by the Dublin Regulation—for which an asylum claim can be submitted only in the first country in which the asylum seeker has been registered—as well as "national" regulations, by which recognized refugees are only permitted to reside and work in that particular country, Dubliners' restlessness reveals a complex panoply of interstitial spaces of autonomy. In this fraught interplay between "illegality" and various tentative forms of "legality," migration categories are shown to be increasingly bureaucratized and yet, at the same time, increasingly blurred.

Considering an analogous but distinct formation of translocal spatial mobilities, Evelina Gambino provides insight into the Gran Ghettò, a spontaneous migrant settlement located in the heartland of agricultural production in the Capitanata Plain in Puglia, southern Italy. Since the 1990s, thousands of migrant workers have traveled to and resided in this shantytown, transforming it into the largest recruiting center in the region for the provision of "cheap" labor for the tomato harvest. Beginning in 2012, Campagne in Lotta, a large political network of "native" Italian and migrant workers, established an activist project in the Gran Ghettò with the aim of breaking the migrant farmworkers' isolation and articulating collective demands for more fair labor conditions. This chapter is an account of that experience and the political struggle that ensued from it. The account corresponds to two separate but intertwined periods of Gambino's direct activist participation in the Campagne in Lotta project as a "militant researcher." The first section analyzes the conditions of life for illegalized migrant workers in the ghetto, with the workers' exploitation by employers explained against the backdrop of the intersections between capital and numerous governmental tools for the control of migrant mobility. The second section concerns Campagne in Lotta's political intervention in the ghetto, based on the appreciation of and contribution to informal networks of migrant social relations.

Gambino contends that these networks constitute the infrastructure of a virtual migrant metropolis, connecting migrants' movements on a transnational (and effectively global) scale. The chapter describes how, during the three years of its existence, Campagne in Lotta has managed to become a part of these traveling relations, moving across the extended space of this migrant metropolis through its diverse projects and the discovery of new sites of intervention as its participants have changed location. The embeddedness of Campagne in Lotta in this geography of migrant mobility, Gambino contends, constitutes its greatest strength and emerges as the precondition for radically new processes of political experimentation and formations of solidarity and struggle to take place.

In contrast to such solidarity projects, in the concluding chapter, Dace Dzenovska examines how the bordering of Europe comes to be diffused throughout everyday life and relies upon citizen involvement through practices of reporting (or informing on) suspected "foreigners," including tenants, neighbors, and even family members. On the basis of a comparative analysis of the bordering practices of the Latvian State Border Guard and the British Home Office, Dzenovska contends that an analysis of "reporting" as a technology of government and an element of public culture is crucial for understanding the kinds of subjects and socialities that contemporary (late) liberal democratic political regimes assume, deploy, and produce, and thus for understanding the polities that they make possible. Inasmuch as this sort of informing has been associated in recent history with the political repertoires of totalitarian states, Dzenovska uses the historical-analytical lens of state socialism to bring into sharper focus the specificities of reporting in contemporary European liberal democratic contexts. The chapter goes on to suggest that state socialism and postsocialist transformations can serve as "portable analytics" that help to illuminate the power of "freedom" to obscure the work of state power in liberal democratic contexts. Notably, it is precisely in the work of bordering Europe within the contours of the "interior" spaces of European everyday life that this sort of power enlists citizens as informers who can assist in the mundane policing and surveillance of migrant "foreign"-ness.

––––

Thus, from Mali to Latvia, from London to Istanbul, from the Strait of Gibraltar to the Evros River, from a refugee camp on the Libya–Tunisia border to a migrant farmworker camp in southern Italy, the chapters assembled in this volume explore the heterogeneous formations of the autonomy of migration and the eclectic assortment of tactics of bordering that have transformed the enlarged and extended space of "Europe" into a variegated borderland (Balibar 2004/2009). The ambitious research and critical analysis compiled here on the borders of "Europe" supply a vital fulcrum for understanding the dynamic tensions and unresolved conflicts that situate the autonomy of migration and the reaction formations of border policing techniques and immigration law enforcement tactics as an indispensable and inescapable centerpiece for European studies today, while simultaneously enriching the wider comparative and theoretical purviews of the overlapping interdisciplinary fields of migration, refugee, and border studies on a global scale.

Acknowledgments

This introduction has been thoroughly enriched by the work of all the contributors to this volume, but has benefited in various ways from the specific critical comments and thoughtful suggestions of Ruben Andersson, Glenda Garelli, Fiorenza Picozza, Maurice Stierl, and Martina Tazzioli, each of whom responded to an earlier draft. In addition to all those directly involved in this editorial project, moreover, this text has been inspired by dialogue and debate within the research network on "The 'European' Question: Postcolonial Perspectives on Migration, Nation, and Race," particularly the discussions during and ensuing from meetings on June 25–26, 2015, at King's College London, which culminated in the collaborative project of the New Keywords Collective on the "crisis" in and of "Europe." Portions of this text were also presented to seminars or conferences at Birkbeck (University of London), King's College London, Goldsmiths (University of London), the Universities of Cambridge and Brighton, as well as the University of California at Davis and Santa Cruz. I am grateful to all those who shared their questions, insights, and criticisms during these discussions, particularly Bob Brecher, Alex Callinicos, Charles Heller, Sandi Hilal, Robert Irwin, Stathis Kouvelakis, Zeina Maasri, Sunaina Maira, Alessandro Petti, Lucia Pradella, Catherine Ramírez, Maurice Stierl, and Eyal Weizman.

NOTES

1. See also the International Organization for Migration's (IOM) "Missing Migrants Project," http://missingmigrants.iom.int.
2. The intensified enforcement at border crossings of easiest passage relegates illegalized migrant mobilities into zones of more severe hardship and potentially lethal

passage. The escalation of migrant and refugee deaths along the U.S.–Mexico border (De León 2015; Dunn 2009; Nevins 2008, 2010; Regan 2010; Rosas 2006; Stephen 2008; Squire 2014; Sundberg 2011; Urrea 2004) as well as in the maritime border zones of Australia (Weber and Pickering 2011) bears a striking resemblance to the parallel proliferation of migrant deaths instigated by the unprecedented extremities and severities of the European border regime—particularly across the Mediterranean Sea but also externalized across the entire expanse of the Sahara Desert (cf. Andersson 2012, 2014a, 2014b; Bredeloup 2012; Lecadet 2013a, 2013b). For a global overview of the escalation in migrant deaths, see IOM (2014) and the IOM's "Missing Migrants Project," http://missingmigrants.iom.int.

3. The most comprehensive database documenting migrant and refugee deaths during attempts to traverse the borders of Europe is "The Migrants' Files," www.themigrantsfiles.com, a data project coordinated by Journalism++, which estimates the total number of European border deaths at more than 30,000. See also IOM (2014); Shields (2015); Spijkerboer (2007, 2013); Spijkerboer and Last (2014); van Houtum and Boedeltje (2009); cf. Carling (2007a) and the IOM's "Missing Migrants Project," http://missingmigrants.iom.int.

4. It remains a matter of speculation whether there was a deliberate rechanneling of migrant and refugee movements by various border policing tactics toward the so-called Balkan route, such as the increasing militarization of the sea routes from Greece to Italy with the launch in June 2015 of the maritime military mission EUNAVFOR-Med, or alternately whether the increasing prominence of this land option was the result of autonomous migratory dynamics (including, of course, the discretionary judgment of so-called smugglers). It is also noteworthy that recourse to the land routes across the Balkans is frequently preceded by comparatively short maritime passages between Turkey and Greece across the Aegean Sea. Nevertheless, while the central Mediterranean routes have remained a primary passage for migratory movements from much of Africa, it seems that movements from the Middle East and beyond, usually via Turkey, have long alternated between two basic options—one passing directly through Greece or Bulgaria, and potentially leading to land routes through the Balkans, and another that involves transit through Egypt or Libya, followed by trans-Mediterranean maritime routes. Indeed, mass deaths by shipwreck began to escalate again during the spring of 2016, and the total number of recorded migrant/refugee deaths in 2016 finally exceeded those recorded for 2015. More than 700 people are believed to have drowned in three shipwrecks in the Mediterranean during the last week of May 2016 alone, marking the deadliest seven days for Europe's borders since the events of April 2015.

5. In response to the versatile autonomous mobilities of migrants, newly mobile and dispersed forms of governmentality and techniques of border control have arisen, provoking William Walters's important call (2014, 2015a, 2015b; cf. 2006) for a more careful critical scrutiny of the proliferation not only of borders and sites of bordering but also the routes and vessels of migratory movement, culminating in what he designates as the "viapolitics" of migration (see also Stuesse and Coleman 2014; Walters et al. n.d.).

6. In addition, as Matthew Carr points out, whereas only 125 people were killed trying to cross the Berlin Wall, at least 150 migrants committed suicide in Germany alone

from 1988 to 2008 because they were confronted with the prospect of deportation (2012:4; see also Ataç et al. 2015).

7. For contributions to the elaboration of the critical concept of the "autonomy of migration," see Mezzadra (2001, 2004, 2011); Mezzadra in Bojadžijev and Saint-Saëns (2006); Mezzadra and Neilson (2003, 2013); Moulier Boutang (1998, 2001); Moulier Boutang and Garson (1984); Moulier-Boutang and Grelet (2001); cf. Bojadžijev and Karakayali (2010); De Genova (2009, 2010b, 2010d); Karakayali and Rigo (2010); Mitropoulos (2006); Nyers (2003); Papadopoulos et al. (2008); Papastergiadis (2000, 2005, 2010); Rigo (2011); Scheel (2013a, 2013b, 2017); Tsianos and Karakayali (2010); Walters (2008).

8. Joint Statement on Mediterranean Crossings of UN High Commissioner for Refugees António Guterres, UN High Commissioner for Human Rights Zeid Ra'ad Al-Hussein, Special Representative of the UN Secretary-General for International Migration and Development Peter Sutherland, and Director-General of the International Organization for Migration William Lacy Swing (April 23, 2015), http://www.unhcr .org/5538d9079.html.

9. As in all of my previous work, I consistently deploy quotes wherever the term "illegality" appears, and wherever the term "illegal" modifies migration or migrants, in order to emphatically denaturalize the reification of this distinction. Otherwise, I rely on the more precise term illegalized (see De Genova 2002).

10. For various contributions to the critique of the discourse of "slavery," see www .opendemocracy.net/beyondslavery.

11. For related work on the implication of humanitarian governmentalities in the sorting and ranking of "deserving" and "undeserving" migrants and the selective deployment of humanitarian "exceptions" regarding migrants susceptible to deportation, see Castañeda (2010); Fassin (2005); Fassin and Rechtman (2009); Fischer (2013); and Ticktin (2006, 2011).

12. The Calais area demarcates a site of border policing between Britain and the Schengen zone (the European area free of border controls or passport checks for citizens from the twenty-six signatory countries). The Schengen area includes twenty-two of the twenty-eight EU member states, plus an additional four countries that are not EU members; Britain, however, is not a Schengen country.

13. The Schengen accord predated the European Union, but was incorporated into the EU's Amsterdam Treaty of 1997, with provisions for some member states to opt out.

14. Slovakian police fired live ammunition at border crossers at the border with Hungary, wounding a Syrian refugee woman, on May 9, 2016 (Cowburn 2016a). A few weeks earlier, Human Rights Watch reported that Turkish soldiers were firing live rounds at Syrian civilian border crossers (Cowburn 2016b).

15. On the wider topic of the externalization of the borders of the EU, see Andersson (2012, 2014a, 2014b); Andrijasevic (2010); Bialasiewicz (2012); Bredeloup (2012); Carter and Merrill (2007); Casas-Cortes et al. (2011, 2013); Collyer (2007); Dzenovska (2014); Feldman (2012); Ferrer-Gallardo and Albet-Mas (2014); Garelli et al. (2013); Hansen and Jonsson (2011); Karakayali and Rigo (2010); Rigo (2011); Soto Bermant

(2014); Tazzioli (2014); Tsianos and Karakayali (2010); van Houtum and Boedeltje (2009); Walters (2009).

16. Subsequently, it was indeed Germany's Chancellor Angela Merkel who reinitiated negotiations between the EU and Turkey that sought to reward Turkey with at least €3 billion in exchange for an expanded role in policing the external borders of the EU and the more effective containment of more than 2 million Syrians and other refugees and migrants. As Merkel put it, such measures would help "keep people in the region," which is to say, keep them out of Europe. In addition, the EU reopened stalled negotiations regarding an extension of visa-free travel privileges to (qualifying) Turkish citizens, as well as the larger question of Turkey's prospective admission to EU membership. See Kanter and Higgins (2015). The "deal" was confirmed on March 18, 2016, allowing Greece to "return" or "relocate" (i.e., deport) to Turkey "all new irregular migrants" arriving after March 20, 2016. For analysis of the legal, political, and ethical vagaries of the agreement, see Collett (2016). As a predictable result of these efforts to more effectively close the Aegean routes, the Office of the UN High Commissioner for Refugees (UNHCR) reported that maritime crossings from Libya in March 2016 had increased to three times the figure for 2015 (Stephen 2016).

17. For more general discussions of the metaphysics of antiterrorism and the rise of specifically anti-Muslim racism in the context of the production of discourses of a "Muslim menace," see De Genova (2007, 2010a, 2010c, 2011b, 2015d); for a discussion of the sociopolitical context of the *Charlie Hebdo* shootings in Paris in January 2015, see De Genova (2017); De Genova and Tazzioli (2015).

18. Replete with the obligatory critiques of the immanence of refugees to the havoc wrought by global capitalism and perfunctory gestures against neocolonialism, Žižek has even transposed his advocacy of "repressive means" (2015) into a call for "military and economic interventions" (2015), and more specifically, the European "militarization" of migration management in the war-stricken sites from which refugees flee, in order to "organize airlifts and regulate immigration" in places such as Syria and Libya (2016b).

19. Indeed, on November 18, 2015, EU member states Slovenia and Croatia, followed by non-EU countries Serbia and Macedonia, abruptly closed their borders to any would-be "asylum-seekers" who could not provide identity documents specifically confirming that they came from Syria, Iraq, or Afghanistan—effectively segregating refugees according to national origin (Associated Press 2015).

1

—

"The Secret Is to Look Good on Paper"

Appropriating Mobility within and against
a Machine of Illegalization

STEPHAN SCHEEL

Reports in the media of spectacular border crossings tend to create the impression that the majority of illegalized migrants enter the European Union (EU) clandestinely, hidden in freight containers or in unseaworthy boats. It is, however, by now an established fact that the majority of illegalized migrants arrive perfectly legally with a valid Schengen visa in the EU and only become "illegal" once it has expired (Collyer et al. 2012; Düvell 2011; EC 2003; Schoorl et al. 2000:101; Sciortino 2004; Zampagni 2013).[1] The importance of visas as a mode of entry for illegalized migrants has also been documented for other destination countries such as the United States, where it is estimated that so-called visa overstayers account for 40–50 percent of the country's illegalized population of 12 million people (Andreas 2000:100; Pew Hispanic Center 2006:3).[2] Likewise, reports on illegalized migration in the United Kingdom (which is not part of the Schengen area) underline the fact that, contrary to public perception, the vast majority of illegalized people in the UK are nondeported rejected asylum seekers and visa overstayers (Sigona and Hughes 2012:6). This observation has also been confirmed for the global level: The IOM's World Migration Report 2010 emphasizes that most of the 10–15 percent of the world's international migrants who are in an irregular situation are, in fact, overstayers (IOM 2010:29). Yet neither the importance of restrictive visa policies for the illegalization of migration nor the significance of visas as a mode of illegalized migration has been sufficiently acknowledged by border and migration studies so far.

This is well reflected by the relative neglect in the border and migration studies literature of the Schengen visa regime, which is the focus of this chapter. The meager but growing number of publications one finds on the Schengen visa regime sits in stark contrast with the attention dedicated to more visible aspects of border control such as detention centers, deportations, militarized border controls under the lead of Frontex, or interception policies in the Mediterranean in border, migration, and critical security studies. It could indeed be argued that much of the research in border and migration studies suffers from the same bias as media coverage and public debate, which, by focusing on more visible and often dramatic forms of unauthorized border crossings and the spectacle of militarized border enforcement, "help to generate a constellation of images and discursive formations, which repetitively supply migrant 'illegality' with the semblance of an objective fact" (De Genova 2013a:1830). The relative neglect of the Schengen visa regime is all the more astonishing given that it affects the access to mobility of billions of people. Phenomena such as the much-debated attempts to cross the Mediterranean in overcrowded boats simply constitute what are, in fact, effects of this vast machine of illegalization, which provokes these and other dangerous forms of border crossing, as I show in this chapter.

Moreover, we know virtually nothing about aspiring migrants' attempts to appropriate mobility to Europe via Schengen visas and the less spectacular border struggles that occur, on a daily basis, in the 3,500 visa sections that the EU's member states maintain worldwide. This chapter uses the introduction of the Visa Information System (VIS), one of the largest biometric databases in the world, as an occasion to compensate for this twofold lacuna in the borders and migration studies literature. Drawing on the autonomy of migration approach (AoM), I engage the Schengen visa regime from the perspective of aspiring migrants in order to investigate how they appropriate mobility to Europe via Schengen visas in the context of biometric border controls.[3]

This question is raised by the AoM's core thesis. As indicated by its name, the AoM suggests that migration features moments of autonomy—that is, moments of uncontrollability and excess—in relation to the attempts to control and regulate it (cf. Bojadžijev and Karakayali 2007; De Genova 2010d; Mezzadra 2011; Moulier Boutang 1993). This claim is in tension with the promotion of biometric technologies as adequate means for " 'filling the gaps' in traditional methods of border control" (Thomas 2005). What makes biometric recognition systems so attractive for border control purposes is their alleged capacity to verify the claimed identity of a person with unprecedented speed and accuracy. One purpose of the VIS is, for instance, to verify that the person seeking to cross the EU's external border is the same individual to whom a Schengen visa has been issued at a consulate. To this end, the fingerprints of all visa holders are captured upon arrival at the EU's external borders and compared to the fingerprint templates that have been created and stored in the VIS when the people concerned applied for visas at the consulates. Thus, the VIS is meant to forestall passports with valid Schengen visas being used by so-called lookalikes, that is, similar-looking persons (Broeders 2007). What this example demonstrates is that the VIS forecloses some of the practices by which migrants could successfully appropriate mobility to Europe. Hence, the introduction of the VIS raises the question: How do migrants appropriate mobility to Europe via Schengen visas in the context of biometric border controls?

Engaging this question provides me—and this is the second contribution that this chapter seeks to make—with the opportunity to introduce the notion of *appropriation* as an alternative concept to theorize migrants' capacity to subvert border controls. To this end, I will identify six features that practices of appropriation share, irrespective of their form. The need for such an alternative concept resides in the limitations of the two concepts that are usually invoked in border and migration studies to theorize migrants' capacity to challenge governmental attempts to control and regulate their behavior. These are the concepts of agency and resistance.

This twofold objective is reflected in the chapter's structure. In the first two sections I show that the Schengen visa regime constitutes, from the viewpoint of aspiring migrants, an unpredictable regime of institutionalized distrust that renders mobility to Europe a scarce resource. The Schengen visa regime emerges as a machine of illegalization that entices multiple practices of appropriation, and thus instigates the very practices it is meant to forestall. In the third section I elaborate on one set of practices by which migrants appropriate the Schengen visa in the context of the VIS. After outlining the central shortcomings of the two concepts that are usually invoked to theorize migrants' capacity to defy border controls, I use this example to illustrate six features that practices of appropriation feature, irrespective of their form.

The following account of the Schengen visa regime and practices of appropriation is based on ethnographic fieldwork that I conducted in and around consulates of Schengen member states in a North African country. During two field visits in 2012, I observed all phases of the visa application and decision-making procedures in a consulate to which I refer in the following only as consulate Z. The reason is that field access was tied to a promise to use the information obtained only in a way that enables neither the consulate nor the country where the research was conducted to be identified. These participant observations have been complemented by interviews with visa applicants, consular staff, and heads of mission of other consulates.

Making Mobility to Europe an Exclusive Affair: The Visa Regime as a Machine of Illegalization

"We are like flies . . . what are we waiting for?" an old woman shouts angrily. Together with dozens of other visa applicants she has been waiting since seven o'clock in the morning outside a large visa section to have her fingerprints taken in order to enroll in VIS. For most people in the queue it is the second day of their visa application. In an attempt to rid itself of the bad image created by queues in front of its buildings in the middle of the capital, the visa section, which receives a large proportion of visa applications in the country in question, has outsourced the filing of visa applications to a private company. Following the instructions on the consulate's homepage, most applicants arrange an appointment at the company's offices, located in a prosperous business district out of town, to submit their application for an additional fee of €25. If their file is complete and none of the required documents are missing, applicants receive an appointment to have their fingerprints taken at the consulate the next day. Many visa applicants regard the new procedure as confusing and complicated. As a surgeon working in a private clinic explains, the visa application procedure is a nuisance for him primarily because it is so time-consuming. The income he loses because he cannot work for two days is more significant to him than the additional fees he has to pay to the private company. Hoping to resume his work at the clinic as soon as possible, he has arrived three hours early for his appointment, like many others who are waiting on the small street behind the consulate. Lorries on their way to the nearby market sound their horns angrily at the waiting people as they try to pass the crowd, which almost completely blocks the road. After fifteen minutes and plenty of shouting, the two security officers guarding the consulate entrance bring the waiting crowd back into line.

What this account illustrates is that the visa application procedure is not only time-consuming and expensive—it is also a daunting experience for applicants, a point that has been greatly emphasized by the existing literature on the Schengen visa regime (Bigo and Guild 2003; CIMADE 2010; Infantino 2013; Maschino 2008; Zampagni 2011). Less has been written about the many people who never join one of the queues in front of the 3,500 consular posts that Schengen member states maintain worldwide because they simply cannot meet the manifold requirements an applicant must fulfill to receive one of the precious entry tickets to Europe.

Each day during my research I encountered people who told me they had never applied for a Schengen visa or had tried once, only to be rejected. One morning, while I was asking people in the queue described above for an interview, a young man approached me and asked me for advice. His name was Mohamed.[4] He explained to me that he had recently tried to apply for a Schengen visa, only to be chased away by the guards in front of the consulate. Laughing at him, they had told Mohamed that his visa application would be refused anyway, advising him to come back in a couple of years when he had found a job and started a family. "Why can I not go to Europe? Why can I not go to [name of country represented by the consulate] to learn about the culture and get to know the people? I have studied European culture and philosophy, so why can I not go there now to get to know it firsthand? What do I have to do to get a visa?" I had no ready reply. I just confirmed what the guards had already told him: his visa application would certainly be rejected because as a young student without a stable financial income he embodied a high "migration risk" in the eyes of consular staff. Each day I encountered numerous others who, unlike Mohamed, had not even dared to apply for a Schengen visa because they "knew" what the guards had told him: they had no realistic chance of being granted a visa. Tarek, a cab driver, had a brother living in Europe but had never tried to visit him because "they would never give me a visa." Walid, a young servant working in the hotel where I was staying, had learned from failed attempts by friends that applying for a visa was "just a waste of time and money."

The accounts of Mohamed, Tarek, Walid, and countless others highlight that it is the very rationale of the Schengen visa regime to render mobility to Europe a scarce resource. This is far from surprising, since "making a division between good and bad circulation, and maximising the good circulation by minimising the bad" (Foucault 2007:18) is the raison d'être of this vast security dispositif. In practice, the Schengen visa regime restricts foreign nationals' access to the EU by introducing an entry ticket, a Schengen visa, receipt of which is subject to conditions that a significant share of the population cannot fulfill and that often do not correspond to local circumstances. People like Mohamed, Tarek, and Walid are excluded from registration and documentation with a Schengen visa through a "wall of documents" they cannot provide and a set of requirements they cannot fulfill (Broeders 2011:59). This is why the Schengen visa regime constitutes a "Paper Curtain" (Lavenex and Uçarer 2004:433) for many citizens from the 124 countries that are subject to a visa requirement, including all of Africa and nearly all of Asia, as shown on the accompanying map.[5]

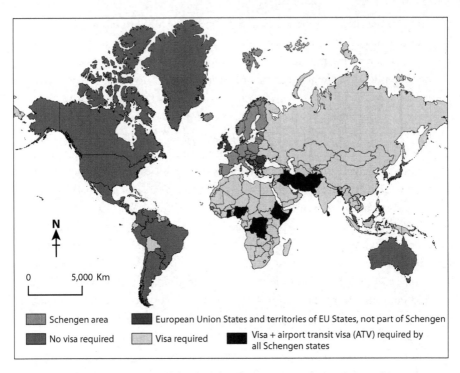

MAP 1.1. Visa requirements for the Schengen area. Source: Migration and Home Affairs Directorate-General of the European Commission

For instance, consulate Z's instruction leaflet enumerates no fewer than ten different types of documents which applicants must provide for a tourist visa: a valid passport, bank statements for the past twelve months, proof of means of subsistence (€88 per person per day) or a declaration from a host that they will cover costs, an employment contract, salary slips for the past three months, a holiday request signed by the employer, a social security card, a print-out of social security contributions, travel insurance for all Schengen member states, and a reservation for a return ticket. Together with the costs of the visa application itself (including not only fees but often also travel and accommodation in the capital), the cost of providing these documents easily amounts to the average monthly income in the country I visited (cf. Zampagni 2011). Moreover, providing some of these documents may prove impossible for many people, as they do not reflect the working and living conditions of a large share of the population. In the context of a large informal economy, cab drivers like Walid may not have a bank account or pay social security contributions (Alpes 2011:116–17).

That the paper requirements for a Schengen visa are often removed from local realities is also admitted by J, who works at an embassy hosting one of the largest visa sections in the country I visited. In the context of a large informal economy, even very rich businesspeople find it difficult to provide documents confirming their wealth, J tells me. The same applies to farmers, who cannot provide evidence of the land they own due to incomplete registers, she adds.

But even if they provide all the requested documents, people like Mohamed, Tarek, or Walid will not be issued a tourist visa by any of the consulates I have visited, because they do not meet the *informal* requirements that guide consular staffs' decisions. The head of the visa section at consulate Z, for instance, considers any application for a tourist visa dubious, because the member state he represents "is certainly not the most attractive tourist destination in Europe." Hence, he only issues tourist visas to people who have previously visited Europe and have a permanent job with a significant income. Likewise, the head of another visa section that does, in fact, represent an attractive tourist destination boasts in an interview: "Anybody who does not earn at least double the average monthly income will not get a visa from me." By setting requirements for a visa that the majority of the local population cannot fulfill, the Schengen visa regime subjects Mohamed, Tarek, Walid, and countless others to the paradoxical freedom "to go anywhere except where one wants to go" (Bigo 2007:26).

But since people "do not decide to stay put just because the receiving state says they are not welcome" (Castles 2004:209), the Schengen visa regime operates, in effect, as a vast machine of illegalization. This becomes apparent if one recalls that boat migration from North African coasts only became a significant phenomenon after Spain first imposed visa requirements on the nationals of all African and Arab countries in 1991, in order to meet the accession criteria for the Schengen area (Carling 2007b:11, 22; de Haas 2008:1307). People like Mohamed, Tarek, and Walid have, in fact, only two options at their disposal to contest their preemptive banishment from Europe through highly restrictive visa requirements: Either they try to appropriate mobility via Schengen visas through practices that involve the clandestine transgression of these strict regulations, or they bypass the Schengen visa regime altogether by engaging in more dangerous modes of clandestine border crossing, which are often facilitated by "smugglers" who charge their clients predatory fees for their services.

Similarly aggressive border enforcement policies have been pursued at the U.S.-Mexico border since the 1990s. One crucial effect of the upscaling of border controls is that it pushes aspiring migrants—like the restrictive requirements for a Schengen visa—"into a wider web of illegality" (Andreas 1998:348), thus provoking the very phenomena tough border enforcement is supposed to forestall.

In the case of the U.S.-Mexico border, migrants' tactics of appropriation have developed from practices of "self-smuggling" to more clandestine forms of border crossing that often involve the services of "well-organized, binational people-smuggling organizations" (Andreas 1998). In the case of the Schengen visa regime, it is a set of highly restrictive formal and informal requirements that efficiently bars a significant share of the local population from applying for a Schengen visa in the first place, which compels aspiring migrants to engage in criminalized practices, such as "corruption," "document fraud," or unauthorized border crossings, in order to appropriate mobility within and against a complex security dispositif whose very logic is to make mobility to Europe a scarce resource. By enticing this "forced fraud" (Garcia 1997), the Schengen visa regime generates this and other forms of "delinquency," such as illegalized migration in unseaworthy boats across the Mediterranean, which are subsequently invoked as evidence by border control authorities for the alleged need to introduce still more and better security technologies, a dynamic that I describe in the next section.

At the Consulate: Encountering an Unpredictable Regime of Institutionalized Distrust

Remarkably, the Schengen visa regime entices not only "have-nots" like Mohamed, Tarek, and Walid to engage in criminalized practices like the manipulation of supporting documents, but also people who are able to provide the requested documents that are needed to submit a visa application procedure in the first place. The reason is that even for those who fulfill the formal criteria for a Schengen visa, the outcome of their application is highly uncertain as they are faced with an unpredictable regime of institutionalized distrust.

Given that it is the very raison d'être of the Schengen visa regime to deflect the mobility of potential migrants, while facilitating the mobility of "bona fide" travelers, it is not surprising that many of the visa applicants I interviewed reported that they felt mistrusted and disbelieved by consular staff. This widely shared experience results from the fact that visa applicants enter the consulates of Schengen member states as "suspects" (Bigo and Guild 2003:93), as the following account from consulate Z confirms.

"Since when have you worked for this company?" the employee at consulate Z asks through the Plexiglas window. "For three months now," replies the woman, who has increasing difficulty holding her young child on her arm. She and her ten-year-old daughter standing beside her have been in front of the counter for more than half an hour. They look intimidated and strained. "You are very lucky," says the employee with a cynical inflection. "Thank you!"—"You are most welcome," replies the employee in an overly friendly voice, while she types under the rubric "Opinion" in the electronic file: "Note the unusually high income the applicant purports to have received for three months now."

After they have left, a young woman approaches the counter. She has completed a master's degree in English at a local university and is applying for a visa to take up an internship with an NGO working with people with special needs. "How did you find this internship?" "Why do you want to work for this NGO?" "Is this the first time you have applied for a Schengen visa?" While the woman replies "yes" to the last question, the employee writes in the "Opinion" section: "Note that the education of the applicant has nothing to do with her envisaged internship." When I ask the employee why she has entered this unfavorable judgment, she replies that the young woman has just finished her studies and is "apparently" looking for work. "Her visa application will probably be refused," she concludes.

This account offers a glimpse of the culture of institutionalized distrust that reigns in the consulates of Schengen countries.[6] Institutionalized distrust has frequently been identified as a central feature of the visa application procedure (Alpes and Spire 2014; Bigo and Guild 2003; CIMADE 2010; Infantino and Rea 2012). The latter has been described as a bureaucratic process in which "suspicion by default" (Zampagni 2013:96) is regarded as "a sign of professionalism" (Alpes 2011:125).

In the following I demonstrate, however, that this culture of distrust is not created by instances of fraud (Alpes and Spire 2014:167), though it is certainly animated by them. Rather, it is already inscribed in the Schengen visa regime's risk management approach. This is reflected in the Community Code on Visas (CCV), the legal basis for the Schengen visa regime. Article 21 states that the principal objective of the visa application procedure is to "assess . . . whether the applicant presents a risk of illegal immigration or a risk to the security of the Member States and whether the applicant intends to leave the territory of the Member States before the expiry of the visa applied for" (EP and Council 2009b:12). Under this clause, the mere wish to travel to the Schengen area becomes the subject of general suspicion. Consequently, the assumption of innocence is reversed in the visa application procedure: consular staff always start from the negative, and it is the applicant who has to convince consular staff that she does not intend to migrate. It is thus the notion of risk itself that creates a culture of institutionalized distrust in Schengen visa regime consulates.

In this context it should be noted that the notion of risk constitutes an indispensable element of the operational logic of the Schengen visa regime. It is through its evaluation in terms of risk that the entire population of a given country is rendered suspect. It is thus the notion of risk which allows those wishing to move to be subjected to in-depth control in their country of departure, before they have even started to move. This dislocation of border controls in both space and time constitutes, in a nutshell, the raison d'être of the Schengen visa regime, as a report for the EMN confirms: "Visa policy is a tool of which the EU and the Member States avail themselves in an attempt to control the mobility of third country nationals prior to their entry into the country, i.e. extra-territorially" (Parusel and Schneider 2012:5). During this extra-territorial control process, applicants have to prove through the answers they provide in an interview and the documents they furnish as evidence for their answers that, contrary to the general suspicion that led to the imposition of a visa requirement in the first place, they do not pose a "migration" or "security risk." A culture of institutionalized distrust at consulates is therefore as integral to the operational logic of the Schengen visa regime as the notion of risk itself.

But how do consular staff "assess" the "migration risk" of an applicant in order to fulfill the core objective of the visa application procedure, and what are the criteria on which this "assessment" is based? The answer in brief is that consular staff do not so much assess but rather ascribe a migration risk to a visa applicant, based on informal criteria that vary from one visa section to the next. It is thus no miracle that many applicants judge the decision making to be arbitrary and unfair (Alpes 2011; Bigo and Guild 2003; CIMADE 2010; Infantino 2013). What underpins these widely shared perceptions is that the Schengen visa regime is, in fact, unpredictable in regard to its decision-making procedure and its outcomes. This unpredictability derives from the discretionary power of consular staff in conjunction with the visa regime's risk management approach, which introduces an irreducible moment of interpretation in the decision-making procedure.

Whenever I asked consular staff how they decide on visa applications, I received the same evasive answer as Alexis Spire (2009:80) in his seminal study on French migration administrations: "on a case by case basis." The head of the visa section in consulate Z (hereinafter: M) defended this case-by-case approach as "sensible," arguing that it would grant consular staff the "flexibility that is necessary to assess each case individually." What this justification of consular staff's "flexibility" in decision making indicates is that discretion constitutes an indispensable element of the operational logic of the Schengen visa regime. Discretion is an irreducible "part of the reality of policy implementation," because it permits street-level bureaucrats working on the front line to adapt abstract laws and regulations to individual cases and local circumstances (Bouchard and Carroll 2002:242; Lipsky 1980:16). Consular staff often emphasized that the definition of any clear-cut decision criteria would prove to be impossible. Since "each dossier is different," as they put it, consular staff have to interpret it to adapt it to the general provisions of abstract laws and regulations. It is thus their task to "assess" the "migration risk" of a visa applicant, the practical implementation of Article 21 of the legal basis of the Schengen visa regime (EP and Council 2009b), that introduces an irreducible moment of interpretation in the decision-making procedure. And it is this aspect of interpretation, which is inherent in any assessment of risk, that makes the decision-making procedure unpredictable for visa applicants, as it results in the application of decision criteria that vary from one consulate to the next.

For consular staffs' decision-making praxis is shaped by a local practical knowledge that varies across visa sections. The reason is that the notion of "migration risk" creates uncertainty not only for visa applicants, but also for consular staff. The task of "assessing" the "migration risk" posed by an applicant compels consular staff to make decisions under conditions of time constraint, incomplete information, and uncertainty. "We cannot look inside people's heads," a senior official responsible for visa policy at a foreign ministry admits in an interview. Since consular staff have no direct access to visa applicants' intentions, their "assessment" of an applicant's "migration risk" is based primarily on interpretation. But this interpretation does not occur in a void. It is shaped by practical knowledge and informal decision-making criteria that circulate among consular staff in the form of stories about legendary cases that function as reference points for their decisions, as illustrated by the following example.

"This applicant shows the profile of a young person from a deprived area in the South who seeks to establish relationships with tourists, enabling him to apply for a visa to Europe. A possible marriage cannot be ruled out." This is one of the many entries by counter staff at consulate Z that features the notions of "risk" and "profile." It illustrates that consular staff interpret a particular combination of certain biographical features as indicators of the presence or absence of "migration risk." But this example equally shows that these interpretations are shaped by local practical knowledge that surfaces in the form of prototype cases. Consular staff "assess" the "migration risk" of an applicant by looking for patterns in the biographical features and narratives of visa applicants in order to allocate them to one of the "profiles" of these prototype cases. In this instance, it is the applicant's age, place of origin, social class, and relationship to his host that serve as indicators for "migration risk," as they correspond to a presumably well-established profile.[7]

Hence, consular staff's decisions are not arbitrary because they are bestowed with a relative coherency by the informal decision-making criteria that circulate among consular staff in the form of advice and stories about legendary cases that are subsequently codified informally as "profiles" and "types" of applicants. This local practical knowledge about certain "profiles" and "types" of applicants is then mobilized by consular staff to negotiate the uncertainty that the task of "assessing" the "migration risk" of an applicant generates for them. Together with a culture of institutionalized distrust and a shared ethos among consular staff, who tend to regard themselves as protectors of national identity and defenders of their national welfare state (Infantino and Rea 2012:74; Spire 2009:58–60), this local practical knowledge imbues consular staffs' decision making with a relative coherency.

While this relative coherency explains why consular staffs' decisions are not arbitrary, their decisions remain, nevertheless, unpredictable for applicants, for three reasons. First, there remains a variance within the relative coherence of the decision-making praxis in each visa section due to the discretionary power of consular staff (Spire 2009:61–79). Second, the informal criteria and prototype cases that inform consular staffs' decisions are not known to visa applicants. Finally, decisions on visa applications remain unpredictable because the practical knowledge that bestows consular staffs' decision-making praxis with a certain coherency within one visa section varies from one consulate to the next.

For instance, M explains to me that he would never issue a visa to a widowed woman wanting to visit her grandchildren in Europe, "because the risk is too high that she stays with her family." He conceives this case as an example where overstaying the visa would present both the visitor and the hosts with a "win-win situation." Following M's reasoning, the widowed woman has an interest in staying in Europe, because she would no longer be alone. The family would in turn welcome her stay, because the grandmother could look after their children. The head of another visa section argues, in contrast, that he would always issue a visa in such cases if the inviting family could sustain the applicant financially, because "an old woman does not do the economy any harm, no matter whether she stays or not." What this example illustrates is that the local practical knowledge informing consular staffs' "assessment" of an applicant's "migration risk" varies considerably from one consulate to the next, rendering their decisions difficult to fathom for visa applicants.

Ironically, it is then the risk management approach of the Schengen visa regime and the attempt to render uncertain future behaviors predictable and governable that make the decision-making procedure unpredictable and its outcome uncertain for visa applicants. Yet the uncertainty that this unpredictability of the decision-making procedure creates for visa applicants "is not equal for everyone" (Alpes 2011:120). Those who regard the visa application procedure primarily as a time-consuming nuisance, like the surgeon in the queue, are those who can be relatively certain of getting a visa because their "profile" corresponds to that of a bona fide traveler. A second group of people, like Mohamed, Tarek, and Walid, can in turn be certain that they will not be granted a visa as long as they play by the rules that render them ineligible for an entry ticket to Europe. For a significant share of people, however, the result of their visa applications is highly uncertain due to a bureaucratic process that is unpredictable because of the irreducible moment of interpretation that decision making by consular staff involves, and the opacity and variability of the informal criteria they deploy to "assess" the alleged "migration risk" of an applicant.

Practices like applying at a consulate that has a reputation for being less "strict" than the representation of the member state that constitutes an applicant's actual travel destination, or concealing biographical features that may be interpreted as indicators of a "migration risk" by consular staff, such as family ties in Europe, are prosecuted as "visa shopping" and instances of "fraud."[8] And they are represented as such by border control authorities, who cite them as evidence for the alleged need to tame the excessive agency of visa applicants through ever more pervasive security technologies like biometrics. However, from the viewpoint of those wishing to move, these and other practices of appropriation constitute indispensable tactics that are necessary in order to negotiate the uncertainty that the visa application procedure generates for them. It is thus the culture of distrust that reigns in the consulates of Schengen member states, in conjunction with the opacity and variability of the informal criteria used by consular staff in their decision making, that prompt people willing to move to engage in practices of appropriation in the hope of increasing the prospects of success for their visa application.

Yet the introduction of the biometric database VIS, which is meant to serve the EU as a multipurpose tool in its self-proclaimed "fight against illegal immigration" (EC 2006), forestalls some of the practices by which people willing to move could previously succeed to appropriate mobility to Europe via the Schengen visa. It is, for instance, no longer possible to hand off passports with valid Schengen visas to "lookalikes," as indicated in the introduction. It is also no longer possible to use stolen blank visa stickers or to manipulate the content of visa stickers in a way that permits the reuse of a visa, either by the person to whom it was issued or by another person. If no corresponding file exists in the VIS, it is very likely that the person concerned will be denied entry upon arrival at the external borders of the Schengen area. For border guards use the VIS not only to verify that the person seeking to cross the border is the same one to whom the visa has been issued, but also to retrieve extensive data on the traveler and her visa application from the database in order to compare it to the information on the visa sticker.[9] Finally, the VIS permits consular staff to detect the lodging of several visa applications at different Schengen consulates, because they can now check, as a senior border guard put it, "if this fingerprint has already applied for a visa."[10] Hence, the introduction of the VIS raises the question of how people willing to move can still appropriate mobility to Europe via Schengen visa in the context of biometric border controls.

Appropriating Mobility to Europe via Schengen Visa: Real, Fake, Fakingly Real, or Real Fake?

During my fieldwork at consulates in North Africa I encountered various ways of appropriating Schengen visas. Due to space constraints, I am only able to present one mode of appropriation here, one that involves the provision of manipulated or falsified supporting documents. I will use this example to outline six features that practices of appropriation share, irrespective of their form. The aim is to introduce the notion of appropriation as an alternative concept to theorize migrants' capacity to subvert border controls and defy migration policy objectives.

The need for such an alternative concept resides in the shortcomings of the two concepts that are usually invoked in border and migration studies to grasp migrants' capacity to challenge and subvert border controls. These are the concepts of agency and resistance. The main problem with the concept of agency is that agency, understood as "the socioculturally mediated capacity to act" (Ahearn 2001:112), always presupposes a structure as its counterpart. The result of this structure–agency divide is a static analysis in which structures and individual and collective forms of agency are analyzed separately and consecutively (for a more detailed account of this argument, see Scheel 2013b). What the notion of agency thus fails to capture is what we often find on the ground: an intricate entanglement of practices of government and subversion. The notion of resistance is in turn problematic because resistance is an inherently reactive concept: it suggests an already existing formation of domination that is to be opposed in a reactive manner. Due to its conception as a "responsive act" (Rose 2002:387), the notion of resistance fails to register the constitutive role that practices of contestation by the governed play in the transformation of regimes of government (O'Malley et al. 1997). In the following I will thus introduce the notion of appropriation as an alternative concept that transcends these limitations of "agency" and "resistance."

During my second visit to consulate Z, a woman applies for a family reunification visa to join her husband, who is already living in Europe. The supporting documents she needs to provide to obtain a long-term national D visa are even more comprehensive than those demanded for a Schengen visa.[11] Instead of the applicant's "will to return," the socioeconomic situation of her spouse is decisive for the positive outcome of her application. Following the laws of the country represented by consulate Z, staff must be assured that the applicant will "not become a burden for the welfare state," as an employee formulates it. Besides a marriage certificate, the woman has to provide evidence that her husband can sustain her and their children financially, and that his apartment is spacious enough to accommodate them. Q, a counter official, flips through the supporting documents the woman has passed through the hatch beneath the Plexiglas window in separate piles. "Your husband's pay slips are too old. Is he still employed?" When the woman replies that he is not, Q advises her to refrain from filing her application. The woman seems puzzled: "Why do you not want to give me a visa? I have given you three pay slips, as stated in the leaflet on your homepage." Q patiently explains that it is not the correct number of pay slips that is decisive for the outcome of her application, but credible evidence that her husband receives sufficient income to sustain her financially. The woman leaves close to tears.

Shortly afterward she returns to Q's counter, accompanied by the security officer guarding the entrance. She wants to know why Q is refusing to process her application. "I have only politely advised you not to lodge your application because it will probably be rejected. If you insist, I am happy to process your application." The woman asks Q to write down how many and what kind of documents are missing for a successful application. Q replies that it is not his job to solve her problems. The woman insists: "So if I bring you three more pay slips, then you will give me the visa?" Q becomes loud: "No! It is not about the pay slips, but that your husband has to receive a stable income so you can prove he can sustain you financially! You have just told me that your husband is out of work at the moment. So do you want to forge the documents or what?"

While we do not know if this is what the woman had in mind, many applicants do, in fact, resort to falsifying and manipulating supporting documents such as employment contracts and social security records. As explained in the previous section, this "forced fraud" (Garcia 1997; Spire 2009:56) is provoked by a highly restrictive visa regime that sets requirements for a Schengen visa that do not correspond to the living realities of a large share of the local population. What the encounter described above indicates is the contested status of the supporting documents. For consular staff like Q, pay slips and other supporting documents constitute a device of control for the verification of the socioeconomic situation of applicants and their hosts. Article 21 of the CCV stipulates: "The examination of an application shall be based notably on the authenticity and reliability of the documents submitted and on the veracity and reliability of the statements made by the applicant" (EP and Council 2009b:12). The example of the woman shows, in turn, that applicants regard the requested supporting documents primarily as obstacles to be negotiated in order to receive an entry ticket to the Schengen area. From their perspective, the falsification and manipulation of supporting documents like pay slips and bank statements constitutes an attempt to repurpose these devices of control into means for appropriating mobility.

Hence, the first feature of practices of appropriation is that they operate through the recoding of the actors, methods, and effects of control into means of appropriation. This capacity of migrants stems from the logic of contemporary border regimes in making people willing to move and, when on the move, complicit in the control of their mobility. Migrants are implicated in the control of their mobility not only as passive objects, but also as acting subjects, because the capacity of border regimes to regulate human mobility derives from, but also hinges on, the active participation of those whose mobility they are designed to govern. Supporting documents like bank statements or social security records are requested by the consulate, but they are provided by the visa applicant. This distribution of the capacity to act in migrants' embodied encounters with border control authorities (Scheel 2013b) also surfaces in the fact that it is Q, the employee of consulate Z, who asks the woman in front of her counter questions in order to assess her eligibility for a family reunification visa, but it is the woman who provides the answers and is thus able to influence the outcome of Q's assessment. It is such active involvement of people on the move in the governance of their mobility that implies that migrants can articulate their capacity to act in ways that convert the means, methods, and practices of mobility control into mechanisms that allow for its appropriation.

This observation indicates the second shared feature of practices of appropriation: they are inseparably intertwined with the actors, means, methods, operational logics, and effects of mobility control. What aspiring migrants and travelers try to achieve through the provision of falsified or manipulated supporting documents is to transform the functional overdetermination of the Schengen visa regime into a pathway to mobility. This functional overdetermination resides in its multiple "objectives of promoting exchanges among civil society, of meeting the demand for skilled labour, of attracting investment and business without enhancing the risk of irregular migration" (Parusel and Schneider 2012:45).

While applicants do not know the criteria that guide consular staffs' decision-making, they do nevertheless have a sense of these criteria. How and where to get a visa is a topic of intense debate in the country I visited, precisely because people are confronted with an unpredictable regime of institutionalized distrust. Hence, a superficial knowledge of consular staffs' informal decision-making criteria circulates in the form of rumors and stories about people whose applications have either been refused or accepted by a particular consulate. These stories and rumors mirror the local practical knowledge consular staff mobilize to cope with the uncertainty generated by the risk management approach. While consular staff use stories about prototype cases as reference points for their decisions, visa applicants infer the "profiles" of these prototype cases from rumors about successful visa applications. Due to these rumors, aspiring migrants sense that they have to provide evidence that they have "something to lose," "something to return to" in their country of origin if they want to convince consular staff of their "will to return." Hence, many applicants falsify supporting documents or manipulate their content in such a way that the fictitious biographies these documents support correspond to the perceived "profile" of a bona fide traveler. "The secret is to look good on paper," asserts Anas, a schoolteacher whom I met outside a large visa section, aptly summarizing this tactic of appropriation.

These features highlight that the notion of appropriation captures—better than the concepts of "agency" and "resistance"—the intricate entanglement of practices of government and control with those of subversion and contestation that we often find on the ground. Instead of obscuring this intricate entanglement through a static analysis that engages "structures" and "agency" in isolation from one another, the notion of appropriation invites scholars to investigate, first, how migrants try to repurpose and recode the actors, devices, and methods of mobility control into means of appropriation, in order to show, second, how this capacity derives from the features of the mechanisms of control themselves that enlist people in the surveillance and regulation of their own mobility.

The reason we encounter an intricate entanglement of practices of control and subversion in the context of migration, rather than open confrontation, is the highly asymmetrical power relation at sites of border control. At consulates, visa applicants must behave within the narrow parameters set by this securitizing site: they must provide all the requested documents, answer all questions asked by consular staff, and—since VIS began operation—have their fingerprints taken. An outright refusal to comply with any of these regulations results in the automatic refusal of a visa. It is these highly asymmetrical power relations that explain why, rather than openly contesting restrictive border regimes, migrants usually try to recode the mechanisms of control into means of appropriation. And it is these highly asymmetrical power relations that likewise compel migrants to execute this recoding secretly and unnoticed if their attempts are to be successful. Practices of appropriation, then, constitute both an "art" (de Certeau 1984:37) and a "weapon of the weak" (Scott 1985). Since practices of appropriation operate—like the tactics described by Michel de Certeau (1984)—in an environment they do not own, remaining undetected—and this is their third shared feature—is a precondition of success for practices of appropriation.[12]

For consular staff are, of course, aware of attempts to appropriate visas through the provision of falsified or manipulated supporting documents. Applicants who provide self-fabricated documents run the highest risk of being detected. Consular staff reported documents containing clumsily scanned stamps or evidently altered names. This shows that appropriating a Schengen visa by staging a fictitious biography backed up by manipulated or falsified feeder documents demands skills, knowledge, and social contacts that not all people possess.

These failed attempts also point out that the recoding of the actors, mechanisms, and methods of control into means of appropriation involves the clandestine transgression of the norms, official regulations, and informal rules of contemporary border regimes. Through the clandestine transgression of the parameters of legitimate behavior laid out for them—and this is the fourth feature of practices of appropriation—migrants initiate a relation of irreconcilable conflict between migration and attempts to regulate it. For consular staff regard migrants' attempts to appropriate a visa through falsified or manipulated supporting documents as nothing less than "document fraud." Each instance of "fraud" which is detected is taken as confirmation of the need for constant vigilance since staff are dealing with "people [who] use all sorts of tricks to get a visa," as M put it. This relation of conflict manifests in dialogues of action between migrants who try to appropriate a visa by providing manipulated documents and consular staff trying to detect these attempts. It is through the study of migrants' embodied encounters with the actors, means, and methods of control that these conflictive dialogues of action can be investigated (Scheel 2013b).

In these conflictive dialogues of action migrants confront devices, actors, and methods of surveillance and control that constitute recuperated forms of previously successful practices of appropriation. One visa section head cites the employment of local staff, who can tell whether the appearance, statements, and behavior of an applicant correspond to her claimed socioeconomic standing, as an important safeguard against the use of manipulated supporting documents. This control measure underlines the importance of impression management in the interview situation. If applicants claim to hold a higher socioeconomic position than they actually do, they need to dress up and prepare for possible questions in regard to their claimed profession. A salesman in a shabby business suit who purports to do business in Europe without speaking a single word of French or English, or without knowing the price of the goods he purports to purchase, will not be believed. Migrants who try to appropriate a visa by providing manipulated or falsified supporting documents have to maintain a strict "dramaturgical discipline" with the script of the fictitious biography their documents are meant to support. They should "not commit unmeant gestures or faux pas in performing it" and should be able cope with "dramaturgical contingencies as they arise," such as an unexpected question from consular staff (Goffman 1959:216).

Any incoherency between applicants' fictitious biographies and their appearance, statements, and behavior in the interview may prompt consular staff to engage in additional background checks. In case of doubt, consular staff may call banks, universities, and employers to verify the information provided by employment contracts, certificates, and bank statements (Spire 2009:93). Staff at consulate Z, in turn, verify the applicant's social security records to check the information given on bank statements, employment contracts, and pay slips. Each day M sends a list of social security numbers from cases that have raised his suspicions to the local administration to verify that the information on the social security records provided is correct and corresponds to an applicant's claimed income. Some member states also send specially trained border guards who use UV lamps, magnifying cameras, and forgery detectors to check passports and supporting documents for traces of manipulation and falsification. If they detect manipulated or falsified supporting documents, the corresponding visa application will automatically be refused. In addition, consular staff may add the applicant's name to the so-called black list.[13]

The stance that it is migrants' practices of appropriation that initiate a relation of irreconcilable conflict between migration and the attempts to control it permits one to read these means and methods of mobility control as attempts to recuperate migrants' practices of appropriation. It is migrants' attempts to appropriate the Schengen visa and the struggles that these attempts initiate that force the European border regime into a permanent process of reorganization (Papadopoulos et al. 2008:77–80). The European border regime emerges as an apparatus of capture that tries to recuperate migrants' practices of appropriation in order to convert them into a driving force of its own development (Shukaitis 2009:37). More precisely, this vast security dispositif tries to harness new forms of knowledge, sociality, and creativity ingrained in migrants' practices of appropriation. From this it follows, first, that migrants' practices of appropriation are enmeshed in a dynamic of subversion of the security dispositif, within which they institute a relation of conflict that then is manifested as the dispositif's attempts to recuperate those same practices. Second, this stance requires contemporary modes of border control to be conceived of as recuperated forms of previously successful practices of appropriation (Shukaitis 2009:48). In this way, to paraphrase Antonio Negri, the notion of appropriation permits scholars to show that it is "by means of a continual theft of the [knowledge] generated by [migrants'] struggles" that the security dispositif "create[s] increasingly complex mechanisms of domination" (2005 [1982]).[14] The concept of appropriation is thus better equipped than the notion of agency with its structure–agency divide and the inherently reactive concept of resistance to capture the constitutive role that practices of subversion and dissent by the governed play in the transformation of regimes of government.

Yet, despite the introduction of ever more sophisticated methods of control and ever more pervasive security technologies like the VIS, there exists one form of manipulated feeder documents that are, in the words of consular staff, "nearly impossible to detect." In the country I visited they are known as "vrais faux" which one can roughly translate as "real fakes." Since "the secret is to look good on paper," people may ask a friend or relative who owns a company to "hire" them in order to obtain the employment contract and pay slips required for a successful visa application, Anas tells me over coffee. "What you need is a skilled job, like an engineer, a teacher, or a receptionist in a large hotel," before adding: "many people do that." The existence of this practice is confirmed by J when I ask her about the authentication of supporting documents. "Many people ask a friend or relative to provide them with an employment contract. These 'real fakes' are nearly impossible to detect, because they are essentially originals."[15]

Even if consular staff call the company that has issued the documents, they will not discover that the applicant is only employed on paper since the person answering the phone will confirm all the information in the documents. Similarly, a request at the social security office will not reveal the employment as fictitious, because the friend who "employs" the person who requires an employment contract is required by law to pay social security contributions for her "employee." In practice, the latter would reimburse her "employer" for the monthly contributions. Hence, the social security records provided by a fictitiously employed applicant are just as "real" as her employment contract and her pay slips:

all these documents are originals, issued by actually existing companies and administrations, but the employment relation they support is fictitious.

What the appropriation of a Schengen visa through "real fakes" demonstrates is that identity remains a "battleground" (Groebner 2004:182), despite attempts to render migrants' bodies a means of mobility control through the introduction of biometric databases. The VIS does not help anyone to verify the authenticity of the supporting documents upon which the decision to issue a biometric Schengen visa is based (Muller 2010:19). Ultimately, the appropriation of Schengen visas through the provision of "real fakes" in the context of VIS confirms that biometric recognition systems are haunted by the very problem they are meant to solve, because "any foreseeable system will be based on exactly the document-based methods of identification upon which biometrics are supposed to be an improvement" (Gold 2012:11).

The fact that this playing with identities is still possible in the context of biometric border controls illustrates, in turn, that moments of uncontrollability of migratory practices—that is, moments of autonomy of migration—emerge, ironically, when migrants stage a convincing performance of *compliance* with the Schengen visa regime's formal and informal requirements. The provision of manipulated documents that are nearly impossible to detect has to be complemented by a credible imitation of the dress codes, behaviors, and biographical features of the bona fide travelers aspiring migrants purport to be. In these performances of compliance with the "profiles" of bona fide travelers, it becomes intelligible why practices of appropriation derive their efficacy not from open resistance to the Schengen visa regime and its discriminating requirements, but from their clandestine subversion, from hollowing them out from the inside.

Paradoxically, it is in these performances of docile compliance that the political quality of practices of appropriation comes to the fore: by staging a performance of feigned compliance with formal rules and informal criteria, migrants take hold of exactly what these rules and criteria are meant to deprive them of: access to mobility. The crucial point is that migrants authorize themselves to take the resources (not rights) of which border regimes seek to deprive them without, and instead of, claiming them from someone. I speak of resources instead of rights here to stress that migrants appropriating mobility do not assert any claims to entitlements like freedom of movement, but rather *take* material and immaterial goods like mobility that are withheld from them. While the language of rights invokes an authority that recognizes and grants rights claimed by subjects, the notion of resources, understood as "material or immaterial goods that can be drawn on by a person or organisation to function effectively" (*Oxford English Dictionary*), immediately links practices of appropriation with debates on the commons.[16] It is this moment of self-authorization that bestows practices of appropriation (and this is their fifth shared feature) with an irreducible political quality. Though migrants try to avoid attracting any attention when they appropriate mobility via a Schengen visa, they nevertheless render border controls, and the legally codified forms of citizenship and socioeconomic status quo that border controls are meant to establish and maintain, as objects of contestation and dissent. Instead of openly opposing restrictive migration regulations and related mechanisms of control, practices of appropriation challenge border controls by staging credible performances of the scripts of mobile subjectivities like middle-class tourists or business people, whose "profiles" are regarded as devoid of any "migration risk." Thus, migrants erode the informal criteria that guide the decisions of consular staff, ultimately plunging the Schengen visa regime into an epistemic crisis. Since "real fakes" are nearly impossible to detect, consular staff can no longer tell whether they are dealing with a "real" or a "fake" tourist, student, or businessman, because the supporting documents provided may not only be "fake" or "real," but could also be "real fakes."

Yet the appropriation of a Schengen visa through the provision of "real fakes" and the successful imitation of the appearance of a bona fide traveler does not signify an unequivocal "victory" of migrants over biometric border control technologies. Rather, it underscores the irreducible ambivalence of practices of appropriation as their sixth and final feature.

What makes practices of appropriation ambivalent is that they are inseparably intertwined with the means and methods of mobility control. The recoding of the devices, actors, operational logics, and effects of mobility control into means of appropriation implies concessions, compromises, and side effects that may prove to be detrimental for migrants and their migration projects in the long run. Migrants cannot completely usurp the means and methods of control for their own purposes. Due to these concessions, compromises, and side effects, practices of appropriation always result in partial, contested, and polyvalent outcomes that imply further struggles over the appropriation of mobility, and each of these struggles features its own set of sites, actors, and stakes. It is thus the irreducible ambivalence of migrants' practices of appropriation that inserts a self-perpetuating dynamic into migrants' struggles over mobility to Europe. The final paragraph of the visa application form, above the field reserved for the applicant's signature, is indicative of this self-perpetuating dynamic:

> I undertake to leave the territory of the Member States before the expiry of the visa, if granted. I have been informed that possession of a visa is

only one of the prerequisites for entry into the European territory of the Member States. The mere fact that a visa has been granted to me does not mean that I will be entitled to compensation if I fail to comply with the relevant provisions of Article 5(1) of Regulation (EC) No 562/2006 (Schengen Borders Code) and I am therefore refused entry. The prerequisites for entry will be checked again on entry into the European territory of the Member States. (as cited in EP and Council 2009b:29)

The statement that a visa does not guarantee entry to the Schengen area indicates that the successful appropriation of a Schengen visa leads to another struggle over the selective denial and direct appropriation of mobility. The struggle that revolves around the conditions of entry takes place upon arrival at the external border of the Schengen area. The first line of the paragraph indicates, in contrast, that migrants will face further struggles over mobility and other resources after a successful border crossing. The appropriation of mobility via the Schengen visa results in a compromise, as it also implies migrants' disenfranchisement by the border regime: living and working in Europe is now possible, but only under the precarious and contested conditions of illegality (Karakayali and Tsianos 2005). After the expiration of their visas, migrants become "illegal," rendering the entire Schengen area a vast borderzone crisscrossed by struggles revolving around the appropriation of various resources such as an income, housing, access to health care, and a permanent residence title. In these struggles the appropriation of mobility remains contested and preliminary as long as migrants are haunted by their data doubles that were created when they initially applied for a Schengen visa and that are stored in VIS in order to facilitate their reidentification and deportation in case of detection by authorities. It is this self-perpetuating dynamic of migrants' struggles over the appropriation of mobility and other resources that makes the relation of conflict that migrants initiate within the security dispositif an irreconcilable conflict between migration and attempts to control it.

Conclusion

Starting from the observation that the central role of the Schengen visa regime in the illegalization of migration as well as in the appropriation of mobility to Europe has not been sufficiently acknowledged to date, I have engaged this complex security dispositif from the perspective of those whose mobility it is meant to assess and control. Drawing on the provision of manipulated or falsified supporting documents as an example, I have shown (and this was the first objective of this chapter) that it is still possible to appropriate mobility to Europe via the Schengen visa in the context of biometric border controls. Adopting the perspective of mobility has allowed me to show, moreover, that these and other practices of appropriation are provoked by the Schengen visa regime itself. The latter constitutes a vast machine of illegalization that, besides creating an artificial scarcity of access to mobility to Europe by setting requirements for a visa that do not correspond to local circumstances, entices applicants to engage in criminalized practices such as "visa shopping" or "document fraud" in order to increase the prospects of success for their applications. While the provision of manipulated feeder documents emerges as a tactic of aspiring travelers and migrants that is necessary in order to appropriate mobility within and against an unpredictable regime of institutionalized distrust, these and other practices of appropriation are framed in terms of delinquency by border control authorities as instances of "fraud" and "betrayal." In this way, migrants' attempts to appropriate Schengen visas are mobilized as evidence for the alleged need to implement more and better security technologies, such as the VIS, a dynamic that Michel Foucault (1980 [1977]:195) has called the "strategic elaboration" of the security dispositif. I could only briefly indicate this dynamic here by characterizing the Schengen visa regime as an apparatus of capture that tries to recuperate migrants' practices of appropriation in order to render them a driving force for its own development. Thus, I have tried to show that the notion of appropriation is better equipped than the inherently reactive concept of resistance to account for the *constitutive* role that practices of subversion and dissent by the governed play in the transformation of regimes of governance. It also better captures the intricate entanglement of practices of contestation with those of surveillance, government, and control than the notion of "agency" with its structure–agency divide. In order to introduce the notion of appropriation as an alternative concept for the theorization of migrants' practices of subversion (and this was the second objective of this chapter), I have used the provision of manipulated supporting documents as an example to outline six features that practices of appropriation share, irrespective of their form. Hopefully, this conception will provide a useful tool to intervene in migrants' mostly silent but inherently political struggles over mobility and other resources by showing that it is the operational logics of today's ever more pervasive border regimes which provoke the very phenomena that they are designed to combat and forestall.

Acknowledgments

The author acknowledges funding from a European Research Council (ERC) Consolidator Grant (Agreement no. 615588; Principal Investigator: Evelyn Ruppert, Goldsmiths, University of London) under the European Union's Seventh Framework Programme (FP/2007–2013), which has supported the writing of this chapter.

NOTES

1. In this chapter I use the criminalizing terms *illegal migrant* or *illegal migration* only if the EU's official terminology is unavoidable. In order to highlight the active role that statist institutions play in the processes that make people "illegal" I will speak of "illegalized migrants" instead (Bauder 2013; De Genova 2002). The notion of "illegalized" migrants thus brings to the fore the processes of illegalization that get concealed by other, apparently politically more correct, alternative terms like "unauthorized," "irregular," "clandestine" migrant, or "sans papiers" (Karakayali 2008). Especially in relation to the mode of illegalized migration described in this chapter, these terms occlude more than they reveal, as many migrants enter the EU neither unauthorized, nor clandestine, nor as "sans papiers."

2. Subsequent figures suggest that this share might have increased: A report of the U.S. Department of Homeland Security (DHS) published in January 2016 suggests that in 2015 alone 416,500 people on short-term visas may have remained in the United States after their "lawful admission period" expired, as the DHS had no record of their departure despite data exchange programs with all commercial air and sea travel providers (DHS 2016).

3. What distinguishes the AoM from other approaches in border and migration studies is that it makes migrants' practices the starting and focal point of any investigation of border regimes or migratory processes (Moulier Boutang 2007). Due to this strategic-analytical prioritization of migrants' practices, the AoM is particularly attuned to migrants' struggles over the appropriation of mobility and other resources within and against today's border regimes. Hence, proponents of the AoM understand migration as a political expression in itself (Bojadžijev and Karakayali 2007; De Genova 2010d; Mezzadra 2011; Papadopoulos et al. 2008). With this impetus, the AoM was introduced as an alternative to the "Fortress Europe" discourse in debates of the antiracist movement in the 1990s (for a more detailed discussion of the AoM's features and relevant debates, see Scheel 2013a).

4. All names in this chapter have been changed.

5. These 124 countries include all African and most Asian states (with the exception of Japan, Malaysia, and South Korea) as well as four South American states, plus Belize, Cuba, and Jamaica in the Caribbean (Council of the EU 2001). For a map, refer to official webpage of the DG Migration and Home Affairs of the European Commission, http://ec.europa.eu/dgs/home-affairs/what-we-do/policies/borders-and-visas/visa-policy/index_en.htm (accessed May 1, 2015).

6. The notion of a culture of institutionalized distrust is inspired by studies of the British asylum system, which invoke a "culture of disbelief" to grasp the generalized suspicion with which asylum-seekers are confronted throughout the processing of their claims (e.g., Griffiths 2012).

7. For the prominence of the notions of "risk" and "profile" in the judgments of consular staff in other consulates, see the works of Federica Infantino and Andrea Rea (2012) and Francesca Zampagni (2013:95–97). This is no coincidence, since an EC handbook on the processing of visa applications explicitly invites consulates to "define 'profiles' of applicants presenting a specific risk" (EC 2010:65). Yet the handbook neither defines what a "profile" is nor outlines procedures for how a "profile" should be drawn up. Moreover, the role of these "profiles" in the decision-making procedure remains entirely unclear as "each individual application shall be assessed on its own merits irrespective of possible 'profiles' having been drawn up" (EC 2010).

8. The pejorative term *visa shopping* refers, first, to the practice of visa applicants filing further applications at the consulates of one or several other Schengen member states after an initial application has already been turned down, and second, to the practice of filing an application at the consulate of a member state other than the one that is responsible for processing the application. Following Article 5 of the Community Code on Visas (CCV), applicants are required to apply for a Schengen visa at the consulate of the member state that constitutes "the main destination of the visit(s) in terms of length or purpose of stay" (EP and Council 2009b:6).

9. An amendment to the Schengen Border Code prescribes the verification of the fingerprints of all visa holders upon entry as mandatory (EP and Council 2009a).

10. To this end, the fingerprint templates and biographical information of all persons whose visa applications have been rejected are stored in the VIS for a period of five years. Following Articles 8(2) and 15 of the VIS regulations (EP and Council 2008) and Article 21(2) of the CCV (EP and Council 2009b), consular staff have to conduct a search in the VIS with the applicant's fingerprints in order to forestall this form of "visa shopping."

11. "D visa" is the official term for a visa that allows its holder to stay in the Schengen area beyond the maximum period of ninety days of a Schengen visa (officially referred to as a "C visa"). Though issuing D visas falls within the sole competence of member states and is not regulated by EU legislation, there are no differences concerning application and decision procedures (Infantino and Rea 2012). While data for D visas is not stored in the VIS, many member states have begun to capture the biometric data of applicants for D visas in national databases, since the necessary infrastructure is already in place due to the VIS.

12. Migration from North African or Turkish coasts to European islands constitutes a noteworthy exception to this rule, as it involves being "rescued" by the coast guard—i.e., recoding these agents of mobility control into a veritable means enabling the appropriation of mobility—and spending some time in detention camps on the island before being transferred to the European mainland. Once there, however, the success of the appropriation of mobility hinges again on remaining undetected and avoiding attracting any attention. For migrants usually disappear to lead a life under conditions of illegality and collectively organized invisibility (Carling 2007b; Papadopoulos et al. 2008). Moreover, the March 2016 deal between the EU and the Turkish government

that facilitated the direct return of migrants arriving on Greek islands back to Turkey has demonstrated that remaining undetected has again become a precondition of success for the appropriation of mobility to Europe by crossing the Mediterranean in often overcrowded boats.

13. Keeping "black lists" of applicants who have breached the visa regime's rules is not foreseen by the CCV. According to M, each consulate keeps its own black list. While visa sections inform each other about "abusive" applicants, it is at the discretion of each consulate's staff to decide whether to add a particular applicant to their black list. M could not tell me how many names were on consular Z's black list, as he could neither evaluate the list statistically nor delete any names from it. Consequently, M sometimes sees hits in the black list, which is searched automatically by the software when he processes a visa application, that were entered more than ten years ago by his predecessor.

14. This reading of the security dispositif as an apparatus of capture is in line with Foucault's analysis of the history of the arts of government. In his discussion of heretical practices diverging from Church doctrine, Foucault argues, for example, that "these counter-conducts . . . have been continually re-utilized, re-implanted and taken up again in one or another direction" by the Church, which "tries to . . . adapt them for its own ends" (2007:214–15).

15. In fact, this practice seems to exist in many countries. In her research on consular practices in Senegal, Francesca Zampagni mentions the practice of issuing employment contracts to friends and relatives (2011:23). "Real fakes" also feature in a newspaper article on the appropriation of Schengen visas in Ivory Coast (Allou 2011). The practice of drawing up "employment contracts . . . for friends or relatives to facilitate the issuing of a visa, though the persons concerned are not actually employed" is also mentioned in a handbook on the issuance of Schengen visas that was published by the EC (2010:57).

16. This is, however, not to say that rights, understood as claims to entitlements that are the subject of contestations and struggles, are completely absent from practices of appropriation. Just as laws are rearticulated and mobilized as tactics for the conduct of conduct by the arts of government (Foucault 2007:99), rights might be mobilized and rearticulated as tactics for the appropriation of resources by the governed.

2

Rescued and Caught

The Humanitarian-Security Nexus at Europe's Frontiers

RUBEN ANDERSSON

On October 15, 2014, a group of undocumented sub-Saharan migrants are caught on video clinging to the triple border fence of Melilla, a Spanish enclave and European Union outpost in North Africa. As one of them, a young Cameroonian, tries to descend via a ladder on the Spanish side, the border guards strike out at him with their batons until he falls. Seemingly unconscious, he is dragged back toward the fences by four officers wearing face masks and gloves. They enter a gate in the barrier and deposit him back on the Moroccan side, like an unwanted parcel returned to its sender.

Spool back a year, to autumn 2013, when the tragedies off the coast of the Italian island of Lampedusa held out the hope of a new European approach to migration controls. "Never again," dignitaries promised as they paid their respects in front of the coffins. Italy promptly launched an extensive military sea rescue mission, Mare Nostrum—yet, as is clear from the violence at Melilla's fences and the mounting tragedies in the Mediterranean, the misery was far from over. Instead, it is getting worse. Almost 4,000 people perished at Europe's external borders in 2015 alone, and more than 5,000 died in 2016, while many more are languishing in desperate conditions beyond the borders.[1]

At first glance, a seeming paradox defines Europe's response to irregular migration. On the one hand, we hear about violence and distress at the borders; on the other, about humanitarianism and human rights. While Italy's navy mounted difficult rescues during 2013–14, the Spanish government was adding razor wire to the fences of Melilla and allowed violent pushbacks into Morocco,

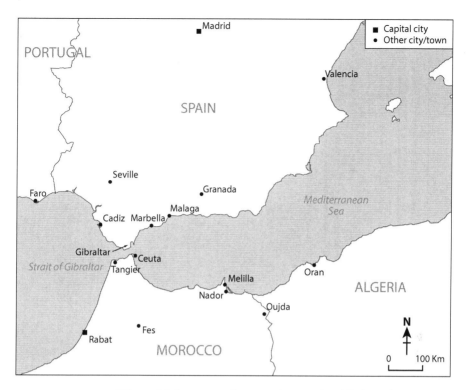

MAP 2.1. Western Mediterranean, featuring Ceuta and Melilla (Spain)

which it eventually "legalized."[2] While the European Commission has called for smoother asylum procedures and responsibility sharing, member states lock refugees up or keep them stranded indefinitely, as happens in Malta as well as in Melilla and its sister enclave of Ceuta (see, respectively, DeBono 2013 and Andersson 2014b). While the EU's Home Affairs commissioner, Dimitris Avramopolous, at one point proposed humanitarian visas, Italy's EU presidency launched a Europe-wide crackdown on undocumented migrants, Mos Maiorum, in late 2014.[3] The scramble in early 2016 to "secure" the Greek–Turkish borders again rehearsed this doubleness in the public debate—crackdowns on the one hand, supposed care on the other. Time and again, any liberal advances seem to be cut short by new draconian measures, motivated by a callous and simplistic quest for "deterrence" at any cost. Yet, as this chapter will show, these two seemingly opposite approaches—which we can gloss as humanitarian and securitarian—are in fact enmeshed and entwined at the borders, in complex and often mutually reinforcing ways.[4]

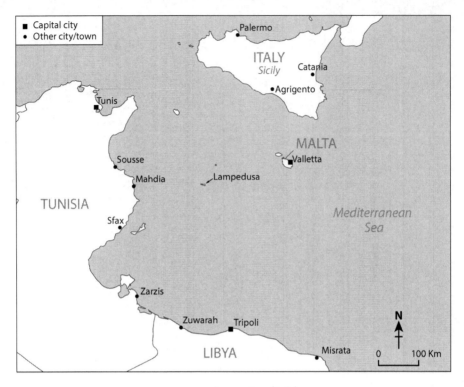

Legend:
■ Capital city
● Other city/town

ITALY
Sicily
Palermo
Catania
● Agrigento

Tunis ■

MALTA
Valletta

Sousse ●
Mahdia

Lampedusa

TUNISIA

Sfax

Mediterranean
Sea

Zarzis

Zuwarah   Tripoli ■
LIBYA   Misrata ●

N

0   100 Km

MAP 2.2. Lampedusa (Italy)

In considering the role of "humanitarian" action at the borders, this chapter builds on a by-now substantial literature on states' use and abuse of humanitarianism (for important interventions, see Barnett and Weiss 2008, 2011; Fassin 2011a; Fassin and Pandolfi 2010). In migration, for instance, Michel Agier (2011:33) has noted how humanitarian action "increasingly finds itself, if not systematically 'trapped,' at least included a priori in the control strategies of migratory flows of all kinds." In this chapter, I will draw up a brief ethnographic and genealogical account of "humanitarian" migration controls in the European case, focusing on what these tell us about the fraught efforts to "fight migration" by land and sea (Pallister-Wilkins 2015). In a key article, William Walters (2011a) has already delineated the emergence of a "humanitarian border" on Lampedusa, where migrant boats have since 2005 been greeted on the island by a joint effort by the police, coast guards, the Red Cross, the IOM, and UNHCR. This "uneasy alliance," as Walters calls it, mixes reception and rejection, care and coercion, in complex ways that reinforce the official border security model—a trend that is also (if not equally) in evidence at other borders across the globe, from the "safety/security nexus" at the U.S.-Mexico border (Williams 2016) to the Australian offshore asylum regime (Dickson 2015).

The Spanish case, which I will focus on below, exemplifies this complex and sophisticated regime of controls, which is increasingly global in scope (Johnson 2014), yet is also refracted through particular national and regional settings. As pioneers within EU external border controls, Spanish authorities have long sought to combine humanitarian, policing, and intelligence-gathering functions in a network of networks—an experiment that came to lay the conceptual groundwork for Italy's Mare Nostrum mission a few years later, and in a rather different sense for the EU-Turkey "collaborations" of 2015–16. Disentangling and exploring the logics behind the European humanitarian-security nexus and networks with reference to the Spanish case will, then, be the topic of these pages.

More specifically, I will here expand on the discussion of humanitarianism in my book *Illegality, Inc.* (Andersson 2014b) by connecting Spain's humanitarian experiments with later developments along Italy's coasts. The first section below will look at the tactics of bordering that humanitarianism enables, focusing on its usage as a justification for more controls and preemptive interceptions, and highlighting how it helps create a self-perpetuating "illegality industry" at the borders. The second section will go a little deeper ethnographically, considering the material and social means that have fomented the integration of aid and policing efforts, while also accounting for how the state co-optation of humanitarianism has led to novel actions by migrants and smugglers in a complex and often counterproductive dynamic. The chapter will conclude with some reflections on how we may understand these intermeshed fields of policing, patrolling, and care at the borders of Europe and beyond—as well as migrants' role within them.

To explore these dynamics, I draw on the notion of "fields" developed by Pierre Bourdieu (1977) and elaborated in studies of border controls by Didier Bigo (2000). In a recent intervention, Bigo (2014:211) delineates what he alternately calls three "fields" or "social universes" of European border controls: the military-strategic field, the internal security field, and the global cyber-surveillance social universe. Officers active in these discrete fields, Bigo posits, hold specific understandings of the border, their task, and their object of intervention: respectively, to patrol and repel people across a solid border; to police and filter them over a liquid border; and to process and profile travelers across a gaseous border. As will be seen, humanitarianism cuts across these fields, leading to overlaps not just among the fields but also with sectors and logics external to them as sea rescue services and aid groups get drawn into the broader effort to "manage migration." While these overlaps are by no means unique to Europe—as seen in the explicit ways in which care has come to "function as a technology of border enforcement" in other settings such as the U.S. state of Arizona (Williams 2015:17)—the chapter will conclude with some further reflections on the specifics of the European case. As the EU is now fracturing under the strain of mounting insecurity and continued refugee flows, but above all because of destructive and short-sighted migration and border policies, the very role and idea of "Europe" is coming to play an increasingly prominent role in the complex humanitarian-security nexus at the borders, in addition to and sometimes in competition or conflict with nation-states.

The Humanitarian Justification

In late October 2014, soon after the show of violence at the EU-funded fences at Melilla, more evidence emerged of Europe's newly draconian approach to migration, this time from London. The UK government, *The Guardian* newspaper reported, was refusing to contribute to future search and rescue operations in the Mediterranean, since such rescues apparently constituted a "pull factor" for those setting out from North African coasts. "Drown an immigrant to save an immigrant" was the new UK policy, as one writer pithily put it—replicating the government's existing "hostile environment" approach to migration inland.[5] Surely inspired by hardline voices in Italy and elsewhere, as well as by Australia's "stop-the-boats" experiment, the UK had for cynical and short-term political reasons helped bring the callous logic of deterrence back to European shores.[6]

Outrage soon ensued. Echoing calls by Amnesty International (2014) and Human Rights Watch (2012), media commentators lined up to urge more humanitarian action and less disregard of human life at sea. These interventions opened up a rare space for considering the ethical dimensions of European migration policy. Thanks to Mare Nostrum, rescues had come to be seen as something within governments' capacity and responsibility; it was now incumbent on European politicians to justify why they would not rescue people on the high seas, rather than the other way round. Yet in the wake of this important debate, we might now also be able to probe further. Doing so involves, first, understanding the role that humanitarian action now plays within the broad field of border controls, as other writers including Martina Tazzioli and Glenda Garelli (in this volume) have argued in the Southern European case. Second, and in an ethnographic sense, it involves understanding the humanitarian-security nexus on its own terms, from the perspective of border workers as well as of the migrants confronting it.[7]

Addressing the first point, as the remainder of this section will do, it is worrisome to see how humanitarian initiatives have accompanied—rather than contradicted—draconian migration controls in recent years. In Ceuta and Melilla, for instance, the triple razor-wire fencing and baton-equipped guards give way to medical care by Red Cross staff for those fortunate enough to breach the barrier. A similar interaction between care and coercion, or between liberal and securitarian measures more broadly, is on display in European deportations of irregular migrants over the past decade. As I have shown elsewhere, the path for such politically controversial removals has often been smoothed by spurious "aid" deals with African states ready to accept deportees, as well as by the participation of humanitarian organizations (Andersson 2014b; see also, e.g., Serón et al. 2011). In North African countries such as Morocco, meanwhile, a similar trend has seen local forces—leaned on by Europe to carry out "border management"—harass migrants and even asylum-seekers until they reach such a point of desperation that they seek out the "assisted voluntary returns" programs managed by the (Western-funded) International Organization for Migration.[8] In these examples, liberal and humanitarian measures are used as a bandage covering the wounds—physical, mental, or metaphorical—inflicted by Europe's authorities and their African collaborators.

The intermixing of care and control in migratory reception and destination settings has by now generated a substantial critical literature, including investigations of the "compassionate repression" traced by Fassin (2005) in the old Red Cross–managed camp for migrants in Calais at the English Channel; the control justifications enabled by humanitarian exceptions in French migration policy (Ticktin 2006, 2011); the conflictive humanitarian stakes of the deadly U.S. desert borders (Squire 2014; Williams 2015, 2016); and the containment functions of largely Western-funded refugee camps (Agier 2011; Agier and Lecadet 2014; Johnson 2014:53). Rather than examining the subtleties of these cases, I will in the remainder of this chapter focus on one specific example of the humanitarian-security nexus: controls and surveillance at maritime borders. Humanitarianism, more than just working as a "bandage" of sorts, has here increasingly served as a key justification for controls on social, legal, political, and even financial levels, with far-reaching consequences at and beyond Europe's frontiers.

———

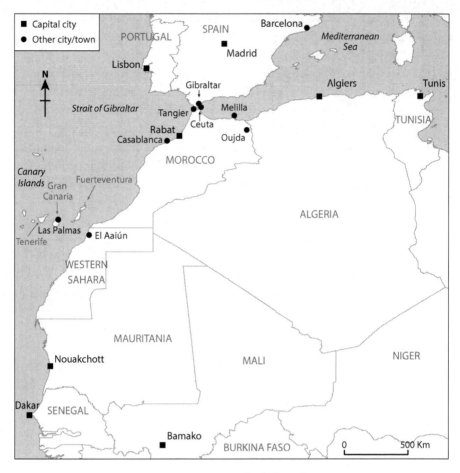

MAP 2.3. Canary Islands (Spain)

As I started fieldwork on irregular migration and border controls in early 2010, I was visiting the state-of-the-art installations of the Spanish Guardia Civil in the Canary Islands. A few years earlier, in 2006, this tourist archipelago had experienced a mass "spectacle" of migration of the kind that has by now become familiar at contested borders on a global scale (De Genova 2002, 2013a): in this instance, thousands of boat migrants arriving from West African coasts as a result of the gradual closure of routes into mainland Spain. By the time of my 2010 visit, the authorities were on top of the "crisis," and arrivals had dwindled, in part thanks to mass deportations and the launch of a large sea patrol mission, Joint Operation Hera, under the aegis of the EU's young border agency, Frontex.[9] Indeed, Spain's interior minister would eventually declare that 2010 had been the best year in a decade for migration control.[10] Given this "success," border officers were more than happy with academic attention from me and others—as long, that is, as it involved looking at their work in its "humanitarian" and technological guise.

The Hera operation, and the large diplomatic drive in Africa and Europe that it involved, positioned Spain in the vanguard of European border controls. Since that time, the Guardia Civil—the security force in charge of patrolling the country's land and sea perimeters—has achieved international recognition for its work on migration, and Spanish border control methods have been envied and emulated by other Southern European neighbors, who have had to deal with larger inflows as routes diverged eastward, away from the Atlantic.

Besides the sharp drop in numbers, Spanish authorities also had another "success" to their credit. Unlike Italy and Greece at the time, they had managed to create a sharp division between the two approaches to controls—securitarian and humanitarian—by applying these to land and sea borders, respectively. The border spectacle in Spain is two-faced: in Ceuta and Melilla, civil guards stand ready to repel migrants behind the razor-wired fences; at sea, their colleagues pull unfortunate migrants out of the water.

Fernando (a pseudonym) was one of the civil guards I met in the Canaries to talk about their work at the sea border, and like his colleagues he was proud of the job he and his colleagues had done to stem the flow of migrant boats. His unit, the maritime service or SEMAR (Servicio Marítimo de la Guardia Civil), had grown quickly since its creation in 1991 and had played a crucial role in controlling migration into the archipelago—and, as Fernando insisted, in saving lives. "The problem is that they arrive completely without security," he said. "If it's a perfect boat, you stop them at sea and tell them to go back." But the boats had to be intercepted and escorted to port, and their passengers often had to be disembarked onto the patrol vessel. The Guardia Civil's migration work, Fernando made clear, was based on "humanitarian assistance" and "the risk to life" at sea.

This assessment, widely shared across the higher rungs of the Guardia Civil, pointed to the role of humanitarianism as an organizing principle in Spain's border work. Humanitarianism, of course, is a convenient trope for the consumption of the media, academia, and the larger public. Besides the Guardia Civil, even Frontex—clearly a "border management" and policing outfit—has at times succumbed to the temptation of styling itself "the largest search and rescue operation on the planet" (Frontex 2010a:37). Tellingly, during fieldwork Frontex responded to my request for a raft of documents on their operations by giving me only a few pages on their strategy on "fundamental rights" and protection for trafficking victims.

However, in addition to recognizing this blatant public relations exercise, it is worth approaching the humanitarian discourse on its own terms. What role does it play, and how does it structure the European response to boat migration—as well as migrants' tactics? Humanitarianism, I will argue, is more than just a bit of PR gloss: it also provides a justification on psychological, moral, legal, political, and even financial levels for preemptive migration controls beyond Europe's borders.

First, humanitarianism constitutes a key line of moral defense for individual border guards—not just toward funders, researchers, the media, and the public, but also vis-à-vis other organizations, not least "real" humanitarian ones. In Spain, officers regularly complained in interviews about having to "play the role of the bad guy," carrying out the "most thankless task" of policing with little recognition for their often dangerous rescue labors on the high seas. A Spanish policeman stationed in Africa, for instance, recalled a public row he had with a Red Cross worker who criticized the policing of the border. "I asked her, who has saved more lives, you or me? You give them blankets, something to eat, and so on when they arrive in the Canary Islands, but we are out there rescuing people." The police work was "99 percent humanitarian," he said. "What I want to do is to save lives. . . . I might have been the bad guy but my conscience is clear."

The biggest and most obvious gap in this account was that with more stringent controls, migrants would use more dangerous routes.[11] This was evident in the increasingly precarious vessels and the longer, more roundabout ways used to enter the Iberian peninsula in recent years, including the Canaries route. "From our point of view," said one Spanish sea rescue chief in a rare note of criticism of the border regime, "the longer the journey is, the bigger the risk and the harder it is to find them when they run into problems."

Individual border guards were aware of the tensions in their task. They found themselves in the difficult professional position of engaging in more controls yet seeing these repeatedly breached; and as their patrols created riskier routes, they had to mount ever more precarious rescues and interceptions. Amid this negative spiral, humanitarianism constituted something akin to the "second-order rationalizations of duties" explored by Josiah Heyman (1995:28) in his studies of the U.S. Border Patrol. Indeed, high-ranking civil guards in interviews constantly strived to "purify" their work as humanitarian (to use the terminology of Bruno Latour 1993).[12] One way of doing this was through the divide between sea and land, as mentioned above, pushing the violent response out of sight and out of mind. This was done quite literally in the video collages that high-ranking civil guards had prepared for visitors to their installations, mirroring similar productions by the U.S. Border Patrol (Williams 2016:31) and by the Italian Navy (Musarò 2016). These videos usually showed boat rescues set to soft, melancholy music, in contrast with other showcase videos on drug controls that followed patrol boats at full speed to adrenaline-fueled rock soundtracks. One comandante, showing me such videos, had also prepared a slideshow describing the four stages of intervention at sea: detection, identification, follow-up, and finally "interception or rescue." I asked him what the difference was between the two. "It's the same, but interception refers more to drugs, migration is usually more of a rescue because it is more humanitarian."

These were not just throwaway comments by a media-savvy comandante, but pointed to a larger role for humanitarianism in legitimizing border controls on the high seas. The legal scholar Matteo Tondini has argued that maritime interceptions "may be in principle legally justified only if retained [as] rescue interventions" (2010:26), and this seems to have been a lesson that high-ranking officers had taken to heart. "We have saved a lot of lives," said one comandante in Madrid as we watched images of African migrants being pulled across to Guardia Civil boats in his office. "We have to avoid them putting themselves in danger." While the first part of this statement sounded almost defensive, hinting at the lack of recognition for his colleagues' rescue work, the second part segued into a justification for extending controls to African coasts, which is what had happened since the 2006 "boat crisis" in the Canary Islands.

The deployment in Joint Operation Hera had been impressive. Guardia Civil vessels patrolled the coasts of Mauritania, Cape Verde, and Senegal in alliance with their African colleagues; Spanish military planes, as well as Frontex-funded ones operated by participating EU member states, circled the open Atlantic; and the Spanish state sea rescue service Salvamento Marítimo scoured the high seas in search of boat migrants. On African land borders, meanwhile, Senegalese and Mauritanian forces had been subcontracted to carry out further controls. Here was a large assemblage of actors, united in the task of "fighting illegal migration" in a preemptive—and supposedly humanitarian—manner. As one Frontex-seconded project manager of Hera said, echoing the civil guards above, "the priority is to save human lives, and this entails [*conlleva*] that all the boats that try to arrive in Spain are intercepted before they arrive at the [Spanish] coasts." The basis for these interceptions, he said, was "saving lives" based on the international convention on the safety of life at sea (SOLAS).

A quick look at the legal debates over the contested space of the seas will help throw some light on the role of humanitarianism in patrolling the Atlantic

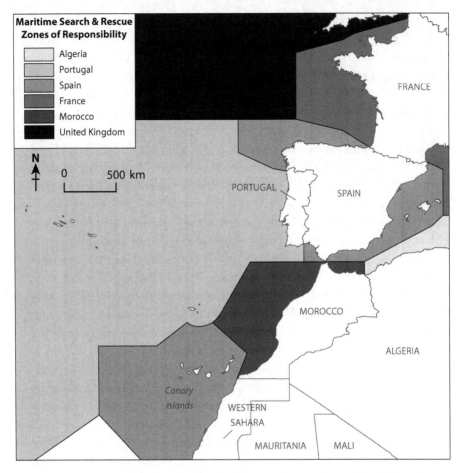

MAP 2.4. Maritime search and rescue (SAR) zones, featuring Canary Islands (Spain)

and African shores. Under international law, national sovereignty extends for twelve nautical miles from the coasts; next follows a "contiguous zone" of limited sovereignty for another twelve miles, and finally the "exclusive economic zone" of up to two hundred miles counted from the shores of the coastal state. Beyond these limits lie the high seas, Mare Liberum. Nominally a nonsovereign space, the "free" seas are still subject to a patchwork of rules under international law. The legal scholars Gammeltoft-Hansen and Aalberts (2010:17) have identified a "new geo-politics of the Mare Liberum" in which amendments to the international search and rescue regime (SAR) and SOLAS have created loop-

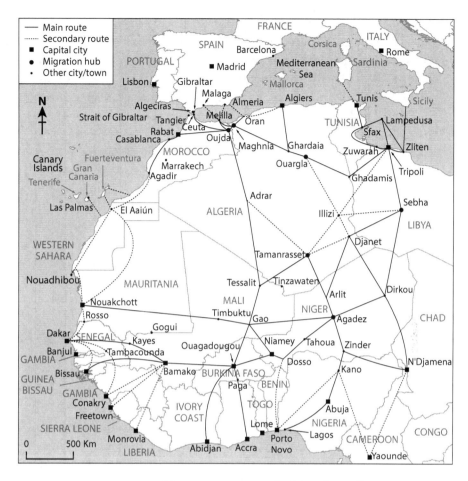

MAP 2.5. Migration routes across the Sahara Desert

holes in which Europe's Mediterranean states can throw off responsibilities for rescue, interception, and diversion onto their neighbors, as has happened between Italy and Malta in recent years. This disavowal of responsibility contrasts with Spain's approach, which has instead used its extensive SAR responsibilities to the full in migration controls. "What matters is helping people," said one Spanish civil guard. "Whether it's at one [nautical] mile, or fifteen, or thirty, or two hundred . . . when helping a boat there is no limit."

In contrast to states such as Malta, Spanish patrols in the Canaries and the Strait saw any migrant vessel as a virtual shipwreck (*náufrago*). In the words of one Spanish sea rescue chief, such a boat was a "danger for navigation" by definition, akin to a bus racing down a highway "without brakes." Such reasoning, on the one hand, provided a political and moral justification for joint patrols in West African territorial waters under Hera, carried out thanks to memoranda of understanding between Spain and Senegal, Cape Verde, and Mauritania. On the other, it enabled early interventions across Spain's vast SAR zone of more than 1.5 million square kilometers, with the Canaries zone constituting two-thirds of this area and reaching the African coastline. In Hera's twin Frontex mission in Spain, the Mediterranean Joint Operation Indalo, the patrol area followed the Spanish SAR zone rather than limiting itself to territorial waters. In the Strait, this zone in fact reached into Moroccan waters, meaning Spanish vessels routinely "rescued" migrant boats right up along Morocco's coasts— overriding the otherwise tense and militarized border.

The blurring of the border in humanitarian patrols may enable more rescues and saved lives, and is in this sense a positive trend. Yet such blurring easily segues into operations that police and divert migrants using a humanitarian justification, as is seen in West Africa.

In Italy before Mare Nostrum, the line between "humane" and "tough" approaches has been much more muddled and mixed, as Cuttitta (2014) has shown in the case of Lampedusa. The muddling was seen, not least, in the landmark *Hirsi* case before the European Court of Human Rights. Confronted with accusations that Italian forces engaged in pushbacks into Libya, Berlusconi's government tried to justify these maritime interceptions as rescue operations. Yet this argument failed to convince the court, in large part because of public assurances that the operations were in fact crackdowns on "illegal migration," and so—the court said—fell within the ambit of European migration law, not least as regards prohibitions on collective expulsions.[13] As legal observers have noted, the potential remains for European forces to follow an exclusively "humanitarian" approach in diverting boats back to North Africa, as long as they adhere to the legal prohibition on sending people back to where they may face harm or persecution (non-refoulement) (Tondini 2012).

In the western Mediterranean, this is the eventual aim of the Guardia Civil, which has actively pushed for a readmissions agreement for third-country nationals with Morocco, on the back of more significant political pressure on Spain's neighbor from Brussels and Madrid. Yet for now, two other "humanitarian" strategies are in place around Spain's Mediterranean borders. First, migrant vessels spotted and "rescued" by Spain in the middle of the Strait of Gibraltar have often been taken to the enclave of Ceuta rather than to the towns of Algeciras or Tarifa on the Spanish mainland. The reason given for this, when I interviewed sea rescue officers, was that Ceuta was the closest safe port. This is usually true in a strict geographical sense, albeit by small margins. Yet the unspoken difference between the two destinations was stark: if taken to the mainland, sub-Saharan migrants would be detained and set free with an expulsion order, unless they had been identified and thus rendered deportable, after a sixty-day time limit. In Ceuta, they could instead be kept indefinitely in an EU-subsidized reception center for migrants, as a presumed deterrent to further entries. Preemptive rescues at sea here fulfilled a policing goal by collectively punishing migrants for their border transgression in an offshore arrangement resembling Australia's "Pacific" (and later "PNG" [Papua New Guinea]) solution.[14]

The second strategy is simply to let North African forces do the job. When spotting a boat with their advanced surveillance systems, Spanish border forces can call their North African colleagues so that the latter then "rescue" the passengers by bringing them back to the coast, regardless of their wishes (and with no consideration of non-refoulement principles). This is hard work, however, and Guardia Civil officers recognized in interviews the limited amount of cooperation by Morocco and especially Algeria in this regard. For this region, the model for the future remains the Hera operation, where the preemptive humanitarian impulse has helped extend joint operations well up to West African coasts, cutting short any intention to cross.

———

The Spanish case also illustrates how "humanitarian" approaches are increasingly serving not just as moral, legal, and political cover for more controls, but also as a reason for more investments. As more surveillance, patrols, and barriers push migrants toward riskier entry methods, new "dual-use" measures—at once aimed at rescuing and intercepting those in distress—keep being proposed, including through the expensive European external border surveillance system, or EUROSUR (Hayes and Vermeulen 2012). EUROSUR, essentially an information-sharing border policing tool, is presented in widely divergent ways, as seen in these quotes, respectively from a Swedish far-right party and from Cecilia Malmström, the (also Swedish) EU home affairs commissioner until 2014:

> Frontex should be strengthened in order to control Europe's external borders. That way we may better prevent illegal activities emanating from outside Europe. As a step in this we also want to see EUROSUR implemented. EUROSUR is a pan-European border surveillance system whose

purpose is to prevent illegal immigration and to fight transnational crime. (Sweden Democrat parliamentary motion, April 2014)[15]

I welcome the launch of EUROSUR. It is a truly European response to save the lives of migrants travelling in overcrowded and unseaworthy vessels, to avoid further tragedies in the Mediterranean and also to stop speed boats transporting drugs. All these initiatives are highly dependent on a timely information exchange and coordinated efforts between the national and European agencies. EUROSUR provides that framework, in full respect of international obligations. (Cecilia Malmström, November 2013)[16]

Saving and policing migrants, it should be noted, are both within EUROSUR's mandate, though the former was only inserted at a very late stage—and has not been much in evidence yet in operations, as Frontex has admitted.[17] However, as noted by civil guards above, the point is almost moot: "interceptions" on the high seas are increasingly coterminous with "rescues." Migrants are at once rescued and caught. This two-faced border response is very useful politically, convincing divergent member states and constituencies; as a corollary, it also provides a mechanism for controls to keep growing indefinitely. This merry-go-round has depended to a large extent on the labors of the European Commission and Frontex, positioned as middlemen between the defense industry, border guard "end users," and intransigent governments (cf. Svantesson 2014). In their quest to depoliticize the (highly politicized) phenomenon of irregular entries by land and sea, pushing it into the domain of expert and technological "solutions," these EU actors have contributed to the creation of an "illegality industry" around migratory routes in which care and control functions alternately clash and merge with each other (Andersson 2014b).

This was clear on the Spanish front, where the Guardia Civil had received EU funding for its SIVE coastal radar system once it switched from principally targeting drugs to "life-saving" migration controls. Elsewhere, too, migration-related investments had been lavished on new Guardia Civil patrol boats, control rooms, and officers, triggering resentment among fellow state agencies such as Customs (see Bigo 2000 on similar turf wars across Europe). In Internet forums for border guards and police, embittered customs officers raged at the Guardia Civil's rapid ascendance despite what they saw as the force's limited skills and competencies. "Gentlemen, no one can stop this," one civil guard replied online, listing the new oceangoing patrol boats, a new Madrid control center, and the multi-million-euro sea border projects led by his agency. "It's not the future anymore, it's the present, and the present of SEMAR is immigration that comes over the sea (among several other themes). There are lots of civil guards seconded today in Mauritania, Senegal, Guinea, etc., and immigration is a priority theme where you cannot save money because of the [risk to] human lives." As more preemptive border controls have contributed to the creation of new and riskier routes, further investments in controls can always be motivated by the fresh human crises sparked at the borders, and so on ad infinitum in a self-reinforcing spiral, as seen in the military operations off the Italian and Greek coasts launched respectively in 2015 (EUNAVFOR-Med) and early 2016 (NATO deployments).

Italy's Mare Nostrum is an example of this ever more entrenched dynamic, yet the operation also shifted the humanitarian-security nexus in important if temporary ways. In its original conception, Mare Nostrum was, as one commentator notes, "modelled on the measures taken by the Spanish government"—that is, of "rescuing" everyone in order to "deter migrants and refugees from even attempting the voyage."[18] Yet, partly owing to the *Hirsi* case prohibiting pushbacks, and partly because many arrivals were refugees and so could not simply be sent back to conflict-ridden Libya, Mare Nostrum soon morphed into quite a different experiment in humanitarian control. As such, it provided a small opening for thinking about other ways of "doing the border," though it also retained its deterrence focus in arresting suspected smugglers on board, a practice that has added considerable difficulties to rescue efforts in recent years.[19] Besides the navy's humanitarian labors, then, we need to see Mare Nostrum within a much broader field of border controls, in which repressive policies at the EU's fenced-off external land borders at Ceuta and Melilla as well as at the Greek and Bulgarian borders with Turkey have diverted migrants toward more dangerous sea routes and into the hands of Europe's humanitarian apparatus.[20] In the ensuing scramble for a response at sea, Mare Nostrum not only improved Italy's battered image after the Lampedusa tragedies; it also boosted the navy's resources at a time of austerity and has allowed it to reassert its position vis-à-vis the many other agencies active at the Italian sea borders, including the coast guard and the Guardia di Finanza. The drawdown of the operation in late 2014 and its replacement with a much more limited Frontex mission was thus not just a humanitarian tragedy, as the rising death toll of early 2015 showed; it also signaled a shift (however temporary, as seen with EUNAVFOR-Med) in the battle over funds and powers at the border.

Humanitarianism, in sum, "works" on several levels: as moral line of defense or professional imperative; as legal and political justification; and as a mechanism for more investments. Yet it would be a mistake to see the "humanitarianization" of migration controls only as an ideological screen for the coercive effort of pushing back migrant boats. It is certainly self-serving, yet given the significant rescue efforts carried out over the past decade in Spain and Italy in particular, we also need to dig a bit deeper into the humanitarian border work. Thus, the next section will look at how specific modes of bordering practice have taken shape around humanitarian action in Spain, giving us a window onto the deep integration of seemingly conflictive sectors in Europe's migration response.

All Aboard: The Humanitarian-Security Nexus

It is worth returning briefly to the three border control fields delineated by Didier Bigo. Writing about the "military-strategic field" of concern to us here, Bigo (2014) says that, to the border guards patrolling the coasts, this border appears solid: as a bulwark, a defense, a wall. As he says, border agencies and officers "may disagree about where to place the 'line'—but not about its necessity" (Bigo 2014:212). However, we see in Spain how what was at first an exercise of "holding the line" soon became an effort of "monitoring a grid."[21] The border was expanding in the joint military-policing-humanitarian efforts in the Atlantic, blurring the lines not just between inside and outside, but between different fields of security—as well as between humanitarian, military, and policing actors and operations. It is this blurring, as well as the interagency tensions and sharing practices it involved, that will be of concern to us in the following pages.

———

"Tarifa Tráfico," as Salvamento Marítimo's control and coordination center for the Strait of Gibraltar is known, lies at the very edge of Europe; it also seems to lie at the top of the world. On a good day, the views across the waters to Morocco, only fourteen kilometers away, are dazzling: the jagged Rif mountains, the stately cranes of the new Tanger Med port, and the massive freight ships plowing through the clear, narrow waters of the Strait are all so near you can almost reach out and touch them.

Adolfo (a pseudonym), a Salvamento chief in his fifties, greeted me at the door. As someone responsible for the search and rescue team scouring the dangerous, fast-flowing waters of the Strait for the constant trickle of distressed migrant boats, he had to have what one Salvamento colleague of his called "rescue in the blood." "Normally I have breakfast with pateras," Adolfo said as we sat down for an interview in his office: migrants usually set off from northern Morocco before daybreak. While the term *patera* literally refers to the small wooden fishing boat used by Moroccans who pioneered the sea route to Spain in the 1990s, it has in recent years become the generic term for "migrant boat" used by all agencies working on migration. Adolfo had seen all kinds of such migrant vessels during his time in Tarifa. Proper wooden pateras were followed by Zodiacs (small, fast boats) and, in the past years, "any buoyant artifact, really." Adolfo brought up pictures on his monitor of the weird and wonderful vessels and their imperiled passengers: migrants using hydropedals, clinging to truck tires, resting atop a surfboard. Subsequently, these had been superseded by what was known among rescue workers as the "toy," a small inflatable boat of the kind used by children on beaches. Adolfo nowadays expected one of two types of vessel for breakfast: the toy, used by four to six people, or the Zodiac, taking between forty and sixty passengers. Two types of migrants used these boats: *subsaharianos* (sub-Saharan Africans) or *magrebíes* (North Africans), as they were known in the racialized sea rescue shorthand.[22] The toys, above all, were used by the sub-Saharans, Adolfo explained; the two groups rarely combined in the same vessel.

The rescue operations often kicked off from the control room of Tarifa Tráfico. Old-fashioned binoculars lined the huge windows through which the whole Strait was visible, but the main action was on the screens, where operators kept track of the 100,000 commercial and other ships passing by each year. Salvamento operators were in constant touch with freight and commercial boats, and also got distress phone calls from the pateras. "The most difficult thing is when we receive a call from a mobile phone and we don't know anything at all," Adolfo said. A few days before my visit, they had found themselves in such a situation; the emergency phone service 112 called the control room after a woman had rung to say her husband was in the middle of the Strait. She gave the mobile number of someone on board the patera, nothing more. When the operators finally got hold of the migrants, Adolfo said, "the only thing they knew to say was 'Tarifa, Tarifa, Tarifa, Tarifa' [their destination]." Knowing what to do in such a situation was hard, every second valuable, any piece of information a treasure. "That's the most complicated situation for us, because where are they? From where have they left? Where can we go look for them?" Adolfo said as we inspected the screens and phone terminals that linked this control room with others run by the Guardia Civil, the Red Cross, and 112. Speaking to passengers, Salvamento operators may only have seconds or a few minutes at their disposal before the mobile battery on board runs out. They prod their onboard contact for clues to the migrants' whereabouts: do they see any freight ships passing by, with big letters on the side? The mobile phone masts covering the Strait give another potential clue, each covering one discrete, though large, area.

Once the patera has been located, the search and rescue mission follows a strict but flexible protocol, developed over the past two decades in the Strait and the Canaries. By 2010, all agencies involved worked hand in glove. Salvamento called the Red Cross and health services, in preparation for assistance once the migrants arrived in port. Guardia Civil launches joined Salvamento ships setting out for a rescue, and its officers usually boarded the orange rescue boat to carry out crowd control and enact authority. Once they reached the migrant boat, the hard rescue work began. Here, frayed nerves and hot tempers could end in disaster. In earlier years, migrants had taken to standing up and moving about as they saw the Spaniards approach, in fright or in expectation of a rescue, making their boats capsize. Members of the Guardia Civil's specialized dive teams, known as GEAS, had to throw themselves into the cold waters or search for hands to grasp, hoping to drag drowning migrants aboard. By 2010 staff had been trained and risks minimized, heralding a first, strange sight of Europe for boat migrants: rescue workers decked out in full protective gear who took them on board, isolated them for "health and safety" reasons, and then safely steered them to port.[23]

As in Mare Nostrum a few years later, this pioneering Spanish-led rescue effort on the high seas depended on utmost coordination and professionalism. However, tensions still affected relations between humanitarians and border guards, as I discuss elsewhere in more depth (Andersson 2014b). Red Cross staff recalled in interviews, for instance, their unease as the guards used crowd control or corralled migrants in their quarters for no apparent reason. However, the initially rough relations gradually smoothed out through the sharing of the humanitarian task, leading to a mixing and mingling in which control and care functions increasingly blurred into each other.

In terms of information-gathering, joint humanitarian approaches helped overcome old firewalls between police, rescue, and reception functions. The Red Cross conducted short interviews with recent arrivals, and Salvamento Marítimo took pictures of migrant boats during rescues. The Red Cross shared and compared their data with the Guardia Civil—information that was then sent on to the Interior Ministry. Salvamento provided the Guardia Civil and police with their footage so that these could ascertain the "captain" (who may simply be a migrant in charge of keeping the course) for detention, as well as the possible origin of the boat. In this way, the images attained value as evidence, temporarily exiting the larger media circuit of border imagery to which the agencies also contributed.

While such images circulated, so did staff, know-how, and resources. In their spare time, civil guards on Fuerteventura volunteered in Red Cross emergency operations in the first bouts of arrivals on this easterly Canary Island. Roles were more clear-cut on the bigger islands and along Spain's mainland coasts, but there too staff switched agencies and roles as job opportunities opened. Equipment circulated as well. The Red Cross not only took over old Yamaha motors from the migrant boats, confiscated by the guards, but also used Salvamento and Guardia Civil launches. The Red Cross, Salvamento, and sometimes the Guardia Civil also held joint exercises, contributing to what one Salvamento chief called a "different feeling" between the agencies working on migration.

In this new social environment, blurred roles also started affecting translation and interrogation procedures. A former Red Cross volunteer in the Canaries, Senegalese by origin, recalled rushing across the island in 2006, often attending to one boat arrival after another the same night. He translated for the Red Cross since "they came to me and spoke, they weren't reticent." He found out where the migrants were from, or made an educated guess. Relations between the Red Cross and police were friendly thanks to an understanding commissioner, he said. "He gave me a job in the end, when you finish you go straight to the police and you have work, you collect data [do interviews], and the government pays, and they paid me very, very well." Here the police could tap into the good will generated by an African Red Cross volunteer to retrieve information from boat migrants. Similar set-ups facilitated the sharing of tasks across agencies in other settings as well.

Migrants' perceptions of these mixed roles were also affected, often in a negative way. It was hard to develop trust with migrants, one Red Cross officer confided; in the early days migrants often mistook Red Cross workers for police. Around the Strait, migrants frequently said they had been picked up by "the Red Cross," which usually turned out to mean Salvamento Marítimo or, at times, even the Guardia Civil. Further south, on African soil, Red Cross volunteers assisting migrants on the deportation route into Senegal said that deportees often refused to see them since they saw the organization as part of the coercive state apparatus they had already encountered elsewhere. Indeed, the "humanitarian" assistance given to migrants in detention, both in the Canary Islands (by the Spanish Red Cross) and in Mauritania (by the Mauritanian Red Crescent, assisted by its Spanish partner), had created a blur around the movement's role in migration control, triggering unease not just among migrants but also among Red Cross volunteers and staff.

These doubts are but one example of the ambivalent and ambiguous position often held by nonstate and humanitarian groups working with some measure of official approval at the border (see, for instance, Williams 2015 on the

U.S. southern desert borders). But they also highlight a larger humanitarian dilemma. A gray zone of humanitarian-security action has in recent decades emerged not just at Western borders, but also in war zones, between combatants and aid workers—as seen, for example, in the military appropriation of the Red Cross emblem in Iraq and Afghanistan (Pandolfi 2010:227). As a result, humanitarianism finds itself, according to anxious voices, at a crossroads. While some trumpet a golden era brought on by the multiplication of aid into billions of dollars and of agencies into the thousands, others see humanitarianism politicized, its universalism questioned, and its workers ambushed (Barnett and Weiss 2008:3). According to Ticktin (2006:33, 2011), humanitarianism has been transformed into a form of politics—an ethical configuration and mode of governance whose efficiency draws on its very apolitical guise.

Humanitarianism has, however, as many scholars note, always been political and intimately linked to militarism.[24] The symbiosis between humanitarians and coast guards was thus not an anomaly; what was unusual was the degree to which humanitarianism transformed the militarized aspects of Spain's sea operations. In the blurred boundaries of the sea realm, it was easy to justify more military deployments or to repeatedly "cross the borders" between humanitarian and state policing agendas, as can similarly be seen in the Mediterranean of 2015–16. One Spanish politician during my time of fieldwork recalled with disapproval the conservative opposition's calls to involve the army in stopping the migrant boats heading for the Canary Islands in 2006, before acknowledging that "it's true that the navy collaborates, but in a humanitarian sense." In his view, they were guardian angels watching out for huddled boat people, not soldiers pushing back an invasion.

Beyond these larger political considerations, in the sphere of day-to-day humanitarian action on the high seas, each agency did hold on to its own institutional imperatives of respectively controlling borders and assisting people. Yet certain shared ways of working were also in the making, thanks to the deep and daily collaborations. Through these constant interactions, a "subfield" of sorts was emerging, partly inside the military-strategic and policing fields discussed by Bigo (2014), yet partly outside them, in the form of the humanitarian imperatives of the NGOs, the Red Cross, and the sea rescue service. In the space where the field of patrolling and the humanitarian subfield overlapped, a humanitarian-security nexus had been created in which it was becoming increasingly difficult to separate the caring from the coercive tendencies, the liberal from the securitarian approaches, and the border guard from the humanitarian.

———

Amid these multifaceted collaborations, it may seem as if migrants and refugees—the targets of interventions—are reduced to the simple roles assigned to them in the border spectacle, either villain or victim. However, migrants and refugees are conscious of Europe's different bordering tactics, and adjust their own actions accordingly. This has serious political ramifications, as was seen in the UK refusal to participate in sea rescues in autumn 2015 because of their presumed "pull" effect—a point to which I will return below.

As I conducted interviews with former boat migrants in Spain and Senegal during my fieldwork, it quickly became clear that they were well aware of border policing tactics in formulating their own. This was true, not least, of the Senegalese fishermen who had once sought the shores of the Canary Islands, often as captains or helpers on collectively funded boats, where their skills at sea could be put to good use in the context of a decline in their traditional trade, thanks in large part to industrial-scale fishing by Europeans off their coasts. As they steered north, they knew when to hug the West African coast and when to enter deeper waters, all in response to where patrolling was most intense. They knew when the Senegalese forces would come on patrol, as word spread and bribes changed hands. They also knew that, if they traveled far enough from the African coastline, they would be taken to Europe and into safety, rather than back to Africa—much as is the case now in the Mediterranean. Getting closer to Spanish shores, migrant guides on board threw their GPS in the water and melted into the background to ensure they would not be seen as captains and put in preventive detention as presumed smugglers (*pasadores*), as was the norm in the Spanish deterrence policy against boat migration.

By contrast, the migrants intending to enter the North African enclaves of Ceuta and Melilla confronted a very different kind of border, and had to adjust their tactics accordingly. When the first undocumented sub-Saharan migrants arrived there in the 1990s, they simply walked across the borders. Then the first fences were built to keep them out, and suddenly a "threat scenario" emerged, as the Guardia Civil recalled in field interviews. The migrants now came running uncontrollably, all at once—the only way of entering and ensuring that at least some of them would get through to the police commissariat in town, thus avoiding informal expulsion by the civil guards at the perimeter. As Spanish policing cooperation with Morocco deepened, increasing crackdowns then fed the desperation among migrants, who came to see the fences around Melilla and Ceuta as a last escape route. As a result, the fences were strengthened again in 2005 with the help of EU funds. In Melilla, triple fences soon rose six meters above the ground, accompanied by sensors, thermal cameras, pepper-spray mechanisms, bright spotlights, and an intricate mesh of steel cables meant to trap any intruder. This mass display of force "worked" for a while, steering migrants toward the dangerous sea route—until 2013 and 2014, when they found new ways across, again using their collective force to ensure a limited number got through. As seen in the spectacular border pictures emanating from Melilla in 2014, showing migrants straddling the fences for hours while guards or locals looked on below, here sub-Saharan migrants actively sought to use their role in the border spectacle in the most ambiguous fashion—rendering themselves visible to Europe's two-faced border regime, at once apprehended as racialized invaders and victims.

As already seen, on the Spanish "front" the two logics of control—humanitarian and coercive—were kept geographically separate thanks to the peculiarity of the southern Spanish borders: the fortified land perimeters of Ceuta and Melilla versus the preemptive rescue domains at sea. These two borders in turn triggered wildly different migrant actions. Yet sometimes this divide was breached, either by authorities or by migrants, or by both in tandem in a mutual mirroring of bordering tactics. The result of this could be unpredictable and tragic, as was the case in early 2014 outside the Spanish enclave of Ceuta.

Before daybreak on the sixth of February that year, hundreds of African men and women were spotted on the thermal cameras of the Civil Guard outside Ceuta as they made their way toward the fences. It was a drearily familiar sight to the sentinels guarding the southernmost frontier of the EU; but this time, it was soon clear, would be different. The migrants first tried entering Ceuta through an opening in the fence reserved for the (officially sanctioned) export of contraband European goods by poor Moroccans. Here, the migrants' advance was foiled; as they proceeded along the fence, reaching the official border crossing, their path was again blocked by Spanish forces. Only one way into the EU remained: by sea. The migrants descended onto the dirt-strewn beach, sliced in two by an extension of the fence. Many of them threw themselves into the Mediterranean, and chaos ensued. In the coming days, it would emerge that the Guardia Civil had fired rubber bullets into the waters to warn off the swimmers, and that, amid the ensuing standoff and panic, fifteen people had drowned in the cold February waters of the Euro-African border.

As described above, migrants have in different ways sought to use and challenge the two-faced border spectacle by placing themselves center stage in it, where they may be apprehended either as humanitarian subjects or else as threatening invaders. At Ceuta's sea perimeter, however, the rules of this game no longer held. The border guards—operating under ruthless orders emanating from their superiors and from Madrid—failed to distinguish between sea and land responses in this ambiguous space at the edge of Ceuta's fence, and used what in a maritime setting turned out to be lethal "crowd control" measures. Here, the Guardia Civil's "purification" of land and sea bordering tactics broke down, leading to the most publicized and lethal transgression by border police seen in Spain in recent years.

If the migrants failed this time in their second-guessing of official bordering tactics, they did not always fail, or not fully so—as seen, for instance, in recent years around the Strait of Gibraltar.

The Guardia Civil happily showed off its advanced coastal surveillance machinery, known as SIVE, to visitors from far and wide—European border guards, visiting dignitaries, journalists, and researchers such as myself. The system was credited with saving lives and halting the boats around the Strait and elsewhere along Spanish coasts. Yet its dazzling technology blinded visitors to how surveillance of the seas had changed the cat-and-mouse game of the sea border, much as fencing, surveillance, and patrols have shifted routes in the U.S.-Mexico case, to take another prominent example of these globalizing migratory dynamics (Donato et al. 2008; cf. Dunn 2009). Most sub-Saharan migrants knew that they might be spotted by the Spanish radars. Moreover, and unlike their Moroccan and Algerian counterparts who feared immediate deportation, they wanted this to happen. In the border game that ensued, everyone—facilitators, migrants, rescue services, guards, and police—had their assigned role. Migrants or their associates called for help before departure, sea rescue boats searched for them and, once they were found, brought them to port for a medical check followed by detention and the hope of eventual liberation.

These dynamics bring us back to the present and Mare Nostrum's dismantling in the autumn of 2014. The UK, withdrawing support for any future sea rescues, contended that this mission had led to more deaths at sea, since it had created an incentive to cross. Was this so? Did conservative UK politicians, and similar voices on the right in Italy and elsewhere, have a point?

Based on the Spanish dynamics I have briefly delineated here, it is undoubtedly true that any new bordering tactic leads to new migrant tactics, and so on ad infinitum. This includes, of course, the incentive to be rescued, and the same must hold true in Italy's case. The question, however, is to what extent in this specific context, and also what relative weight should be given to this factor. As is painfully evident from the millions displaced within Syria and in its vicinity, the main driver of boat migration in 2014 has without doubt been vicious conflict, along with repression in other large "sending" states such as Eritrea. But beyond these "push" factors, another one needs to be brought into the equation: the repressive response to migration on land.

Libya is in chaos; there, militias and gangs now routinely "arrest" sub-Saharan migrants and often subject them to prolonged detention and human rights abuses before eventually (or hopefully) setting them free upon the payment of a "liberation fee" (Amnesty International 2015). Here, the Gaddafi-era use of migrants as a bargaining chip in relations with Europe has evolved into something even more insidious—a new, violent racism directed at people seen as fair game both legally and socially. This is also happening, to a lesser extent, in Morocco, where closer cooperation with Spain and Europe on migration controls has led to ever more repression and harassment of sub-Saharan migrants by police and even vigilante groups, pushing them toward an irregular exit.[25]

Again, bringing the discussion back to my initial observations, we need to see the dynamics at sea in relation to the much larger field of border control around it. This includes, besides the coercive European response at fenced-off land borders and the violence and harassment in collaborating third states, draconian new policies in Israel and Saudi Arabia, both of which have long been important destinations for migrants and refugees from the Horn of Africa. As many scholars are increasingly pointing out (see, e.g., Johnson 2014; Jones 2012), and as I have argued elsewhere (Andersson 2016), we are seeing a parallel globalization of the punitive border security response and of irregular migratory routes, with tactics from "above" and "below" colliding with each other in a deadly game.

At this time—as the securitarian response is being copied-and-pasted into new settings across the rich world, and as poorer neighboring states have come to collaborate in controls with little regard for human rights considerations—the fear of repression and persecution (rather than the lure of rescues) must thus be seen as a major factor in fomenting sea departures. Indeed, as early as January 2015, the EU's cruel experiment of cutting sea rescues because of their supposed "pull effect" was falling apart: the number of crossers during that month was up 60 percent over the previous year in the Mediterranean, and hundreds were again perishing in the waves, with much larger drowning incidents taking place that spring.[26]

Besides the pressure to depart, the more subtle changes in behavior after departure also need to be taken into account when evaluating the UK's and similar positions on deterrence. With Mare Nostrum, as in the Canary Islands in 2006 or in the Strait more recently, passengers now want to be detected, since they know they will be taken to Europe, not pushed back to Africa. As seen above, this is a subversive act insofar as it short-circuits the advanced and expensive border surveillance machinery. If European politicians are sincere in wanting to limit deaths at sea, however, it is also in their interest for migrants and refugees to seek such rescues. That way, after all, the crossers run less risk than if they (and their smugglers) seek more dangerous routes to avoid detection.[27] Migrants or refugees and border workers can here come to collaborate in a brief and positive humanitarian moment on the open seas—a moment, as has been seen, that is nevertheless surrounded by a large field of violence, coercion, and deterrence stretching out on both sides of the maritime border.

Conclusion: Beyond the Borders of Europe

Humanitarianism on the high seas, it has been argued here, on the one hand has to be grasped from within, in order to see what it does and which relations and projects it creates for the various agencies working on migration at the borders. On the other hand, it has to be understood as but one "militaro-humanitarian moment" (Fassin, quoted in Walters 2011a:154) in a larger field of controls. This field stretches well beyond the Euro-African border as well as far inside it, into European space, as seen in the extensive migration policing operations there or the prolonged detention or limbo experienced by refugees across the Union.

Rather than branching out toward the larger global picture, as I have done elsewhere (Andersson 2016), I will in this conclusion address a key theme of this volume, namely the shifting position and meaning of "Europe" itself within the "refugee crisis," as the continent's experiment with a supranational project has lent itself to quite historically specific tensions in the field of migration and border controls. At the Union's external borders, we regularly see a two-faced image of "Europe" in the newscasts: at once draconian and humane, hostile and welcoming—a tense and fractious polity that, through its closed routes to legal entry for certain kinds of travelers, has allowed the deaths of thousands at its borders.

In a recent essay, Nicholas De Genova (2016a, 2016b) puts what he calls "the 'European' Question"—what "Europe" is, and who belongs in "it"—firmly in relation to its various postcolonial and migrant Others. He writes: "In the extended aftermath of the end of the Cold War and especially now, amid the shocks of the global capitalist crisis, the European question has become a problem of a new significance and magnitude—above all, in Europe itself" (De Genova 2016b:76). Looking at this European Question from the border, we can see how the humanitarian-security nexus delineated in these pages serves as one potent element in a narrative and enactment of "Europe." Through the Union's constitutive outside, so well represented by the ragged and desperate boat people seeking "our" shores, the European question initially seems to receive a positive answer. "We" inhabit the space sought by those Others, and can assure ourselves of our continued relevance in the world; we are those who save, who decide, who remain in control, despite our floundering economies and member-state squabbles. This is certainly how boat migration into Spain has been perceived on the national stage in the past decade, even well before the crisis: as a chance to prove the country's once so insecure "European-ness" through political acumen, humanitarian expertise, and an impressive deployment of patrols and cutting-edge technology. Later, once the economic crisis hit, the spectacle of the border was briefly reduced to the simplest of messages— Red Cross volunteers wrapping sub-Saharan migrants in blankets in an upbeat Coca-Cola–sponsored advertisement, encouraging TV audiences to get the country moving once more.[28]

Despite the UK and far-right protestations over life-saving measures, then, Europe's two-faced border response has often presented a flattering image, even if that image has been torn apart by the mounting number of avoidable deaths since 2015. Whether "we"—European citizenry—are of the right or left, nationalist or liberal, Southern or Northern European, we have regularly congratulated ourselves as we have witnessed unfortunate passengers being rescued on the high seas. This is the "Europe" by which we want to be seen: the repository of freedom, democracy, and human rights, professionally coming to the rescue of the world's "huddled masses" with the help of all our latest technology. All the while, off-stage, migrants are quietly bundled through a fence or chased through the streets of Tangier or Tripoli—safely beyond the border that separates lawless existence from Europe's "area of freedom, security, and justice." In these vicious dynamics, "Europe"—as idea and political project—emerges as deeply compromised by its double move at the borders.

This will surely have negative repercussions on Europe's perception from the outside and its standing in the world, as is already evident to those of us studying migrants' own changing views on the European "dream" that once motivated their journeys. Needless to say, it will also affect Europe's attractiveness as future destination for willing workers compared with other regions, crucial at a time when many EU countries are rapidly aging and global competition for labor is set to intensify. But none of this need bother the security professionals with whom this article has been principally concerned. Returning to Bigo (2014), we can see how humanitarianism—as PR gloss, multilevel justification, and intricate daily activity—has blurred distinctions between the three fields of border control, yet strengthened those at the top of the hierarchy within the military-strategic field in particular, while simultaneously bolstering the position of politicians beholden to short-sighted domestic agendas. In Italy the navy has benefited from the drive to "humanitarianize" the border, while in Spain it is the "mixed" body of the Guardia Civil that has seen a boost to its symbolic, political, and financial capital. As Bigo (2000) showed many years ago, this type of militarily organized police force, like the gendarmerie in France, has been ideally positioned to take advantage of the new transnational security environment in which migration becomes a major European preoccupation. Situated at the threshold of the civilian and the military spheres, the Guardia Civil, by invoking and enacting both securitarian and humanitarian responses, has managed to establish itself as a "hub" agency with links to the Spanish military, national police, Frontex, aid organizations, and the state sea rescue service—as seen, not least, in its state-of-the-art control and coordination centers in Madrid and Las Palmas.

Meanwhile, in the Brussels sphere where the defense lobby meets with the eurocrats, the gains from the humanitarian-security nexus are similarly manifold. It has not only justified further investments in technology and patrols by pleasing all sides, as seen above; it has also fueled attempts to get third states to "cooperate" more in "border management" (that catch-all term), preemptively cutting "risk to life" before Europe has to deal with it. Through such interactions, Europe's "illegality industry" keeps being reinforced while the space for criticism gets progressively reduced—leaving actors such as Amnesty International and Human Rights Watch merely able to call for more "humanitarian" patrols at the border, rather than a fundamental rethink of Europe's counterproductive "fight against illegal migration."

A "theology" of border control now holds sway not just across Europe, but far beyond its shores. The calls for more barriers and patrols may on the one hand be a blatant attempt to quell familiar voter anxieties through a securitization of migration and borders (see Chebel d'Appollonia 2012), yet beyond this politics of fear lie the more complex humanitarian-security terrains discussed in this chapter, in which motives, methods, and objects of intervention are increasingly mixed up. In the "doxa" of border controls (Bourdieu 1977), unspoken assumptions dictate what the problem is, what our options are for solving it, and importantly where we should look—that is, toward the physical or juridical borderlines, whether with our liberal/humanitarian or nationalist/securitarian glasses on. On a theoretical level, one key challenge is to see beyond the repressive and disciplinary nature of controls to account for the productive aspects of Europe's attempts to halt migratory flows: the new social realities and roles created by border thought and praxis.[29] Politically speaking, understanding the humanitarian-security nexus at play at the sea borders is key to moving beyond the current impasse, in which the only two options available are those of more "tough" and more "humanitarian" controls—both blindly taking the borders of Europe as their main reference point and the racialized migrant, pitiable and threatening by turns, as their wayward object of intervention.

NOTES

1. See "Mediterranean Sea: Data of Missing Migrants," report by the Missing Migrants Project of the International Organization for Migration (IOM), http://missing migrants.iom.int/mediterranean.

2. On the razor wire, see http://www.theguardian.com/world/2013/nov/01/razor-wire-divide-morocco-melilla-inhumane. The battle over pushbacks in Melilla has been complicated by the interior minister denying that these are even taking place, since migrants have not entered Spain—according to him—until making it past the border guards, an argument repudiated by jurists as invalid. See, for instance, http://www.eldiario.es/desalambre/Rajoy-incumplimiento-extranjeria-obligacion-controlar_0_318468919.html.

3. On Avramopolous's hearing in Brussels, see http://eulawanalysis.blogspot.co.uk/2014/09/mr-avramopolous-goes-to-brussels.html; on Mos Maiorum, see, for instance, this news report: http://www.vice.com/read/the-eu-held-its-biggest-ever-anti-immigrant-crackdown-933.

4. A slightly different, or complementary, way of framing these two tendencies is to talk of a national security versus a human security focus in controls; see, e.g., Adamson's (2006) discussion of migration and securitization in Europe.

5. For the latter quote, see http://www.telegraph.co.uk/news/politics/11192208/Drown-an-immigrant-to-save-an-immigrant-why-is-the-Government-borrowing-policy-from-the-BNP.html; for the original *Guardian* story revealing the UK position, see http://www.theguardian.com/politics/2014/oct/27/uk-mediterranean-migrant-rescue-plan.

6. On the Australia comparison, see http://www.theguardian.com/commentisfree/2014/oct/29/the-uk-is-now-turning-its-back-on-migrants-dying-at-sea-have-we-learned-nothing-from-australia?CMP=twt_gu.

7. For one example of a comment piece denouncing the UK position, see http://www.theguardian.com/commentisfree/2014/oct/28/britain-refusal-help-migrants-inhumanity?CMP=twt_gu. The double task here of unmasking and understanding echoes Fassin's call for "critical thinking located at the frontiers" of humanitarianism, between "insider" and "outsider" perspectives (Fassin 2012:245–46).

8. On the IOM in Morocco, see not least this scathing assessment by Hein de Haas: http://heindehaas.blogspot.co.uk/2012/10/ioms-dubious-mission-in-morocco.html.

9. On Hera, see Andersson (2014b) and Carrera (2007).

10. For the interior minister's intervention, see http://tinyurl.com/9cwlh73.

11. One pioneering study (Carling 2007b) found no evidence that more surveillance had led to more risks and deaths. However, this study was hampered by the fact it only looked at Spanish sea borders, when in fact controls there have displaced migrant routes elsewhere, toward the Sahara desert and routes into Italy and Greece, which have to be assessed for any full quantitative assessment of fatalities. The difficulty with this, of course, is that the further away from the border that migrants perish (at sea or in the desert), the harder it is to have any figures at all.

12. Awareness of the consequences of more surveillance—longer and riskier routes—has been spelled out, to give just one example, in the Guardia Civil's celebratory book on their SIVE radar system (Guardia Civil 2008), as well as in Frontex statements of more recent years.

13. See judgment at http://hudoc.echr.coe.int/sites/eng/pages/search.aspx?i=001–109231 as well as discussion in Tondini (2012) and Di Filippo (2013).

14. On offshoring practices and the Australian case, see Mountz (2011).

15. See http://sverigedemokraterna.se/wp-content/uploads/2014/04/SD-vårbudget motion-2014.pdf (in Swedish; my translation).

16. See http://europa.eu/rapid/press-release_IP-13–1182_en.htm.

17. See Frontex acting director's statements at http://euobserver.com/justice /124136.

18. Quotes from a piece by Don Flynn on the Migrants' Rights Network website: http://www.migrantsrights.org.uk/blog/2014/11/refugees-mediterranean -violence-and-war-driving-flows-not-people-traffickers?utm.

19. The risk of arrest and long sentences has meant smugglers have increasingly come to "delegate" the captaining function to migrants or refugees on board; it has also led to many cases of captains abandoning the rudder as they see patrol vessels approach, triggering tragedies at sea.

20. On this changing landscape of routes, see, for instance, Amnesty International (2014).

21. Quote from Feldman (2012:95). "Hold the Line" was the name of a U.S. border control operation at El Paso, Texas, which began in September 1993 (Dunn 2009).

22. A third group is that of minors, since they fall under a different legal regime from that of adults.

23. Besides the full safety gear, workplace health regulations at sea borders also included special insurance covering tropical illnesses for Salvamento staff, and separate ventilation for rescued migrants on large Guardia Civil patrol boats.

24. The larger debates on the politicization of humanitarianism will not be discussed here; see Fassin and Pandolfi (2010) and Feldman and Ticktin (2010) for two important interventions.

25. On repression in Morocco, see the discussion in Andersson (2014b) as well as Human Rights Watch (2014).

26. On the developments of early 2015, see, e.g., this Amnesty International dispatch: https://www.amnesty.org/en/articles/blogs/2015/02/lampedusa-dramatic-chronicle-of -the-latest-mediterranean-tragedy/.

27. For a discussion of the risk of dying at sea during and before Mare Nostrum, see, for instance, Amnesty International (2014). It has to be emphasized that better detection of boats also produces a higher official "death count," thus skewing official figures negatively in terms of Mare Nostrum's efficacy.

28. See http://www.youtube.com/watch?v=FTHn8X895cI.

29. This observation stems from Walters's (2011a) challenge to think beyond Foucault's "toolbox" in understanding the dynamics at contemporary borders.

3

Liquid Traces

Investigating the Deaths of Migrants at the EU's Maritime Frontier

CHARLES HELLER AND LORENZO PEZZANI

If geography expresses in its very etymology the possibility of writing and therefore reading the surface of the earth, the liquid territory of the sea seems to stand as the absolute challenge to spatial analysis. The waters that cover over 70 percent of the surface area of our planet are constantly stirred by currents and waves that seem to erase any trace of the past, maintaining the sea in a kind of permanent present. In Roland Barthes's words, the sea appears a "non-signifying field" that "bears no message" (Barthes 1972:112). Furthermore, its vast expanse and the lack of stable habitation on its surface lead events at sea to occur mostly outside of the public gaze and thus remain unaccounted for. The deaths of illegalized migrants at sea and the violation of their rights are no exception.[1] While, between 1988 and November 2012, the press and NGOs reported more than 14,000 deaths at the maritime frontier of the EU—including more than 7,000 in the Sicily Channel alone—the conditions in which these occur have rarely been established with precision, and the responsibility for them has seldom been determined.[2] Many more lives have been lost without being recorded other than in the haunting absence experienced by their families and friends.

It is in relation to the challenges posed by this liquid frontier that we started the Forensic Oceanography project in the summer of 2011 in an attempt to document the deaths of migrants at sea and violations of their rights. This endeavor was spurred by the new demands for accountability that emerged in the aftermath of the Arab uprisings, which represented a moment of paroxysm and rupture in a number of respects. The revolution in Tunisia and the civil war in Libya led to the sudden reopening of the central Mediterranean's clandestine migration routes. While this context saw an intense movement of people, the precarious conditions in which the crossings occurred led to a record number of deaths. However, as we will see, these deaths occurred while this very maritime space was being monitored with unprecedented scrutiny due to the NATO-led military intervention in Libya. The crossings and deaths were occurring in a space populated by a large number of Western states' military ships and patrol aircraft, and there were strong indications that military forces were failing in their obligation to rescue migrants in distress, despite possessing the requisite means of surveillance to witness their plight.

This was particularly apparent in the incident now known as the "left-to-die boat" case, in which sixty-three migrants lost their lives while drifting for fourteen days in the NATO maritime surveillance area, despite several distress signals relaying their location, as well as repeated interactions, including at least one military helicopter visit and an encounter with a military ship. By precisely reconstructing these events and the involvement of various actors within them, we demonstrated that traces are indeed left in water, and that by reading them carefully the sea itself can be turned into a witness for interrogation. The contemporary ocean is in fact not only traversed by the energy that forms its waves and currents, but by the different electromagnetic waves sent and received by multiple sensing devices that create a new sea altogether. Buoys measuring currents, optical and radar satellite imagery, transponders emitting signals used for vessel tracking, and migrants' mobile phones are among the many devices that record and read the sea's depth and surface as well as the objects and living organisms that navigate it. By repurposing this technological apparatus of sensing, we have tried to bring the sea to bear witness to how it has been made to kill. In this, our analysis also goes against the popular imagination of the ocean as a void lying outside history and beyond the reach of society.

Migrants die not only at sea but through a strategic use of the sea. As this particular incident exemplifies, even when they drown following a shipwreck or starve while drifting in its currents, there is nothing "natural" about their deaths. After all, as Ellen Churchill Semple noted long ago in her *Influences of Geographic Environment* (1911), the sea has a fundamentally dual and paradoxical nature, both restricting and enabling human movement. In her geographic deterministic frame, Semple argued that among many different types of "natural boundaries" that "set more or less effective limits to the movement of peoples and the territorial growth of states," "the sea is the only absolute boundary, because it alone blocks the continuous, unbroken expansion of a people" (214). Yet, in another passage, she also remarks that the sea can be "domesticated" to bring people into contact: "Man," she writes, "by appropriating the mobile forces in the air and water to increase his own powers of locomotion, has become a cosmopolitan being" (292). We can reread Semple's comments today in the light of the concept of "geopower" proposed by Elisabeth Grosz (2012), through which, as Duncan Depledge summarizes, she underlines how geographic environments are endowed with "forces contained in matter that precede, enable, facilitate, provoke and restrict 'life'" (2013:1), but that, conversely, political practices shape the way this geopower operates, and affect the ways some are empowered and others restricted by it. Through such an understanding of geopower, we can hold on to the dual nature of the sea Semple perceived so astutely, but strip it of the geographic determinism that marked her formulation, and emphasize instead that it is the agency of humans—from their invention of new means of navigation to the policies that determine who can and cannot access them—that plays a central role in making the sea oscillate between a medium enabling circulation and one adding friction to movement and life.

Our project thus could not limit itself to reading the sea in order to document specific incidents, but demanded that we attempt to understand the conditions that have led the sea to become so deadly. As we will demonstrate, the Mediterranean has been made to kill through contemporary forms of militarized governmentality of mobility which inflict deaths by first creating dangerous conditions of crossing, and then abstaining from assisting those in peril. This governmentality is shaped by the complex legal structure and mode of governance of the sea that enables state actors to selectively expand or contract their rights and obligations. What emerges from these conditions is a form of violence that is diffused and dispersed among many actors and which often, as in the case we have investigated, operates less through the direct action of a singular actor than through the inaction of many. As a consequence of this form of systemic violence, the specific responsibility for deaths and violations at sea is difficult to detect and prove. Before describing the strategies and methodologies we applied to collect the testimony of the sea so as to reconstruct the "left-to-die boat" case and others, it is first necessary to chart the broader political, juridical, and technological conditions through which the sea was made to kill—conditions that we have mobilized against the grain in the task of breaching the impunity of the actors involved.

Maritime Governance: Beyond the
"Freedom vs. Enclosure" Divide

In *The Nomos of the Earth* (2003 [1950]), the German jurist and political theo-rist Carl Schmitt epitomized a vision of the sea as an anarchic space in which the impossibility of drawing longstanding and identifiable boundaries made it equally difficult for European states to establish a durable legal order or found claims of sovereignty. "The sea," he wrote, "has no character, in the original sense of the word, which comes from the Greek *charassein*, meaning to engrave, to scratch, to imprint" (42–43).[3] Thus Schmitt described the fundamental dis-tinction on which geopolitics has been predicated for many years: the binary division between a solid land, where territories can be clearly demarcated and where order may be imposed, and a sea where borders can be neither traced nor held and where freedom reigns absolute. This opposition found its expres-sion in the evolution of maps of the world which, from the early seventeenth century onward, tended to represent (European) land in great detail in terms of geographic morphology, human-built environment, and political boundaries, but signified the territory of the surrounding sea as an abstract and frictionless geometric space open to navigation.[4] While idealizations of the sea as empty and lawless still persist (Helmreich 2011; Sekula and Burch 2010), recent his-toriography of empires as well as geographical scholarship on maritime gover-nance tell us a different story, in which the oceans have long been crisscrossed by multiple regimes of appropriation and juridical differentiation.

Historians of empire have effectively shown how, in the early modern period, "trans-oceanic trade and colonization created significant new international conflicts and constellations of power outside existing arrangements" (Mancke 1999:232). This situation fostered the proliferation of differential zones of var-iegated sovereignties that were "integral to empire" (Benton 2010:132; see also Stoler 2006:139), and this both on land and sea. Until the mid-nineteenth century, according to Lauren Benton, "empires did not cover space evenly but composed a fabric that was full of holes, stitched together out of pieces, a tangle of strings" (2010:2). These historians thus qualify the ideal type of the sovereign territo-rial state to which Schmitt alluded, by revisiting its emergence from within the messy history of the empire-state form (Cooper 2005). Furthermore, geogra-pher Philip Steinberg has also demonstrated how maritime governance imposed by (Western) states and capital has always oscillated throughout modernity be-tween two poles: on the one hand, the desire to divide up the waters of the earth in a way that would mirror the carving up of territorial boundaries on land; on the other, the vision of the oceans as commons, open to free navigation—the "free seas." However, rather than an either/or application of these seemingly opposed tendencies, what we observe throughout this period is rather their productive entanglement.[5] This productive tension is at work in one of the founding moments of maritime law, commonly referred to as the "Battle of the Books" (1580–1650), which centered around the opposition between the vision of a free sea expressed by the Dutch jurist Hugo Grotius in his 1609 text *Mare liberum* (The free sea) and the defense of maritime division and control formulated by the English scholar John Selden in *Mare clausum* (The closed sea) in 1635.[6] But this apparent contrast conceals a deeper convergence. While Selden, by noting that "*mare clausum* can go only so far as one can assert effective control," endorsed negatively the idea of freedom for the high seas (Steinberg 2001:97, 105),[7] the concept of the "freedom of the seas" coined by Grotius routinely led to the use of coercion to ensure the smoothness and security of trade routes or block those of competitors (Benton 2010:106). As Steinberg writes, "Freedom requires policing and mobility requires fixity, and both of these activities require continual efforts to striate the ideally smooth ocean" (Steinberg 2011:271).

For both poles in the governance of the seas, the ability to map, measure, and exercise surveillance over the maritime space was fundamental. This knowledge did not precede its application in the service of power, but was inextricably bound to war, trade, and imperialism in its very production. It was the coupling of scientific epistemologies and Western commercial and military networks of empire spanning the globe that enabled systematic measurements to be sampled across vast distances, and generated increasingly detailed knowledge of the winds, currents, tides, depths, landmasses, and living organisms that constitute the ocean's global system.[8] This understanding of the seas was essential to secure and fast navigation, as well as to charting maritime territory and life in a way that would eventually enable its division, exploitation, and regulation. While Schmitt was indeed right to state that the sea itself cannot be carved up and possessed in the same manner as land, the same is not true of the resources located within the water and in the soil under it, or the traffic that floats on its surface. By going beyond his land–sea binary and by being attuned to the vertical dimension of maritime spaces, we are able to decipher a much more complex form of governance than the simple opposition between territorial control and deterritorialized flow.

The tension between, and coexistence of, the tendencies of enclosure and freedom in the governance of maritime space has resulted, on the one hand, in a form of unbundled and spatially variegated sovereignty, and on the other, in a governance in motion that seeks to compensate for the impossibility of controlling the entire liquid expanse, by focusing on the control of maritime routes and the mobile people and objects that ply them. Whereas in 1702 the extension of the territorial waters could be defined by Cornelius Bynkershoek as the area covered by coastal states' cannon-shot range, with the governance of routes largely dependent on the presence of ships along key corridors, today a far more complex jurisdictional regime and mode of governance has been enabled by the contemporary technological apparatus discussed below, which transforms the maritime space into a dense and extensive "sensorium" (Coté 2010; Latour 2006:104–7). In this situation, as we will see with reference to the Mediterranean, multiple lines of enclosure that run parallel to the coastline and dissect the surface and volume of the ocean into partial sovereignty regimes intersect with diagonal and ever-shifting lines of control that attempt to follow routes of maritime traffic. These sets of lines do not simply coexist, for, as we will see, the carving up of partial sovereignty regimes is the very legal basis for governance in motion to expand and contract selectively in policing the "free seas."

Lines of Enclosure: Unbundled Sovereignty at Sea

The successive stripes of jurisdiction, which, by dissecting both surface and volume of the sea, determine the current legal architecture of maritime territories (Suárez de Vivero 2010), are mainly codified by the 1982 United Nations Convention on the Law of the Sea (UNCLOS). After establishing the criteria for determining the position of the so-called baseline—the ideal line that usually corresponds to the low-water line along the coast—the convention further defines several jurisdictional zones, over which states exercise decreasing degrees of control and exclusive privilege. These include, among others, "territorial waters" that extend up to twelve nautical miles from the baseline, within which states have full sovereignty; the "contiguous zone," covering up to twenty-four nautical miles, within which states may further exercise certain border police functions; the "exclusive economic zone" (EEZ), which may delimit a zone up to two hundred nautical miles from the baseline, within which coastal states have exclusive control over natural resources both in the water (such as fish) and under the soil (such as gas or oil). Beyond this zone lie the "high seas," where no state can exercise its full sovereignty nor subject any part of them to its jurisdiction.

While the high seas are "free for all states and reserved for peaceful purposes," they do not become as a result a legal vacuum, since the rights and obligations of each actor and state are framed by international law. The jurisdiction of states applies to vessels flying their respective flags, and each vessel thus becomes a small piece of floating state jurisdiction, transforming the high seas into an international space in the strongest sense, since all states are potentially in contact with each other (Cuttitta 2007). Finally, vessels and coastal states also have particular obligations: among these, of central relevance for our investigation into the "left-to-die boat" case, are the duty of vessels to provide assistance to people in distress and the obligation of coastal states to coordinate rescue operations. For this purpose, search and rescue (SAR) zones have been established across the high seas by the 1979 International Convention on Maritime Search and Rescue (SAR), delimiting the geographic areas within which particular states have a legal responsibility to coordinate rescue operations.

What emerges from this process of enclosure of the high seas by various and sometimes competing jurisdictional regimes, is the image of a space of "unbundled" sovereignty (Sassen 2006), in which the rights and obligations that compose modern state sovereignty on the land are decoupled from each other and applied to varying degrees, depending on the spatial extent and the specific issue in question (Steinberg 2011:207). As a result, a patchy legal space constituted by overlapping and often conflicting fragments has emerged. The Mediterranean is a paradigmatic example of this phenomenon, which is therein reproduced at a smaller scale but with increased rapidity and intensity. Until recently, most Mediterranean states had refrained from extending exclusive claims beyond their territorial waters, for fear of getting entangled in thorny legal conflicts and of reducing the navigational advantages guaranteed by the high seas. Since the beginning of the 1990s, however, under changed geopolitical conditions, the Mediterranean has entered a phase of accelerated juridicalization, and zones of exclusive maritime use have proliferated, extending national jurisdiction into what used to be high seas (Andreone 2004:7–25). These are zones of environmental protection and resource conservation which are often not even provided for by the UNCLOS, but which further subdivide the high seas according to specific functions such as fishing, ecological, and archaeological protection. The complexity of these maritime jurisdictions has in turn created numerous disputes involving states as well as fishing, oil, and shipping companies, and which are often fought through scientific campaigns to map and measure the size of fisheries, the morphology of the seabed, and the presence of minerals located under it (Suárez de Vivero 2010).

These overlaps, conflicts of delimitation, and differing interpretations that have been the by-product of the recent carving up of the sea are less malfunctions than an exacerbated expression of the structural condition of global law, which, as Andreas Fischer-Lescano and Gunther Teubner have argued, results from deep contradictions between colliding sectors of a global society (2004:1004). Furthermore, as we will see in relation to the policing of illegalized migrants at sea, this condition has become an integral part of the capacity of states and other actors to apply rights and abide by obligations at sea selectively, according to their interests, expanding and contracting their jurisdictional claims at will—for example, in order to intercept migrants or to evade the obligation to rescue people in distress. This unbundled and elastic sovereignty is key to the operations of the mobile governance exercised to police the so-called "freedom of the seas."

Lines of Control: Governance in Motion through Scopic Systems

In addition to the lines of enclosure running parallel to the coastline discussed above, the Mediterranean is crisscrossed by diagonal and ever-shifting lines of control that emerge as maritime governance attempts to follow routes of maritime traffic and police the "freedom" of the high seas.[9] As Michel Foucault had already noted in the late 1970s, this inextricable articulation between freedom and control is characteristic of forms of mobility governance in (neo)liberal societies, which operate by "maximizing the positive elements, for which one provides the best possible circulation, and [by] minimizing what is risky and inconvenient, like theft and disease, while knowing that they will never be completely suppressed" (2007:34). While the Mediterranean's waters are central to global trade—with an estimated total of 200,000 commercial ships crossing it annually (Abdulla and Linden 2008:8)[10]—this dense traffic and the maritime space itself are perceived though the lens of security as being constantly under threat: from international terrorism, criminality, illegal fishing, pollution, and, of course, illegalized migration.

To detect threats amid the productive flow of vessels and goods, states deploy means of surveillance, military and border patrols, and rescue agencies. In addition to national initiatives, NATO's Operation Active Endeavour was launched in the wake of the events of September 11, 2001, to act as a deterrent and protect civilian traffic in the Mediterranean. Policing has thus become an increasingly structural part of the supposed freedom of the high seas. The exercising of the "right of visit" is an indication of this. While, according to the UNCLOS, this right allows officials to board a vessel on the high seas in "exceptional circumstances," it has come to be used to justify an increasing number and array of interventions, including the routine interception of migrants (Papastavridis 2011b).[11] Nevertheless, the deployment of aerial and naval forces remains insufficient to police the vast waters of the Mediterranean. The sorting out of "bad" traffic from large quantities of "good" mobilities within an extremely vast space necessitates the assemblage of a sophisticated and increasingly automated technological apparatus of surveillance.

For the purposes of surveillance, the coasts of the Mediterranean, as well as state-operated vessels, are equipped with radars that scan the horizon around them by sending out high-frequency radio waves that are bounced back to the source whenever they encounter an object, indicating these "returns" as an illuminated point on a monitor. Automated vessel-tracking data for large commercial ships (AIS) or for fishing boats (VMS) is sent out by a transponder on board via VHF radio frequency and captured by either coastal or satellite receivers, providing a live view of all registered vessels.[12] Optical satellites generate imagery by capturing reflected energy of different frequencies such as visible and infrared light, while satellites equipped with synthetic-aperture radar (SAR) emit a radio signal and create an image based on variations in the returns. Both "snap" the surface of the sea according to the trajectory of orbiting satellites and are used to detect unidentified vessels or track pollution.

The constant emission and capture of different electromagnetic waves these technologies utilize confers a new material meaning upon Fernand Braudel's metaphor of the Mediterranean as an "electro-magnetic field" in terms of its relation to the wider world (Braudel 1976:168). These technologies do not simply create a new representation of the sea, but rather constitute a new sea altogether, one which is simultaneously composed of matter and media. The current aim of the different agencies striving to govern the sea is to assemble these different technologies so as to achieve the most complete possible "integrated maritime picture." This is both a technological and an institutional challenge, since it requires the interoperability of agencies from different countries (both within and outside the EU) across different fields of activity. Through this assemblage emerges what Karin Knorr Cetina has called, with reference to financial markets, a "scopic system": "When combined with a prefix, a scope (derived from the Greek *scopein*, 'to see') is an instrument for seeing or observing, as in periscope. . . . A scopic system is an arrangement of hardware, software, and human feeds that together function like a scope: like a mechanism of observation and projection" (2009:64).

While the assemblage of technologies and institutions that constitute the Mediterranean's scopic system enable a "vision" of the sea that far exceeds that of its ancestor the telescope, it is still far from producing the totalizing panoptic view that state agencies and surveillance companies regularly call for. For a start, agencies come up against their limits when faced with the huge quantity of data generated by the dense maritime traffic and the increasing deployment of remote-sensing technologies. To deal with the resulting information overload, surveillance agencies are increasingly resorting to the use of algorithms that allow the automatic detection of "anomalies" so as to distinguish "threats" from "normal" maritime traffic.[13] An even bigger challenge is posed by the task of detecting the kinds of small boats used for clandestine migration—such as ten-meter rubber boats or fifteen-meter wooden boats—within such a vast area. In this respect, all solutions to date have run up against the conflict between resolution and swath: while the detection of small boats necessitates high-resolution means of sensing (such as SAR satellite imagery), this can only be achieved for small geographic areas, thus leaving much of the maritime area unattended.[14] As such, the Mediterranean's scopic system operates a form of incomplete and patchy surveillance that runs up against the frontiers of information quantity and resolution.

Recognizing the impossibility of monitoring the entire space of the sea and the totality of traffic that populates it, state agencies focus the attention of their mobile governmentality on the main vectors and lines of sea crossing. At work then is a form of "viapolitics," a concept coined by William Walters (2011b) to describe a politics that takes as its object routes and vehicles. For Walters, "vehicles and their infrastructures are nodes, relays, surfaces, volumes in a dispersed and uneven governance of population and territory" (2011b). The modality of governance of the maritime frontier is thus deeply shaped by—and to a certain extent consubstantial with—the surveillance apparatus that enables it. For if the border exists only in its violation, the latter must first be detected either by human perception or its various technological extensions. Conversely, the strategies of invisibility enacted by clandestine migrants so as to slip through the cracks and gaps in this surveillance apparatus are essential to subverting the violent border regime that operates at sea.

The Contested Frontier: Mobile Knowledges, Elastic Borderings, and the Politics of Irresponsibility

Like the ocean, the mobility of people has proven particularly difficult to govern throughout history. In the past twenty years, severe restrictions have been imposed on the movement of people across the Mediterranean with the introduction of Schengen visas and the progressive externalization of border controls into the maritime frontier and onto North African states (Migreurop 2013). This brought an end to the phase following World War II in which "guest-worker" programs and postcolonial relations promoted an influx of migrant laborers into European countries, who frequently crossed the sea by ferry. The recent restrictions on the movement of non-European migrants have, however, proven unsuccessful in curbing "unwanted" migration flows.[15] Migration from the southern shores of the Mediterranean has continued, but in a clandestine and precarious form, employing, among other methods, crossing the sea in unseaworthy vessels.

Those wanting to cross the Mediterranean despite being denied access to formal and legal modes of doing so had to create a new transport infrastructure, constituted as much by actual vessels as by interpersonal relations and knowledge of borders. Faced with governmental agencies' interlinking of their means of surveillance to form an "integrated maritime picture" so as to control mobility, illegalized migrants developed their own social networks through which information and services are exchanged (Alioua and Heller 2013:175–84). As the work of sociologist Mehdi Alioua has shown, contrary to common perception, resorting to smugglers is usually limited to particularly difficult stages in the crossing of borders, whereas the majority of migrants' trajectories are organized autonomously and collectively. Through their mobility, migrants progressively generate a shared knowledge, which allows them to orient themselves in new environments and know where and how to cross borders undetected. This collective knowledge and practice of border crossing has a deep and ambivalent aesthetic dimension, in that it hinges on the conditions of appearance of the migrants (Rancière 2006). The very term *clandestine*, from the Latin *clandestinus*, meaning "secret" or "hidden," points to their aim to circulate undetected—literally, under the radar; this is also why most crossings begin at night. However, this desire to go undetected is always weighed against the risk of dying unnoticed at sea, as in the "left-to-die boat" case when, in distress, the migrants did everything they possibly could to be noticed and rescued.[16]

In response to the continued capacity of illegalized migrants to reach the southern shores of Europe, through a series of policies and practices, the Mediterranean has been progressively militarized and transformed into a frontier area that allows border operations to both expand and contract far beyond the legal perimeter of the EU, thus adding further friction to the mobility of migrants. In an important report submitted in 2003 to the EU Commission by Civipol—a semi-public consulting company to the French Ministry of the Interior—the authors explain that in order to "hold a maritime border which exists by accident of geography," it is necessary to go well beyond an understanding of the maritime border as delimited by EU states' territorial waters (8, 71). To exploit the geopower of the sea and use its physical characteristics to reinforce the border, surveillance has to cover "not just an entry point, as in an airport, nor a line, such as a land border, but a variable-depth surface" (8). The unbundled sovereignty at work on the high seas enabled European and non-European coastal states—assisted since 2001 by NATO as part of its Operation Active Endeavour and since 2006 by Frontex (the European border management agency)—to deploy maritime border patrols using boats, helicopters, airplanes, and the aforementioned surveillance technologies to intercept incoming migrants. Through these means of governance in motion, the line of the border has become elastic, expanding and contracting with the movement of patrols. However, the increasing militarization of the maritime frontier of the EU has not succeeded in terms of the stated aim of stopping the inflow of illegalized migrants; rather, it has resulted in the splintering of migration routes toward longer and more perilous routes of crossing.[17] This is what has turned the Mediterranean into the "deadliest route" for migrants in the world, the epicenter of those "landscapes of deaths" that characterize global borders (Nevins 2002:144; Weber and Pickering 2011).

It is thus the strategic use of the maritime environment as a frontier zone that has turned the sea into an unwilling killer. Seen from this perspective, the sea stops being a mute background onto which tactics of border enforcement unfold and becomes a constitutive element of boundary making in the same ways in which border guards, national and international institutions, and surveillance systems are.[18] The fact that such policies remain active despite policymakers' knowledge of their "failure" to keep migrants out is a reminder of the productive dimension of illegalized migration. It makes it possible for governments to engage in a never-ending "war on migration" whose benefits include attracting the populist vote, keeping the surveillance and military industries buoyant, and, last but not least, providing the labor market with a ready supply of deskilled and precaritized laborers. This is the obscene supplement of the spectacular scene of border enforcement to which Nicholas De Genova (2013a) rightly draws our attention.

As a result of these policies and militarized practices, once traveling at sea, migrants frequently find themselves in difficult situations of distress, due to a variety of factors such as failing motors, vessel overload, or loss of direction. However, as soon as they enter the Mediterranean Sea, they enter a space of international responsibility. We have already noted the obligation of vessels at sea to provide assistance to those in distress, and for coastal states to coordinate rescues within their respective search and rescue (SAR) zones. The strategic mobilization of the notion of "rescue" has at times allowed coastal states to justify police operations on the high seas, or even within foreign territorial waters to which they would otherwise have little legal access, thus blurring the line between policing and humanitarian activities.[19] But along with rescue comes the burden of disembarkation, which in turn entails responsibility for processing possible asylum requests or deporting migrants in accordance with the so-called Dublin Regulation.[20] To avoid engaging in rescue missions, states have strategically exploited the partial and overlapping sovereignty at sea and the elastic nature of international law (see Gammeltoft-Hansen and Aalberts 2010:18; and Suárez de Vivero 2010).

The delimitation of SAR zones has been the first battlefield. In the central Mediterranean, Tunisia and Libya have refrained from defining the boundaries of their SAR zones, while Italy and Malta have overlapping SAR zones and are signatories to different versions of the SAR convention, a situation which has led to repeated standoffs.[21] The latter have been exacerbated by the lack of clear definitions of concepts such as "distress" and "assistance" under international maritime law, enabling divergent interpretations (Papastavridis 2011a). Moreover, coastal states' unwillingness to accept the disembarkation of migrants has led to an increased reluctance on the part of seafarers to allow those in distress to board their vessels, in some cases fearing criminal liability for "facilitating illegal immigration." In such ways, the international legal norms established to determine responsibility for assisting those in distress at sea have been used precisely for the purpose of evading and deferring this responsibility. As a result, many migrants have been left unassisted, leading to human tragedies. It was precisely this politics of irresponsibility that was at work in the unfolding of the "left-to-die boat" case.

While Italy and Malta had been informed of the location and distress of the passengers, with the vessel still outside their SAR zones (but soon to enter their zone of overlapping and conflicting responsibility), they limited themselves to sending out distress signals to vessels transiting the area and informing NATO command, which was monitoring the maritime surveillance area within which the passengers were located. However, during the period of the international military intervention in Libya, NATO followed a practice of minimal assistance, the aim of which was to ensure that the migrants could continue their journey until they entered the Italian or Maltese search and rescue (SAR) zone so that they would become a concern for those states.[22] While this did occur in several instances, in the case of the "left-to-die boat," the evaluation of the distress of the migrants and the minimal assistance provided to them (a helicopter visited them twice and dropped a few bottles of water and biscuits) were clearly insufficient, as they soon started to drift back to the Libyan coast, left to merciless winds and currents that inflicted on the passengers a slow death.

If migrants thus die at sea from a range of direct causes such as dehydration, lack of food, the ingestion of salty water, and drowning, all of which are related to the geopower of the sea, it should be clear from the above that it is through the enforcement of migration policies imposed by the EU and their articulation within a particular maritime legal and governance regime that the sea has been turned into a deadly liquid, the site and means of a rising number of deaths and structural violations of migrants' rights. What has emerged is a form of violence that is exercised less by effecting a destructive force against a given actor, than by creating the conditions in which the sea becomes a liquid trap and refraining from helping those who are caught in it. In this, the governmentality of migration at sea constitutes an example of a form of biopolitical power described by Foucault, one that is exercised not only by actively sustaining and protecting the life of certain populations, but also by causing the death of others by simply abstaining from any form of action. To paraphrase his famous summary of this form of power, one could say that the maritime border regime "makes flow and lets drown."[23] The migration regime thus produces a form of structural violence that kills without touching and is exercised by several actors simultaneously (Pezzani 2015). As a consequence, the responsibility for the deaths and violations that are its structural product is shared, diffuse, and thus difficult to address. While migrants' rights organizations have been documenting the deaths of migrants for a number of years and have denounced the deadly policy of the maritime border regime, it was not until 2011, with the radical geopolitical shifts brought about by the Arab uprisings and the military intervention in Libya, that new possibilities for addressing this form of violence arose.

2011: Ruptures in the Migration Regime and Renewed Opportunities for Accountability

In relation to the context outlined above, 2011 represented a moment of paroxysm and rupture in a number of respects. The Arab uprisings led to a temporary power vacuum in Tunisia that enabled more than 28,000 people to cross the sea to Italy during that year. This intense mobility in the immediate aftermath of a revolution is a clear indication that the aspiration to freedom and justice of the Tunisian people was directed not only toward the way their country was governed, but also extended toward the imposition by the EU—with the active participation of the Ben Ali regime—of a violent and discriminatory migration regime within and beyond Tunisia's borders.[24] The uprising in Libya, on the other hand, led less to the seizing of a new freedom than to forced displacement. The entrenched civil war in Libya and the ensuing NATO-led military intervention forced almost 26,000 people to cross the sea to reach the southern shores of Italy, with Gaddafi's regime playing an active role in forcing migrants onto boats, with the aim of using them as weapons of war. With boats loaded to the point of collapse and without regard for even the minimal safety measures usually provided by smugglers, over 1,822 recorded deaths occurred in the central Mediterranean during 2011, one of the all-time highs.[25] However, these deaths occurred at a time when the militarization of the EU's maritime frontier had taken on entirely new dimensions, with the usual agents of the low intensity "war on migration" joined by a large number of additional military ships and patrol aircraft deployed by Western states off the Libyan coast in support of the international military intervention. Their mission included the surveillance of a wide maritime space off the coast of Libya in order to enforce an arms embargo.[26]

In this context, a coalition of NGOs was formed with the aim of identifying direct responsibility for these deaths. Their claim was that, given the means deployed, it would have been impossible for military and border control personnel to have failed to witness the distress of migrants at sea.[27] The "left-to-die boat" incident provided a case in point and the coalition decided to focus on this paradigmatic incident to launch a legal case claiming liability for nonassistance of people in distress at sea. In support of this endeavor, together with the architectural firm SITU Research, we produced a ninety-page report which, by mobilizing a wide range of digital mapping and modeling technologies and by relying on an unorthodox assemblage of human and nonhuman testimony, reconstructed and mapped as accurately as possible what happened to this vessel.[28] Having outlined above the conditions that have turned the sea into a deadly liquid, we are now in a position to explain how we brought the sea to bear witness to the conditions that have led it to kill.

As should now be clear from our discussion of the scopic system assembled to monitor maritime traffic, it is no longer true—if it ever was—that the sea entirely resists being written. The maritime space is constantly registered in optical and thermal cameras; sea-, air-, and land-borne radars; vessel-tracking technologies; and satellites that turn certain physical conditions into digital data according to specific sets of protocols, determining the conditions of visibility of certain events, objects, or people. While many of these remote sensing means remain exclusively in the hands of states and their agencies, certain types of automated vessel-tracking data (automatic identification system, or AIS), meteorological data, as well as satellite imagery are available to the public. Moreover, parallel civilian networks also supplement these sensors: migrants frequently film their crossings with mobile phones, while networks of ship- and plane-spotters post photographs of naval activities, thereby contributing to documenting, transmitting, and archiving events at sea. Through this vast process of imaging and dataization of the maritime space, the sea has become a vast and extended sensorium, a sort of digital archive that can be interrogated and cross-examined as a witness. This is precisely what we did in order to produce our report: in the absence of external witnesses, we corroborated survivors' testimonies by interrogating the very environment where these events took place—the sea itself.

But in a context in which remote sensing is so central to the process of policing illegalized migration, and the success of clandestine border crossings hinges on not being detected, how does one avoid becoming complicit with the governmental attempt to manage migration by shedding light on the transgression of borders? The use of these technologies and other sources of information demanded that we position ourselves strategically in relation to their usual application by border agencies. While the latter perform an ambiguous act of unveiling practices of clandestine migration while concealing the violent political and legal exclusion that produces this clandestine status in the first place (De Genova 2013a), as well as the numerous legal violations the migration regime generates in turn, our approach needed to invert this strategy. We aimed not to replicate the technological eye of policing, but to exercise a "disobedient gaze" (Heller et al. 2012), one which refuses to expose clandestine migration but seeks to unveil instead the violence of the border regime, and in the process disrupts the "partition of the sensible" (Rancière 2006) imposed by the border regime onto the sea. Applying this strategy to the "left-to-die boat" investigation entailed redirecting the light shed by the surveillance apparatus away from clandestine migrants and toward the act of policing the sea, and spatializing the practices of different actors so as to reinscribe responsibility within the space of the unbundled sovereignty at sea.

As described in more detail in our report, we mobilized various remote sensing and mapping technologies to reconstruct the events and determine the degree of involvement of different parties in several ways. In this endeavor, it has been crucial to couple a robust understanding of the technical characteristics of these technologies with a thorough analysis of the web of economic, scientific, and political relations in which they are embedded and which shape both their potential usage and the epistemological frame they impose on the world.[29] Only then was it possible to insert ourselves within the complex chain of production that their use involves, in order to locate specific nodes from where information could be extracted and repurposed toward the spatio-temporal reconstruction of the events and actors involved in the incident.

First, we reconstructed the trajectory of the migrants' boat up to its point of drift, by georeferencing the position of the migrants' distress calls made using a satellite phone, and by reconstructing the boat's speed and route based on detailed interviews with the survivors. But to determine the entire trajectory of the boat during its fourteen days of deadly drift, we also had to bring the winds and the currents to bear witness. An oceanographer reconstructed a model of the drifting vessel by analyzing data on winds and currents collected by buoys in the Sicily Channel. In this way, we determined that the migrants' vessel remained for the majority of its trajectory within the NATO maritime surveillance area.

With the migrants' boat's trajectory determined, and the knowledge of its distress by other vessels operating in the area at the time established by tracing the different distress signals that were sent out, the key question became: Which ships were in its vicinity and failed to respond? To answer this, we relied on synthetic aperture radar (SAR) satellite imagery, which, analyzed by a remote sensing specialist, allowed us to establish the presence of a number of ships in the immediate vicinity of the migrants' boat. However, the relatively low resolution of the images (1 pixel represents 50 m² or 75 m²) did not allow us to locate migrants' boats (usually small wooden and plastic vessels), but only the bigger military and commercial vessels. The resolution of the image thus became a highly political issue, in that it determined the frontier between the visible and the invisible, and separated the practice of a disobedient gaze from an uncritical act of revealing that risks complicity. In the process, not only were we using against the grain a technology usually used for surveillance, we were repurposing the very images surveillance produces: the availability of those SAR images was probably due in the first place to the military operations in Libya, since there was a sharp increase in the number of available images coinciding with the days of the conflict.

In a third strategic use of surveillance technology, this time in line with the claim made by the coalition of NGOs, we turned the knowledge generated through surveillance means into evidence of responsibility. While the military had deployed exceptional means of surveillance to enforce the embargo and detect any threat at sea, the knowledge they generated also made them aware of the distress of migrants—and therefore responsible for assisting them. After collecting several official statements by military officials celebrating the technical capability of the means of surveillance deployed in the Mediterranean, we carried out a detailed analysis of the range and precision of their sensing technologies in order to prove that the naval assets in operation at the time of the "left-to-die boat" case had the means to detect the drifting migrants' boat. Since, as Bruno Latour reminds us, with the capacity to sense events should come "sensitivity"—the capacity to respond to them—the lack of response despite the knowledge generated by surveillance became in this case evidence of guilt (Latour 2013). In this way, we attempted to close the gap which the politics of irresponsibility tries to leave open between the possibility of sensing a certain event (of distress) and the obligation to intervene.

FIGURE 3.1. Map reconstructing the chain of events of the "left-to-die boat" case.
Charles Heller, Lorenzo Pezzani, and SITU Research

While many questions remain open in terms of the identities of the different actors involved—crucially, the two helicopters and the military ship that entered into direct contact with the migrants have not yet been identified—we were able to provide a precise reconstruction and to point to the implication and failures of several actors, including NATO and the coalition of national militaries, the Italian and Maltese Coast Guards, the fishing and commercial vessels present in the area, and Gaddafi's troops. Because of this multiplicity of actors and the partial and overlapping juridical regimes with which the migrants' boat intersected, the question of who should be held responsible for the structural violence perpetrated against the passengers emerged. While the fragmentation of juridical regimes at sea so often allows for the evasion of responsibility, in this case it was mobilized strategically toward the multiplication of potentially liable actors and of forums where they could be judged and debated. Not only were several legal complaints lodged in the courts of France, Italy, Spain, and Belgium against unknown parties for nonassistance to people in danger at sea—each time generating press attention—but several other initiatives took place in parallel: two documentary investigations were screened on television as well as at festivals;[30] a report was published by the Council of Europe, leading to several hearings with representatives from different states; and finally, the case was presented in many venues to activist and academic audiences across Europe and North Africa. Each of the forums, with their respective languages, rules, and technologies, became a space of judgment. But even managing to address the responsibility of the numerous actors involved would have been insufficient if the multifarious policies of exclusion, militarization, and evasion of responsibility that shaped the incident in the first place were not themselves put on trial. While demanding accountability for all the deaths of migrants at the maritime frontier of the EU has not been possible so far within the forum of the law and its particular language, the different actors investigating this case had to go beyond the realm of the law and venture into that of politics. In this way, they denounced the violence of the denial of freedom of movement and the deaths it generates, which no amount of compliance with legal obligations will be able to undo.

Conclusion: Liquid Lands

It has been necessary to follow the meandering route of the history of the governance of the seas and its intersection with the policing of the mobility of people in order to understand the conditions under which the sea has been made to kill, and which have led to the structural violations of the rights of migrants. Only through a "hand-to-hand" struggle with this network of geographic, aesthetic, technological, legal, social, and political conditions were we able to reinscribe history and responsibility onto a sea of impunity. Understood in these terms, incidents such as the "left-to-die boat" shed a new and harsh light on contemporary forms of maritime governance and migration management. The image of the Mediterranean that emerges is that of an environment crisscrossed by "a thick fabric of complex relations, associations, and chains of actions between people, environments, and artifices" (Weizman 2012:6). It is the totality of this field of forces that constitutes the particular form of governance that operates at sea. With regard to the policing of illegalized migrants, we have seen that the selective expansion and retraction of sovereignty that this space enables has led to a form of governmentality that, although highly militarized, diverts and modulates movement rather than blocking it, blurs the line between humanitarian and policing functions, and inflicts death on a large scale by creating conditions of precarious crossing and by refraining from acting to save those caught in this liquid trap.

The fantasy of a soft governance that would make the movement of people and things simultaneously orderly and productive is a mere chimera, since there will always be subjects who refuse this order, and attempts to tame them can only lead to deaths and legal violations on a structural basis. The deaths at the maritime frontiers of the EU are, in this sense, the necropolitical ghost that haunts this vision of neoliberal governmentality (Mezzadra and Neilson 2013:174). They will continue unabated as long as the current migration regime and governance of the seas prevails. While European publics seem to have come to accept these deaths as a necessary lesser evil, documenting violations, filing multiple contentious legal cases, and supporting the mobilization of the relatives of the migrants lost at sea in their struggles to shed light on what has happened to their family members may be seen as inserting "grains of sand" into the migration regime's mechanisms, blocking them temporarily, forcing them to change slightly.[31] In this process, an important shift has occurred: states, the military, and other actors at sea no longer have a monopoly over watching. Civil society demands that the increased capacity to monitor the sea be accompanied by an increased level of responsibility, using the same sensing technologies against the grain to follow the (in)actions of the different actors who operate in the frontier space of the sea, reinscribing responsibility where they attempt to evade it. But if the change that may be effected through such a practice is only in its infancy, we already observe the tendency of maritime-like forms of governance being exported onto land, in a striking inversion of Carl Schmitt's land–sea binary.

While the challenge for Schmitt, as we saw, was to impose onto the ocean a form of power characteristic of the land, the sea has become a laboratory in which new forms of contemporary governance have been devised and experimented with and are now being brought to bear on the land. As at sea, border functions on the land have been decoupled from the limits of the territorial border and are becoming increasingly dispersed and mobile, able to follow ever-shifting routes. From the notion of "Routes Management," which revolves around the charting of clandestine migrants' routes, to that of "Integrated Border Management," which seeks to control migration "before, at and after the border," practices of border control seem to have increasingly done away with fixed territorial thinking (Casas-Cortes et al. 2013). In a move that echoes the practice of maritime governance over several centuries, their focus seems instead to be on following the routes of migrants as they move across different geographical and political spaces. Rather than the solidification of the sea—a term that was suggested by the collective Multiplicity (2002) to describe the progressive invasion of the terrestrial logics of bordering into the sea—what we observe here is rather a "liquefaction of the land." In this sense, the sea should not be considered as exceptional in respect to land, but rather as a limit condition that more vividly illustrates the current transformations of territorial borders, where the spatial imaginary of the border as a line without thickness is stretched into a deep and uneven tridimensional zone (e.g., Weizman 2007).

However, there would be another, more desirable way to draw inspiration from the sea, one that is still out of sight of the hegemonic public view and policy circles. Viewing the world "from the sea," from the perspective of the constant movement of the liquid element that defies the appropriation of the ocean, one might be able to perceive the unruly freedom of human mobility which, far from being an anomaly, has been a constant throughout history, and persists in spite of the multifarious practices that try to tame it.

NOTES

An earlier version of this chapter was previously published in the edited volume *Forensis* (Forensic Architecture 2014).

1. We use several different terms to refer to people who cross borders without authorization. Because this terminology is highly politicized and contested, it is useful to indicate which terminology we use and why. Within European media and policy uses, the terms *illegal migration* and *clandestine migration* are frequently used to point to the evasion or violation of the law, and both terms have negative connotations. In this article, we alternate between using the terms *illegalized migrants* and *clandestine migration*. We use the term *illegalized* to highlight that illegality is a product of state law rather than an intrinsic feature of migrants. The term *clandestine migration* may seem problematic in that it is marked to such an extent by the language of power; yet in its etymological connotations of hiddenness and secrecy, "clandestine" accurately describes the strategies of migrants who, having been denied access to legal means of entry into a state, must cross borders undetected. As such, we refer to "clandestine" migration when pointing to the strategies of migrants. For the politics of the language of migration, see Bauder (2013); De Genova (2002, 2013a); Düvell (2008).

2. See http://fortresseurope.blogspot.com/p/la-fortezza.html and http://www.unitedagainstracism.org/pdfs/listofdeaths.pdf (accessed December 2013).

3. For an insightful discussion of this work, see Steinberg (2011).

4. For an important historical review of the shifting practices of cartography of oceans in relation to changing forms of governance and ideologies, see Steinberg (2001:99–109, 2009b).

5. Philip Steinberg (1999) traces this period back to a 1493 papal bull. The bull was formalized and amended the following year by the Treaty of Tordesillas.

6. English translations of these Latin texts have been published as Hugo Grotius, *The Freedom of the Seas, or the Right Which Belongs to the Dutch to Take Part in the East Indian Trade*, trans. Ralph Van Deman Magoffin (New York: Oxford University Press, 1916), and John Selden, *Of the Dominion, or Ownership of the Sea: Two Books* (New York: Arno, 1972).

7. It should also be remembered that both thinkers were writing from the perspective and in the service of mercantilist states which were challenging Iberian maritime supremacy. See Miéville (2006:211).

8. Before the emergence of relatively independent scientific institutions, oceanographic knowledge was produced by sailors involved in military and commercial activities. Even at the turn of the nineteenth century, scientists frequently operated within naval institutions and relied on their infrastructure; the fact that the ships associated with the pioneers of oceanography were exclusively military is a striking expression of this. For a general overview of the emergence of oceanography, see Garrison (2009:22–44). For more specific and theorized examples, see Reidy (2008) and Burnett (2009:185–255).

9. This is in fact a longstanding characteristic of governance at sea. Lauren Benton shows how since early modern times imperial visions of the ocean were "organized around the discovery and militarization of maritime passages" (2010:106). This tendency was also stressed in U.S. Navy admiral and geostrategist Alfred Thayer Mahan's work on sea lanes and maritime logistics in the late nineteenth century.

10. This report further notes that approximately 30 percent of international sea-borne volume originates from or is directed toward the three hundred ports in the Mediterranean Sea.

11. For the United Nations Office of the High Commissioner for Refugees (UNHCR) specification of those practices that should be covered by the term *interception*, see UNHCR (2003). For the use of the "right to visit" as the basis for interception, see Parliamentary Assembly of the Council of Europe (PACE) (2011).

12. AIS (automatic identification system) is a ship-borne transponder system designed for maritime safety and in particular for collision avoidance. It provides information as to identification, position, speed, and course. This live data is made publicly accessible on various websites such as marinetraffic.com. While mandatory for large commercial ships, the carriage of AIS is not required for certain categories of ships such as warships. VMS (vessel monitoring system) data is mandatory for fishing vessels longer than 15 m and is used to monitor fishing activities. While VMS operates in very much the same way as AIS data, it remains tightly controlled by state agencies. See European Commission/Joint Research Centre (2008).

13. Such techniques are already being implemented by NATO; for example, see Commander Brian Finman, "Keeping the Med Safe—How It's Done," NATO Review, May 19, 2010, http://www.nato.int/docu/review/2010/maritime_security/EN/index.htm. EU agencies are still developing this practice, with the "Blue Hub" project of the EU's Joint Research Council (JRC) leading the way. See http://ipsc.jrc.ec.europa.eu/index.php/Projects/318/0/ and https://bluehub.jrc.ec.europa.eu/ (accessed September 2013).

14. See the tests of the use of SAR imagery for the detection of small vessels described in European Commission/Joint Research Centre (2011).

15. There are several more specific reasons for this, including the need for un- or de-skilled migrant labor in EU economies, the constraints imposed on liberal democracies by the human rights regime, and because, once established, migratory networks tend to become self-sustaining and relatively autonomous from policies. See De Guchteneire and Pécoud (2006).

16. Here too social networks proved central: like many hundreds of people before and after them, the passengers in distress used a satellite phone to contact Father Mussie Zerai, an Eritrean priest living in Rome who has defended migrants crossing through Libya for several years, and whose phone number has circulated by word of mouth.

17. This effect is explicitly recognized in the Civipol report, which notes that while the majority of clandestine migration by sea uses "focal routes" of which "geography dictates the locations—straits or narrow passages where Schengen countries lie close to countries of transit or migration," they observe that "when a standard destination is shut off by surveillance and interception measures, attempts to enter tend to shift to another, generally more difficult, destination on a broader and therefore riskier stretch of water" (2003:9). The effect has also been widely observed in academic literature; see, for example, de Haas (2008).

18. The way in which (hostile) environments have been actively deployed and incorporated into the logic of border enforcement, thus underlying the latter's "more than human" and "hybrid" character, has been analyzed in depth in particular in the context of the U.S.-Mexico desert border. See, for instance, Sundberg (2011) and the brilliant book by de León (2015).

19. This was the case, for instance, of Spain (see Andersson 2012:8). This was also the argument mobilized by the Italian government in the trial of Hirsi et al. at the European Court of Human Rights, as discussed in Tondini (2010).

20. The Guidelines on the Treatment of Persons Rescued at Sea (adopted in May 2004 by the Maritime Safety Committee together with the SAR and SOLAS amendments) contain the following provisions: "The government responsible for the SAR region in which survivors were recovered is responsible for providing a place of safety or ensuring that such a place of safety is provided." MSC Res. 167(78), 2.5, Doc. MSC 78/26/Add.2 (May 20, 2004).

21. This dispute is well summarized by Gammeltoft-Hansen and Aalberts (2010:21): "Italy has signed the 2004 amendments to the SAR and SOLAS conventions that stipulate that the migrants should be disembarked on the territory of the state within which's [sic] SAR zone its vessel is identified or intercepted. Malta, however, due to the size of its SAR zone, has refused to ratify these amendments for fears that it would impose unrealistic obligations to disembark migrants rescued by other states and private vessels. Malta consequently maintains the interpretation that the coordinating country's obligation is to disembark rescued persons at the nearest safe port of call. This has led to tensions between Malta and Italy following a series of incidents where migrants were rescued in Malta's SAR zone yet closer to the Italian islands Lampedusa and Pantelleria. The result has been lengthy standoffs during which migrants have died, and a number of confrontations between Italian and Maltese naval vessels literally trying to block each other from entering its territorial waters and disembark rescued migrants."

22. See the precedents we discuss in our "Report on the Left-to-Die Boat" (Heller et al. 2012:37).

23. In his March 17, 1976, lecture, Foucault addressed the form of power over life—biopower—which emerged in the nineteenth century. Foucault argues that in the classical theory of sovereignty, the right of life and death was one of sovereignty's basic

attributes, but was mainly exercised negatively, in the taking of subjects' lives. The new power over life that emerged in the nineteenth century is much more productive in that it revolves around the care for life and death, and is inflicted less through direct action than through the lack of care. In the process, the right over life and death was radically transformed: "sovereignty's old right—to take life or let live—wasn't replaced, but it came to be complemented by a new right which does not erase the old right but which does penetrate it. . . . It is the power to 'make' live and 'let' die" (Foucault 2003:240–41).

24. The work of Jean-Pierre Cassarino (2013) is an important reminder not only that these policies were imposed by the EU on Tunisia within highly unequal relations, but that the Ben Ali regime instrumentalized externalization policies to forward its own goals of political and social control.

25. UNHCR, "Mediterranean Takes Record as Most Deadly Stretch of Water for Refugees and Migrants in 2011," briefing notes, January 31, 2012, http://www.unhcr .org/4f27e01f9.html (accessed September 2013).

26. Vice Admiral Rinaldo Veri, commander of the NATO Maritime Command in Naples responsible for embargo enforcement, stated on April 4, 2011, that "anyone who believes they can sail through NATO's layers of surveillance and interdiction needs to think again." NATO, "VADM Veri Holds Press Conference aboard ITS Etna," April 4, 2011, http://www.jfcnaples.nato.int/page167503642.aspx (accessed September 2013).

27. For the initial press release by the French NGO GISTI (Groupe d'information et de soutien des immigrés), which made the explicit connection between surveillance and responsibility, see the GISTI press release of June 9, 2011, http://www.gisti.org/spip .php?article2304 (accessed September 2013).

28. The report and other material we produced in relation to this case can be found here: http://www.forensic-architecture.org/case/left-die-boat/ (accessed September 2013). The following is a summary of key events:

1. The migrants' vessel left the Port of Tripoli between 00:00 and 02:00 GMT on March 27, 2011, with 72 migrants on board. In the frame of the military operations in Libya, NATO was enforcing an arms embargo in the Central Mediterranean, which was consequently the most highly surveilled area of the sea in the entire world at that time.

2. At 14:55 GMT on March 27, the boat was spotted by a French aircraft which transmitted its coordinates to the Maritime Rescue Coordination Centre (MRCC).

3. After proceeding in the direction of Lampedusa for 15–18 hours, the migrants placed a distress call by satellite phone. The vessel's GPS location was determined at 16:52 GMT on March 27 by the satellite phone provider Thuraya. Shortly thereafter, MRCC in Rome signaled the boat's distress and position to all vessels in the area. It further alerted Malta MRCC and NATO HQ allied command in Naples.

4. The migrants' vessel continued its course for approximately two hours before being flown over by a helicopter. As the satellite phone was thrown into the water shortly after this sighting, the last signal detected by Thuraya at 19:08 GMT on March 27 thus probably corresponds to the location of the helicopter

sighting. Around the same position, the passengers approached several fishing boats but their requests for help went unheeded. They were then visited for a second time by a military helicopter that dropped just a few biscuits and water before leaving. Between 00:00 and 01:00 GMT the passengers resumed their course NNW toward Lampedusa.

5. At approximately 07:00 GMT on March 28, after having probably entered the Maltese Search and Rescue (SAR) area, the vessel ran out of fuel and began to drift SSW.

6. The boat drifted SSW for 7–8 days before it encountered a military ship between the 3rd and 5th of April. Despite approaching them in circles and witnessing the distress of the passengers, the ship left without assisting them.

7. The boat continued to drift until April 10, when it landed southeast of Tripoli at Zlitan. Upon landing, sixty-one migrants were dead and eleven were still alive. Two more died shortly thereafter.

29. Concerning satellite imagery, see Kurgan (2013); Parks (2009); Parks and Schwoch (2012). For critical perspectives on GIS and mapping, see among others the works of Pickles (1995, 2004), as well as Crampton (2010).

30. Emiliano Bos and Paul Nicol, *Mare Deserto* (Switzerland, RSI, January 24, 2012), 52 min.; Stefano Liberti and Andrea Segre, *Mare Chiuso* (Italy, Zalab, 2012), 60 min.

31. Following the "left-to-die boat" case, we have continued to collaborate with the migrants' rights movement through different investigations and by developing a new online and participatory mapping platform, WatchTheMed, http://www.watchthemed.net/.

4

———

The Mediterranean Question

Europe and Its Predicament in the Southern Peripheries

LAIA SOTO BERMANT

In the introduction to this volume, Nicholas De Genova invites us to problematize the question of Europe (see also De Genova 2016a, 2016b). The
European Question, he argues, is a question about limits, about exclusions,
about the definition of "non-Europeans." It is therefore a question that refers us to the political and epistemic history of European domination, in relation both to Europe's southern neighbors and to its internal peripheries. Based
on ethnographic fieldwork conducted between 2008 and 2009 and, briefly,
in 2013, this chapter considers the constitution of Europe as a political, economic, and cultural project from the point of view of one of its most controversial borderlands. A 12-km² enclave located in northeastern Morocco,
Melilla has been under Spanish sovereignty since the late fifteenth century.[1]
In the early 1990s, when Spain joined the Schengen area, Melilla became,
along with Ceuta (the other Spanish enclave in Morocco), one of Europe's
southernmost borderlands. In the late 1990s, following the arrival of the
first groups of sub-Saharan African migrants, Spain built a three-meter-high
fence around Melilla. A few years later, when the inefficacy of the old fence
became apparent, the EU financed the construction of a six-meter-high,
three-tier fence equipped with manned control posts, infrared cameras, and
acoustic sensors and motion detectors. Morocco then came under mounting
pressure to control its side of the border, and military "clean-up" operations
on the Moroccan side of the border became common practice. Since then,

Melilla has played a crucial role as a buffer zone between the two continents, operating as a first line of defense in the control of migration flows into Europe.

The Thin Red Line

The first time I saw the Gourougou, a volcanic mountain located some two kilometers southwest of the Spanish enclave of Melilla, in northeastern Morocco, I was in a car with my Moroccan hosts. It was the summer of 2008, and I had just begun my doctoral research in the Moroccan province of Nador, across the border from Melilla. The Spanish enclave had been in the spotlight a few years earlier, following a violent episode at the fence that had left fifteen sub-Saharan African migrants dead, but the border had been relatively quiet since then. In Melilla, the CETI (Center for the Temporary Stay of Migrants) hosted a permanent population of around six hundred migrants. Most of them had been living there for years, waiting for a decision from the Spanish government—either an expulsion order or, in a few exceptional cases, a *laissez-passer*, a legally ambiguous term for a safe-conduct that allows undocumented migrants to travel to mainland Spain without granting them asylum or residency permits. "That's the Gourougou Mountain," said Fatima as she pointed toward it. "That's where the blacks used to hide. Now there's only monkeys!" she added, laughing. By then I had grown accustomed to hearing stories about "the blacks" (*los negros*). "The blacks," people told me, used to live up on the mountain and come down to the cities to beg and scavenge for food. "But now they are all gone," explained Fatima. "The Moroccan military put them all in a truck, took them to Oujda [near the border with Algeria], and left them there."[2]

Five years later, in September 2013, I received a message from a friend in Melilla. The message said: "This will interest you: 200 immigrants jumped over the fence last night. It gives me goose bumps." Along with the message came a video, clearly a copy from a recording taken by one of the fence's infrared security cameras, showing hundreds of African migrants jumping over the fence in the middle of the night. The number of "break-ins" had increased drastically since 2012, and it would continue to rise exponentially over the following year (Sánchez 2013), turning Melilla into a regular headline in the national and international news. The CETI was at full capacity, hosting three times as many migrants as it had originally been designed for, and the Spanish government had begun to use helicopters to patrol the fence at night. By then, rumors about illegal deportations carried out by the Spanish military police at the fence, which I had first

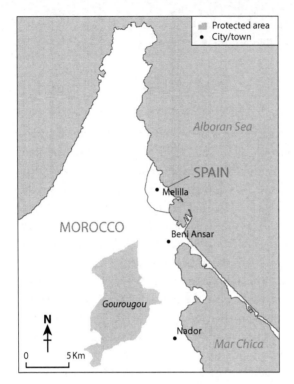

MAP 4.1. Melilla (Spain)

heard from an NGO activist in 2008, were spreading. But there was no evidence of this illegal practice—that is, until April 2014.

On the third of April 2014, around two hundred African migrants tried to jump over the fence that separates Melilla from Morocco. Like many before them, they had been hiding in the Gourougou for months, sleeping in improvised camps, with barely any food, water, or medical assistance, waiting for an opportunity to break into the European enclave. On that morning, a large group set out toward Melilla, marching down the side of the mountain in single file, armed with make-shift hooks to climb over the fence.[3] The Moroccan gendarmerie was on alert and ready to deter any possible break-ins, and only twenty-seven of them made it past the first line of defense. By the time they reached the fence and began to climb, the Spanish military police (Guardia Civil) were waiting for them on the other side. On one side of the fence stood the Moroccan gendarmerie; on the other, the Guardia Civil. Many had faced this situation before, and the course of action had always been to scale down on the Spanish side and turn themselves in at the police station as "asylum-seekers." This would entail taking up residence in the CETI and joining the hundreds of migrants indefinitely stranded in Me-lilla. However, the increasingly frequent "expedited removals"—which involve (illegally) handing incoming migrants back to the Moroccan military through one of the service gates of the fence as soon as they set foot on Spanish soil— had made migrants wary, so, instead of climbing down on the Spanish side, they sat atop the fence and waited. They held on for ten hours, until their exhausted bodies gave in and they surrendered—only to be "returned" to Morocco, as they feared, through one of the service gates. But this time something was different. For the first time, the long standoff between the migrants and the Spanish Civil Guard was caught on camera and reported live in the national and local media.

Less than two weeks later, the journalists, photographers, and cameramen who had witnessed the standoff firsthand released a statement on Facebook. "Up until yesterday," it read, "the Civil Guard stopped us from doing our job and taking photographs of these facts, establishing a 'security perimeter' to which we had no access. However, yesterday, not only did they allow us to see firsthand how a group of men tried to jump over the fence but we were in fact invited to witness, photograph and record how . . . they were later handed over to the Moroccan military."[4] As journalists, the statement continued, they had an obligation to report these events, but they also had a duty to speak out and denounce the fact that the sudden invitation to film illegal deportations was in support of a more general, fear-mongering strategy to justify violent secu- rity measures at the fence and normalize expedited removals (expulsiones en caliente, literally "hot deportations"). Since then, as predicted, the stream of news pieces, videos, and photographs showing the "assaults" on the fence has been continuous, and today Melilla's "dirty secret" (Davies 2010; cf. De Genova 2013a) is no longer a secret. Journalists, NGO workers, human rights organ- izations, and activists have become routine bystanders to these controversial practices—and, with them, the Spanish public at large.

Predictably, the increased visibility of these "border spectacles" initiated a national conversation over the nature and legitimacy of "immediate returns." Spanish immigration law grants procedural safeguards to migrants who enter the country irregularly, including the right to seek asylum, the right to appeal against administrative sanctions, and the right to a lawyer and an interpreter. Thus, when the Spanish minister of the interior justified the illegal expulsions, he had to do so by arguing that the migrants had not in fact reached Spanish territory. The border, he claimed, "is not tied to a particular geographical location, but to the line of defense of the Spanish police and Civil Guard." The deportations, it followed, were not deportations, but "rejections at the border" (rechazos en frontera). The choice of words, of course, was deliberate; if the deportations were classified as "rejections at the border"—that is, if the migrants had been detained before they reached Spanish territory—then the safeguards asylum-seekers are guaranteed under European and international law (including the right to non-refoulement) would not apply. The legality of expedited removals, therefore, hinged critically on the precise definition of Spain's (and, consequently, of Europe's) border.

Lawyers, jurists, and human rights organizations insistently voiced their opposition to this ad hoc border policy, and the EC commissioner for human rights publicly criticized the Spanish government's position.[5] But in March 2015 the Spanish Congress approved an amendment to the current Law on Public Security that provides a legal basis for the summary expulsions in Ceuta and Melilla. The new text codifies the concept of "rejections at the border" into law, stating that migrants who try to cross the borders of Ceuta and Melilla without authorization "will be rejected in order to prevent illegal immigration into Spain." The clause does not specify the protocol to follow when migrants are intercepted inside Spanish territory, and does not provide a clear definition of where the border lies. What it does, however, is institutionalize the legal ambiguity that has informed border control policies since Spain joined the EEC in 1986. Much like the deportation of migrants through the border with Algeria and the "clean-up" operations of migrant settlements in the Gourougou Mountain regularly performed by the Moroccan military, Spain's "rejections at the border" are a paradigmatic example how the constitution of labor migration as a security problem (Bigo 2002) has led to the normalization of unlawful practices in border enforcement (Chalfin 2012).

In a climate of ever-increasing "moral panics" (Cohen 2011), and amid popular accusations that migrants absorb employment opportunities and public resources, the complexity of the EU's border regime has opened up a space of legal ambiguity that allows for the implementation of novel surveillance mechanisms. Among these are the twin strategies of border outsourcing (that is, expanding border controls with the assistance of third countries) and insourcing (the strengthening of internal border control through surveillance agencies, increased rates of deportation, and the proliferation of internment centers) (Coutin 2010; Guild and Bigo 2010). This process of dislocation has transformed the dynamics of border control in the EU's southern borderlands, generating a complex relationship of dependency between centers and peripheries organized around the generous financial packages allocated by the EU for border control. Indeed, closing Europe's border has become a big business (Andersson 2012, 2014b; Chalfin 2012), but not only for the security industry. In peripheral areas like Melilla, for example, the local economy as a whole has come to depend on these funds. Thus, EU subsidies have been used to finance not only the adequate maintenance of the fence, security equipment, and personnel, but also numerous development projects ranging from basic infrastructure (a water desalination plant, a refuse dumping ground, an industrial park, and an incinerator plant, to name but a few) to transport communications, the rehabilitation of public spaces, and the development of training programs to encourage the growth of the private sector in the city.[6]

In the case of Morocco, too, it is increasingly evident that the more international pressure is put on Melilla to adhere to EU asylum-seeking regulations, the more funds are being diverted toward less hospitable tactics in Morocco. Indeed, the Moroccan government has been building its own barbed-wire fence around Melilla—a fence that, according to local NGOs, has been at least partially financed by EU subsidies allocated to Spain for border control. These "border experiments" expose the shifting nature of contemporary borders (Coutin 2010; Green 2013; Weber 2006), as territorial boundaries are redefined ad hoc to suit the changing interests of the state and circumvent questions of legitimacy. This also seems to be the rationale behind the project of "externalizing the camps" submitted to the European Commission by some European governments (Balibar 2004). The drama played out in Melilla, then, is representative of a wider process of reconfiguration.

But this global trend toward increased securitization should not blind us to the changing and conflicting forces at play in border management. We know that the same countries that are determined to secure their borders are actively engaged in the construction of free trade partnerships with the very same neighbors from whom they seek to protect themselves (Andreas 2000; Heyman 2012). However, the extent to which the tension between mobility and immobility governs on-the-ground decisions in the management of borders is too often forgotten. The construction of border security as an exclusively political problem (not only in media and policy circles but, more crucially, in academia) effectively conceals this tension, making it appear as if processes of border demarcation and management were the result of a unified and coherent strategy. The case of Melilla shows that this is hardly ever the case, and that, while there is indeed a distinctly neoliberal articulation between securitization and free-market transnationalism (Sparke 2006), border regulations are often the result of a complex history of interlocking interests at local, national, and supranational levels. In order to understand the novel uses that different actors are making of spatial constraint as a solution to handle the conflicting pressures generated by global capital (Harvey 2001), then, we must move beyond traditional understandings pitting mobility against enclosure and ask the question of whose interests the opening or closing of borders serves (Cunningham and Heyman 2004; Newman 2006).

"Back then, crossing the border only took about twenty minutes. We all used to go to Beni Anzar every Sunday for lunch, or to have Moroccan tea and pastries! But now, now it takes at least two or three hours to cross the border with all the contraband! I used to take customers through the frontier at least four or five times a day, but now, now I won't do it for less than one hundred euros! It's because of the blacks (los negros), you know, that's why they built the fence."

I heard these words from a taxi driver in Melilla, as we were driving away from one of the main checkpoints toward the city center. I remember looking around and noticing the heaps of rubble, discarded plastic wraps, and cardboard boxes lying on the pavement. A few men were still loading their cars with goods—backseats lifted, spare tire removed, doors unhinged—for one last trip across the border. By then I was acquainted with this less visible (and in some respects less spectacular) side of the border. I had seen the crowds of frontier workers gathering around the checkpoints in the early morning hours, and knew firsthand that the taxi driver was not exaggerating when he said it takes two to three hours to get out of Melilla; the lines of cars can reach a kilometer on any given morning, and Melillans plan their daily journeys around the smuggling "rush hour" to avoid being stuck in traffic. At the very same time as the group of African migrants began their fateful descent from the Gourougou Mountain on the third of April, then, old Mercedes loaded with smuggled goods blocked the roads leading up to the crossing point of Beni Anzar, and hundreds of smugglers lined up by the crossing point of Barrio Chino to collect the large, heavy bundles of blankets, clothes, and toiletries to be smuggled into Morocco. Indeed, the border of Melilla functions as both a barrier and a conduit (Nugent and Asiwaju 1996).

To understand how this system of selective permeability works and how it came about, however, we must take a closer look at the history of the enclave. Melilla was among a number of military outposts (*presidios*) established by the Spanish along the North African coast in the late fifteenth century. For over three centuries, the enclave operated as an offshore military prison for political deportees, vagabonds, and Gypsies (Pike 1983). Melilla's population (which also included soldiers, governors, priests, and a military elite) survived thanks to intermittent shipments of foodstuffs and basic goods from mainland Spain. Raids and counter-raids with neighboring Berber tribes were frequent, and the enclave was under constant threat of attacks and sieges, not only from Berber tribes but also from the troops of the Moroccan sultan (Driessen 1992). Nevertheless, the walls of the citadel were far from impermeable. Shortages of food and other necessities were recurrent, and the Spanish had to rely on commerce with local tribes to ensure the provision of basic supplies when shipments from Spain failed (Martín Corrales 1988). This was a highly regulated form of exchange that took place near the walls of the citadel with the assistance of the *moros de paz* (Moors of peace), who usually lived in settlements near Melilla, and belonged to what were known as frontier tribes (*cábilas fronterizas*). In these markets, basic commodities such as meat, vegetables, fruit, grain, wood, and water were exchanged for money, textiles, medicines, tools, weapons, and ammunition (Calderón Vázquez 2008). Small-scale trading, then, took place alongside raiding most of the time.

The rise of the enclave as a regional commercial hub began in the mid-nineteenth century, when Ceuta and Melilla were declared free ports (1863), and the enclave began to operate as a key transit point for British and French manufactured goods in North Africa. Trade routes linked the presidio with Taza, in Morocco (153 km southwest of Melilla), and with Oran and Algiers in Algeria. Caravans from Algeria, sometimes traveling for as long as sixteen days, came to buy sugar, tea, cotton, and candles in Melilla. Others traveled from the south of Morocco to sell chickens, eggs, wax, vegetables, cattle, leather, and wool, and to buy manufactured products to be exported to the Moroccan hinterland. Similarly, tribesmen from the outskirts of Melilla traveled to Taza and other Moroccan towns to sell English cotton and candles bought in Melilla and bring back cattle or other products of interest to the French or the English. As trade flourished, the number of civilians living in the enclave began to grow and, in 1879, the Junta de Arbitrios (Board of Taxation) was created to collect taxes from this trade. In an attempt to make the enclave self-sustaining, the Spanish crown allowed local authorities to manage customs duties, and Melilla gradually began to tax incoming merchandise to finance the urbanization of the enclave.

With the consolidation of Melilla as a transit hub for regional and international commerce, interest in the region grew, attracting small communities of Jewish and Indian traders who settled permanently in the enclave (Driessen 1992). The urbanization of new territories around the old citadel also facilitated the accommodation of a new population of both unskilled labor and merchants (Bravo Nieto 1996), and, as Spain's colonial policies shifted focus from Central and South America toward North Africa, Melilla acquired new political and military significance. Spain's colonial project in northern Morocco consolidated Melilla's economic standing in the region and further strengthened networks of exchange across the border. By the time of Moroccan independence (1956), large numbers of Moroccans had settled in Melilla in search of work in

Christian households or for Christian employers, and kinship, employment, and trade networks straddled the border. Transit across the border was fluid, and "frontier workers" moved in and out of the enclave with ease.

Over the course of the following decades, the volume of trade from Melilla into Morocco grew to become a fundamental source of revenue for both the enclave and its neighboring border towns. As Moroccan emigration to Europe grew, new trade routes opened, and, with the increase of migrant remittances, a large market of consumers emerged across the border (Soto Bermant 2014).[7] Commodity trade increased considerably during those years and, by 1981, one in five Melillan residents were making a living through commercial activities (García Velasco et al. 1985). It was then that the trade in goods bought in Melilla and taken across the border clandestinely (to avoid paying Moroccan customs duties) to be sold at a higher price in Morocco became a "way of life" (Driessen 1999). Thousands of poor families in the province of Nador began to make a living through small-scale, subsistence smuggling in groceries, blankets, toiletries, and watches; Moroccan emigrants already settled in Europe began to take advantage of their regular trips to their homeland to smuggle secondhand cars, clothes, and trinkets into Morocco; and, soon enough, a number of professional smuggling networks developed to control the trade in certain luxury goods, such as tobacco, alcohol, and electronics (Driessen 1999; cf. McMurray 2001; Planet 1998). By the mid-1990s, cargo shipments filled with manufactured goods coming from Europe and Asia reached the port of Melilla on a weekly basis (Planet 1998).

By the time Spain joined the Schengen area and the porosity of the Spanish border became a "problem," then, the whole region was organized around an informal economy built around the border. This frontier economy came under threat as soon as Spain was required to pass a new immigration law (1985), introduce visa restrictions on Moroccan citizens (1991), and build a security fence along the perimeters of the two North African enclaves. Spain had little choice but to comply with EU directives and seal the enclaves off from the neighboring hinterland, but in order to protect the local commercial sector a complex system of selective permeability was developed. Thus, and parallel to the gradual closure of the border, a series of steps were taken to preserve the unrestricted movement of commodities across the border. The first of these steps was to keep both Ceuta and Melilla outside of the European Free Trade Association to preserve their local control over customs duties and their privileged status as ports of entry for European and Asian manufactured goods. Hence, when Spain joined the EEC, the Spanish government negotiated to have the enclaves classified as "special zones." In practice, this meant that goods imported to the enclaves would be exempt from EU customs duties, thus preserving price differentials between Melilla and Morocco.

However, the preservation of cross-border trade networks also required a certain degree of mobility for the local population. Thus, when Spain introduced visa restrictions on Moroccan citizens, a formal agreement between Spain and Morocco created an exception for Moroccans from the provinces neighboring the two Spanish enclaves. This guaranteed the availability of a cheap army of "frontier workers" to service the enclave (as waiters, cleaners, domestic workers, manual laborers in the construction sector, and so forth) and, more importantly, to move goods between the two sides of the fence, independently of increased border security measures. Strict controls at the airport and at the port ensured that these frontier workers remained on the African continent and did not make use of their "privileged" status to access (mainland) Europe. Indeed, this was not so much a process of exclusion as a process of inclusion through illegalization (De Genova 2002).

These "border acrobatics" (Ferrer-Gallardo 2007) transformed the social, political, and economic landscape of the region. In order to allow frontier workers daily access to the enclave, it was necessary to redefine the category of "migrants" and produce a distinction between two classes of Moroccan citizens: those with access to Melilla and those without. Then it was necessary to provide the infrastructure to make this distinction operative: opening checkpoints exclusively for "locals" (Melillans and Moroccans from neighboring Nador), ensuring that the largest checkpoint had separate lines for Moroccan neighbors and Moroccan "foreigners," and assigning a number of military policemen to check identity cards and passports at each crossing point. This legal and socio-spatial redefinition of border relations had (un)foreseen effects. Stricter controls at the checkpoints meant that contacts, financial resources, and residency documents became necessary for smuggling, making it increasingly difficult for petty smugglers to remain in the trade. It was not long before a professional smuggling industry run by wealthy entrepreneurs and serviced by hired couriers (*porteadores*) took over the trade in clothes, blankets, foodstuffs, toiletries, and electronics. Within less than a decade, products smuggled in from Melilla were sold throughout Morocco through nationwide networks of distribution, and the smuggling industry was generating revenues to the tune of €600 million per year (López-Guzmán and González Fernández 2009).

The professionalization of the smuggling industry had critical consequences for the way in which cross-border trade is organized. Many subsistence and petty smugglers were incorporated into the industrial army of couriers hired by professional smugglers to take the goods across the border, while unemployed

Moroccans from further inland (mostly women) moved into the area in search of work in the smuggling industry (Aziza 2008). Today, hundreds of people (thousands, by some estimates) are employed in moving goods between Melilla and Morocco on a daily basis. The goods are wrapped together into heavy bundles (sometimes weighing up to 100 kilograms) that couriers carry across the border on their backs, for, as long as the goods are physically carried by an individual, they are classified as personal luggage, and Morocco has to let them in duty-free. Of course, everyone knows that the women who carry these loads are porteadoras, but informal agreements with the Moroccan officers on duty, who supplement their meager income with the bribes they receive from smugglers, guarantee the unproblematic passage of goods.

Earnings as a courier are meager, and the job is typically taken up by the most vulnerable—mostly women (widows, divorcees, and former prostitutes), but also old men—as a last resort for subsistence. This is often seen as an alternative to begging or prostitution. Every morning, couriers gather in a barren field by the crossing point of Barrio Chino to collect the bundled merchandise from middlemen. Competition between them is fierce, for often there are more couriers than bundles to carry, and fights break out regularly. But the risks do not end there. The border itself has three narrow passages with revolving doors at each end, through which the thousands of smugglers must pass, with the merchandise, in order to reach the other side of the border. Each of these passages is known as "the cage" (*la jaula*). The crowds are large and accidents are not uncommon. In January 2009, to take a particularly tragic example, a courier was crushed to death in "the cage" by fellow smugglers (Cembrero 2009).

Outcasts in their own land and structurally excluded from any kind of formal belonging in the Spanish enclave, Melilla's couriers are trapped in "a condition of permanent insecurity" (Balibar 2004:15) from which many benefit. Suppliers are exempt from legal responsibility, as are the intermediaries who place the orders and the merchants who sell the goods. Import and export companies, of course, profit from the legal ambiguity surrounding this trade, as does the commercial sector at large. But even more important are the revenues that smuggling generates for Melilla's treasury. In fact, it has been estimated that the city collects between €40 and €50 million annually in customs duties from these imports, accounting for between 35 percent and 55 percent of the city's annual budget (López-Guzmán and González Fernández 2009). With these revenues, the public sector employs over 40 percent of the enclave's population (Mayoral del Amo 2005). In fact, the local government is the largest employer in the city, rivaled in importance only by the informal smuggling sector itself, and civil servants in Melilla are the beneficiaries of a monthly bonus known as "residency compensation pay," which makes them the best-paid public employees in Spain.[8] The hidden connections between the comfortable lives of Melilla's middle class and the miserable conditions of those who "service" the enclave constitute the relatively invisible underside of the border spectacle. This is, indeed, the dark side of Melilla's "welfare state," and in this too the Spanish enclave stands as a paradigmatic example of processes that are present elsewhere, though perhaps in a less easily discernible form.

I have argued elsewhere (Soto Bermant 2014) that places should be understood not as a substratum that underlies relations of exchange, but as a product of these relations. Places, as Harvey (1996) puts it, are social and material "permanences" carved out of processes of flow and exchange. Borders, then, ought to be understood not simply as entities that divide and separate, but as socio-spatial assemblages that produce the spaces they demarcate (Green 2013), transforming old sets of relations and generating new ones along the way. Spain's incorporation into the European Community changed the ways in which the border was organized and cross-border relations were managed, but, in doing so, it also resignified the two political spaces it brought into existence. In the remaining section of this essay, I turn to this process of resignification and explore how deep-rooted narratives pitting Christians against Muslims and Spaniards against Moroccans took on a new meaning when Melilla went from being a far-flung, long-forgotten territory in North Africa to being Europe's southern gatekeeper.

Europe and the Mediterranean Question

With its roots firmly placed in the ancient world, Europe has been constituted, at different times and in different voices, as a paradigm of enlightened values, progress, and civilization. As Pagden (2002) argues in *The Idea of Europe*, the basis of this vision was the conviction that the rule of law, understood as the power to harness men's naturally competitive and violent instincts through social institutions, was necessary for a society to flourish, and that this was the only sustainable project of civilization. This particular way of life, Pagden shows, was intimately associated with the urban environment. Thus, despite the diversity of Europe's populations and the critical importance of agricultural production throughout much of its history, Europe was conceived in political and intellectual circles as an eminently urban space. This urban environment was associated with a certain conception of order defined and implemented by the state (conceived as the maximum guarantor of the law) and of man as an eminently political animal. Where, then, did that leave all those who did not belong within the confines of this civilized, urban space? Beyond the limits of the city, Aristotle answered, there could be no life but that of "beasts and Gods" (cited in Pagden 2002:41).

In ancient Greece, only free, adult men enjoyed the rights of citizenship. In Rome, too, only the unenslaved could enjoy the privileged political and legal status that came with citizenship. Those who were excluded were the uncivilized barbarians, from the Greek βάρβαρος (*barbaros*), a term that was used as an antonym for πολίτης (*politēs*), that is, "citizen." As Pagden (2002) explains, there is a distinctively long trajectory to the conception of "Europe" as a collective identity in which "the Others" have played a constitutive role, from the Christian crusades against Moors and Ottomans that reopened trade routes on the southern and eastern coasts of the Mediterranean in the Middle Ages, to the more recent Islamophobic formulations following south-to-north labor migration patterns. Of course, what "Europe" meant then and what it means now are entirely different things, and one must indeed be careful not to read these processes teleologically (Herzfeld 1987). But it is important to remember that the production of Europe as a conceptual object—which preceded its production a political space—is tied to violent processes of exclusion and assimilation (Baumann 1995) that can hardly be called modern. Already in the twelfth book of Virgil's *Aeneid*, when the gods decide to bring an end to the war between Trojans and Latins and Juno agrees to allow the two peoples to intermarry and create a new race, it was on condition that the new race "will look like the Latins, will dress like the Latins, will speak like the Latins, and their customs—their mores—will be Latin" (Pagden 2002:35).

Paradoxically, it would be precisely the Mediterranean, home of the Latins, which would later pose a challenge to the conception of Europe as a beacon of progress and civilization. Throughout Europe, the experience of colonialism and imperialism had given rise to a new language to think and talk about "the Orient" (Said 1978). The question of Europe was being redefined through a colonial project grounded in a discourse that pitted white against black, West against East, Christian against Muslim, and civilization against savagery. Spain was peripheral to this project, but its Muslim past weighed heavily on European imagery, and the lure of the Arabian romance drew many European travel writers to portray the Andalusian landscape as a primitive and exotic land, a remnant of times past. Starting in the late eighteenth century, then, when the heritage of Al-Andalus resurfaced in the idealized and exoticizing accounts of French and Anglophone writers (most famously Washington Irving, but also Prosper Mérimée or Joseph Townsend), the Mediterranean, and particularly the Iberian Peninsula, came to be constituted as an "Orient à la carte: exotic enough to be interesting, but not so different as to be considered completely alien" (Tofiño-Quesada 2003:143).[9] Through their writings, Spain came to occupy, conceptually, a liminal position between Europe and Africa, Christianity and Islam, the East and the West:

> Spain, even at the present day, is a country apart, severed in history, habits, manners, and modes of thinking, from all the rest of Europe. It is a romantic country, but its romance has none of the sentimentality of modern European romance; it is chiefly derived from the brilliant regions of the East, and from the high-minded school of Saracenic chivalry. (Irving 1998 [1861]:620)

But the myth of primitive Spain was an autochthonous production as much as a foreign projection (Corbin 1989). For more than seven centuries (AD 711–1492), the Iberian Peninsula was partly under Muslim control. During that time, as the Christian military takeover of the lost territories (later known as the Reconquista) gained momentum, the notion of a common identity became intimately tied to the struggle against the "Muslim invader." By the time of the fall of the last Muslim stronghold in Granada (1492), the systematic opposition between Christianity and Islam had become the foundation of a collective identity whose boundaries were traced according to what was then known as "purity of blood" (*limpieza de sangre*).[10] This is what José Jimenez Lozano (1966) would later define as "biological Catholicism," and Américo Castro (1987) characterized as the "castist discourse."[11] The construction of a collective Spanish identity during the Middle Ages, then, was inseparable from the encounter with a historically consecutive sequence of Others that originated with the Moors and later came to incorporate Jews, heretics, Protestants, Lutherans, Gypsies, and Africans. It was in opposition to these Others that a notion of "Spanish-ness" (*españolidad*) tied to Christianity (and, more specifically, to Catholicism) developed (Soto Bermant 2007; see also Castro 1987; Stallaert 1996). Indeed, every society produces its own strangers (Baumann 1995), and, in producing them, it produces itself.

Over time, Spain's ambivalent relationship with its Muslim past came to dominate all discussions about the identity, development, and "fate" of the country. The gradual decline of the Spanish Empire throughout the eighteenth and nineteenth centuries, and particularly the loss of most of its American colonies in the early nineteenth century, contributed to Spain's self-perception as a marginal power (Carr 1982). At a time when Europe was enjoying a period of increasing prosperity, Spain remained stagnant, and Spanish intellectuals found in the mythical time of Al-Andalus a key to the question of Spain's peripheral position vis-à-vis the rest of Europe. It was thus that Europe's orientalization of Spain found its echo in the work of nineteenth-century Spanish writers, whose work reflected Spain's self-perception as situated, both symbolically and geographically, at the interstices between "the West" and "the Orient" (Tofiño-Quesada 2003; Morales Lezcano 1988).

The angst over the extent of African/Islamic influence over Hispanic culture haunted Spanish intellectuals until well into the twentieth century. The painful experience of the hundreds of thousands of Spanish workers who migrated to northern Europe during the 1950s and 1960s, fleeing poverty and hunger to work in German factories, only strengthened these liminal imaginaries and, at a time when the Spanish coastline was becoming a favorite destination for northern European tourists, the stark contrast between the economic hardship faced by Spaniards and the relatively comfortable situation of their European neighbors became plainly evident.

It was only after Spain's incorporation into the European Economic Community that a new discourse about the natural "European-ness" of Spain began to emerge alongside the question of Spain's African heritage (Suárez-Navas 2004). It was then that Spain embarked on a material and symbolic process of Europeanization to join the ranks of "civilization" and rid itself from the visions of decadence and backwardness that haunted the collective imaginary. During that process, the configuration of a new physical, political, and conceptual border between Europe and Africa actively engaged Southern Europe in a process of "re-fronterization" (Suárez-Navas 2014) that turned networks of mobility into "illegal migration flows," and foreign workers into a reserve army of labor that Europe could recall when necessary. This was a long and difficult process that entailed the bureaucratization of the migratory process. The government had to enact a new immigration law and set up the necessary infrastructure for border control before it could join the "path of modernization." Yet Spain rapidly embraced the cost of being admitted into this exclusive "club," and began to operate as a gatekeeping area for the flows of North African labor.

Over time, however, and particularly during the recent financial crisis, it would become clear that not only Spain but all Southern European countries had been made responsible for guarding an idea and an entity to which it was not clear that they themselves belonged.[12] Indeed, while neighboring EU countries were being recruited to defend the integrity of the European Union through neighborhood policy agreements, the very "European-ness" of Southern Europe was being called into question (Mufti 2014). Logically, the repeated threat of withdrawal of European-ness during the crisis, along with the EU's endorsement (or, perhaps more accurately, imposition) of budget cuts and austerity measures, have taken a toll on the legitimacy of the European Union in

Southern European countries. Dissenting voices in Spain, Greece, Italy, and Portugal have gained increased visibility, and there is a growing skepticism about the "European project" among ordinary citizens. Yet even the most radical political alternatives in Southern Europe have stopped short of calling for the withdrawal from the EU. This reluctance is grounded in more than just economic reasons; in the southern peripheries, "Europe" operates as a powerful conceptual barrier against the threat of an African "contagion."

In Melilla, where the risk of African "pollution" literally lies next door, this colonial imagery has never lost its appeal. The complex relationship that developed during the Reconquista between religious identity, national identity, and notions of genealogical purity found a particularly fertile ground in this North African borderland, where the nearby presence of the Muslim "Other" was always imagined as a threat to the identity of the enclave (Soto Bermant 2015). What Europeans had imagined of Spaniards in the nineteenth century, peninsular Spaniards imagined of the inhabitants of the two North African territories, who saw their "European-ness" doubly questioned. Little wonder, then, that the growth of the autochthonous Muslim population over the past few decades has been constructed as a "problem." The danger, as anthropologist Mary Douglas (1966) noted long ago, is one of blurring boundaries. Even today, Melillans of Spanish descent refer to themselves variously as "Spaniards" or "Christians," categories that are both conceptually opposed to "Muslims," used to refer both to Moroccans and to native Melillans of Moroccan descent.

When Spain joined the European Union, the Christian–Muslim dichotomy was reworked to incorporate the language of multiculturalism that was blossoming in Europe (Soto Bermant 2015). Melilla became the "Land of Cultures," and "Christians" became "Europeans." It was then that the term *Europe* itself acquired a certain "semantic density" (Ardener 1987) and began to operate as an authoritative discourse of exclusion pointing not so much to what one is, but to that which one is not: whatever else they may be, Europeans are not Africans. The old Christian–Muslim opposition thus gained a new lease on life under the Europe–Africa rubric, and the defense of the enclave's right to protect itself from the "avalanche" of migrants became entangled with older concerns about the identity of Melilla as a place. "I don't know how this is going to end," someone wrote in a closed Facebook group following the break-in attempts in the summer of 2014, "but there are hundreds and hundreds of them and we need to stop it." "This is not racism," commented someone else, "just worry for our city, we have Sub-Saharans, Algerians, Moroccans."

Large-scale political projects of mutual self-definition might indeed have a longer history and play a far more important role in contemporary place-making processes than we usually think (Graeber 2013). Despite the negative effects that increased border control has inevitably had on the lives of Melillans, the new security measures were a small price to pay for the protection of an imaginary of progress, civilization, and modernization from which they had long been excluded, and for the defense of a collective narrative of origins that was challenged by the enclave's geographical location. In marking a physical, and most importantly a conceptual boundary between Europe and Africa, the new security fence gave material expression to the enclave's predicament, pulling it out of its structurally liminal position. Indeed, as writer Marcello di Cintio (2013) put it, the fence "does not defend, it defines." The relationship between Melilla and the Rif (and therefore also between Spain and Morocco, between Christianity and Islam) was then resignified as a relationship between Europe and Africa, and Melillans embraced the apparent opportunity to settle once and for all the question of their "European-ness." It is perhaps somewhat ironic that, from the point of view of Europe's "centers," it was precisely the enclave's peripheral position—in other words, its "African-ness"—that turned it into the perfect gatekeeper.

Conclusion

As an object of study, "the border" is a relatively recent invention. Historians, geographers, and political scientists have been concerned with territorial boundaries since at least the latter half of the nineteenth century, but the study of borders itself only became an established academic field over the last quarter of the twentieth century, when migration became a growing political concern in Europe and in the United States (De Genova, Mezzadra, and Pickles 2015). Since then, calls for the comparative study of borders have been numerous in the social sciences. Yet "borderlands" remain elusive both conceptually and empirically (Piliavsky 2013), and borders themselves, not least the European border, have proven to be surprisingly difficult to define (Álvarez 2012; Balibar 1999a; Green 2010).

The invention of the border, at least as we know it today, is inseparable from the institution of power as sovereignty, and, certainly, the territorialization of space (that is, the transformation of space into territories controlled by state power) is a precondition for the emergence of politics in the modern sense of the term (Balibar 2004). But in the era of "post-fordist" capitalism (Harvey 1989), the proliferation of spatial borders and "borderings" suggests that struggles for the control of space extend beyond and cut across national boundaries. This is evident in the constitution of transnational institutions such as the European Union, where member states have renounced certain aspects of sovereignty in favor of a supranational authority whose ever-shifting borders respond to an equally shifting political and economic agenda. But it is perhaps more recognizable in the emergence of novel types of "borderings" (Sassen 2009), from tax havens and offshore trading centers, to maquiladora factories, gated mining complexes, export-processing zones, and other "capital-attracting enclaves" (Ferguson 2005). Offshore migrant detention facilities such as Christmas Island in Australia, Lampedusa in Italy, and Ceuta and Melilla in North Africa are, therefore, variations on a theme. Indeed, the proliferation of new and relatively unregulated spaces of "exception" (Agamben 2005), where certain activities can take place with minimal intervention by the state, but which are nevertheless created by the state (Palan 1998, 2003), points to important transformations in the relationship between power, space, and territory (Sassen 2006, 2009; Yeung 1998).

I want to suggest that, at least in some respects, borders are no different from these other forms of "bordering"; they function as entities that simultaneously divide and define, and, in doing so, generate new sets of relationships between the socio-spatial units they bring into existence. They do not simply enclose national territories, they define spatial relationships, and, as such, they provide an instrument to gain (or bar) access to geographically distributed resources. This way of conceptualizing borders allows us to critically interrogate the assumption that "mobility" and "immobility" respond to necessarily opposing and mutually exclusive interests, and see instead the tension between these two dynamics as intrinsic to the workings of global capital. The European Commission's policy briefs make it perfectly clear that immigration policy is a function of shortages and/or surplus of labor within the EU,[13] and the EU's Neighorhood Policy Agreements leave little doubt that the establishment of free trade areas and the development of a "climate conducive to foreign direct investment" are as important as the "effective management of migration flows" in its relation with neighboring countries.[14]

This is not to say that Europe speaks with one voice. There is no question that there is an uneven distribution of power within the European Union, and that different interests and shifting alliances come into play in the competition between centers and peripheries, states and regions. The principles of segmentation indeed apply to a far broader range of events than anthropological lineage theory once suggested (Dresch 1988). But where does that leave "Europe" as a racial and cultural project? Perhaps, as Shore (2000) argues, "Europe" is little more than a strategy used by the political class to seek legitimacy. But it is certainly in the name of a distinctive European identity that a host of everyday bordering practices are being implemented in Europe, often without much controversy. The acceptance of social surveillance systems and control mechanisms, even when they are in manifest violation of the very "European" values they purport to protect, points to the increased significance of discursive activities of place construction that occur outside the institutional sphere. The ideology that sustains the European project may well have been designed in the offices of EU bureaucrats, but if we want to understand how this project operates on the ground—how and why, that is, "Europe" has become a master signifier in discourses of exclusion that serve to legitimate the current deportability regime—we need to turn our attention to the zones of intimacy that flourish in the backstage of public culture (Herzfeld 2005; Shryock 2004).

The productivity of the ethnographic encounter should not be limited to revealing the limitations of global "formalizations" through the exploration of local complexity and contingency. Rather, as Hannah Appel (2015) has argued, ethnographic intimacy should be used to trace the processes "through which complexity and contingency are often so effectively mustered into capitalist projects," lending global "formalizations" the appearance of coherence, stability, and legitimacy. It is therefore not so much a matter of "the global" taking on different meanings as it is "localized," but of local conflicts and struggles being redefined and resignified by recourse to the authoritative narratives generated on a global scale. "Europe," of course, does not mean the same to a bus driver in London, a schoolteacher in Melilla, or a human rights activist in Paris. But it is precisely this amorphousness—the fact that it can be made to fit different contexts and, therefore, different struggles—that gives it such a wide appeal. In Europe's southern borderland, where a few centimeters can make the difference between "flexible citizenship" and "bare life," and where colonial imagery is still alive and kicking, "Europe" operates as a powerful discourse of distinction and exclusion. Memories of the time when the dividing line between Europe and Africa stood north of the Pyrenees are only too recent, and both the desperate pleas of migrants in the Gourougou and the ever-worsening conditions of frontier workers and smugglers serve as a constant reminder of the dangers of falling on the wrong side of the line.

NOTES

1. Ceuta and Melilla are not enclaves in the strict sense of the term. "Technically, for an exclave (enclave) to exist it must be (a) part of one country, (b) completely surrounded by the territory of another state" (Catudal 1974:116). Following Catudal's definition, Melilla and Ceuta belong to the category of "coastal territories," for they are "regions along the sea coast of one state but administered by another" (Catudal 1974:111).

2. Due to a lack of deportation agreements with sub-Saharan countries, most of the migrants arrested in the Moroccan military's raids are driven back to the border with Algeria, where they are released and left to their own devices. These irregular practices have been widely documented by journalists and human rights organizations. See, e.g., Médecins Sans Frontières (2005) and Groupe Antiraciste d'Accompagnement et de Défense des Étrangers et Migrants (2010).

3. It is worth noting that not all migrants try to enter Melilla by jumping over the fence. Only the most desperate, the poorest, take that risk. Those who can afford it pay smugglers for a ride in the false bottom of a car, near the engine or the exhaust pipe, or simply buy fake passports.

4. Full text available at https://twitter.com/Sanset81/status/455987241144553472.

5. Andalucía Acoge, SOS Racismo España, and La Asociación Pro Derechos de la Infancia-Prodein came together to file a lawsuit against illegal deportations carried out on July 18, 2014, when a group of migrants who had successfully trespassed the first two fences but had not reached the final fence were fetched by Moroccan forces and taken out to Morocco, and August 13, 2014, when a group of Malian migrants had reached the third fence and the civil guard forced two of them to climb down on the Spanish side and returned them to Morocco. The court initially determined that there was enough circumstantial evidence to go through with the trial, but on April 7, 2015, the court ruled that because there is no clear definition of where the border is located under Spanish law, the return of migrants did not constitute an offense. The full text of the lawsuit is available at http://estaticos.elmundo.es/documentos/2014/09/15/citacion_comandante.pdf (accessed October 24, 2014); the final ruling is available at http://www.asylumlawdatabase .eu/sites/www.asylumlawdatabase.eu/files/aldfiles/Regional%20court%20Melilla%20 push%20backs.pdf (accessed April 26, 2017). See also http://www.hrw.org/news/2014/10 /30/spain-abandon-abusive-migration-plan (accessed November 24, 2014).

6. For the period between 2000 and 2006, the EU allocated over €164 million to projects in the Spanish enclave and, in 2012 alone, over €48 million in EU funds were assigned to Melilla for border control. Full details are available online at http://www .fondoseuropeosmelilla.es/plan_comunicacion/cuaderno.pdf.

7. The 1960s had been a time of economic growth in Europe, and countries like Germany, Belgium, France, and the Netherlands had signed labor recruitment agreements with Morocco in order to satisfy a growing demand for cheap labor. Moroccans had emigrated en masse during those years, and the remittances they sent home drove up demand for manufactured goods in Morocco.

8. The "residency compensation-pay" (*indemnización por residencia*) is paid in the Balearic and Canary Islands, Ceuta, and Melilla (with Ceuta and Melilla having the highest compensation rates). In Melilla, the payment ranges from €312.87 for the lowest-income jobs to €881.48 for the highest, amounting to a 50–60 percent increase over the basic salary paid in mainland Spain.

9. See Gifra-Adroher (2000) for examples of American writers and Hontanilla (2008) for British authors.

10. Literally, *Estatutos de Limpieza de Sangre* translates as "Statutes of Blood Cleanliness." The statutes worked as a seal of warranty. The imposition of an Estatuto de Limpieza de

Sangre limited access to certain social institutions to Christians who could prove that their lineage was "clean"—that is, not mixed with Jewish or Muslim blood—and that their ancestors had not been prosecuted by the Inquisition.

11. According to Castro (1987), this particular understanding of religion resulted in a hierarchical social organization based on a system of "castes" where the preservation of the purity and nobility of one's lineage was dependent on the avoidance of any unnecessary intercaste contact.

12. When the budget cuts began to hit the most vulnerable segments of the population in Southern Europe, freedom of movement within the EU was suddenly restricted, and Germany announced that it would withdraw the residency permits of European citizens who had been living in Germany for over six months without remunerated employment.

13. "As a result of growing shortages of labor at both skilled and unskilled levels, a number of Member States have already begun to actively recruit third country nationals from outside the Union. In this situation a choice must be made between maintaining the view that the Union can continue to resist migratory pressures and accepting that immigration will continue and should be properly regulated, and working together to try to maximize its positive effects on the Union, for the migrants themselves and for the countries of origin." Communication from the Commission to the Council and the European Parliament, 2000, "On a Community Immigration Policy," available at http://eur-lex.europa.eu/LexUriServ/LexUriServ.do?uri=COM:2000:0757:FIN:EN:PDF.

14. See, e.g., the EU's Action Plan for Morocco, available at http://trade.ec.europa.eu/doclib/docs/2006/march/tradoc_127912.pdf.

5

———

Europe Confronted by Its Expelled Migrants

The Politics of Expelled Migrants' Associations in Africa

CLARA LECADET

The Specter of Europe

In a crowded conference room in the center of Bamako, Mali, on March 15, 2008, men sitting in the audience raised their hands, asking to be put on the list of speakers, then one after another, gave their full names to the moderator in charge of organizing the order in which they would speak, stood up, and took their places on the platform. They formed a long queue, and each one in turn stepped up to the microphone to express his anger, set out his demand, tell his story, or say how difficult he found it to express himself publicly. Together with the militant association members who had organized that day's event and who were themselves speaking, these men shared the experience of having been expelled, some recently, others long ago, from a country to which they had migrated. The meeting was set up as their event, to allow this cohort of anonymous men to say something, however briefly, about the experience which united them all. It aimed, at least symbolically, to convert the taboo and failure around deportation into a political issue that transcended individuals while simultaneously involving them intimately. Each of these men was to have the chance to transform the wound of personal humiliation into the reassurance of collective protest.

The Malian Expelled Migrants Association (Association Malienne des Expulsés, AME) was created in 1996 in Bamako. Their organization of events dedicated to giving expelled migrants the chance to speak out, and to setting up a front against expulsion policies, marked the entry of new actors onto the public stage (Lecadet 2012a). The place taken by AME in social and political life in Mali was in opposition to the progressive implementation of the European policy of "returning" (deporting) "illegal" migrants, and also to corresponding practices within Africa and the rest of the world (De Genova and Peutz 2010). The media events, demonstrations, and debates organized from 1996 onward by members of this association and its supporters made deportation a burning issue and gave expelled migrants the status of an advance guard in contemporary social struggles in Mali. Their initiative became a popular cause and revitalized the actions of the working-class left in Mali from the year 2000 onward. The legitimacy that they won, and which they had always demanded politically, was based on this process of gathering the experiences of expulsion from individuals who were directly affected by such measures. They had to move outside the traditional frameworks of legal mediation and political representation in order to establish their political existence. This positioning and these struggles transformed political constraints and exclusions imposed by the state into a source of protest and allowed a new collective identity to emerge.

Expelled migrants are in fact the nebula of the European project, its spectral shadow. While they are a central concern in the process of building a European migration policy focused on the return of undocumented immigrants, they cease to be a subject of concern once they have been removed. The disappearance of expelled migrants from the national scene in the European countries from which they have been deported, and the failure of these nation-states to acknowledge them, remain nonetheless an inextricable part of the sociopolitical life of the self-enclosed "national" and united "European" realms, fueled by the symbolically powerful instrument of expulsion. The way in which the European Union progressively set up its own legal framework for expulsion (Carlier 2007), right up to the adoption by the European Parliament in 2008 of "a directive establishing common standards and procedures for Member States, whereby illegally staying third-country nationals may be removed from their territories," seemed utterly oblivious of individuals, even while taking care to guarantee human rights, at least in principle. The gathering of expellees to expose their situation and articulate claims runs counter to the invisibility that is an inherent consequence of European and national deportation policies. This chapter argues that the "expelled migrants" were given a name through their shared experience of political constraint and collective subjectification (Foucault 1994). Their name, as in numerous other social and political protests, is also the name of the harm that was done to them (Rancière 2007).

Their organization as a group made visible a small part of what Peter Nyers has called a "deportspora," referring to that "abject diaspora" which results from the intensification of expulsion practices throughout the world (Nyers 2003), or what Daniel Kanstroom has analogously called, not without irony, "the new American diaspora," with regard to the unprecedented growth in the number of expulsions from the United States (Kanstroom 2012). This diaspora is a predictable but unforeseen result. It uncovers a figure from the unconsidered and largely hidden side of expulsion that embodies the outcome of the process of state exclusions and contests them (Lecadet 2012b). A troublemaker both within and without, this figure uncovers what the expelling countries refuse to acknowledge, while redefining the terms of political participation in his country of origin or the country through which he travels.

Expelled migrants thus show a negative image of European political structures, in both the definition of the EU's methods of statutory membership and its geographical rights. The citizenship that underpins it (Balibar 1991a; Costa-Lascoux 1992; Hansen 1999), as well as the control measures set up at its constantly moving, fragmented, and diffuse borders (Andersson 2014b), produce this excessive mass, a cohort of anonymous people sent back to the airports of African capitals on specially chartered planes or individually on commercial flights, and also in police lorries to the desert borders between Morocco and Algeria, between Mauritania and Mali, between Algeria and Mali (Lecadet 2013a, 2014a, 2014b), or between Libya and Niger (Brachet 2009), a more or less direct consequence of the externalization of the frontiers of Europe to third countries (Blanchard 2006; Haddad 2008; Hyndman and Mountz 2008). Thus, expelled migrants are also figures who embody the questions posed by the demarcation of European space and the extension of its rights beyond European soil. European return policy has indeed been strongly encouraged and supported by a policy of cooperation with third countries, including economic partnerships and shared migration control, norms, and legislation. The rise of the expellees was therefore a way of confronting European migration politics both inside and beyond the borders of "Europe."

The campaigns led by AME have enabled the emergence and spread of a critique of European migration policy by expellees, in a period punctuated by the various stages of the European communitization of a policy of "returning" (deporting) "illegal" migrants, and their corresponding dramas at the threshold of the Spanish enclaves of Ceuta and Melilla, in the Mediterranean, and in the places where expelled migrants arrive (Fekete 2006). This political critique—in conjunction with the stand taken by the Malian left, "illegal" migrants' associations, and networks for the defense of migrants in Europe—has given rise to a political demand on both Europe and Mali.

In the wake of AME, numerous expelled migrants' associations were created from the year 2000 onward, not only in Mali, but also in Togo, Cameroon,

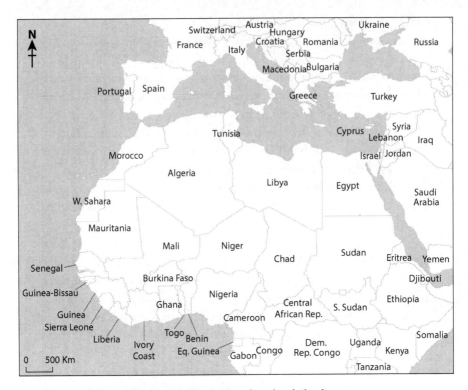

MAP 5.1. Europe's southern borderlands

and Senegal, although by no means did all of them enter into direct political confrontation with Europe or their own state. The complexity and heterogeneity of the expelled migrants' associations in Africa springs first of all from the diversity of national contexts and the possibility or difficulty of protest. They are also due, however, to opposing positions taken by associations: while some choose to denounce expulsion and the criminalization of migration through political confrontation, others adopt more consensual means of protest, favoring the care of expelled migrants by humanitarian organizations or even taking part in campaigns for the respect of migration law led jointly by national governments, the International Organization for Migration (IOM), and the European Union (EU) (Pécoud 2012). The response to Europe was thus nothing if not heterogeneous.

The genetic link between the conditions and places of expulsion and the emergence of protests by migrants themselves allows us to understand the politicization of their experiences and their day-to-day existence. Their groupings in their countries of origin, in those through which they have traveled, or in those to which they have been sent, enable us to comprehend the social and political reorganization caused by expulsion, as well as the different positions to which these give rise. The analysis of the issues raised by the politicization of expellees in Africa is an extension of studies of the progressive institutionalization and increased legal intervention regarding measures for the deportation of foreigners in the United States (Kanstroom 2007, 2012; Ngai 2004) and in Europe (Fischer 2013; Noiriel 1991). It allows us to connect the institutional, political, and social issues relating to expulsion mechanisms and policies around foreigners in a country illegally, with their impact on the countries to which the expelled migrants are sent. For present purposes, it enables us to see how the reconfiguration of political space, provoked in particular by the European Union's desire to set up a "global approach" to migration, influences the very nature of protests on the African continent, with the diffusion of certain slogans and the gathering of some of the expelled migrants' associations in demonstrations along state borders which they contest. The forced reintegration of expellees into the society they left raises new questions relative not only to the possible status of such migrants, their (re)registration as citizens, and the possibility and forms of protest, but also to the messages that they want to bring to public attention, relating principally to criticism of, or allegiance to, state policies.

The Emergence and Evolution of Expelled Migrants' Associations in Africa

In October 1996, prompted by the feeling that if expulsion policies were to be criticized effectively and pressure was to be brought on governments, then expelled migrants needed to become visible in the public arena, Ousmane Diarra, a Malian shopkeeper expelled from Angola, founded the Malian Expelled Migrants Association (AME). Together with other compatriots, some of whom, like him, had been expelled from Angola, and with others expelled from Zambia, Tanzania, and Europe, he regularly visited the Ministry for Malians Abroad, only to be told that the fate of expelled migrants was not part of their responsibilities, and was referred to the High Council for Malians Abroad, a body representing the diaspora which in fact has very little power. After many informal meetings on the premises of the Delegation for Malians Abroad and vain appeals to the government, Diarra and his supporters created an association whose name symbolized the reappropriation of the expelled migrants' position by affirming their collective existence. Thus the name of the association, a reminder of their forgotten existence yet also a proclamation of it, moved expelled migrants from anonymity to a collective assertion of the experience of rejection, and was part of the action through which a long list of forgotten people forged for themselves a name that acknowledged the harm that had been done to them.

The reasons for this movement seem few, but in fact they were a significant step forward in relation to the shameful silence surrounding expulsion (Tounkara 2013): making expelled migrants the object and the agents of protest in public life, promoting solidarity among migrants, and welcoming those who had been expelled. Lacking their own space, the expelled migrants sought to find a space in which they could provide evidence for their rights and also, and perhaps above all, in concrete terms, provide a place, if only a temporary one, for those who returned destitute and often without family or friends. Little by little, AME gained credibility and forged a reputation for itself on the ground by putting in place reception measures, with those arriving at Bamako-Sénou airport being greeted by a member of the association and provided lodging on the association's premises (Dünnwald 2010).

It also brought to the fore issues relating to the return of expelled migrants and their possible or impossible reintegration in their country of origin: their treatment and their welcome on arrival; the possibility of legal action to recover lost possessions or unpaid wages, for the right to go back, or to return to their professional lives; as well as the joint responsibility of governments in putting in place such measures. These legal, social, and political issues opened up the unconsidered and what was often seen as politically indeterminate field of life after deportation. Guided by the principle of self-help, AME aspired to give expelled migrants an organization for collective representation and participation, which would enable them to make their voices heard in public life and influence the political choices made by the Malian and European authorities.

"The Voice of the Expelled Migrant"

"The Voice of the Expelled Migrant" is a manifesto of several pages, drawn up in 1997 shortly after the creation of AME. The conciseness and effectiveness of its title show the importance of the question of language and the various issues around speaking at events, and the different language registers used in collective action. The desire to impose a name and an identity was in fact, from the 1990s onward, an explicit motive behind various protests (Von Busekist 2008). The subversive, antiestablishment, not to say revolutionary dimension of words spoken by individuals who are socially marginalized or whose existence is denied politically (De Certeau 2008) is often considered a political act.

In "The Voice of the Expelled Migrant" we can find echoes of issues raised by the sans-papiers movement in France in the same period, relating to autonomous struggles and the importance of naming as a rallying factor (Cisse 1999; Diop 1997). In similar fashion, the emergence of expelled migrants onto the public stage is linked to a process of speaking out on expulsion and on its double status as an experience and a political issue. In this founding document, the signatories stated the need for collective action in the face of the Malian government's indifference to their fate and the repeated refusal of their request for a meeting. Malians living abroad, they wrote, were nonetheless active contributors to the economy and the political life of the country. Instead of recognizing these contributions, however, the Malian government was complicit with the practices imposed by other countries to the detriment of its own nationals: the expelled migrants therefore regretted having been kept at a distance from negotiations between the Malian and Angolan governments on the question of goods confiscated from Malians expelled from Angola, and furthermore accused the Malian government of facilitating the deportation of Malians from France by making money from the passes issued by its consulate, without which expulsions could not be carried out.

The originality of the central argument, which determined the nature of subsequent protests, was to make the expulsion of Malians an issue relating to colonial and postcolonial history (Mbembe 2000). When France, which had held sway over the former French Sudan up until the proclamation of independence by the Malian Federation in 1960, closed legal access to migrant workers in the 1970s, this reopened the "wound" of colonial history. Memory and history form the background of the expelled migrants' move to collective action. The violence which they suffered, being used and then rejected by France, found its echo in the sacrifice of the tirailleurs (infantrymen recruited in the French colonial territories) in the service of the French army (Gary-Tounkara 2013; Mann 2003):

> C'est cette France pour la 1ère et la 2ème fois, de 1914–1918, 1939–1945, qui est venue ramasser des millions d'Africains, des bras valides je veux didu bétail et produit alimentaires dont personne ne peut estimer, qui sont partis pour ne plus revenir.

> [It was France who, for the first and second time, in 1914–1918 and 1939–1945, gathered millions of Africans, able-bodied men, cattle, and food products of inestimable value, who left, never to return.]

But the postcolonial government was also implicated: the inability of the Malian state to protect its nationals was presented as the major reason for the unilateral nature of expulsions, the flouting of rights, and the confiscation of goods without any compensation being demanded from the expelling nations.

"The Voice of the Expelled Migrant" was thus first and foremost an address to the state of Mali. The final appeal illustrates the desire of the expelled migrants to have a government capable of imposing real political force to prevent expulsions and to obtain the restitution of lost possessions:

> L'Association Malienne des expulsés sollicite aujourd'hui la force vive et décisive malienne dans cette lutte afin que les biens confisqués en Angola, en France ou ailleurs soient immédiatement restitués sans conditions; que les expulsions soient immédiatement arrêtées; que les autorités diplomatiques maliennes en France soient remplacées; que les expulsés se retournent dans leurs pays hôtes; que des mesures sécurisantes soient prises pour protéger les personnes et leurs biens.

> [The Malian Expelled Migrants Association today calls for strong and decisive Malian action in this struggle, for goods confiscated in Angola, France, or elsewhere to be immediately and unconditionally handed back; for expulsions to be stopped with immediate effect; for Malian diplomatic authorities in France to be immediately replaced; for expelled migrants to return to their host nations; and for safety measures to be taken to protect individuals and their goods.]

Expelled Migrants, Heralds of the Parties and Media of the Malian Left

The first notable action by AME, which rapidly earned it the reputation of an autonomous, antiestablishment force, was a march organized in 1997 to demand the freeing of seventy-seven Malians who had been sent back from France on "Debré's 38th charter flight" and imprisoned by the Malian authorities on their arrival in Bamako after the death of a French policeman during a riot inside the plane. AME roundly denounced the double punishment suffered by the migrants, considered as criminals and punished as such. The prisoners were freed two weeks later and AME, backed by a very politicized support committee, continued its intervention via communiqués and media interviews, which condemned the conditions in which migrants were detained and expelled in Europe and Africa, and tried to convert the social taboo of expulsion into a truly political issue, including the responsibility of the Malian government. AME benefited from significant media coverage in opposition, left-wing, and communist newspapers. Radio Kayira, created in 1992 by militants from the democratic movement to promote popular expression and the claims of associations defending the most vulnerable (peasants stripped of their land, migrants) and baptized "the radio of the voiceless," gave a great deal of air time to AME and publicized their protests: at the same time, the SADI party, led by the deputy Oumar Mariko, who was also the owner of the radio station, made expelled migrants a feature of his political activity.

This revolutionary party in the tradition of African socialism, based on Marxist and collectivist theories (Ndiaye 1980), made expelled migrants the figurehead of its denunciation of a neocolonial, capitalist system organized by Europe with the complicity of African states. The "Declaration on the Repression of African Immigrants," published on October 16, 2005, following the death of migrants at the border fences of the Spanish enclaves of Ceuta and Melilla, pointed out Europe's responsibility in the impoverishment of the African continent and in setting up a repressive policy on African immigrants:

> Au lieu d'apporter des réponses politiques aux causes structurelles de la pauvreté et la misère qui gagnent le continent Africain, lesquelles sont les résultats des politiques d'ajustement structurel et du pillage néocolonial de ses ressources stratégiques par les sociétés multinationales, l'Europe continue de surélever les grillages de fer et déployer des fils de fer barbelés. Les immenses richesses stratégiques (comme l'or et le pétrole) sont pillées sans vergogne, tandis que les victimes de ce pillage, c'est à dire l'immense majorité des africains sont interdits de franchir l'espace Schengen. Quel paradoxe!

> [Instead of bringing a political response to the structural causes of the poverty and destitution spreading through the African continent, and which are the result of structural adjustment policies and the neocolonial pillage of its strategic resources by multinational companies, Europe continues to build barbed-wire fences. Immense strategic wealth (such as gold and oil) is shamelessly plundered, while the victims of this, namely, the great majority of Africans, are forbidden to enter the Schengen area. . . . What a paradox!]

The formulation of proposals for the better protection of Malian nationals abroad was pressed at the national level, along with an attempt to erect barriers to the unilateral imposition of European migration policy on the return of foreigners illegally within its borders. The party also took part in an international political movement against the imposition of restrictive migration policies by the European Union, carried forward by several Latin American countries.

The expelled migrants thus contributed to a renewal of the left-wing working-class struggle. AME was supported by *Sanfin*, the newspaper of the workers' movement in Mali, which regarded the struggles of the expelled migrants as an extension of the struggle of the working class, a position which AME seized upon by gradually putting itself in the avant-garde of contemporary social movements in Mali. *Sanfin* claimed an affiliation with the African Independence Party, founded on September 15, 1957, in Thiès, Senegal, a pan-African, working-class, anticolonialist, socialist party related to various national liberation movements across the world. Through its chief editor, Mohamed Tabouré, who had stood by the expelled migrants from their first meetings in 1996, the paper developed a radical critique of French and European policies. The anti-imperialist credo of *Sanfin* stressed the effect of imperialist pressures and the directives of a worldwide system on measures for the forced return of migrants. Leaders thus regularly attacked the question of development aid, trying to show its increasingly close links to migration issues (Daum 1997).

AME, however, kept away from any political label likely to diminish the originality of its stand and the credibility of its actions. Although the SADI party was an essential support for AME in parliament (in January 2010, the SADI-PARENA parliamentary group was the main opposition alliance in the Malian national assembly and published a communiqué in which it called on the government to act against the expulsion of Malian nationals abroad), AME maintained a defiant approach to all forms of institutional politics, which led it to keep its distance from parties, even when the most politicized members of its supporting collective wanted to use their close links with the association as an argument in their electoral campaign in 2010. This desire to seek representation for expelled migrants, which was at odds with traditional politics and which questioned the representative nature of the association itself (in reality, only a very small number of migrants were involved in collective action), raised the issue of their room for action and what forms of action the expelled migrants could use.

The Complexity and Heterogeneity of the Movement

If AME was a pioneer, this was in part because it existed in a political context which allowed for its emergence and the rapid spread of its slogans. The democratic liberalization of the country in 1991 allowed those on the margins of society to take their place in public life (Daum and Le Guay 2005). From the year 2000 onward, other associations created by expellees appeared in various African countries. The disparity of their political contexts, however, demonstrates the difficulty that expelled migrants faced in creating a space they could call their own. Each association had to adapt to the political constraints that hindered or authorized its existence. In Togo, where in 2008 Togolese migrants expelled from Germany had founded the Togolese Expelled Migrants Association (Association Togolaise des Expulsés, ATE) following the Mali model, demonstrations were limited by the sway the regime held over public life, and the expellees, the majority of whom had fled Togo for political reasons, experienced hostility and distrust from the authorities on their return (Basaran and Eberl 2009). The exile of a large number of political opponents of the regime following the failure of the transition to democracy in the early 1990s had led the regime to suspect the diaspora of working abroad for its overthrow. Upon their return, the expelled migrants, immediately classed by the police at Lomé airport as enemies of the regime, were often imprisoned during the 1990s and into the early years of the twenty-first century, or had to negotiate their freedom through influential contacts or by resorting to bribery with significant sums of money. Their association, in a country in which all forms of opposition were silenced, was built up discreetly and by a very cautious approach to the issues tackled in their public meetings.

Thus, rather than choosing direct confrontation with those in power as AME did, ATE pursued more unifying and consensual questions, such as legal forms of migration and the contribution made by the diaspora to the Togolese economy. It was similar to a number of associations that were beginning to form, such as Attac Togo or Visions Solidaires, which were trying to build bridges in Lomé between the authorities and the demands of civil society, and which, in December 2010, organized the first Togolese social forum. If ATE and AME were inspired by the same aims—to bring expellees together, to improve the conditions in which they returned, to promote the emergence of an organization and a way of telling their own stories—it also had to legitimize its contribution to public life without offending a wary dictatorship. Because of politics and corruption, associations of expellees in Togo and Cameroon had long been waiting for official acknowledgment that would legalize their existence. Unlike Mali, these countries, which had almost always discretely recognized the sovereignty of other countries in relation to their migration policies, had never considered their migrants as an essential part of national construction: the issue of emigration simply had no place in public debate. ATE and the Cameroonian association Welcome Back Cameroon, founded in 2006, thus claim their links to AME's pioneering initiative: Razak Aboubacar and Oscar Eyezo'o, the presidents of these associations, consider AME's founder, Ousmane Diarra, as a seminal figure in the organization of expellees.

The overall picture of expelled migrants' associations is, however, complicated. The gathering of expellees through associations can turn into cooperation with international agencies and an allegiance to state policies. In Cameroon, where the power of associations was growing and where in the early 2000s there were an increasing number of NGOs working on projects financed by Europe and the United Nations (notably on migration and citizenship), many associations dealing with migration were created—sometimes out of necessity, but often through opportunism. The contrasting picture provided by these associations in Cameroon led to a number of initiatives and campaigns that set the defenders of free movement against those who were leading dissuasive campaigns against what IOM called "the dangers of illegal immigration." These differences of position in the face of migration policy issues reveal tension and dissension even among associations of expellees, showing that the politicization of expellees gives rise to a variety of actions around deportation, which cover the whole spectrum, from alliance with, to opposition to, political authorities. Statements by expelled migrants' associations could occasionally be seen to converge with European political interests. For instance, the Cameroonian Repatriated Migrants Association for the Struggle against Clandestine Migration (Association des Rapatriés et de lutte contre l'Emigration Clandestine du Cameroun, ARECC), created in 2005, chose a radical position, since these young expellees from the Spanish enclaves of Ceuta and Melilla led media campaigns warning of the dangers of clandestine migration. On their own initiative and backed by the experiences they had been through, they mounted a photographic exhibition showing migration tragedies, which toured various large towns in Cameroon with the aim of encouraging young people to conform to migration laws. Robert Alain Lipothy, the president of ARECC, was also completely opposed to the idea that expelled migrants could become protesters; he passed harsh judgments on the protests against expulsion in Mali and in other African forums, which he considered pointless unrest. He had no illusions as to the impact of these demonstrations, and considered that the authority of governments was undisputed. Their action was part of a dissuasive campaign by public authorities and the IOM, which also took place in Mali, Senegal, and other African countries, aimed at discouraging young people from leaving. Self-help by expelled migrants could thus be used by governments as part of their injunction to respect legal forms of migration.

Mirrored Policies: European Policy as a Catalyst of Protest in the 2000s

The creation of the Schengen area in 1985, which set up an infra-European area of free movement, and removed border controls outward to Europe's external frontiers, had a major impact on the redrafting or adoption by the countries of the European Community of policies aimed at regulating the issues of residence and the expulsion of foreigners. European states have very diverse histories in regard to immigration and the affirmation of national identity. The effects of the European project and of these individual national histories have contributed to the development of a return policy at the European level which nonetheless leaves individual countries with a fair amount of room for maneuver. The agreements reached at the European level thus produced a progressive redrafting of immigration policies at the national level, while the basic principle of expelling foreigners became a community given (Carlier 2007:270–71). The years from 1990 onward therefore saw harmonized methods in relation to sharing information about illegalized migrants and sending them back (Carlier 2007:259). In 1991 the member states of the Schengen area signed an initial readmission agreement with Poland, which obliged the latter to authorize the readmission of any of its nationals subject to an expulsion decision. Other communal readmission agreements were to follow. The liberalization of borders within Europe was thus accompanied by an increased preoccupation with the question of harmonizing immigration and asylum policies. After 1994, several member countries, supported by the UNHCR, proposed the relocation of asylum claims to countries that were the source of migration (Noll 2003), and asked for a collective system for the rapid return of those asylum-seekers whose status as refugees was not recognized and who needed no other form of international protection. This system would be based on readmission agreements negotiated collectively by the EU with the countries of origin (Rodier and Saint-Saëns 2007). Joint flights for expelling illegal immigrants were considered at the European level at a meeting of the interior ministers of the G5 in 2005, and were put in place in 2010 jointly by Great Britain and France for the expulsion of Afghans. These different elements came together in a formalized return policy with the adoption by the European Parliament of the "Directive on Common Standards and Procedures in Member States for Returning Illegally Staying Third-Country Nationals" in 2008. This seemed to mark a turning point in the development of a European migration policy, as it gave systematized and regulated scope for the expulsion of illegalized migrants.

Up until 1995, the idea of drawing up bilateral agreements on the readmission of illegal migrants existed only in recommendations in European legislation. It constituted the negotiating base from which each member state would have to work with third countries. Against the background of this common framework set out by Europe, everything was still to be drawn up, and each country had wide room for maneuver in which to conclude partnerships with countries with which, for historic, economic, and/or political reasons, it had a special relationship. Rather than agreements dealing exclusively with the readmission of migrants, which were politically risky (because they could well be seen as a form of unilateral action), countries preferred mixed agreements in which readmission appeared as a simple "migration clause" in, for example, an economic partnership. What had been seen as a possibility, case by case, by the European Council became the norm in reality. A subsequent decision by the Schengen executive committee, dated December 15, 1997, raised the issue of the methods by which individuals were to be identified within the framework of readmission agreements, and established a list of indicators and evidence that would prove the illegality and the identity of the migrant. These agreements were not only the subject of discrete negotiations, but were not always immediately identifiable. A number of countries signed such agreements, while others regularly opposed any moves to facilitate the expulsion of their nationals, but in very few countries was this issue a matter for public debate led by the media.

The movement led by AME and FORAM (Forum for a Different Mali) from 2008 until early 2009 against the signing of such readmission agreements by the Malian government was a first. In the call for mobilization against readmission agreements by the associations' collective Overseas Migrants (MOM) on June 4, 2009, Mali is cited as an example of a successful joint movement by two countries against the signing of such agreements. This call stressed the need to dissociate public funds from the development of migration clauses which offended the dignity of the individual. The campaign launched by AME and FORAM in 2008 was at first presented as a continuation of European protests against the extension of the powers of Frontex, the European agency for the surveillance and enforcement of Europe's external borders; the involvement of AME in an international movement opposing expulsions increased its legitimacy and credibility locally. The originality of the campaign lay in the fact that the questions raised by the identification process underlying the expulsion of illegal immigrants in Europe brought new demands to the fore in relation to the migrants' countries of origin.

A movement aimed at pushing the state to become fully involved in the protection of its nationals in relation to expulsion methods, and even in preventing them, was supported by AME as well as by a part of the press and the Malian political class. At the head of this movement, AME developed a statement that went further than simply denouncing expulsion, exposing more technical and less well known aspects of the practice of sending migrants home. It warned against any suggestion that Malian police should accompany expelled migrants on their return journey, as was proposed in a pilot project, which would help to strengthen the feeling that the Malian state was complicit in the expulsion of its nationals. It also condemned the fact that increased expulsions in North Africa had transformed Mali into a country in which migrants of all nationalities ended up, and it labeled as "a human dumping ground" the ghettos of Tinzawaten, where undocumented migrants were left by Algerian police after being collectively deported from Tamanrasset, Algeria, after an exhausting three- to four-day journey in the desert, and where they had settled self-organized shelters according to their different nationalities (Lecadet 2013a).

Demands concerning state policies were addressed both to the states which expelled migrants and to those which received them. Demonstrations and public statements took place on the margins of negotiations with the Malian authorities led by the French government envoy, Patrick Stéfanini. They involved a number of demands: freedom of movement, the sovereignty of the Malian state as an argument against the subjugation of its policies to French migration prerogatives, and a denunciation of the inhuman nature of expulsions. The movement against readmission agreements gave substance to the claims of this association by linking its statements on the disgraceful conditions of expulsion to a wholly political demand in relation to the Malian state. The stigmatization of European policy and the denunciation of the criminalization of migrants were accompanied by an injunction to the Malian state in terms of the protection and defense afforded to its nationals. Diarra pleaded in favor of a review of the balance of power between countries in carrying out these measures, so that one country would not always have to submit to the policies of another, and said that he wanted to contribute to setting up a policy that would be designed from the migrants' point of view. In October 2008 AME's campaign widened, targeting the European directive on returning illegally staying third-country nationals and the treaty on immigration and asylum. Taking part in a counter-summit on October 17–18, 2008, against the second Euro-African summit on immigration (held in Paris on October 20–21, 2008), it restated its desire for the organizations defending migrant rights to take up the question of freedom of movement. AME then actively participated in marches organized by the Euro-African network on migration in Congo, Mali, Mauritania, Cameroon, Benin, and Morocco. Other demonstrations on migration took place in Africa and

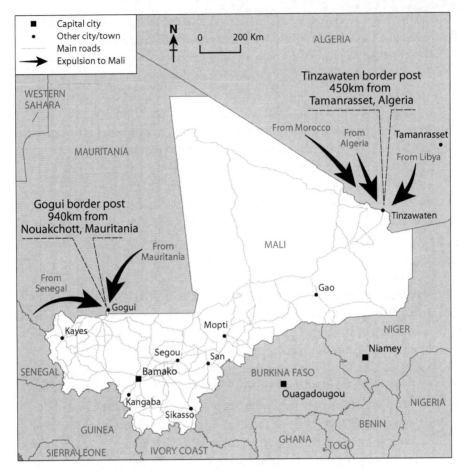

N

0   200 Km

ALGERIA

WESTERN
SAHARA

MAURITANIA

Tinzawaten border post
450km from
Tamanrasset, Algeria

From Morocco
From
Algeria
Tamanrasset

From Libya

Gogui border post
940km from
Nouakchott, Mauritania

From
Mauritania

MALI

Tinzawaten

From
Senegal

Gogui

Gao

Kayes

Mopti

NIGER

Segou
San

Niamey

SENEGAL

Bamako

BURKINA FASO

Kangaba

Ouagadougou

NIGERIA

Sikasso

BENIN

GUINEA

GHANA   TOGO

SIERRA LEONE   IVORY COAST

MAP 5.2. The frontiers of deportation to Mali

Europe. The movement against the signing of readmission agreements took
on such momentum that the president of Mali, Amadou Toumani Touré, announced in his New Year's greetings to the country on December 31, 2008, that
he would be holding a forum on emigration. Sympathizing with the difficulties
experienced by Malian migrants and pointing to the restrictive nature of migration policies, he called for a public meeting on these questions that would
go beyond what he judged to be the sterility of moral indignation. The demonstrations by expelled migrants thus had the paradoxical effect of pushing the
president to a real politicization of the debate on expulsions, toward which the
government had always shown prudence, if not a wait-and-see policy.

On Saturday, January 10, 2009, a meeting was held at the headquarters of AME. A statement was made reaffirming the view of civil society organizations that the government must not sign the agreements. Aminata Dramane Traoré defended the idea of a resistance specific to Mali. Insofar as some of the demonstrations were based on the European policy agenda, the final refusal of the Malian government to sign the agreements was the main outcome of this protest (Soukouna 2011), thus revealing the communitization of European expulsion policy.

European policy and the politics of expelled migrants thus mirrored each other. The opposition to European policy represented by AME illustrates Jacques Rancière's view that politics cannot be reduced to the institutions that organize the distribution of activities and roles in a society, but emerges from those very fractures and tensions between the practice of governments and what they produce in terms of the formation of collectives in the struggle (Rancière 2007). These movements created a space of political confrontation and critique, which illustrated a struggle taking place not only at the national level but also at a point of tension in the unequal balance of forces between states.

The figure of the expelled migrant was born out of a doubly impossible, doubly forbidden political affiliation. Undocumented migrants are usually denied the political rights accorded to citizens of the respective nation, and in this sense, the emergence of collective sans-papiers movements in France was seen as a crisis of citizenship and democracy (Balibar 1999a ; Terray 2008). For Étienne Balibar, these migrant struggles made it essential to consider the idea of a republican citizenship that would give migrants access to certain aspects of citizenship, even without formal nationalization.

The issue of the relationship of migrants to the state and to citizenship also arises from the point of view of their country of origin. In the 1980s, the progressive organization of the Malian diaspora under pressure from the state, which thus hoped to maintain links with, and control over, financial operations and the money contributed by migrants to their country of origin, went hand in hand with the emerging criticism of a double standard in the citizenship status given to migrants. Political criticism of differentiated citizenship, according to whether an individual was either an "immigrant" contributing to the general well-being of all, or an expelled migrant marginalized by public authorities, indirectly showed expulsion to be an experience of material loss, moral harm, and social delegitimization in a special report on migration published in the review *Jamana* in 1987: "This is so that humiliation should end, so that the migrant should not be considered a full citizen [only] when he is earning and when all is going well, and then left on one side when he comes face to face with problems: illness, expulsion without compensation, etc."

The issues around citizenship raised by illegalized migrants in Europe and those who are expelled to their country of origin and rejected yet again together constitute the figure of the expelled migrant. It is by affirming this doubly impossible existence in politics that this figure acquires its distinctive political identity.

The European "Global Approach":
Toward a Depoliticization of Expulsion?

The European Union has been in favor of a global return policy, in which third countries would agree to both migration control and expulsion. The unilateralism of expulsion policies would thus be overtaken by a return policy recognized and accepted by all the parties involved. In 1994 the European Commission published a paper on asylum and migration policies which promoted a global approach to migration control that would go beyond any internal national policy, with the aim of integrating elements of security, trade, and development. The idea of an approach to migration control favoring reciprocity shows clearly the way in which the European Union tried to overcome difficulties in the practice of expulsion by creating a political model combining politics and economics, thereby shielding it from criticism of the unilateral and hegemonic nature of expulsion. At the European Council meeting in Seville in 2002, the European Union advocated a "global approach to migration" which aimed to create cooperation between the countries of origin, transit, and residence of migrants in the implementation of European migration policy. Antje Ellermann has analyzed the genesis of this "global approach" to return in relation to Germany (Ellermann 2008). The post-expulsion period was thus the object of increased political commitment by individual countries, international agencies, and NGOs, anxious to legitimize forced return by paying greater attention to the difficulties it generated in the countries of origin. Migration policies which were developed and put into practice at different levels and which involved various agencies (governments, international agencies, NGOs, private organizations, etc.), tried to reconcile expulsion practices with measures aimed at assisting returning migrants, following the classic procedure of adding a humanitarian touch to the repression which such policies represented (Agier 2003).

The controversial establishment of the Centre for Migration, Information, and Management (CIGEM) in Bamako in 2009, a pilot project of the European

Union, was part of this process of legitimizing return policy through increased partnerships with third countries. Born out of cooperation between the Malian government and the European Commission responding to the migration phenomenon, CIGEM aimed to help Mali define its migration policy in response to the preoccupations of migrants—those returning as well as expatriate Malians. The first invitations by this institution in 2009 were to finance associations to welcome and assist expelled migrants. While AME refused to respond, wanting to avoid reinforcing expulsion measures through the politically organized management of reception centers for expellees, other associations did set up reception centers for expelled migrants thanks to this funding. These included the Association for Central African Expellees in Mali (ARACEM), created in 2006 by Roméo N'Tamag and Patrice Boukar, two Cameroonian cousins who had been expelled from Algeria; the Association of Migrants returning to Kidal (AMRK), founded in 2008 by Modibo Diakité in Kidal to help expellees from Algeria; and the Association for Return, Work, and Dignity (ARTD), which grew out of a regrouping by Aminata Dramane Traoré of expellees from Ceuta and Melilla in 2005. Though ARACEM regularly took part in debates organized by AME, it focused on the social insecurity experienced by expellees; from 2009 onward it gradually put in place a humanitarian-style welcome system, offering lodging and medical care to expelled migrants from Algeria and Libya, in partnership with the NGOs Medico International and Médecins du Monde. ARTD, a partner of the IOM, also organized the reception of expellees in Bamako in 2011, and followed up on projects sponsored by the IOM for the long-term integration of expelled migrants in their country of origin.

The close relations between the expelled migrants' associations created in Mali and the northern NGOs, as well as with international agencies in charge of migration issues, transformed them into administrators of social and medical help for expellees. The establishment of CIGEM as well as subsidies from the IOM and various NGOs transformed autonomous self-help initiatives by expelled migrants and led to the emergence of a post-expulsion scene in which European political interests met humanitarian-style management. CIGEM's financing of expelled migrants' associations in 2009 on the one hand, and the increased partnerships between these associations and European NGOs on the other (Médecins du Monde, Medico International, CIMADE), was both a vital resource for them, since they had previously received no public funding, and a strong influence reorienting their activities toward strictly humanitarian post-expulsion work. This structural dependency meant that there was a hiatus between the emergence of expellees as an autonomous political force and the formatting imposed by the humanitarian framework—making these associations a hybrid product of self-help and Western humanitarian concern. In some ways, they became part of the extended reach of expulsion measures, which they supplemented with their social or humanitarian contribution.

The awareness campaigns by the Ministry for Malians Abroad and African Integration and the IOM on the dangers of illegal immigration (Pécoud 2012) can also be seen as part of this "European global approach," since they were aimed at dissuading migrants from leaving home. Although in Mali they were considered by most protest associations as simply agents for the implementation of European migration policies, some of these associations did in fact testify to the risks of the venture. Such opposing views on the part of these associations demonstrate the coexistence of AME's demands on behalf of expellees with the participation of other associations in the prevention of unregulated migration led by the Malian government and European politicians. Similar tensions were at work in Cameroon when the Camaroonian Repatriated Migrants Association for the Struggle against Clandestine Migration (ARECC) chose to run media campaigns on the dangers of clandestine immigration.

While AME thus managed to raise a dissident voice that the Malian government could no longer ignore in its talks on migration policy—in 2008, the "Bamako Appeal" asked the Malian government to fight against expulsion—the association was also increasingly asked to take part in consultations on establishing a national migration policy, which the Malian government was holding under combined pressure from the EU and agencies overseeing migration (IOM, CIGEM), with the aim of harmonizing migration policies in Europe and Africa. Furthermore, members of AME met several times with representatives from the European Parliament in 2010 and 2011, and in 2011 took part in a consultation meeting on a global approach to migration organized by the EU in Dakar. The commitment by the EU to address questions raised by post-expulsion conditions, as well as its proactive policy on the adoption of a legal migration framework by African countries, had an effect on the makeup of the associative picture which the expellees had initiated.

Opposition to Expulsions in a New Political Arena

The public recognition of self-help movements is an ambiguous process. AME's first meetings with the Minister for Malians Abroad and the French ambassador in Bamako in 2008 showed the symbolic weight of the pressure brought to bear by the association against the readmission agreements, but they were also indicative of the interest shown by the Malian and international political class in the "global approach" to migration policies promoted by the EU. The presence of CIGEM and the IOM in Bamako made inevitable the drawing up and adoption by the Malian parliament of a legislative framework on migration in 2011, a process that was subsequently interrupted by the war that broke out in Mali in 2012. These bodies all consulted AME during the process. Seizing the opportunity to have its voice heard by the political authorities, the association was nevertheless wholly aware of the political exploitation in which they were involved. Those meetings with the French ambassador were certainly helpful in ensuring that submissions on family reunification for expelled individuals were examined, but the ambassador also tried to bring up again the unsigned joint agreements on managing migration flows, and used the association's network to inform migrants that they could now make appointments with the French consulate via the Internet. At a hearing in November 2011 in the French Senate, at the invitation of the socialist Senator Richard Yung, the association raised questions relating to the situation of the sans-papiers in France and expellees in Mali, but it also accepted expulsion as an inherent part of European policy from then on.

The paradoxes of AME's political legitimization can be seen in the difficulty it has had in holding on to a purely oppositional position and not becoming an alibi for the construction of institutional policies. Consultations with various elements of civil society are a part of that search for consensus which is a crucial ingredient in the workings of European political institutions. All struggles founded on the self-help organizations of marginalized people probably run the risk of exploitation and hybridization. Combining the consultation process with maintaining a critical stand is a difficult balance when politics is itself operating at various levels. The different levels at which AME was involved were emblematic of the concerted action by governments, the EU, NGOs, and international agencies in trying to set out the foundations of policies governing migration. AME was thus caught between its initial drive—encouraging representation for expelled migrants and opposing measures that oppressed them—and its progressive inclusion in the political consultation process. This double bind calls into question the possibility and significance of a policy for expellees, the room for action, and also the risks of exploitation run by a protest movement that tries to establish the collective existence of people with no political status.

These different levels of involvement are, however, equally emblematic of the makeup of the protest arena and of a political critique that goes beyond state boundaries. Worldwide migration forums, social forums in Africa and Europe, workshops organized by African networks, forums and summits organized by networks for the defense of migrants' rights in Europe and across the world— all make up a transnational mobilization arena that seems to be the start of a movement running counter to the powers that are reconfiguring politics through attempts at a "global approach" to migration. Social forums and counter-summits are constitutive of what looks like a "global public space" characteristic of the 2000s, when some issues took on global characteristics and followed a process of transnationalization of social movements (Baeza et al. 2005).

These forums in fact produce means of collective representation for migrants, as can be seen in the adoption in 2006 of the World Charter of Migrants (coordinated by Ousmane Diarra, president of AME), which was proclaimed again in Gorée, on the fringes of the World Social Forum in Dakar in 2011. The creation of the World Assembly of Migrants, of which AME is a founding member, in Bouznika in 2008, and of Justice without Borders for Migrants, of which it is president, is also part of this effort to increase representation for migrants, which extends beyond national limits and ensures a better defense of their rights. Establishing a dialogue on migration on an African and worldwide scale, in which civil society organizations are regularly consulted and encouraged to formulate recommendations, opens up yet more representative areas for AME and other migrants' associations, while also involving them in a process, the final aim of which remains nonetheless the strengthening of the development and implementation of migration policies promoted by international authorities. By way of example, a workshop was held in Bamako in 2010, in which associations pooled their ideas on intraregional migration in West Africa, and high-level talks on migration were organized in New York in 2013 under the aegis of the United Nations. AME's history is caught in this tension between the desire for representation for those who have up to now been deprived of a political existence, and its incorporation into a general process of legitimizing the coercion of migrants. Slipping from radical protest demanding change in the political paradigm into a more or less forced allegiance to a policy on expellees put together by governments, international agencies on migration, and NGOs exposes expelled migrants' associations to the reproach of being nothing more than a tool for perpetuating expulsion.

The Expulsion Frontier Is the Mobilization Frontier

The existence of joint protests by expelled migrants' associations in Africa, however, sometimes allows us to overcome the disparities and difficulties of discrepant national contexts. The link between some of these associations and the alter-globalization movement, and their partnership with European antiracist networks, as well as the networks that they have built across the African continent, explain the implementation of such joint protests. These occasions are rare, as associations develop first and foremost at a local and national level, and deal with urgent problems arising from the expulsions experienced by people from each particular country. Nonetheless, the organization of social forums in Africa enables these associations to meet and to devise action in public life on issues related to borders, freedom of movement, and expulsion. Such action operates at both national and transnational levels and in so doing tries to surpass and subvert the barriers that migrants find along their routes. The caravan that left Cotonou for the World Social Forum in Dakar in February 2011 was conceived as a way of representing a border to be crossed and defied. The associations working together in this operation used each stage of their journey to denounce the corruption endemic in the practice of border guards and the rackets to which migrants are prey. This targeted action brought together issues of circulation and mobility with the multisited, transversal character of migrant movements. Here, ATE and AME met in communal action, leaving aside for a while their individual projects in their respective countries and the difficulties posed by their emergence as political entities.

These mobilizations challenge the concept of borders by inventing new forms of protest demonstration that are mobile, multisited, and that refer directly to the mobility and autonomy of migrants as they travel. In this regard, the use of the term *caravan* to designate the coalescence of migrants' associations in bus convoys moving from city to city, publicly alerting authorities and the general public in all the places they visit to migrants' needs and rights, is highly symbolic. The Malian mobilizations and, more broadly, mobilizations across the African continent, are trying to promote the idea of a shared mobility. They are taking place in a space beyond the merely national scene and beyond the traditional divisions between countries. The notions of "bilateral struggles" or "the convergence of struggles" mentioned in exchanges and interactions between collectives of illegalized migrants, networks in defense of the rights of migrants in Europe, and associations of expelled migrants in Africa, are all equally a part of this attempt to carry out joint actions across frontiers, as well as to find ways of coming together in Europe as well as on African soil. European migration policy is a catalyst for these new mobile, transnational scenes of protest. No doubt this phenomenon is not entirely new or unprecedented: it has its roots in the nineteenth-century workers' movement and in other attempts at unity and coordination on an international scale. The fact that newspapers defending the interests of the working class in Mali played an active role in the campaign denouncing the bilateral agreements between France and Mali suggests that the theme of migration is in the process of preparing the ground for, and giving a contemporary meaning to, the idea of a multisited, trans-local struggle.

Conclusion

The creation of associations by expellees in Africa has brought about a shift from the invisibility and disregard of expellees caused by the increasing importance of deportations from Europe since the 1990s, to their emergence and affirmation as public figures. The emblematic case of the movement carried out by AME in Mali illustrates the possibility, although a marginal one, for expellees to become political actors with a significant influence in national political discussions. It shows a renewed form of belonging and participation for rejected citizens, at both the national and international levels, but it also reveals all the critical issues that remain unaddressed by deportation policy and practice.

The process of collective subjectification at work in the movements initiated by the Malian Expelled Migrants Association and other such associations of expellees in Africa thus seems emblematic of the issues ensuing from European return policy, in terms of the reception, rights, and citizenship of expelled foreigners. These movements are scattered and diverse across Africa. As I have demonstrated, they give rise to protest but also create contradictory forms of allegiance, cooperation, and complicity with state policies.

The politicization of expellees in Africa shows the extent to which the militant social figure of the expelled migrant crystallizes the issues at the heart of the Europeanization and internationalization of control measures and governance in the field of migration. It is impossible to envisage the very remarkable responsibility exercised by expelled migrants other than within this multisited, fragmented dimension, actively involved in the expulsion process, and the internationalization of both the struggle against these practices and the measures that seem to give a humanitarian dimension to the repressive policing of the process. Thus, the self-organization of expelled migrants across Africa has been an important manifestation of the constitutive role of the autonomy of migration in transnational struggles over the ongoing production and consolidation of the borders of Europe.

6

———

Choucha beyond the Camp

Challenging the Border of Migration Studies

GLENDA GARELLI AND MARTINA TAZZIOLI

"Choucha does not exist anymore." This is the laconic comment we kept hearing from the United Nations High Commissioner for Refugees (UNHCR) representatives when, during the summer of 2014, we insisted on getting an update on the status of the refugee camp that the UN agency itself had opened in Tunisia in 2011, just a few kilometers from the Libyan border and in a military zone in the desert, to accommodate people fleeing the Libyan civil war. Variations of the same declaration of the camp's nonexistence came from the NGOs and Tunisian institutions that were variously involved with Choucha, which we kept pressing for information.

Yet the presence in March 2015 of approximately 150 people[1] who had been living at Choucha since 2011 tells a rather different story.[2] Despite its official closure on June 30, 2013, the Choucha camp still exists. While UNHCR closed the camp—declaring the emergency of Libyan war refugees in Tunisia over and sanctioning Choucha as a success story of migration management—refugees still live on the site where the camp used to be, where all humanitarian infrastructure has been dismantled and from which the humanitarian actors have fled. Refugees have no place to call home other than this stretch of desert, now a de facto war zone because of intensified unrest on the Libyan side of the border. It continues to be as a "Voice from Choucha" that refugees report about their struggles at the camp on the blogosphere, and it is still at the same site, that is, eleven kilometers from the Ras Jadir border post, that drivers crossing the border into

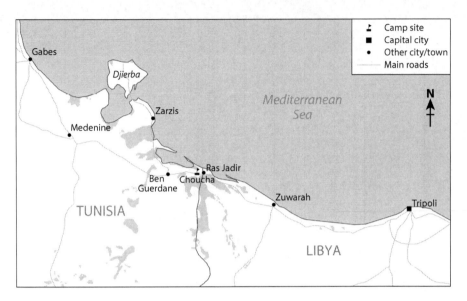

MAP 6.1. Choucha (Tunisia)

Tunisia occasionally throw bread and water for those stranded at Choucha. And, finally, Choucha camp remains a destination for journalists, photographers, and activists who document the struggle of Libyan war refugees.

Choucha during the Time of the Official Camp

Before focusing on the story of Choucha after the camp's closure, let us briefly trace the history of how the camp came to be. The UNHCR opened the camp in the aftermath of the outbreak of war in Libya in February 2011 to host Libyans displaced by the war.[3] As soon as the war started, hundreds of thousands of Libyans as well as third-country nationals who had been living and working in Libya fled to Tunisia and Egypt. In those turbulent days, Tunisia made the decision to keep its border with Libya open. This resulted in the entry of about one million people fleeing the Libyan turmoil into Tunisian territory in the span of just a few months.

Choucha was the first refugee camp ever opened in Tunisia, reaching its peak occupancy in May 2011, with about 22,000 people. When war escapees crossed into Tunisia, IOM identified and registered them at the of Ras Jadir border post (Tazzioli 2012), transferring Europeans to the airport of Djierba for repatriation and all other war escapees to the camp of Choucha—including people who could not return to their countries of origin for fear of persecution, or because their countries did not organize returns. These people were third-country nationals—mainly from African countries—who had been living and working as migrants in Libya. Since Tunisia did not have any refugee legislation or a reception system (despite being a signatory of the Geneva Convention), UNHCR was in charge of processing asylum claims in the country. In the summer of 2012, the UN agency issued its first refusals of asylum claims, which also resulted in a spatial reorganization of the camp, with refused refugees marginalized in the outer fringes of the camp. Starting from October 2012, UNHCR stopped providing services for this group, interrupting food provision and access to water and electricity. In June 2013, when the camp officially closed, about four hundred migrants were still there. Most of them were "rejected refugees," but the group also included some statutory refugees who were not resettled abroad. Their enduring presence at the officially closed camp was a form of protest: by persisting on the site of the refugee camp, they continued demanding to be resettled in Europe as Libyan war refugees.

Far from being simply and mainly a Tunisian issue, Choucha camp played a crucial role in the European politics of migration and refugees' containment, in at least three ways. First, as a refugee camp, Choucha also functioned as a spatial trap, where refugees ended up stranded at the camp for years. In this sense, the humanitarian camp worked as a space of containment (a forced pit-stop) for those who were headed to Europe.

Second, Choucha contributed to the ongoing process of transformation that has been investing the EU politics of externalization with the increasing deployment of "humanitarian borders" (Walters 2011a) alongside practices of pre-frontier enforcement. As many have argued, the frontiers of Europe no longer coincide with its geopolitical borders if one considers the spatial outcomes of EU migration policies. Even the notion of "externalization," we suggest, should be reframed in light of the existence of places like Choucha, which as one of the many humanitarian borderzones of Europe, function as European frontiers.

Third, the Choucha refugee camp was the first international laboratory for a specifically humanitarian politics of migration containment in Tunisia: European actors and international agencies contributed the construction of a humanitarian space of containment in Tunisia, despite both open and indirect opposition from Tunisian authorities (Garelli and Tazzioli 2016b). Such European and international refugee management efforts on Tunisian territory, however, ended up failing the people who fled the Libyan war. In fact, these people ended up stranded in remote places like Choucha,[4] or abandoned and illegalized as "migrants" in Tunisian towns (Storiemigranti 2015).

Methodological Notes: The Camp beyond Its Temporal
and Spatial Borders

While Choucha camp still clearly exists according to ethnographic and public media evidence, its juridical status has changed over time: since UNHCR terminated its jurisdiction and archived the Choucha camp as an example of successful humanitarian intervention, the "camp" in which refugees still live is not technically a refugee camp any longer.

As humanitarian actors dismissed the presence of refugees living on-site as the accidental presence of "illegals,"[5] "people not of our concern,"[6] and "nomads living in the desert,"[7] we became interested in documenting the humanitarian invisibilization of refugees still living there, and their enduring struggle. We propose the notion of Choucha beyond the camp to refer to the material conditions of people still living on the site of the camp, in humanitarian abandonment; it is these material conditions that we take as our critical vantage point on the humanitarian regime. In fact, the people at Choucha are still struggling for international protection and resettlement despite the institutional termination of the refugee camp and state initiatives to evacuate its residents.

If "Choucha does not exist anymore" for the humanitarian actors—or rather, more precisely, for the United Nations High Commissioner for Refugees—what are the avenues to document the existence and the struggle of people at Choucha "beyond the camp," beyond its juridical delimitations, beyond its official physical and temporal boundaries, beyond its epistemological borders, and, finally, beyond the "discipline" of the camp—understood both as a scholarly order within the regime of refugee studies and as a political order within the politics of the humanitarian regime?

Thus, there is a double "beyond" at stake here, namely jurisdictional (the continuing struggle of people at Choucha camp after its official closure) and governmental (the governmental hold over people's lives "beyond" the boundaries of the humanitarian regime). Let us expand on this last point. The humanitarian regime—the governance of refugees—does not concern only those who are recognized as refugees by humanitarian agencies (i.e., "people of concern" in UNHCR jargon); humanitarian governance also looms over its very "waste," namely the people whose claims to international protection are rejected by humanitarian actors or the people whose status is recognized but are somehow not given the protection they are formally entitled to (Agier 2011).

Governing by nongoverning is a powerful way of having control over people's lives: producing refugees and asylum-seekers as "people not of concern" corresponds to their illegalization and further vulnerabilization on Tunisian territory. For instance, when UNHCR closed Choucha, the camp still hosted an array of subjects whom the humanitarian government was also ready to close "with," not only those to whom it refused refugee status to but also "not-resettled refugees" (i.e., those whose right to international protection and resettlement was recognized by UNHCR but to whom the agency was not able to provide asylum in a safe third country). The asylum system impacts the lives of those to whom it gives refugee status as well as the lives of those it rejects: all the different migrant-subjects upon whom it still employs a "hold" and whose lives it controls. Indeed, people "not" of UNHCR's concern (e.g., rejected refugees) are also governed by the humanitarian regime: being not of concern does not mean escape from the "humanitarian hold" over one's life. It implies being governed by humanitarian technologies precisely as subjects excluded from the field of "international protection." Rejected refugees are eminently governed subjects, "despite" and "through" their being not of concern. So the government of the rejected or the government of the "margins" of the field, of the subjects marginalized within the humanitarian regime, is in fact situated at the very core of the functioning of refugee governmentality. This chapter therefore underscores the necessity of monitoring the impact of the humanitarian regime on the lives of those whom it seeks to remove from its concern, those who are placed "beyond" the discursive space of humanitarian concern by UNHCR but whose lives are still ruled by humanitarian borders (Fassin 2011b).

By following the effects of the humanitarian regime beyond the camp, we also aim to bring refugee studies out of the confines of the camp itself, so to speak. Grounding our research in the space between Tunisia and Italy, we follow the lives of people at Choucha as they leave the camp in permanent or intermittent ways. Hence, our focus is a migration space or, better, the "migration struggle-field" of people who have passed through Choucha camp. By "migration struggle-field," we mean, on the one hand, an area of crossing and a site for migration containment strategies and detention, and, on the other hand, an area that can also be considered a "space of governmentality." The humanitarian regime certainly works through various instances of humanitarian and border spectacles, be they of vulnerable lives or of rescued lives, as many scholars have underlined (Cuttitta 2012; De Genova 2002, 2013a; Sossi 2007). But it also works through less spectacular yet equally binding technologies whereby refugees are governed through a process of identity reshuffling, where refugees are illegalized, and where humanitarian subjects fall out of concern. Such change in how one is classified by humanitarian actors has very specific spatial consequences: refugees' illegality on Tunisian terrain while in processing and afterward; different and contrasting strands of formal rights or non-rights to presence for different groups; the migrant-ization of refugees due to normative anomalies (e.g., the presence of non-resettled-status refugees in a country where asylum legislation that is not yet fully functioning turns them into undocumented migrants).

We propose the notion of "people of Choucha" as an intervention against such identity reshuffling. Following the practices of self-naming in which various migrants and refugees have engaged (e.g., Refugees of Lampedusa in Hamburg), we propose to refer to the group at the center of this chapter as the "people of Choucha." This name, in fact, breaks through the partitions created by migration policies (undocumented migrants, labor migrants, refugees, etc.) and the humanitarian regime (rejected, status, nonresettled—refugee) among people who were displaced by the Libyan civil war and who ended up going through the experience of Choucha, either the UNCHR-run camp and/or its afterlife, which we trace in this chapter.

Beyond Bordered Spaces of Exception

In August 2014, 150 people lived at Choucha camp. If no longer an official UNHCR camp, Choucha was certainly a refugee camp hosting people who had fled the Libyan war and who had been stranded in the desert for almost three years—in processing, in limbo, and in abandonment. Talking with representatives of the national communities in a café in Ben Guerdane—a town close to the campsite of Choucha—in August 2014, we found out that it was not only rejected refugees who were currently residing at the camp (those whom UNCHR insisted on classifying as "people not of our concern" in our many interviews with them) but also status refugees.

Why would status refugees—those whose right to international protection UNCHR has recognized—seek refuge in such a desert esplanade where shootings and warfare on the Libyan side of the border are heard a few kilometers from the camp? "If you don't have Tunisian documents,[8] a job, and a place to stay, what can you do? At least at Choucha you don't have to pay rent."

Thus, despite the camp's official closure by UNCHR, Choucha has become a centripetal force attracting a vast array of displaced people: long-standing and/or returning Choucha residents (rejected refugees, non-resettled-status refugees, people targeted for local reintegration) and a few new residents as well (people who are still escaping from Libya and also, in some instances, people who were rescued at sea by the Tunisian National Guard).[9] Mainly, Choucha has become a sort of reference point for those who moved to Tunis, or to towns in southern Tunisia, such as Medenine or Ben Guerdane. People leave the camp to find a job, but they either keep living at the camp permanently or move back occasionally to save some money on rent. To account for such a relational geography, one needs to move "beyond the camp" and refocus analytical attention on the transformations that Choucha has undergone, when the official story of the UNHCR camp is that it is closed, and now that the site is not run by international humanitarian agencies but by the refugees and migrants themselves.

The issue of space is certainly one of the most effective perspectives on migration in the critical literature. In particular, the literature on refugee camps and migrant detention centers has called attention to the ways in which migrants are governed, blocked, and contained "through" and "in" space. Migrations are managed through many polymorphic spatial technologies that transform places into more or less official zones of detention (Martin and Mitchelson 2009). Moreover, moving beyond the walls of detention centers, critical scholars have pointed to how certain natural spaces are transformed into places of containment—for example, the Australian islands serving as offshore processing centers for asylum claims (Mountz 2011). Critical migration scholarship—especially within refugees studies—stresses the exceptionality of spaces of detention and zones of containment, pointing to the temporal suspension and spatial strandedness of people's lives or to abuses in detention centers. The reference to Giorgio Agamben's theory of the state of exception has been paramount in these conversations, both in migration studies and in refugee studies (Bailey 2009; Edkins 2000; Hanafi 2009). However, the paradigm of the exception has been the target of criticism by scholars who instead highlight the many governmental regimes, legal statuses, and institutional processes that crisscross migrant lives in the camp and which variously qualify them as "governed subjects" (Fassin 2014; Garelli and Tazzioli 2014; Mezzadra and Neilson 2013).

The space of the camp is a bordered zone in which migrants are governed by humanitarian actors and the exclusionary criteria of asylum, and whose mobility is constantly monitored. In this regard, there is a wide literature that addresses the peculiarity of a life conducted in a camp—that is, in the case of refugees' continuing permanence in the space of the camp (Agier 2002; Grbac 2013; Ramadan 2013; Sigona 2015). Our argument for an analytical move "beyond the camp" builds on such criticism of the paradigm of exceptionality in the study of processes of migration and refugee management. We contend that such a bordered approach tends to overlook the processes through which people are governed, contained, and stranded beyond a bounded zone of processing or containment, such as, for instance, a refugee camp. The government of people's freedom of movement does not only operate through sheer blockage—as, for instance, in incarceration, detention, or encampment; it also works through mechanisms of spatial and temporal suspension of people's lives "beyond" the regime of visibility sanctioned by such institutional technologies' lifespans (e.g., a UNHCR-run refugee camp and the UNHCR calendar for the camp's closure). Looking at the space of Choucha now that it is no longer an official UNHCR camp allows a mapping of the long range of the humanitarian hold on people's lives and sheds light on how people's movements and lives continue to be contained, hampered, and finally governed even beyond the institutional borders of the refugee camp.

To put it differently, the hold over migrants' lives enacted by governmental technologies functions also by abandoning and yet still governing people stranded in a place like Choucha (both during and after UNHCR's management of the camp), by creating juridical impasses for those processed by the humanitarian regime (e.g., non-resettled-status refugees who are considered illegals on Tunisian territory), and by leaving Choucha residents no other option than—as a UNHCR official told us at the Zarzis office in January 2013—to go back to Libya or "make themselves invisible in Tunisia." Or, rather, as a refugee put it for us at Choucha in the summer of 2014, this governmental hold on their lives left people no other option than living in the desert at Choucha camp and eventually being arrested at some point as undocumented migrants in Tunisia, or risking their lives crossing the Mediterranean by boat to "Europe."

Moving beyond and outside the boundaries of the camp does not mean overlooking the specific function of zones of detention and containment or the economy of power within refugee camps. Rather, it means situating the supposedly bordered space of the camp in a broader economy of governing mechanisms of spatial strandedness and temporal suspension. It is precisely this stepping out of the boundaries of the camp that we call for when we focus on the conditions of people's life in the camp after its official closure. From this vantage point, the camp looks rather like a hub: a dense cluster of techniques of containment and partitioning on the part of its authorities and a contested site of coping and resistance strategies on the part of its residents. Camps tend to amplify the visibility of bordering mechanisms where formal and informal restrictions on mobility, direct surveillance, interviewing processes, and daily life routines sanctioned by humanitarian agencies come into full light.

Looking at the site of Choucha after its official closure and in the midst of its enduring functioning as a refugee camp, as a sort of migratory hub, allows us to shed light on the enduring hold over refugees' lives of the humanitarian regime, even after the camp's closure. In other words, it allows the camp to be seen from the point of view of people who have been living there for three years: only an interrogation that challenges the camp as a space of exception and a spatially closed space allows one to see what happens to the people of a camp after its institutional termination. In other words, by challenging the borders of technologies for governing refugees and the boundaries of the discipline of refugee studies, it is possible to shed light on the situated struggles of people governed by the humanitarian regime and on the various governmental techniques directed by the humanitarian regime toward people "of concern" and "not of concern."

A second reason sustaining our attempt to move beyond the boundaries of the camp and beyond a focus on the camp as a bordered space concerns the productivity of borders. Building on the conversation that claims that camps are not spaces of mere exception where people are stripped of all rights and reduced to a bare existence, our ethnographic research at Choucha points to the productivity of the experience of the camp itself, concerning bordering mechanisms in a broader sense, and the subjects that these mechanisms shape and transform through regulatory frames, emergency measures, juridical statuses, and further layers of vulnerability. We refer here to the economy of power that sustains life in the space of the camp and show that people in the camp are the object of heterogeneous governmental techniques that shape migrants' subjectivity, stranding them for months or years in that space, labeling them with different migration profiles, and forcing asylum-seekers to maintain their lives at a minimum level. Consequently, we argue for a twofold dislocation in the study of camps: on the one hand, a dislocation away from the spatial fix of the camp form, and, on the other hand, a dislocation away from the temporality of migration policies (e.g., the temporality that establishes the beginning and the end of a humanitarian space by issuing an opening and a closing day). In the case of Choucha, for instance, spaces of humanitarian reception and struggle both predate and postdate[10] UNHCR's jurisdiction over the site of Choucha as an official refugee camp.

It is not merely a question of showing how arbitrary measures pertaining to the governance of the camp are normalized. Rather, looking at the ways in which people are governed by the humanitarian regime, "exceptionality"—for example, the exceptionality of the camp as a space—appears as the mark of the exceptionalization of migrants' mobility as such, that is, as the institutionally produced partitions that mark and distribute different forms of displacement and movement into migration and asylum-seeking (and the politics of international protection statuses). Such a process of institutional exceptionalization becomes particularly evident when—moving beyond the boundaries of the camp (from those instituted by UNHCR policy to those instituted by academic practice), and following the journeys of the people of Choucha—we see how their movements are incessantly hampered by or subject to the "exclusionary sorting" of the humanitarian.

The exceptionalization of people's mobility as that of undocumented migrants can be grasped only by situating the camp within the assemblage of different formations of capture and spaces of governmentality that haunt migrants during their journeys. In other words, it is only by taking together the fixed and bordered spaces of containment (such as, for instance, the refugee camp) with a "governmentality on the move"—or, as William Walters puts it, a "viapolitics" (Walters 2014)[11]—that it is possible to map the work on an economy of exceptionalization at large. In fact, following migrants' troubled displacements beyond the camp, one sees how their whereabouts are channeled, hampered, and even turned into a target for military intervention along the way. For instance, the "military and humanitarian" operation of search and rescue, known as Mare Nostrum, that Italy launched in October 2013 and terminated at the end of 2014, is a compelling example of a governmental hold over migrants when their lives are depicted as "in danger" and therefore calling for the exceptional intervention of military force in an operation of "rescue." In these spaces of governmentality, in which migrants' itineraries and projects are temporarily stopped, the camp represents a fundamental machine of deceleration and interruption of migrants' spatial practices of mobility.

Spatial Economies of Invisibilization beyond the Camp

The statement that "Choucha does not exist anymore" became clear in its governmental vision and spatial outcomes during the summer of 2014, as we were trying to follow the evolution of humanitarian government and struggles dealing with the humanitarian regime. Let us offer three examples of the "humanitarian" spaces we encountered "beyond" the camp of Choucha and as direct enactments of its termination by humanitarian actors.

Medenine, August 5, 2014: The major town in southeastern Tunisia, located about seventy kilometers from the port of Gabes and on the state highway route to Libya, Medenine is one of the sites of post-Choucha humanitarianism in Tunisia. It is here, in fact, as well as in other nearby cities, that the various humanitarian actors formerly involved with managing refugees from the premises of Choucha camp are reorienting the focus of their activities.

We had heard about the Medenine *foyer pour les réchappée de la mer* (hosting center for those rescued at sea) as we were trying to follow the paths of those who decided to leave Choucha camp to try to cross the Mediterranean by boat into Europe. The Tunisian National Guard, we had heard, was rescuing people whose boats were found in distress. Upon landing, the Red Crescent, in collaboration with UNHCR, was in charge of handling those rescued. During our interviews (August–October 2014), the inexorable and rather pedestrian "humanitarian logistics" that developed at Medenine for handling those rescued from the sea started to unfold: upon arrival in Medenine from the port of rescue, people were divided in two groups and assigned to different spaces: those coming from so-called unsafe countries were placed in a building managed by UNHCR, and their asylum claims were registered by the international organization; those coming from so-called safe countries (which, through our interviews, we reconstructed to mean mainly Nigeria, Ghana, Senegal, and Cameroon) were instead placed in a dilapidated building, left with no food and water, and abandoned with no information of any kind about their options (including, of course, the possibility of asking for a form of international protection). Even if people hosted here were deliberately denied the possibility of asking for some form of international protection, however, they were still "managed" by humanitarian actors as people rescued from the sea. So it is still under the humanitarian regime predicament that their presence in Tunisia is to be analyzed.

It is this latter foyer that we had the chance to visit in early August 2014. Located close to the city center, in an anonymous building with no indication of its function, the foyer was possibly an even more disorienting humanitarian locale than Choucha camp itself. Hosting about eighty people of various nationalities in a decrepit building, with only a few mattresses on the floors, crammed rooms, and no regular food and water supply, those "rescued" from the sea seemed to have ended up on a path to a slow but sure further exacerbation of whatever vulnerable situations they were trying to flee when they set sail across the Mediterranean. Most people with whom we had a chance to talk were sleeping as we entered the building around noon. With no food or water in days, no documents, and no information on their situation, their sleep felt like a survival strategy. While at Choucha refugees started organizing themselves during the early months of the camp's existence, Medenine seemed very far from the possibility of achieving any kind of spontaneous organization. Even from an infrastructural standpoint, Choucha looked to us more organized than this abject and destitute site.

Yet it is this wrecked location that humanitarian actors have chosen as one of the sites of humanitarian intervention after Choucha. The political visibility that Choucha camp had for over two years, both in Tunisia and in Europe, and the possibility of renewed media attention to the area due to the continuing conflict on the Libyan side of the border, served to make UNHCR reorient its efforts toward a strategy of prevention against the possibility that something like Choucha—that is, a clearly visible and large site of struggle—could exist once again on Tunisian soil. Hence the humanitarian regime converged upon a strategy of dispersal, scattering people in different cities and in small numbers.

It is worth noting that, in parallel with the institution of places like Medenine, the humanitarian regime was engaged in a deliberate attempt to dismantle Choucha, not just by terminating the "humanitarian camp" designation of the site and changing its land-use protocol, but also by a deliberate strategy of abandonment of the people who were still there, including many people suffering with illnesses.

The space of Choucha has clearly not been of "humanitarian" concern for a long time, since humanitarian organizations stopped providing medical care and food in 2012, and have never visited the camp since its official closure. However, this does not mean that Choucha is simply abandoned or that institutional control is withdrawn from it. The opposite is true. The "humanitarian invisibility" that UNHCR produced for those still at the camp after its official closure was sustained by the militarization of the space of Choucha, where the Tunisian army came to be stationed. The military is the institutional actor "beyond the camp" at Choucha, replacing the humanitarian regime in managing the very same stranded refugees stuck in the Ras Jadir borderzone.

Zarzis, August 2011–August 2014: In 2012 UNHCR settled its local office for managing the refugee camp of Choucha in Zarzis, a few kilometers north of the camp's site. Zarzis is a coastal tourist town lined with hotels and resorts. In the aftermath of the Tunisian revolution, the tourist industry struggled throughout the country as Europeans stopped targeting the Tunisian coast for their vacations. In Zarzis, however, some of the hotels were soon repopulated by the humanitarian regime's personnel involved in the management of Choucha camp—the staff and representatives of IOM, UNHCR, the Danish Refugee Council, the Red Cross, Save the Children, and Islamic Relief.

The UNHCR office in Zarzis became a symbolic site for Choucha refugees' struggle, with protests and sit-ins organized by refugees in front of it. Two years after its opening, the office relocated to a remote street, and removed the UNHCR logo from the outside of the building—a retreat from the public eye and from the persistent claim of those still at Choucha to be of concern for UNHCR (Garelli and Tazzioli 2014). The homepage of the Choucha refugees' blog, "Voice of Choucha," features a picture of a protest banner reading: "UNHCR Finish Your Job."[12] This call to accountability has been the persistent demand of the rejected and nonresettled refugees at Choucha. Clearly, this is also the message from which UNHCR has been persistently trying to disassociate itself: when UNHCR officers keep repeating that "Choucha does not exist anymore" and declare that people still at Choucha are not "people of concern" for humanitarian agencies, UNHCR is pronouncing Choucha to be a completed project and disavowing any form of accountability for the lives of those still there: camp closed, case closed.

Such a retreat from the public eye is seen also in the reluctance to talk at all about the experience of Choucha on the part of UNHCR. Even journalists and researchers are not welcome anymore at the Zarzis office, and are directed to the main office in Tunis. We finally managed to meet with a representative of the Zarzis office in person only after insisting to the guard at the front door that we would not leave otherwise. (We were not received inside the office; the representative came out to meet with us in the street, outside the gate.) UNHCR even refuses to meet asylum-seekers: during the summer of 2014, we were informed, it was the Croissant Rouge that was charged with registering the new arrivals of third-country migrants in Medenine and, eventually, bringing people to UNHCR should they express a desire to claim asylum, a situation that is hard to picture after having seen the buildings at Medenine, above all the one for people from "safe" countries, but also for those presumed refugees from "nonsafe" countries.

Tunis, Alouina neighborhood, 2014: Despite ongoing negotiations involving the European Union, UNHCR, and the Tunisian government,[13] Tunisia does not have a proper asylum system, and it is UNHCR that operates there with regard to issues of international protection, supported by local organizations but with a full mandate on asylum claims processing and adjudication.

The claim that "Choucha does not exist anymore" by UNHCR was matched by the organization's support of "local integration programs" where nonresettled-status refugees and rejected refugees were offered settlement in Tunisia through specific humanitarian programs, despite the refugees' insistent claim that Tunisia is not a safe country for them. What is relevant for the "beyond-the-camp" perspective is this sort of humanitarian displacement, wherein the humanitarian agency disengages from its own visible and spatially located activity in the camp at Choucha in favor of a devolution of humanitarian government to small-scale integration programs across Tunisia.

This is certainly a sort of retreat of humanitarian government—from its rationale as well as its provision of protection—despite the rhetoric of democratization that matched the promotion of local integration programs. Asylum is currently one of the main stakes in the political discourse pertaining to the democratic transition in Tunisia: the existence of a regime of international protection is presented as a test and a milestone to qualify Tunisia as a truly democratic country. Indeed, the respect for human rights and the compliance with international humanitarian standards are seen by European countries as the token that Tunisia owes to Europe in exchange for the role of privileged economic partner.

Such dispersal at large of humanitarian action, however, has so far coincided with the incorporation of layers of informality into the humanitarian regime. As a matter of fact, statutory refugees who have accepted local integration in Tunisia explained to us the paradoxical capture in which the promoted "integration" locks them: "We are here, without any residence permit, in the same situation we were in three years ago. We are refugees but we are still illegal migrants in this country."[14]

The arrival of almost one million people in 2011 from Libya has certainly represented a new phenomenon in Tunisia, which has historically been a country of emigration. The political visibility and the volatile context at Choucha camp, on the one hand, and the huge number of arrivals of people from Libya on Italian coasts on the other, convinced the European Union to put pressure on the Tunisian government to fully implement a refugee law.

Despite Tunisia's reluctance—worried about becoming a pre-frontier of Europe—the announced asylum law and the exemplary effort made by Tunisia in keeping the Ras Jadir border open in 2011 for asylum-seekers, contributed to the crafting of a discursive space about "security" and "safety" for refugees that, in the event, turned out to be a spatial trap for the people at Choucha. Indeed, confronted with the refugees who demanded to be resettled in a safe country, UNHCR responded by stressing that Tunisia is now a proper democratic and secure state.

However, the "unruly mob" that is still at Choucha camp, and the migrants rescued at sea and brought to Medenine, are not included in this space of protection; they are considered "nomads in the desert" or "people free to go back to Libya," as humanitarian organizations' representatives put it to us in January 2013 and then again in August 2014. The underlying message was that the refugee camp at Choucha—a hub of unruly migrants—should not exist anymore. This is what UNHCR and all humanitarian actors argue, thus erasing the political visibility of the camp and reinforcing the invisibility of the people who are still living there.

It is important to clarify that the "humanitarian" erasure of lives at Choucha does not so easily refute the persistence of Choucha residents' claim to presence and to their demand to be resettled in a third county. The ongoing and thorny presence of the people of Choucha, their refusal to leave despite the eviction notice, their protests, endure and disturb the politics of erasure performed by governmental actors. In *Economies of Abandonment*, Elizabeth Povinelli focuses on practices and forms of life that remain below the threshold of the political, describing them as "quasi-events" that are not perceived by any politics of recognition, since they are not even contemplated in the space of the political and "never quite achieve the status of having occurred or taken place" (Povinelli 2011). It is precisely by looking at these "unperceived" but noisy practices, and considering them for what they put into place, that it is possible to avoid the posture of "seeing like a state" (Scott 1998). It is, in other words, in a focus on what lies below the threshold of visibility in the humanitarian regime that it is possible to identify a politics of erasure (on the part of humanitarian and state actors) from the effective disappearance of a place like Choucha and the people who have been its residents. To put it more directly: the disappearance of subjects and spaces from the public scene does not coincide with the disappearance of their "incorrigible" presence (De Genova 2010d), their spatial persistence, or their "strategies of existence" (Sossi 2007). As Povinelli eloquently puts it:

> People may be bracketed by liberal procedures for proceeding in the face of alternative social projects and worlds, but these brackets do not vaporize them. . . . Large groups of people may be, as Dipesh Chakrabarty put it in another context, consigned to the "imaginary waiting room of history." But they are living within these waiting rooms. Whether one wishes they would or not. (Povinelli 2011)

The approximately 150 people we met at Choucha in the summer of 2014 were definitely "bracketed" by humanitarian actors. Yet they persisted in disrupting this humanitarian invisibilization; they persisted in their claims for redress at the very time they were declared "not of concern" by humanitarian actors. In the process they produced an "excess" within humanitarian politics, the politics that otherwise sought to bracket them as a residue. We are interested in accounting for the persistence of political claims, spatial practices, and subjectivities that are instead targeted for invisibilization by humanitarian and migration policies. More than simply denouncing the thresholds of (in)visibility that the humanitarian regime enlists in a place like Choucha, we are interested in accounting for the residue in excess that is produced by such persistence. In other words, we are interested in what is left out of concern by the politics of the humanitarian but that nonetheless persists and exceeds the terms of its political and juridical definition, instantiating autonomous spatial practices that, despite their political erasure, remain there and assert themselves.

As a former resident of Choucha camp told us, some of those who arrive in Europe decide to change their names in order to forget everything related to their life at the camp. They want to start a new life after Choucha, since that camp has been like "a suspension of our existence for over three years." As we said in the beginning, Choucha "beyond the camp" also has an important temporal dimension that refers to migrants' life after the official closure of Choucha in June 2013. Indeed, from that time onward, Choucha has become an officially nonexistent place. "Choucha does not exist": this was the answer given to us by UNHCR and all the actors involved in the management of the camp. But despite their political effacement, around four hundred people in the beginning and then, after one year, about 150 people, were still living in the camp. Others—the majority—left, trying to reach Europe or moving to various Tunisian towns. Thus, migrants' life after Choucha must be located both within and beyond the spatial boundaries of the camp.

The dispersal of Choucha residents after the official closure of the camp makes it difficult to map the diachronic dimension of "Choucha beyond the camp." How does one visualize the space-time of the "after-camp" on a map? How does one even gather this information? For instance, how can one map the final destinations, juridical conditions, and life situations of those who arrived in Europe? One can imagine what happened: maybe some activists met them in some town's public parks, or at a railway station, or in some Italian harbor where those whose boats were rescued by the Italian Navy were brought after October 2013. Trying to follow the hampered journeys of former Choucha residents and the various forms of humanitarian capture to which they have been subjected (at the camp, when rescued by the Italian Navy, and finally when identified in Italy and housed in a hosting center), we see that a homogeneous humanitarian regime does not exist.

During the functioning of the camp, people at Choucha were monitored by a humanitarian gaze that controlled their mobility and regulated their daily life. In a certain way, this was also true for rejected refugees. While UNHCR categorized them as "people not of concern," or, as one representative put it for us, "people not of our concern," they were actually controlled by various humanitarian and military actors (the Tunisian Army, UNHCR, the Red Cross, IOM, Islamic Relief, and the Danish Refugee Council), and their movements out of the camp were allowed only as long as they were limited to the nearby city of Ben Guerdane. However, when the camp was officially closed in June 2013, people who decided to remain at the camp came to be somehow "deprived" of the "status" of subjects of the humanitarian regime. Both refugees and rejected refugees have since been described by humanitarian agencies and by the Tunisian government as mere "nomads" and "people living in the desert with tents."

Those who left Choucha and crossed the Mediterranean once again became targets of humanitarian concern, lives to be saved at sea by the Mare Nostrum mission. Here we see at play the "identity reshuffling" (Tazzioli 2015a) that protean humanitarian politics continues to produce, even once migrants from Choucha arrive in Europe. Their movements were regulated by the same procedure used for all migrants rescued by the Italian Navy: most of them were fingerprinted and put in spaces and facilities used as temporary "hosting centers" (tent camps, sports stadiums, buildings, and barracks). Some succeeded in escaping. Others, like the Eritreans and Syrians, for instance, were not identified by Italy, in a sort of informal but deliberate act of institutional disobedience performed by the Italian government against the Dublin III Regulation by casting a blind eye toward those who were most likely to be granted asylum. Lacking the political strength to propose a change to the Dublin Regulation (and particularly to the provision forcing asylum-seekers to file their claim in the first country of entry), which Italy had formerly voted for, the Italian government decided to oppose this provision by not implementing the fingerprinting of asylum-seekers that would require them to seek asylum exclusively in Italy and in no other European country. However, this tactic of the Italian state to informally allow migrants to enter Northern Europe did not mean that crossing the Italian borders was easy. Many were blocked in Italian towns for weeks, and the rail stations of some of those towns—such as Milan, for instance—became places of prolonged and indefinite waiting, temporary junctions from which to eventually carry on the journey.

At Choucha, the generalized abandonment after the official closure of the camp has certainly further hardened the conditions of life for the people still living there. Actually, the lack of food and water is not new for the rejected refugees, since UNHCR had already stopped their provision in October 2012. However, people persisted in that desert: that an unlivable place like Choucha should have become a site of struggle upset both the Tunisian authorities and the humanitarian agencies that formerly managed the camp. Indeed, by persisting in that space of tents despite its official closure as a refugee camp, and defining themselves as "subjects of the humanitarian regime" because of their being stranded in the desert for over three years, residents of Choucha came to represent an unruly scant multiplicity that refuses the regime of exclusionary access to asylum. If the figure of the mob, as Claudia Aradau and Jef Huysmans illustrate, corresponds to the ungovernability of those people who are irreducible to the demos (2009), the out-of-place position of the people at Choucha camp depends on what can be called an unassimilable excess. By denying them refugee status, UNHCR illegalized the presence of these people in Tunisia and multiplied the numbers of "residual" people produced at Choucha by the humanitarian regime. However, while many left for Europe or settled in Tunisian towns, a few—namely a group of about 150 persons, whose numbers continued to decrease as months went by—decided to stay as the "remainders" that result from the very exclusionary politics of asylum. In fact, the presence of remainders as the subjects excluded from the space of international protection is a mechanism that is functional to the reproduction of the asylum system; there are residues, as in the case of the rejected refugees at Choucha, who represent an excess, a scant multiplicity that cannot be erased.

Detention and Deportation Regime for the People "of" Choucha

Looking at the space of the camp after Choucha means also moving away from the camp premises and at times even away from Tunisia. Once the camp closed, in fact, rejected and status refugees who lived there stopped being considered people of humanitarian concern, not only by UNHCR but also by local police authorities. The site was threatened with eviction by the National Guard, and its residents were increasingly targeted for detention as undocumented migrants on Tunisian territory.

We learned of this carceral experience for the refugees "of" Choucha only by chance, when one of them got in touch with us from the detention center of Al-Wardia in Tunis. The main publicly known detention center for migrants in Tunisia, Al-Wardia hosts not only third-country nationals who commit felonies but also undocumented migrants, asylum-seekers, and status refugees, including entire families with children, as our fieldwork in August 2014 documented. Our report, published by Storiemigranti (2015), denounces several violations of detainees' rights in detention and documents the criminal practices by which the Tunisian National Guard manages detainees' exit from the detention center.

What, in fact, is the way out of detention for refugees at Al-Wardia? As our interviews with former Choucha residents and their fellow inmates documented, the only ways to get out of detention were to either pay for one's own deportation (to the country of birth, or to a transit country) or to be deported by Tunisian authorities to the border with Algeria, in a remote desert zone which had become a site of terrorist training. Interviews in the Storiemigranti report document weekly deportations of migrants and refugees who could not pay their way out of the prison. A refugee who was able to survive his exit from

Al-Wardia reported that during his two months of detention in 2014, about 400 people were deported: about 240 were deported to Algeria and about 180 to Turkey. The Storiemigranti report focuses on the logistics of deportations to the borderzone between Algeria and Tunisia:

> They deport them clandestinely. They give them a bottle of water and they abandon them there. Some people got lost in the desert and died or, like the Nigerians who were with them, walked a lot but finally found themselves again in Tunisia, finding again the Tunisian policemen.
>
> When the Somalians who were detained in my cell were deported, the guards put pressure on me, saying that if I did not have the money to buy my repatriation's ticket, they would have deported me to Algeria as they did with my comrades. (Storiemigranti 2015)

The camp after the camp coincides with the space of detention and with the geography of deportation. In both instances, refugees are not only abandoned as humanitarian subjects but also put in situations of dire risk to their lives. One of the enduring political claims of refugees at Choucha (during and after the camp) has been that they are all refugees "of" the Libyan conflict and hence they should all be resettled in a safe third country, regardless of their countries of birth. In this chapter, we have supported this claim by illustrating the furthering of their vulnerability as people "of" Choucha, as refugees who have spent four years in the desert at the Tunisian border with Libya, first in an officially designated refugee camp run by UNHCR and then on the premises of the same camp abandoned by humanitarian actors or at the different sites of destitution to which that abandonment led—the many camps following the official closure of the refugee camp that the people "of" Choucha have been experiencing as subjects who are simultaneously abandoned but also governed by the humanitarian regime.

NOTES

1. While official numbers recording presences are unavailable since the camp was formally closed, representatives of the national communities agreed to document the number of people living at the camp in July (about 150 people) and November 2014 (about 100).

2. At the time of preparing the final revision of this chapter in November 2015, the population of Choucha residents had decreased to forty people.

3. Tunisian citizens from Ben Guerdane—the Tunisian town closest to the Libyan border—started hosting people fleeing Libya before UNHCR opened its camp. This Tunisian "popular chain" of solidarity (Garelli et al. 2013), however, was mainly directed toward Libyan citizens and not migrants who had been living in Libya.

4. For documentation of other "humanitarian spaces" of abjection in Tunisia, see Garelli and Tazzioli (2016b).

5. Phone interview with UNHCR representative in Tunisia, July 2014.

6. Zarzis, interview with UNHCR officer, January 2013.

7. Zarzis, interview with Croissant Rouge representative, July 2014.

8. Even status refugees do not have an official residence permit issued by the Tunisian government.

9. We refer to migrants who left Libya by boat headed to Italy and who were rescued while their boats were in distress by the Tunisian National Guard. Some chose Choucha as their residence after the experience of the hosting center in Medenine.

10. For humanitarian reception before UNHCR arrival at the border with Libya in the context of the 2011 conflict, see Garelli et al. (2013) and Tazzioli (2012).

11. "Even though all migration involves journeys, it is only under specific conditions and with particular effects that the journey, the route, its vehicles and the complex social relations that underpin any journey become objects of expert knowledge and counter-knowledge. We are in the presence of viapolitics only when migration is problematized from the angle of the journey, and the vehicles, authorities, markets, infrastructures, and subjectivities that mediate that journey" (Walters 2014).

12. Voice of Choucha blog: http://voiceofchoucha.wordpress.com.

13. Mobility Partnership, http://europa.eu/rapid/press-release_IP-14–208_en.htm.

14. Tunis, interview with a refugee from Cameroon now settled in the city of Tunis, August 2014.

7

———

"Europe" from "Here"

Syrian Migrants/Refugees in Istanbul and
Imagined Migrations into and within "Europe"

SOUAD OSSEIRAN

Getting to Greece is like catching a fish with its water.
—HAMID TO THE AUTHOR, Istanbul, 2012

This chapter explores the ways in which Syrian migrants/refugees in Istanbul conceptualize "Europe" and the "EU" space beyond the established political boundaries or the official constructions of EU authorities.[1] The chapter emerges in a context where Syrian migrants/refugees have been fleeing the fighting in Syria since 2011 and many are making their way into Europe. Syrian migrants/refugees are thus more involved at present in the politics of Europe and the EU as constructed spaces than ever before. The chapter takes as a premise that Europe and the EU are not stable or set entities, but continuously changing spaces that are conceptualized differently by different actors (cf. Massey 2005:10–11). Hence, I place "Europe" and the "EU" in quotes in various parts of the text to highlight where the usage of these terms may diverge from ostensibly objective referents, and to thereby underscore that these spaces are neither predetermined nor stable conceptualizations. As Mezzadra (2011:122) explains, "Europe is, of course, a social construct that artificially unifies diverse locales [which] present very different migration histories and landscapes." Syrian migrants/refugees thus invoke their own discrepant imaginings of Europe and the EU, contributing thereby to how these spaces are always in process rather than stable or fixed (cf. Massey 2005:10).

Syrian migrants/refugees' imaginings of European and EU spaces emerge in their exchanges about other migrants/refugees' movements into Europe. They also emerge in their discussions about migratory and asylum policies in different EU states. Syrian migrants/refugees in Istanbul (and elsewhere) continuously share information about all these issues as a way of thinking about and preparing for their own prospective movements. They exchange information about the spatial, temporal, and legal aspects entailed in moving across borders into and within Europe. In the process, they develop their own conceptualizations of Europe and the various countries within the EU. In the chapter, I will examine the ways Syrian migrants/refugees residing in Istanbul and intending to move on to Europe configure Europe and the EU in their stories about others' migrations, and their attempts to comprehend the asylum and migratory regimes in different countries in Europe. I argue that Syrian migrants/refugees configure Europe and the EU not in terms of core and periphery, or centers and margins, but rather in more fragmentary ways that draw attention to some spaces and overlook others. In their accounts, Syrian migrants/refugees bypass certain countries by evaluating them as spaces where they do not want to remain, or where they cannot stay permanently. Syrian migrants/refugees thus depict certain spaces in Europe and the EU as spaces of temporariness, and some spaces in particular are constituted as only possibly temporary (cf. Papadopoulou 2004). Migrants/refugees assess these spaces as merely temporary in response to state tactics of bordering and to the asylum regimes in place in different states.

Syrian migrants/refugees' imaginings of Europe and the EU, developed through others' movements across borders, are then part of "a politics of migration" (cf. De Genova 2010d; Papadopoulos and Tsianos 2013; Squire 2011).[2] Their classification of spaces within Europe as temporary or permanent, whether in their discourses or practices, relates to the interplay between the "politics of migration" and the enactment of a "politics of control" (Mezzadra 2011:121). Migrants/refugees' practices consistently outpace states and border agencies in their attempts to enact a politics of control. The struggle over bordering extends beyond the border, inasmuch as state and border agency practices also operate within the space of the nation-state. An important part of state bordering practices is the institutionalization of certain forms of migrant presence as always potentially temporary (cf. Rajkumar et al. 2012). Notably, migrants/refugees respond dynamically to this sort of institutionalized temporariness by various acts of rebordering of their own, as evidenced in their movements and their discourse. Syrian migrants/refugees en route within Europe actively seek to pass through certain states without remaining, or alternately avoid them entirely. In their discussions about Europe or the EU, Syrian migrants/refugees analytically disregard or displace borders in order to bring spaces of temporariness or permanence into sharper focus. Here Syrian migrants/refugees' discussions of Europe and the EU space constitute it differently from the official delineations of the EU as a political entity or the imaginings of European elites, and thereby contribute to a discrepant production of the space of Europe (De Genova 2016b; cf. Lefebvre 1991 [1974]). In imagining and telling stories about Europe, Syrian migrants/refugees emerge as narrators (or authors) whose practices add to the production of multiple "Europes." Following Curry (1996:7), one of the ways people constitute places is by recounting stories about them. The stories they share counter any "self-producing story of Europe" (Massey 2005:71). Their autonomous migrant/refugee authorship is not contingent upon their adoption of European elites' or EU state actors' conceptualizations of "Europe."

This chapter will begin by presenting the context for Syrian migrants/refugees' presence in Istanbul and exploring the concept of "transit." I will then discuss the ways in which migrants/refugees' collective information about moving into and within Europe construct "Europe" and the EU space. Syrian migrants/refugees approach Europe not only through others' movements but also through information about asylum, fingerprinting, or benefits in different states. Migrants/refugees share information about these different issues while preparing for their journeys and also while they are en route. Their exchange of information and imaginings of Europe and the EU may be understood to be part of a "politics of migration," even when migrants do not necessarily explain their discourse in self-consciously political terms or account for their actions as political.

Syrian Migrants/Refugees in Turkey

Following the start of the uprising in Syria in 2011, Syrian migrants/refugees began coming to Turkey (and Istanbul), fleeing the violence in Syria. Syrian nationals have been present in Istanbul (and other parts of Turkey) from prior to the start of the uprising in Syria, but the uprising and subsequent violence has prompted unprecedented numbers to come to Turkey. The Turkish state responded to the influx by granting Syrian nationals entering Turkey temporary protection (Yınanç 2013). The Turkish state's offer of protection (albeit conditional), its political support for the Syrian political opposition, and its position at the border of the EU space are all factors that made it more attractive than other countries in the region. Syrian migrants/refugees have gradually settled in most neighborhoods in Istanbul. They have been incorporated into the (predominantly informal) labor force, as well as bringing capital and starting businesses in the city. Many Syrian migrants/refugees have chosen to reestablish their lives in Istanbul, while others approach their presence as an interim phase within their larger migratory plans.

Syrian migrants/refugees have been subject to different statuses since the start of the influx. The various statuses affect their presence and access while in Istanbul. With the start of the influx into Turkey in April 2011, the Turkish state officially designated those entering to be "guests" rather than refugees or asylum-seekers. Soon after, the state announced that all Syrian nationals present in Turkey are under the "temporary protection" of the Turkish state (Yınanç 2013). Turkey did not at the time of the announcement have a regulation or law pertaining to temporary protection, and "guest" continued to be used as an official reference (AFAD 2013). In October 2014 the state released the Regulation on Temporary Protection (Regulation No. 29153), which outlines the terms and conditions for Syrian migrants/refugees' presence in Turkey (İneli-Ciğer 2014; Yınanç 2013). Based on the regulation, Syrian nationals present in Turkey are referred to as "persons under temporary protection." Syrian migrants/refugees have thus been assigned various statuses since the start of the influx into Turkey. Aside from official statuses, many Syrian nationals nonetheless explain their presence in Turkey as a forced presence and affirm that they are "refugees." Others interpret the concept negatively and refuse to use the term *refugee*. In this chapter, I use the duality migrant/refugee as a means of recognizing and maintaining the tensions between people's different terms of self-identification. This emphatic duality also serves as a reminder of both the significance and instability of official political categories and juridical statuses in affecting the lives of those to whom they are applied.

In this chapter, I focus on the ways Syrian migrants/refugees discuss Europe and the EU space while preparing to move on to Europe. The accounts and circumstances explored in this chapter arose during ethnographic research with Syrian migrants/refugees present in Istanbul. I undertook primary fieldwork from July 2012 to December 2013, supplemented by subsequent research during an extended period of residence in Istanbul thereafter. As part of the fieldwork, I undertook participant-observation with Syrian migrants/refugees who were planning to move on to Europe, and others working toward remaining in Istanbul for the foreseeable future. As time passed, more interlocutors voiced similar expectations of continuing to Europe. The participants mentioned in the chapter had been present in Istanbul for varying periods of time, ranging from around two months to as long as two years or longer. Despite the longer-term presence and economic activity of some of them, they continued to insist on their eventual migration to Europe. For many individuals and families, Turkey, while offering safety from the violence in Syria, did not offer the same possibilities for rebuilding their lives that many migrants/refugees imagined Europe to offer. The comments included in this chapter arose either in response to direct questions or in the course of larger conversations that arose as a result of particular situations or circumstances. In most instances, my interlocutors were either planning their own journeys or speaking about the recent attempts or journeys of others. From the stories and information shared, I focus on the aspects pertaining to their imagining of EU-rope and the EU space in a bid to understand how these spaces are conceptualized beyond maps or institutionalized political boundaries.

Constituting "Transit"

"Transit country," "transit migration," and being "in transit" are categories and terms increasingly used in discussions of migration within academia, international organizations, and policy making (Papadopoulos et al. 2008; cf. Collyer and de Haas 2010; Coutin 2005; Düvell 2010; İçduygu and Yükşeker 2010). EU agencies and other bodies routinely use these terms to describe Turkey and many other non-EU states bordering the Schengen space. Despite their apparently prosaic descriptive character, these teleological categories and terms are always political and part of "a discourse of migration management" (Oelgemöller 2011:408; Papadoloulos et al. 2008:162). The categorization and relations that ensue partially demonstrate the relations of power in operation, whereby the EU can designate other states in particular ways and seek to affect their actions (cf. Andersson 2014b). The EU uses "transit country" as a way of pressuring neighboring states to change their laws, take on the responsibility of securing the borders of the EU space, and accept the deportation of migrants and rejected asylum-seekers to their territory (Papadopoulos et al. 2008:162–63). The project of securing the EU space thus extends well beyond the borders of the EU and neighboring states to a focus on migratory routes (Hess 2010:433; cf. Andersson 2014b). States along migratory routes into the EU are called upon to change their laws and practices to alter migrant and refugee presence (Düvell 2010:421). The demand is either for migrant and refugee presence to be facilitated through legal or institutional measures, or alternately that regulations be instituted enabling EU states to deport migrants/refugees back to these countries.[3] EU bodies thus seek to intervene in the configuration of migrants/refugees' journeys, their desired destinations, and the conditions of their presence in the

EU after they arrive. To this end (asymmetrical) partnerships are established with states removed from the EU space in a bid to control migratory routes (cf. Andersson 2014b; Papadopoulos et al. 2008:165). The borders of "Europe"—as sites for the enactment and enforcement of bordering the space of the EU—are pushed ever further away from the states neighboring the EU space. *Transit* becomes a term that is applied to both near and distant spaces—to the point that it is applicable to virtually the entire world (Hess 2010:433). Similar to Coutin's (2005:199) analysis of the U.S. case, EU bordering agencies in the process of externalizing the border beyond immediately adjacent states displace the border in certain ways while upholding and fortifying them in other ways.

By focusing on "transit countries" and spaces outside of the EU, EU state bodies deflect attention from the ways that migrants move around once within the EU space. It also situates the "problem" of "transit" elsewhere, and facilitates calls for the EU to demand that the states in question take action (cf. Oelgemöller 2011). Düvell (2010:418) highlights that official EU documentation never refers to Poland, Austria, Italy, or France as "transit countries," "despite the significant flows through these countries" to elsewhere in the EU. The alternative to the repeated demarcation and reinscription of the border is to identify the continuum between the EU spaces and spaces outside the political boundaries of the EU. Sabine Hess (2010) develops the idea of the "transit zone" as a way of criticizing the category "transit country." Her analysis illustrates how migrants connect spaces within and outside the EU through their movement. The transit zone is then an analytical tool evoking a different mapping of EU and non-EU space and confounding the boundaries of the EU. Such discrepant mappings are a way of moving beyond approaching the EU as a closed space that expands and contracts based solely on official EU authorities' actions or directives, such as admitting new member states (cf. Massey 2005:106).

Migrants/refugees' discourses and practical trajectories once within the EU space further enhance the concept of transit zones. Papadopoulou (2004), for instance, examines the case of Greece through the experience of Kurdish interlocutors who were present in Athens for varying periods of time. Their decision to move on was affected by the lack of infrastructure available for asylum-seekers and refugees as well as the difficulty of obtaining refugee status. The lack of infrastructure directed them to move on to elsewhere within the EU (Papadopoulou 2004:171). Although already physically present within the EU space, they qualified these spaces "within" differently, and sought to move on. Vigh (2009:105) similarly explains how young men from Bissau approached their presence in Portugal as a launching point to move elsewhere in the EU, given the racism they faced in Portugal. Migrants/refugees' movement *within* the EU space, therefore, is best understood to be, at times, a continuation of their movement *into* the EU space—toward "Europe." Researchers are consequently faced with the task of analyzing the continuities of migrants/refugees' movement and, in the process, their autonomous practices of rebordering "Europe."

Transit is constructed on multiple levels. In the context of Turkey, it is constructed by EU bodies and agencies and by international organizations working on migration, labeling Turkey as a transit country that migrants pass through en route to Europe.[4] According to Oelgemöller (2011:413), Turkey was one of the first countries identified as a "transit state" by the EU. Its role as a "transit country" is usually attributed to its geographical position as a crossroads between Asia and Europe (İçduygu 2004). "Transit" is also constructed through the laws and regulations governing different categories of migrants' and refugees' presence within Turkey. Thus, migrants' and refugees' decisions to come to Turkey and then remain or move on are likewise affected by the legal framework in place. Turkey's previous regulation (No. 1994/6169) concerning asylum-seekers and refugees and its current law (Law No. 6458) on migration (as of 2014), which establishes criteria for organizing migrants' presence and outlines the available pathways to citizenship, directly influence migrants/refugees' prospects for remaining. Thus, while a signatory to the 1951 Convention on the Rights of Refugees and the subsequent protocols, Turkey maintains a geographical limitation whereby only people fleeing conflicts in Europe can apply for refugee status and be resettled in Turkey. Asylum-seekers from everywhere else are referred to as conditional refugees, and while they are protected and can remain in Turkey, their status does not enable them to become citizens.

Beyond the differential provisions of the legal framework, Turkey is approached differently by a variety of migrants and refugees. Consequently, "transit" is constituted through migrants' and refugees' autonomous subjective orientations, especially by those planning to move on, as well as through their differential experiences of presence in Turkey. Some migrants and refugees come to Turkey with the aim of remaining, while others approach their presence as transitory within their larger migratory projects. For Iraqi Chaldean refugees waiting in Istanbul to be resettled elsewhere by the United Nations High Commissioner for Refugees (UNHCR), their presence in Turkey is presumptively and emphatically temporary (Daniş 2007). Brewer and Yükşeker (2009) highlight that migrants and refugees from various African states have rather different circumstances. Turkish-speaking Bulgarian migrants come to Istanbul as migrant labor (cf. Parla 2009, 2011). Some approach their presence as temporary in the long run and aim to return, while others seek to settle permanently in Turkey and apply for citizenship. Similarly, Biehl's (2015) ethnography of the Kumkapi neighborhood in Istanbul illustrates how migrants and refugees from various countries, ranging from former Soviet states to African countries, make discrepant decisions about remaining, moving on, or returning. Yaghmaian's (2005) interlocutors of various nationalities actively sought to move on from Istanbul to Europe, and some repeatedly attempted to cross the border with Greece or Bulgaria. Either seeking safety due to the difficulties and persecution they had experienced in their countries of origin, or due to a desire to reach "Europe" to make their lives there in a space of imagined possibility, some of these diverse interlocutors did not stop at Greece or Bulgaria at all, but instead sought to first go further west. Without clarity regarding their future or possible presence in Turkey and no end in sight to the fighting in Syria, many Syrian migrants/refugees approach Europe as a place of possible long-term security. They risk crossing multiple borders in their search to attain this security. Beyond legal frameworks or internationally designated governmental categories of mobility, migrants and refugees make their choices and then tactically alter their plans with unforeseen changes in their life circumstances and opportunities. As with any space of "transit," therefore, a multiplicity of migratory movements and ambitions exist among migrants and refugees coming to Turkey.

"Transit" is consequently a political concept used to encompass a myriad of aims, whether deployed by migrants to describe their experiences in certain spaces, or by states as part of a politics of control aiming to restrict movement into the EU space. Transit, rather than being a self-contained or delimited concept pertaining exclusively to spaces outside Europe or the EU, however, extends in many instances into the EU. "Transit" can potentially continue even once migrants and refugees have supposedly "arrived" at their destination as they face new borders, social or linguistic or legal, which they have to overcome (cf. Coutin 2005; Mountz et al. 2002; Yaghmaian 2005). While referring to a multiplicity of meanings, the term *transit* nonetheless still holds potential as an analytical category, particularly once it is reinterpreted through the critical lens of the autonomy of migration.

Europe and the EU: Politics of Knowledge

Syrian migrants/refugees' discussions about "European" states and ways of moving between EU states give rise to particular imaginings of "European" space. They swap stories about others' experiences en route or their own previous attempts to cross various borders. Migrants/refugees circulate information about other migrants' border-crossing practices and migratory regimes' responses to their practices as a way of negotiating the prospective risk they might face in their own projected movements. The information they gather is in part produced by EU bodies as they continuously devise and refine tactics of bordering in response to migrants/refugees' presences and movements. Papadopoulos and Tsianos (2013:190–91) describe the information and knowledge that migrants/refugees share as part of a "mobile commons" that migrants/refugees create while on the move. They explain this concept as part of a larger politics of mobility that migrants/refugees enact by moving and then by circulating information about moving, thereby facilitating the movement of others. For migrants/refugees, exchanging information is a central part of crossing borders and arriving, given the constantly changing state responses to different migratory movements and arrivals (Papadopoulos and Tsianos 2013; cf. Yaghmaian 2005). In light of the tactics of bordering, migrants/refugees depend on updated information as a resource with which to render their attempts successful. In the process of exchanging stories and information, migrants therefore create a common fund of information. The fund is accessed and augmented by migrants/refugees who have already arrived at their desired destinations, those en route, and others still seeking to move on. Migrants/refugees in a variety of places, not just Turkey or Syria, access this knowledge through their social networks and social media.

Migrants/refugees share information or stories about the near past or present of others whom they know or have heard about. In these exchanges, the vagaries of the near future take precedence over the dreams of a more distant and uncertain prospect of building a new life in Europe (cf. Guyer 2007). Given their focus on the near future, they are also more likely to tell anecdotes from the near past of recent migratory movements rather than recount the details of events in the more distant past, unless the older narratives serve a comparative purpose in relation to analyzing current practices or policies. If someone tells stories or supplies information about much earlier migrations, these are told with particular instructive aims beyond the goal of contributing to general knowledge. For most migrants/refugees, current practice and future action are the main concern. They share the information and stories as a way of explaining what is to come, what to expect, and what to try to avoid (cf. Vigh 2009:92). Through these exchanges, they present their mode of thinking about their near futures through the actions and lives of others. In the discussions, Syrian migrants/refugees bridge their present (before they move on) with their desired future of arriving in an elsewhere, in "Europe."

For many migrants/refugees, the stories of others' journeys and the information about various countries help them to cope with the uncertainty of their as-yet incomplete journeys, whether as cautionary tales or by inspiring hope and confidence (cf. Cruikshank 1998). Migrants/refugees' sharing accounts of others' journeys is encouraged by their successes. Similarly, stories of difficulties or incidents of violence that have happened to individual Syrian migrants/refugees or groups while en route are circulated as warnings. Most migrants/refugees are aware, usually without speaking of it directly, that they face the risk of injury, violence, or death in undertaking the attempt. Many migrants/refugees who use Facebook or other forms of social media rely on these forms of media to circulate information and stories about attempts or violence experienced en route. Information disseminated through social media is discussed with family members or friends as a means of assessing and verifying the accuracy of various sorts of information. A great heterogeneity of migrants/refugees participate in creating this sort of communicative nexus and attempting to understand what is entailed in border crossing through information that is circulated both within their direct social circles and in considerably more extended ones online. Through this communal fund of information, migrants/refugees create and cultivate a shared reality of movement into, across, and within Europe. In the process, or potentially as a by-product, Syrian migrants/refugees produce their own imagined "Europe" and their own discrepant conceptions of the spaces of the EU. Even sometimes apart from their own direct experiences, migrants/refugees come to "know" these spaces through the collective fund of information exchanged (cf. Curry 1996).

In discussing the information that Syrian migrants/refugees exchange, I will focus on the ways migrants/refugees construct Europe and the EU space. Migrant/refugees' exchanges about movement and space contribute to creating these spaces rather than serving merely as a discursive commentary on social relations or action (cf. Jiménez 2003). Doreen Massey (2005:10) argues that spaces are produced by relations, and to the extent that socio-spatial engagement and the nature of these relations are altered, space "is always in the process of being made." More or less directly informing and instructing one another's mobility plans and border-crossing practices, Syrian migrants/refugees sharing stories and information about journeys—and by extension, about "Europe"—may therefore be understood to be a political action that creates spaces of a European elsewhere from within the "here" and "now" of migrant/refugee Istanbul. It is an example of their authorship as mobile actors whose movement is implicated in constituting Europe and the EU space. In discussing Europe and the EU space from the standpoint of their mobility projects, elaborating a distinct migrant/refugee knowledge of the borders and bordering of Europe and the tactics of border crossing, Syrian migrants/refugees become active participants in creating these spaces in ways European elites and states would never have intended or anticipated.

Europe—An Idea and a Space

"I do not want to go to Europe for the sake of Europe, but because I am tired of carrying the responsibility of the children," Amira said in January 2014. Amira, a woman from Qamishli of whom we will hear more further along, was at the time waiting for word about the family reunification procedures her husband had initiated in Germany. She waited for around nine months for him to be granted political asylum in Germany and then began waiting anew for the family reunification process to be completed. Amira recognized that many migrants/refugees had illusions about Europe or about the lives they would lead there. She, on the other hand, believed her existential security would come from joining her husband—not from her reaching Europe. The idea of Europe as a space of possibility and security to which Amira alluded is not exclusive to Syrian migrants/refugees. Young men in Bissau compared Bissau to Europe, highlighting how they perceived Bissau as stagnant (Vigh 2009). The young men faced difficulty in becoming proper "adults" in Bissau given the economic situation and limited possibilities. They wanted to migrate to Europe as a way to fulfill the next expected stage in their life course. In a similar manner, Hage (2005:470–71) explains that his Lebanese interlocutors repeatedly highlighted that the potential to "become" was perceived to lie always outside of Lebanon. Similarly, many of the Iranian migrants and refugees whom Yaghmaian (2005) interviewed expressed their feeling of being immobile in Iran, prompting them to make their way westward. For many Syrian migrants/refugees, Turkey, while offering a space of security (albeit temporarily), is not perceived as a space of possibility. Many Syrian migrants/refugees face uncertainty about their futures in Turkey and have to rebuild their lives from scratch there without state or institutional support. The situation is compared with "Europe," where migrants/refugees insisted that most states would grant Syrian migrants/refugees permanent status and provide them with some modest support, thus enabling them to begin to rebuild their lives without having to worry about their basic subsistence.

In their discourses, imaginings, and movements, Syrian migrants/refugees construct a European/EU space of their own rather than adopting a construction imagined by others in Europe or the EU. Most Syrian migrants/refugees explained that they wanted to go to "Europe" and spoke of Europe in terms similar to Papadopoulou's Kurdish interlocutors in Athens: "In fact, for many migrants the destination is Europe, understood as a broad space of safety, protection, and opportunity" (Papadopoulou 2004:174). For most Syrian migrants/refugees, given the uncertainty of the overall situation in Syria as well as their tenuous predicament in Turkey, the security (financial and existential) offered to refugees is part of the attraction of going to "Europe," despite the risks, difficulties, and costs of arriving.

At the same time that migrants spoke of going to this generic Europe, however, they also described Europe and the EU as differentiated spaces. Syrian migrants/refugees distinguished among various spaces within Europe and set up their own evaluative hierarchies of EU member states. The hierarchies were based on the respective states' migration and asylum policies, and their policies toward Syrian migrants/refugees in particular. For many Syrians, the promise of permanent residence, social provisions, and the speed and possibility of family reunification processes all affected this hierarchy of EU states. The hierarchy set up EU states not as core or periphery but more as spaces of greater or lesser temporariness or permanence.

Transit Zones

Migrants/refugees' imaginings of Europe and the EU space entered into the narratives of other migrants/refugees' movements across borders into Europe and their movements once inside Europe. In their anecdotes, Syrian migrants/refugees tended to position Greece, Bulgaria, Italy, and France as spaces that they move through rather than remain in. Migrants/refugees also omitted other states along the route, so that at times it seemed as if the mobile protagonist of each narrative leapt across geographical space. The states on which migrants/refugees focused as spaces to merely move through acquired the qualities of transit zones.

These zones of "transit" extended far into Europe and the EU. While in Istanbul, preparing to move on, Syrian migrants/refugees were therefore concerned with devising strategies by which to avoid moving through them altogether, or for eventually (as promptly as possible) moving on from them. I met Hamid in Istanbul in early October 2012 through a mutual contact. The first time we had spoken, he was in the detention center in Edirne following an attempt to cross the border into Bulgaria. He returned soon thereafter to Istanbul, and I met him in the Aksaray neighborhood several times before he moved on again. A single man in his early thirties, he had come to Turkey alone, leaving behind his family, as well as parents and siblings, on their farm in

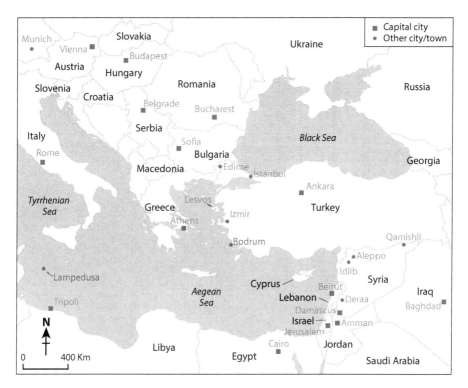

MAP 7.1. Southeastern Europe and the eastern Mediterranean

Idlib. He entered Turkey legally by land and made his way to Istanbul with the aim of continuing to Europe. He had come to Istanbul with very little money, prompting me to ask him why he had not stayed in the south of Turkey, or in the state-run camps in the southern Turkish provinces set up for Syrian migrants/refugees fleeing the fighting. He replied, "They are camps: no matter how great it is, your freedom is limited. You will see the fence every day." During the three weeks that followed his failed border crossing, we met repeatedly in Aksaray for tea. He would relay to me news of his latest plan or talk about his previous attempts. He had already tried to cross the border twice—once to Greece and the second time to Bulgaria. He had attempted both times with other migrants because he did not have the money to hire a smuggler. He told the stories of their attempts with good humor but remained anxious, preoccupied with finding a way of continuing. Eventually, he found a new companion with whom to move, and he planned to cross to Bulgaria and to go from there to Austria or Germany.

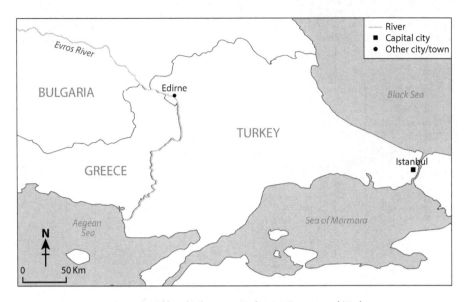

MAP 7.2. Land border between Bulgaria, Greece, and Turkey

During our first meeting, I asked him why he decided to change his route from Greece to Bulgaria following his first attempt. He said by way of explanation that the man with whom he was crossing the first time had lived in Greece previously and had a permit that allowed him to work there. Hamid compared himself to his former travel companion and explained that the man had options in Greece—prospects for remaining. As Papadopoulou (2004) has explained, remaining permanently in Greece is possible only if migrants have work authorization. In contrast, Hamid framed his prospective presence in Greece as one without possibilities. Hamid continued, "I can do nothing there." Later on in the same conversation, Hamid said, "Getting to Greece is like catching a fish with its water."[5] His reflections on Greece, taken together, served to reaffirm his desire to continue onward to Germany or Austria. Rather than it being a matter of his inability to arrive or remain in Greece, however, he chose to change his route to Bulgaria because he believed it was easier to move on from there than from Greece. Migrants continued from Greece by purchasing a counterfeit or original look-alike passport, moving through official channels by transiting through the airport, or they went by boat to Italy, or sought crossings by land. Crossing by land involves crossing several borders, one at a time, and some of the Balkan states en route are not EU member states. Many migrants therefore preferred to seek other routes. In addition to these considerations, various migrants/refugees explained during the summer of 2012 that the routes out of Greece were effectively "closed." Migrants/refugees increasingly decided to go to Bulgaria on the basis that continuing from Bulgaria involved crossing fewer borders, and routes from Bulgaria were reportedly "open" at that time. There was also less information in circulation at that point in time about how EU states such as Germany or Austria handled the cases of migrants/refugees who were first fingerprinted in Bulgaria.

Hamid's remark referred to his assessment of more or less viable routes, based on the information in circulation in the mobile commons of migrants/refugees, and thus exemplified the rebordering that migrants first enact mentally in talking about routes or nation-states, and then enact practically and materially in physically crossing those same borders and territories in their efforts to eventually arrive at their desired destinations. Hamid's comment figured Greece as a kind of dead end, a bounded place. Furthermore, he dismissed the importance of crossing the Turkish–Greek border or being in Greece. Without the means of continuing from Greece, by plane or with a smuggler, crossing the border to Greece was simply unrewarding and not worth the effort. The metaphor of a fish and its water is suggestive of a reciprocal relationship with the world (cf. Lucht 2012). Migrants take the risk of crossing the border to reach a place of greater security—existential and/or financial. They exert effort and endure the hardship of the border crossing, but arriving in Greece is unfulfilling unless migrants have the means of moving on from there (cf. Yaghmaian 2005). Even though Greece is part of the EU, it does not offer the same possibilities for existential security that are available elsewhere in "Europe" (cf. Papadopoulou 2004). Hamid thus positioned Greece, like Bulgaria, as states that migrants merely move through rather than states they would aspire to move to. Thus, these states, despite their EU membership, were seen to constitute parts of an extended zone of transit that begins in Turkey, and for Hamid, entering them was merely a continuation of his situation in Turkey rather than offering the promise of a substantial change in his circumstances.

Familial Ties and Movement

Various EU states' approaches to the arrival of Syrian refugees and the reception given to them have affected Syrian migrants/refugees' choices of heading to Europe and where they plan to seek asylum once in Europe. Many migrants wanted to resettle in particular European countries because of familial ties or the presence of friends already established there. They therefore differentiated and evaluated EU space through familial or other familiar relations. Other migrants chose states where they had no connections, favoring them based on their positive perceptions of their laws or policies regarding asylum-seekers and refugees (cf. Papadopoulou 2004:181), especially Syrian nationals. The possibility of family reunification and the speed of procedures, whether asylum processing or family reunification, were factors about which migrants/refugees routinely inquired, and which they often considered paramount in making their decisions about where to go. Leila, a single woman in her late thirties with family in Germany, explained in October 2012 that she preferred to go to Sweden, as the situation was better for Syrians there than in Germany. Sweden was processing Syrian asylum claims faster than Germany and was providing Syrian refugees with permanent residence, housing, and financial support. Faced with various national bureaucracies administering asylum, Leila chose her destination in order to prospectively exercise greater control over her time and her future. She wanted to feel secure about her status quickly and to be sure of the provisions available to her, rather than prioritizing living close to her siblings. Whereas in 2012–13 many Syrian migrants/refugees favored the idea of going to Sweden because of its response to the arrival of Syrians seeking asylum, by the summer of 2015, Germany had become the destination of choice following that state's response to the increasingly large number of Syrian migrants/refugees crossing into Europe at that juncture (Hall and Leichfield 2015). In contrast, the Danish state's announcement that it would confiscate refugees' valuables and money in excess of US$1,000 was baldly intended to direct potential asylum seekers to go elsewhere (Dearden 2016).

Many migrants/refugees appreciated the prospect that they would be able to move around freely once they had attained "legal" status in a Schengen member state. Abu Rezan, a father from Qamishli with four sons over the age of eighteen, explained in the winter of 2013 that he no longer cared if all the family ended up in the same EU member state. Like Leila, he wanted his family to arrive to safety even if they were not physically close to one another. At the time we spoke, one of his sons had already gone to Germany from Istanbul using a counterfeit passport, and Abu Rezan did not think it likely that the whole family would end up in the same country. He accepted that his family would be dispersed across the EU. His resignation was a compromise in the face of the uneven regime of divergent security and border controls. His compromise was significant: like other Kurdish male heads of families (and many other Syrian fathers, generally), he preferred to keep his family together. By keeping his family together, he would have a better chance of maintaining his relations with his children and his position as a figure of authority within his family. Nevertheless, his first priority was for his family to arrive to safety (existential safety), even if separately and at the expense of his own position as patriarch.

Kenan, Amira's husband, had come to Turkey with his family prior to the start of the uprising in Syria. They are Kurdish, from the city of Qamishli in northern Syria. A family of eight, they came to Istanbul with the aim of continuing to Europe. Their attempt failed, their money ran out, and they decided to remain and eventually to claim asylum, as Kenan had indeed had problems with the regime in Syria. They underwent their first interview with UNHCR and were already awaiting a second interview when the uprising started in Syria. In November 2011, the Turkish state announced that all Syrian nationals in or entering Turkey would be under the temporary protection of the state. Following the announcement, their file with UNHCR was put on hold. I was introduced to the family in December 2012. Kenan complained about their situation generally, and specifically about their UNHCR application. His teenage daughters were working to support the family, and there was no promise of changes in the family's situation in the near future, especially as the possibility of being resettled through UNHCR had been abruptly undermined. He slowly started to talk during subsequent visits about continuing alone or with his eldest son to Germany or Sweden. He insisted that his eldest son, Ciwan, come with him as the young man was over eighteen and would not be included in any family reunification process. Kenan intended to apply for family reunification to bring over his wife and other children once he had acquired refugee status. His decision to cross was a move to end his family's waiting rather than continuing to depend on UNHCR for a possible change in their situation.

Kenan and Ciwan attempted to cross the border into Europe in February 2013. They were caught in Istanbul hiding inside a truck boarding a container ship headed to France. They were initially held in a police station close to where they had been caught, and were subsequently moved to Yabancılar Şubesi, the Foreigners' Unit jail of the Turkish National Police, in the Kumkapı neighborhood near Aksaray. When I came to visit, Amira, his wife, explained what had happened to them and how they were caught. During the conversation, I asked her where Kenan had wanted to go. "He did not care as long as the country has family reunification. They were going to head to France first and then Kenan was going to see if anyone he knows there would get him to Sweden. Still Germany does family reunification, Sweden, Holland, Austria. . . . France does not give asylum, they give you a paper that says you have fifteen days to leave, it does not matter to where."

Amira has relatives living in various European states, and she knew of the different nation-states' policies from them and from other migrants/refugees in Istanbul. Amira effectively positioned France outside the larger European regime of asylum in which the other European states she mentioned were understood to participate. The "France" of which Amira spoke was merely a "transit" country—one that institutionalized asylum-seekers' presence as an expressly temporary presence. States issuing migrants/refugees a document ordering them to leave (regardless of the direction they go) institutionalize temporary presence and render migrants/refugees' continued presence "illegal." The high rate of rejection of asylum petitions thus establishes the conditions of migrants/refugees' persistent presence in France as that of mere (illegalized) "migrants" (cf. Hess 2010:434–35). Similarly, Hess discusses the practice of issuing "release permits" in Greece. Migrants held in Greek detention centers who opted against seeking asylum with the Greek authorities were detained for three months and then released with a paper similar in substance to what Amira described. Such detention centers were thus "transit" stations where asylum-seekers remained for a time and then from which they continued their journeys. Such centers serve to interrupt movement temporarily instead of halting it, operating in effect as decompression chambers (Mezzadra and Neilson 2003; cf. Andrijasevic 2010:158–59; Karakayali and Rigo 2010:133–34; Papadopoulos et al. 2008:196–202), from which migrants/refugees are induced to move on. "France," as Amira described it, held a similar quality as a virtual detention center, writ large on the scale of an entire nation-state. In her framing, by withholding any possibility of settling under legal forms of authorized presence such as refugee status, such countries left moving on as the only viable option available to asylum-seekers. Highlighting the hierarchy of EU member states according to their greater or lesser beneficence in granting asylum, Amira described the larger migratory regime that differentially establishes the disadvantageous conditions under which migrants/refugees can remain in some countries only as rejected (illegalized) asylum-seekers.

Other migrants contributed to this sort of alternative mapping of Europe and the ranking of distinct EU states by drawing on similar ideas of temporariness or permanence predicated on asylum policies and regulations. Majed and his brother Hani, whom I met in Istanbul in October 2012, are Palestinians who had been living in the city of Deraa in southern Syria. Both in their early thirties and married with young children, they had participated in the uprising in Deraa and were wanted by the regime in Syria. Due to their precarious situation with the regime and the continued fighting in Deraa, they decided to head to Europe. They planned to make the journey and then send for their families once they had secured refugee status. They said they wanted to go to Sweden, as it was understood to be giving "permanent residence, a wage, and a house" to Syrians who were arriving there and seeking asylum. Majed explained that he had been studying maps of Europe while still in Syria in preparation for the journey.

They came to Istanbul with the names and numbers of a few smugglers, which they had gathered from friends and neighbors in Deraa who had already gone to Europe. I met them the day after their arrival in Istanbul. They described their journey to Istanbul and the smugglers with whom they had spoken thus far. One was an Iraqi smuggler with whom their neighbor from Deraa had migrated. He moved people from Istanbul by plane to France or Italy, and he had warned Majed over the phone, "The country you get to, you have to seek asylum in!" As we sat, Majed tried to convince his brother that they should go to Italy, because their neighbor who had moved with that smuggler had succeeded to continue on from Italy to Sweden. The discrepancy between the smuggler's warning (that they must seek asylum in the state in which they arrive) and their neighbor's eventual arrival in Sweden was perplexing. They turned to me at that point, asking, "How is that possible?" "I don't know," I responded. Hani then telephoned his wife in Deraa to ask, and she reported that the smuggler had instructed the neighbor on how to present herself to UNRWA,[6] and then they had assisted her onward to Sweden.

"They took her?!" I asked, a little incredulous.

"Yeah, they took her. See, Italy does not give asylum," Majed explained.

Italy was perceived as having low refugee approval rates,[7] but Majed reframed this perception as a situation in which Italy simply did not have any asylum policy. He constructed Italy as a country that migrants/refugees pass through without having any legal recourse, such as seeking asylum, to remain. By insisting on the prospect of an inevitable link between the country of first arrival, registration as asylum applicants, and consequent permanence, the smuggler's depiction of the European asylum regime had contradicted the well-founded perception of Italy as a place from which refugees and migrants could or must move on. They knew that seeking asylum in one EU state would limit their opportunity to claim asylum in another EU state. In moving on from Italy, their neighbor's experience seemed to supply the proof that arriving elsewhere in Europe, via transit through Italy, truly was possible; it was just a matter of understanding precisely how it had happened. Hani's wife's explanation included the intervention of an international agency that had apparently facilitated the neighbor's continued movement, and thereby seemed to reaffirm the idea that refugee presence in Italy is a matter of institutionally imposed temporariness.

In both Amira's and Hani and Majed's discussions of Europe, migrant/refugee presence within certain spaces is configured as institutionally temporary. They spoke of the spaces in question as places of transit, places through which migrants/refugees pass without the possibility of remaining permanently. Migrants/refugees reframed the incidence of low asylum acceptance rates in particular nation-states as if there were actually no asylum policies whatsoever. Whereas Amira listed several states (in contrast with France) that were understood to offer the possibility of remaining and therefore of family reunification, Majed and Hani spoke of their neighbor's journey from Italy to Sweden as one of virtually uninterrupted and expedited movement. Remarkably, Hani's wife's explanation omitted the countries in between, compressing them as if they were merely a corridor connecting Italy and Sweden.

Fingerprints

The divergent migratory and asylum policies, the disparate economic situations, and migrants/refugees' heterogeneous desires were all factors that affected migrants/refugees' imaginings of various EU states, and consequently their choices of where to go and how. Migrants/refugees depend on the assessment of these factors in their decisions to continue beyond Greece or Bulgaria. Migrants/refugees' constructions of European states as places of relative permanence or temporariness were partially informed by the asylum and refugee policies of the states in question. Bulgaria or Greece were therefore imagined as places of temporary presence, in contradistinction with other parts of Europe that were constructed as prospective sites of plausible resettlement and potential permanence (cf. Collyer and de Haas 2010; Papadopoulou 2004). Consequently, migrants strategically sought information about how to ensure that their presence in Greece, Bulgaria, or Italy would in fact prove to be temporary. In particular, they discussed measures to avoid being fingerprinted in these countries, as they understood that fingerprinting would affect their opportunities to seek asylum elsewhere in Europe.

Many Syrian migrants/refugees in Istanbul, concerned about fingerprinting, spoke of how being fingerprinted in some EU states acted as a permanent mark, while being fingerprinted in other EU states did not limit their ability to claim asylum elsewhere. Being fingerprinted attested to a relationship with a particular state, or potentially with several states. Through fingerprinting, EU member states (potentially) affect migrants/refugees' lives and futures. Fingerprinting also created a textured hierarchy of states whereby being fingerprinted in some states could be dismissed, while in other states it had consequences. Syrian migrants/refugees explained why they needed to avoid being fingerprinted, as well as explaining the differences between various fingerprintings. Some migrants/refugees intending to move on through Bulgaria, for example, denied that it was even an EU member state. They insisted it was outside the EU in order to reassure themselves and those moving with them that it was possible to claim asylum in another EU state even if they were forced to register as seeking asylum in Bulgaria first. They reaffirmed that documented presence in Bulgaria, in the form of fingerprints or an asylum claim, was negligible in their overall plan to arrive elsewhere. These sorts of spatial imaginings introduced a textured hierarchy of the various states extending transit zones beyond the simple categorization of countries as "EU" or "non-EU" member states. The differences among various EU member states' fingerprinting practices thus added to the migrants/refugees' discrepant imaginings of "European" spaces and EU states by reaffirming their sense of a graduated hierarchy among the various countries.

Migrants knew that being fingerprinted in one EU state meant their case might not be processed elsewhere or, if processed, then only with difficulties (cf. Hess 2010:434). Hamid insisted that being fingerprinted in Bulgaria did not affect claiming asylum elsewhere, as migrants/refugees were only fingerprinted on paper and not electronically. He contended that migrants in Bulgaria have the option of seeking asylum or not, and that their files are "thrown out" after six months. He also claimed that Bulgaria was not part of the EU, so being fingerprinted there had "no effect." In the process, he categorized being fingerprinted on paper as merely an interruption of movement rather than a veritable foreclosure of the possibility of arriving and being processed for asylum elsewhere. In speaking of Bulgaria as a place where it was simply a matter of the migrants/refugees' choice to claim asylum or not, Hamid raised questions about the ways that seeking asylum elsewhere in Europe is presented, in effect, as an institutionally mandated imperative rather than a choice. The Bulgarian migratory regime he evoked was one that maintained temporariness and represented interruption, making migrants and refugees move on rather than keeping them in place.

For migrants/refugees, as a result of the EU's asylum regime, the objective is to ensure there is no trace of their presence or movement while they are en route (cf. Coutin 2005).[8] Notably, the active or directed effort to disguise or conceal movement once across a European border marks a striking contrast with Syrian migrants/refugees' approach to their presence in Istanbul. In Istanbul, Syrian migrants/refugees are a rather visible presence: Arabic is spoken openly in the streets or on public transport, there are Syrian restaurants in various neighborhoods in the city, and even smuggling is discussed openly in Aksaray and other parts of the city. Syrian migrants/refugees' need for discretion and their efforts to limit their visibility begin only once they are at the border with Europe, whether they are trying to cross by land, sea, or through the airport. At the borders of "Europe," Syrian migrants/refugees hide themselves to avoid being caught by the Turkish gendarmerie, who serve as outsourced enforcers of the European border regime, such that being caught will result in delaying the migrants' journeys or their having to sort out alternate routes. Migrants/refugees' need to hide themselves continues once they are within so-called European space, especially in the case of Greece, as there is the possibility of being returned to Turkey if they are apprehended at the border. It is, supposedly, only when they arrive at their destination, regardless of where their final destination may be, that it is no longer necessary to hide. In seeking to erase or minimize the evidence that they were ever "there"—whether "there" is in Turkey, Greece, Bulgaria, or Italy—migrants and refugees seek to disclose having been "there" only in their narratives. Syrian migrants/refugees are required to explain the route they took to arrive at wherever they claim asylum, but recounting which states they passed through is different from having been fingerprinted in a particular state while en route. Their narratives of being en route pose no threat of rejection or expulsion, whereas fingerprints, documented evidence of their presence as asylum-seekers, potentially do.

Kenan tried to continue from Turkey three more times and succeeded on his third attempt. He and a cousin paid a smuggler for their passage. They hid inside a truck that was going to travel through Bulgaria, Hungary, and Austria to reach Germany. At one point en route, Kenan's cousin felt that he was going to suffocate. They got out of the truck, and were soon afterward stopped by the police. They were in Hungary. They were fingerprinted and told to make their way to a detention center in the capital. They managed to continue to Austria, and from there they went to Germany by train. They were stopped by police soon after entering Germany, and they claimed asylum. I asked Amira when she told me the story of their passage if they would be returned to Hungary because they had been fingerprinted there. She explained that her husband had been told that being fingerprinted in Hungary would not affect his claim for asylum in Germany. She said that Austria returned asylum-seekers fingerprinted in Hungary, but Germany did not. Kenan therefore had no other option than to continue on to Germany once he had crossed into Austria, because the fingerprints taken in Hungary were a trace that would have prevented him from remaining permanently in Austria.

Stories and information about fingerprinting add to the imagining of Europe and EU space by mapping those spaces as variegated ones involving greater or lesser potential temporariness and permanence. These migrant/refugee perspectives and experiences counter representations of "Europe" as a uniform, integrated, harmonized space. Migrants/refugees approached fingerprints as traces that, depending on the particular state in question, could affect migrants/refugees' lives profoundly, or alternately might have no effect whatsoever. Regardless of the effect of being fingerprinted, however, fingerprints attested to a relationship with a particular state. For Syrian migrants/refugees, the objective was to avoid forming such relationships with states through which they wanted simply to transit, in order to guarantee that they could finally seek asylum somewhere desirable. By exchanging information about the complexities and vagaries of fingerprinting, Syrian migrants/refugees thus constituted a "Europe" and an "EU" space according to their own autonomous mobility projects and aspirations.

Conclusion

This chapter has explored the ways in which Syrian migrants/refugees imagined Europe and the EU space in accounts related in Istanbul about their own and other migrants/refugees' mobility projects. Through their stories, Europe and the EU space become knowable and known for the would-be migrants/refugees. These accounts highlight the ways that "Europe" and particular countries within the EU are constituted as uneven sites of temporariness and permanence. In the process, the multiple borders within Europe and the EU come to be blurred, shifted, displaced, or unhinged through migrants/refugees' practices, first in their imaginings and narrations and then in their eventual border-crossing trajectories. This dislocation of the borders of Europe evokes and exposes unforeseen "transit zones" within and across Europe. At the same time, as some state spaces are approached as sites of temporariness or permanence, other state spaces are ignored or disregarded altogether in migrants/refugees' stories and assessments of routes, asylum regimes, or fingerprinting. Thus, in their accounts of their own and others' journeys, migrants/refugees draw attention to certain spaces, creating in the process a heterogeneous "Europe" and a fragmented "EU" that are the objects of knowledge of a mobile commons that pools insights and shares experiences from one mobility project to the next. In their stories, migrants/refugees, while unsettling and displacing borders, never cease to account for and appraise the control apparatuses of states and their techniques of border policing. Their engagements therefore bring to the fore the continual negotiation that is at the heart of the larger politics of mobility that emerges between autonomous movement and tactics of bordering. Indeed, migrants/refugees' imaginings of the discrepant spaces of "Europe" or the EU incorporate into their analyses the very politics of control that states and border agencies seek to implement. They do not, however, take "the border" or the control instituted there as the definitive limit of those imagined spaces. Rather, their imaginings of a more fractured Europe—indeed, a Europe constituted by its many contradictory borders—opens up the possibility of other "Europe(s)" different from those demarcated and enforced by the constrictions of EU institutions and European elites in their campaigns of border control.

Acknowledgments

The author would like to acknowledge the financial support awarded by the British Institute at Ankara (BIAA), which made part of the fieldwork in Istanbul possible. The author would like to thank Professor Nicholas De Genova for his feedback and comments throughout the process of research and writing, Taras Fedirko for his comments and feedback on various drafts, and Dr. Zahira Araguete-Toribio for discussions on the themes included in the chapter.

NOTES

1. While it is by now customary to refer to these people as "refugees," I opt instead to characterize them as "migrants/refugees" to underscore the inherent experiential, epistemic, juridical, and political instability between these categories as "governmental contrivances" (see De Genova, this volume), as will be further elaborated below.

2. Migrants/refugees' movements, especially over the summer of 2015, prompted EU states to rearrange their borders and engage in various acts of rebordering within the Schengen area (New Keywords Collective 2016; cf. Kallius et al. 2016; Kasparek and Speer 2015).

3. Notably, Turkey and the EU signed an agreement on March 18, 2016, which allowed the EU to return migrants and refugees who arrive on the Greek Islands from Turkey (EU Press Office 2016). Based on the agreement, the EU recognizes Turkey as a "safe third country," making it possible for Greece to return asylum-seekers to Turkey. With the agreement, Turkey has moved from being designated a country of "transit" to a country of "return," changing the relationship between the EU and Turkey. The agreement potentially alters the ways migrants/refugees (Syrians and others) may move, not only from Turkey into the EU space, but also how or if they may ultimately be able to seek asylum once within the EU.

4. EU–Turkey agreement of March 18, 2016.

5. Hamid's comment bears similarity to a line Yaghmaian (2005:227) found written in Persian on a door in an informal migrant and refugee settlement in Patras, Greece: "Patras, the open prison."

6. United Nations Relief and Works Agency for Palestinians in the Near East. This UN body is active only in the countries of the Near East.

7. See EUROSTAT (2014) for approval rates in Italy in the years 2012 and 2013.

8. Following the EU–Turkey deal in 2016, migrants/refugees' approaches to narrating the routes they have taken may change. The deal will have effects on the ways in which migrants/refugees move, as well as on how they eventually arrive.

8

———

Excessive Migration, Excessive Governance
Border Entanglements in Greek EU-rope
MAURICE STIERL

The idea of migration as something excessive underlies many critical or autonomist conceptions that have emerged as a challenge to orthodox, economistic, or static understandings that regard migration simply as a response to clearly reducible factors that "push" or "pull," or as quasi-passive reactions to socioeconomic needs and pressures. To the contrary, it is argued in accounts associated with the autonomy of migration (AoM) literature, there is an unpredictability of migration, a stubbornness, an inherent recalcitrance that subverts, mocks, or overcomes attempts at (border) control and the figuration of "the migrant" in policy which seems to always violate human diversity, inventiveness, and potential.[1] Migratory subjects are said to "exceed" control, in the original sense of the term: to "go over a boundary or specified point," to "be greater in number or size than," to "go beyond what is allowed or stipulated," to "surpass."[2]

This chapter inquires ethnographically into the idea of migration as an excessive force. While excess seems, by definition, to escape measurement, it should not remain merely a hopeful, at times romanticized assumption. It has to surface somewhere and somehow, even if only momentarily in particular movements, gestures, or anecdotes. Citing several encounters in Athens, during my fieldwork in autumn 2013, with communities in (arrested) transit seeking to "irregularly" escape Greece toward Western European countries, I explore how individuals and groups attempt to overcome Europe's many borders and thereby collide with forces that seek to restrict, manage, or block them.[3] Through an engagement with the narration of diverse migration experiences I examine how, if at all, practices of migration and everyday contestations in the "borderscape" of Athens can be understood as struggles that contain an excessive potentiality, even in increasingly restrictive and violent conditions (Rajaram and Grundy-Warr 2007).

Michel Foucault's short essay "Lives of Infamous Men" (1994) serves as a way to further think through these encounters in Greek transit and questions of excess. Tracing collisions of "infamous" subjects with forms of authority, Foucault not only elaborates on the often painful fate of those who drew the sovereign's attention to themselves but also points to all those lives that remained unacknowledged, hidden in the void of history, unencumbered by sovereign might. At the same time, Foucault gestures toward the changing relationship between excess and control in times of an emergent political authority that functions not through clearly determinable sovereign centers but through "networked" forms of power, regimes, or dispositifs. With the vanishing of the king and his crude but awe-inspiring forms of punishment, (sovereign) control itself transformed, diffused, and expressed itself productively though no less violently. Whereas excess could be understood as the king's teasing counterforce, contemporary governmental regimes question such duality and complicate the relationship between control and excess, so that accounts of migration that seem to re-create or build upon such dichotomous understanding need to be rethought.

The contemporary European border regime, I argue, is excessively violent in its own right. Through diffuse border practices that routinely act on racialized markers of perceptibility, this regime enacts excessive and horrible forms of border control throughout and beyond sovereign spheres, causing types of suffering that do not necessarily vanish with the overcoming of physical borders but often linger on as fear, trauma, and depression. Violent forms and effects of control can be thought of as excessive as they surpass moments of sovereign decision-making "at the border." There is a productivity to forms of contemporary border control that saturate not only moments of collision between those in transit and border guardians but also moments of anonymity, imperceptibility, and escape. This is, of course, not to put in doubt the ability of those on the move to creatively and continuously subvert certain border configurations, but rather to ask for a more cautious and subtle understanding of migration's excess, its entanglement with forces of control, the racialized rationalities that underlie European border control, and their increasing spatial and temporal displacement. Instead of remaining attached to a conception of migration as autonomously (or ontologically) primary, it is argued that more attention needs to be paid to migration's entanglement with forms of border control. It is in this way that we begin to understand how a politics of perceptibility, but also one of imperceptibility, can be an effect of governmental strategies of border enforcement as well as their subversion and distortion. Beginning with an understanding of border entanglements invites a closer interrogation of what forms of human creativity, diversity, and excess are expressed and violated in the process of migration.

This chapter is organized in four sections. Section 1 points to the assumption of migration's excess and ontological primacy in the autonomy of migration literature. Therein, notions in the semantic field of excess, such as autonomy, creativity, stubbornness, imperceptibility, or unruliness, have frequently been employed to characterize the capacity of people in transit to escape or exceed (certain forms of) border control.

Section 2 briefly outlines the current borderscape of Greece before turning to several encounters with Jaser, his family, and members of the Yazidi Syrian community, all of whom sought to leave Greece and travel toward Western European countries. Jaser's family succeeded in enduring in an environment of unwantedness, and eventually overcame multiple border obstacles. While their story is one of (excessive) movement, their experiences of being stuck where they did not want to remain and of various horrible border collisions cast light on contemporary border effects that contain an excessively productive violence that impinges on people in transit and often stays with them, even after overcoming physical borders.

Section 3 further elaborates on these ethnographic encounters by alluding to Foucault's short essay "Lives of Infamous Men," in which he traces collisions of "infamous" subjects with the king's authority. In his writing, Foucault points to the excess that lies within anonymity, which seems close to the understanding of autonomy developed in the AoM approach. However, Foucault gestures also to the changing relationship between control and excess in times of governmental authority with consequences for the ways in which anonymity as well as autonomy can be thought.

Section 4 shows how the experiences of Jaser and his family were shaped by the diffuse but violent effects of the European border regime. Both memories of horrible border collisions and their racialized perceptibility meant that living imperceptibly did not translate into anonymous freedom but into fearful hiding, severely impacting on their migration project. It is argued that (dualistic) accounts of excess and control need to be rethought and conceived as intimately and necessarily co-constitutive forces that fold into one another and form border entanglements where excess can be detected in violent border collisions as well as in the will to struggle and move on.

Section 1: Excessively Autonomous Migration?

The question of excess seems to, implicitly or explicitly, reverberate throughout conceptions of migration as proposed by the autonomy of migration literature. Therein, a reductive understanding of migration as passive reactions or objectifiable processes is repudiated and abandoned. Instead, migration is thought of as a primary force whose mobilities often escape (border) control, possessing, Rutvica Andrijasevic and her colleagues note, a "moment of independence vis-à-vis political measures seeking to control them" (Andrijasevic et al. 2005). In many accounts associated with AoM, notions in the semantic field of excess are regularly employed to foster an understanding of migration's supposed autonomy: escape, creativity, potentiality, uncontrollability, supplement, independence, surplus, stubbornness, imperceptibility. Ranabir Samaddar's conception of autonomy as "governmentality's other" (2005:10) seems to productively fold into the AoM approach, and is shared by many of its proponents. He proposes an understanding of autonomy as "practices that give birth to the political subject whose existence is in contradistinction to the existence of the governmental realities of this world" (2005:10). For Samaddar, autonomy functions as a "symbol for the emerging patterns of new spaces in politics, spaces that speak of rights, and justice" (2005:10). He suggests that "autonomy always points to the supplement that remains after (the task of) government has been achieved" (2005:9–10). Connecting processes of migration with such an understanding of autonomy, Michael Hardt and Antonio Negri seem to capture an underlying sentiment of the AoM when they state: "A specter haunts the world and it is the specter of migration. All the powers of the old world are allied in a merciless operation against it, but the movement is irresistible. . . . The legal and documented movements are dwarfed by clandestine migrations: the borders of national sovereignty are sieves" (2000:213).

Similarly, Yann Moulier Boutang notes that while forms of repression may be utilized to counteract migratory movements, it would be impossible to fully tame them.[4] Similarly, Nicholas De Genova detects in freedom of movement a "defiant reminder that the creative powers of human life, and the sheer vitality of its productive potential, must always exceed every political regime" (2010b:59). Moreover, Dimitris Papadopolous, Niamh Stephenson, and Vassilis Tsianos interpret escaping subjects as protagonists of social transformation, who dwell as "new elusive historical actors . . . in the world of imperceptibility and generate a persistent and insatiable surplus of sociability in motion" (2008:221). Papadopolous and Tsianos argue elsewhere:

The spectre of migration will never become a new working class. It will always remain a spectre, which comes in the night through the backdoor of your nation on a smuggled vessel, by using false papers, by crossing hundreds of miles of snowed mountains, by changing one's own identity, by destroying the skin of one's own fingertips with acid and a knife to avoid identification, by overstaying a visa, an au pair contract, or the regular tourist period of stay.... The spectre of migration will always be with us, among us, more real than anything else: cleaning your home,... taking care of your kids, fixing your computer, fixing your car, providing sex, providing care,... living in the flat next door. Migrants do not hold the place of a historical or a political subject as such, rather they tend to become imperceptible to history.... But the more they do this, the more they change history by undermining the sovereign pillars of contemporary societies. (2013:187)

Papadopolous and Tsianos suggest that the AoM approach "is about training our senses to see movement before capital (but not independent from it) and mobility before control (but not as disconnected from it)" (2013:184).

For many AoM scholars, thinking of migration as autonomous allows one to move away from conceptions that portray migration's subjects primarily as vulnerable, passive, or abject victims. Instead, their mobilities constitute political mobilities, often able to escape forces of control that seek to monitor, regulate, capture, or deter them. Migration, then, becomes "a creative force within [social, cultural, and economic] structures" (Papadopolous et al. 2008:203). Sandro Mezzadra argues that AoM shows "how the 'politics of control' itself is compelled to come to terms with a 'politics of migration' that structurally exceeds its (re)bordering practices" (2011:121). And Manuela Bojadžijev and Serhat Karakayali (2010) hold that such a gaze allows "exploring migratory lines of flight as social movement in the intermediate zones, where migration slips out of the hands of regulative, codifying, and stratifying policies."

This specter of migration that is frequently referred to forms a crucial dimension in the AoM literature. Conceived as something that is always at work, migration actively transforms the social, makes worlds, not as a collective subject implementing political programs or demanding political change, but as a multitude of people on the move excessively changing politics. There is, it seems, an anarchic unruliness to migration itself when understood as an ungovernable current or force transcending political spaces, thereby challenging and altering these spaces and politics, even if imperceptibly and inaudibly. Migration, thus, is thought of as a mobile force that, while subjected to increasingly repressive and governmental forms of control, finds, or rather creates, subversions. These subversions, other than in mainstream "left" accounts or definitions of what constitutes the political, are always already political, and excessively so, without having to formulate a manifesto or even claim their politicality (Mitropoulos 2006:131).

By drawing attention to the political moment of migration per se, AoM scholars have importantly intervened in traditional discourses of migration by problematizing and considerably departing from traditional taxonomies underlying not only the discourses and practices of contemporary border and migration regimes, but also widespread and dominant currents in "migration studies." AoM does not regard migration as a problem that requires governance and is critical of accounts, produced and reproduced often in languages of policy and research that suggest how to "better" understand, direct, monitor, or deter migration or its paths and patterns.

Migration's supposed excessive autonomy, while inherently difficult to grasp, requires ethnographic exploration. Rather than a hopeful taken-for-granted assumption, migration's (border) subversions are material realities, and as such must have observable effects, even if only as fleeting moments and gestures. The ethnographic inquiries of the following section revolve around questions of excess and control in a borderscape that various individuals, families, and groups in transit continuously seek to subvert and overcome in order to travel on to other EU-ropean countries—Greece.

Section 2: Stuck in Greece

Contemporary Greece constitutes an agglomerate of Europe's border dilemmas. Situated at EU-rope's periphery, its geographical location close to Turkey has turned Greece into one of Europe's main entry points for people on the move, and for many years now it has drawn the gaze of EU-rope's border regime and the heightened attention of its border enforcement practitioners. While peripheral, Greece as a "border area" has become a central EU-ropean concern. As Étienne Balibar observes: "border areas—zones, countries, and cities—are not marginal to the constitution of a public sphere but rather are at the center. If Europe is for us first of all the name of an unresolved political problem, Greece is one of its centers, not because of the mythical origins of our civilization . . . but because of the current problems concentrated there" (2004:2).

Various interlinking national and EU-ropean border reinforcements and policies were enacted within a few years' time, further securitizing, militarizing, and externalizing the Greek–EU-ropean borders. For the first time ever, in 2010,

EU-rope's external border agency Frontex deployed its Rapid Border Intervention Teams (RABIT) along the Greek–Turkish border; they were replaced in 2011 by the reactivated and extended Joint Operation Poseidon (land and sea).[5] Frontex also became more permanently present in Europe's eastern Mediterranean region by opening its first Operational Office (FOO) in Greece in 2010.[6] Through a bilateral migration pact agreed to in the same year, Turkey accepted the return of "illegal migrants" from Greek territory, and in 2013 the EU followed suit with the EU–Turkey Readmission Agreement in order "to establish, on the basis of reciprocity, procedures for the rapid and orderly readmission, by each side, of the persons having entered or residing on the territory of the other side in an irregular manner."[7] The 12.5-kilometer-long Greek fence on its land border with Turkey was completed in late 2012, while, in the meantime, Greek detention facilities were either newly erected or extended and "for the most part financed by the European Union."[8]

These intersecting dynamics need to be seen as a response to the mounting political pressures exerted by EU member states on the Greek government to further securitize its external borders and prevent transitory movements toward Western European countries. While before, following the Dublin Regulation, EU member states would routinely deport those who "irregularly" traveled into their territories back to Greece, this changed after a ruling by the European Court of Human Rights (ECHR) in 2011 (Clayton 2011:758). The Afghan interpreter "MSS" entered Greece in 2008, became registered on the Eurodac system, traveled on to Belgium, and was deported back to Greece. In his complaint about his treatment by Greece and Belgium, the ECHR found both countries in violation of Articles 3 and 13 of the European Convention on Human Rights concerning "MSS's conditions in detention, his general living conditions and the inadequacy of the asylum determination system" (Clayton 2011:763). The MSS ruling had far-reaching consequences as most EU member states suspended deportations to Greece. In turn, with one deportation destination fewer on the map, EU member states began to demand the "sealing off" of Greece's internal EU-ropean borders.

Reacting to a Frontex report in 2012 in particular, which suggested that two-thirds of detections of "illegal entries" into the Union occurred along the Turkish–Greek border, the Greek government was publicly denounced and urged to rapidly react or face serious repercussions.[9] Austrian Interior Minister Leitner criticized Greece's inability to shut its "open barn door" while France's President Sarkozy as well as Germany's Interior Minister Friedrich threatened to expel Greece from the Schengen area or to selectively reestablish national border controls.[10] Shortly afterward, the Greek government deployed 1,800 police officers to the Greek–Turkish border ("Operation Shield") and, in August 2012, launched the police operation "Xenios Zeus," named after the god of hospitality, first in Athens and later in Patras.[11]

In view of these dynamics, only briefly pointed to here, it becomes clear that, for EU-rope, Greece constitutes a particularly problematic border area, central not merely in matters of austerity politics but also in matters of migration deterrence. Especially the Greek capital of Athens has become a space where the "concentration of problems," as indicated by Balibar, is starkly observable, where Greek–EU-ropean border politics are played out within a dense urban borderscape. It is here that the Greek government's police operation Xenios Zeus, in less than six months, stopped "almost 85,000 people of foreign origin on the streets of Athens [who were] taken to a police station for examination of their identification papers and legal status" and "4,811 [were] arrested for illegal entry and stay in Greece—a criminal offence—and detained pending deportation."[12] Those arrested in these large-scale police sweeps, based almost entirely on ethnic profiling, faced incarceration for many months, subsequently extended to up to eighteen months in order to make migrant life "unbearable," as suggested by the Greek chief of police.[13]

For those who succeed in entering the Greek mainland, Athens constituted a significant site of rest, (re)orientation, sometimes work, and new identities and documents, but also one of homelessness, hunger, unbelonging, racist attacks, and police controls. For many merely a stepping stone to a beyond that promises a future of arrival, family, work, and security, Athens has, nonetheless, become the unwanted "home" for thousands of people in transit. "Being stuck" in Athens and Greece is a common phrase uttered by those in transit whose movements and lives have involuntarily come to a halt. It is here that, while stuck in a situation of tremendous anxiety and uncertainty, possibilities of escape are envisioned, located, and enacted.

Encounters in (Arrested) Transit

I first meet Jaser in front of the Greek Council for Refugees in Exarcheia, Athens.[14] Waiting in line to ask for an interview with lawyers of the Council, I notice a man in his early thirties who tries several times to draw the attention of the Council's doorman, but fails. Standing quite close to him I can see a pile of documents in his hands. They are all in German, including the card of a German insurance company. I approach him and ask him, in German, what he came here for. He turns around, his face lights up. "You speak German?" he asks. "Ich bin Jaser." He says that he has visa problems but that he is a resident of Germany. Detecting my visible confusion, he indicates that this is a longer story. We step aside, leave the queue, and go to a café around the corner. Jaser is eager to tell his story.[15]

> I have lived in Germany for seventeen years and have not seen my family in Syria for seventeen years. I asked to see my family in Greece who came due to the war and violence. I came to Athens to hug my family but became convinced that in Greece it is very difficult to live. On the 10th of October 2013, I came via Switzerland to Athens and on the 23rd of October I had to return to Germany. At 11 AM in the morning I went to the airport in Athens. I got my boarding card and when I went through the police control the police said that my documents were not my documents. They said these papers belonged to somebody else. I asked him to return my papers but he said no. They took me to the police station in the airport and I spent six hours there. In the end they hit my ear really hard. I have witnesses; my cousin and a good friend were there, for example. He could not react as he was scared to be arrested. I went to the German embassy but they said they could not do anything about it. I have work and appointments in Germany. Now I had to apply for new papers and I will lose my job and miss my appointments. I will be in difficulties in Germany.

I read through the documents; they are issued by the German embassy in Athens in case of lost visa documents. Jaser has difficulties understanding the six pages of complex officialese. Following residence law paragraph 25, Jaser obtained a temporary right to reside in Germany for humanitarian and personal reasons. His local administration granted his "vacation in Greece" and issued the relevant papers.

We try to complete the visa forms, but Jaser's case is different; there is no box asking for details on the loss of visa documents due to police abuse. We take a taxi to the German embassy and together we ask for advice. The embassy staff knows Jaser; he has been here several times before asking for help but was merely handed documents and told to ask for help at the Greek Council for Refugees. The council is a special charity offering "legal and social advice and services to refugees and people coming from third countries who are entitled to international protection."[16] The facts that Jaser does not fall into this category and that the council is not capable of helping filling out documents in German should be blatantly obvious to the embassy staff.

We indicate that several passages of the form do not apply to his case. Jaser recounts his story, not for the first time. Unimpressed and losing patience, the staff member notes: "If the police control migrants they usually fill out a protocol that the migrant then receives." Surprised, we indicate that the police recording an incident in which they used excessive force, tearing both Jaser's travel documents and his eardrum, seems unlikely.[17] "I have not heard of such problems before, he needs to fill out the form saying he lost his visa." While tempted to refer to the many reports on police abuse in Athens and Greece in general, it seems wiser to do what she says. Although the embassy is aware of his right to reside in Germany, and has already obtained his details, issuing a visa would take a "couple of weeks, maybe longer."

Jaser invites me back to the flat in the area of Neos Kosmos, where his family stays. The flat is tiny, three rooms for twenty-five people. It is hot and smoke-filled; the single window is only slightly ajar. They are all from Syria and came to Greece in the last three years, some as recently as two months earlier. As religious Yazidis they belong to the wider Kurdish community, a non-Muslim minority frequently persecuted in the Middle East, most recently by ISIS fighters in Syria and Iraq. Jaser translates for me, and his brother-in-law, Nihad, recounts the story of how Assad's soldiers came to his house and demanded money.[18] Wanting to escape the constant harassment by Syrian authorities, instead of paying, Nihad decided to flee with his two wives and eight children. They traveled via Turkey and were smuggled into the Evros region of northern Greece. "We were just let out in a forest and then caught by the police. We had thirty days to leave the country and stayed at the police station for seven days."

They traveled on to Athens, where they slept outdoors at a playground for a few days until they met other Syrians and found a flat. The police evicted them, and again they stayed at the playground. They begged for money, found food in garbage containers, and eventually moved into their current flat in Neos Kosmos. Nihad was arrested and stayed in detention for several months. "My family ate from the garbage or cooked grass from the forest. Then I was arrested three times and put in prison for three months each time because my papers had expired. . . . Now I am scared to leave the house."

Nihad's recollections come to a close, and a relative of his, Ziad, tells the story of how he fled the war in Syria with his family only six weeks earlier. In Turkey their fingerprints and passports were taken. First imprisoned and beaten by the police, they were then discarded into a large refugee camp where Ziad's sister was sexually abused. For thousands of euros, three hundred per child and six hundred per adult, his family was taken to northern Greece, where Ziad had to leave his parents behind—they were too weak to walk on and they have not heard of them since.

We exchange numbers and promise to meet again, two days later, at the Doctors of the World for health checkups on some of the children and Jaser's swollen ear.[19] However, only a day later I get a phone call: "Jaser prison, Jaser prison." Accompanied by a friend who speaks Greek, we hurry to the police station, where the police inquire repeatedly about my origin and seem not fully convinced by "Germany/EU."[20] Their disinterest in our presence is palpable; rolling cigarettes and joking around, their contempt for us is hardly concealed. We seek to explain Jaser's particular situation. They seem to know but state that they would have to make some background checks first before releasing him. While an order by Major General Emmanuel Katriadakis of the Greek Ministry for Public Order and Citizens' Protection announced that Syrians would be detained for just a few days so that their origin could be verified, various cases of arbitrary detention have emerged in contradistinction to such an order.[21] With the assistance of a Greek migrant rights lawyer, Jaser gets out of prison the same night, after having been subjected to the distinctly Kafkaesque predicament of being jailed for not having the documents that the police themselves had taken away from him.

In the following weeks Jaser, his family, and I meet frequently, talk to doctors, lawyers, journalists, and activists. Walking down the road, always looking out for the police, Jaser points to "the people smugglers" who had asked whether he wanted to pick up people from the north. "Look into my wallet, I have two euros left and they told me I could earn 2,500–3,000 euros by driving up once but I won't do that, I am not a criminal." Jaser introduces me to the "Yazidi community" that has gathered in Neos Kosmos, some distance from Muslim Syrian communities. In many encounters I am exposed to the plight of those who escaped war only to live in poverty and social marginalization in EU-ropean Athens—traumatized children, wounded young men, and sick elderly who are unable or unwilling to make use of Greek health services. I meet Nizar, whose ten-year-old daughter was raped by smugglers when he could not immediately pay the money they requested.[22] "Back in Asia, where we live, so many people die, there is no god. I thought god would be in Europe but if he is not here, he does not exist." Also scared to be arrested, Nizar hardly leaves his small, run-down but overpriced flat.

Jaser just wants to leave Greece. His papers, however, are not ready for weeks. Living among his many relatives in this noisy flat causes pain to his injured ear. He is constantly tired and afraid to use up the cigarettes he has left. We meet, once again, in the flat with a lawyer and human rights activist who inquires into the different legal situations of the family members. There are potential cases of family reunification with relatives who already reside in Germany. The question of whether or not to apply for asylum in Greece, however, remains unresolvable. A registration would allow family members to move around Athens without being arrested and detained, but what if they escaped to Western Europe and the ending of deportation to Greece got lifted in a few months or years? Would one trade future uncertainties for a present ability to move more freely within clearly defined bounds, or would one choose a present of insecurity, constant hiding, and possible detention, for a potentially less threatening future—a present or future of potential confinement, both effectively folded into the Greek asylum regime, leaving only unpredictable variables and impossible choices?

The lawyer takes note of every case, and then, suddenly, Jaser's aunt, who had remained silent throughout, starts speaking. Yes, she has a case as well, a case against the Greek state and its border guards, who pushed her child into the Evros River right next to her, drowning and "disappearing" her soon-to-be-married daughter. Everybody in the flat goes quiet, the older women in the room start sobbing. Jaser has difficulty translating, we have difficulty listening. Cautiously, the lawyer expresses her deep sympathies, hugs the mother. She asks about dates and times, whether the body had been found or not. No, it has not. The Greek state did not search for her, but other migrants did. Many, about thirty, traveled up north from Athens to search the Evros for the body. It remains unfound, and obsequies have already taken place both in Germany and in Syria. The mother does not want to start legal proceedings. She does not want to mention her daughter again.

Jaser escapes Greece about five weeks after his planned departure. This time he is not stopped. He has lost his job in Germany, has trouble with the job agency and his girlfriend, who have difficulty believing his story, and he lacks the money to pay the bills that pile up in his flat. But at least he made it out of Greece. He speaks to his family in Athens every day. He tells me in December how his old uncle had died in the tiny flat, and for days the police and emergency services refused to pick up his body. They were collecting money to send the body to Turkey, where his children live precariously.

In January 2014, Jaser calls me, this time with good news. "Remember my brother-in-law's second wife? She left Greece with her mother and two children and is now in Serbia, and I expect them to be in Germany in three days. . . . And I have more news. Remember my niece? She arrived in Germany yesterday. She went through Serbia, Romania, and so on, Hungary, you know, but anyways, she is now at my place, at home." In May, Jaser informs me that "they are all now in Germany, not a single person remains in Greece."

Section 3: Infamous Migrant Lives?

In many ways, the story of Jaser and his family can be read as a story of migration's excess. Against all odds, border obstacles were overcome, eventually, after months and years of hardship and struggle. Many of the family members traveled without documents to and throughout Europe. Some secured falsified documents, while others located legal routes for at least some sections of their journeys. Continuous messages from Jaser announced more and more arrivals in Germany, until, finally, the family was nearly completely reunited. This version retains hopefulness, as it can be read as giving evidence for the (AoM) assumption that migration forms a stubborn force that exceeds the many guardians of Europe's diffused borders.

At the same time, the family's experiences of homelessness, loss, murder, rape, and fear were experiences of extreme violence, a violence that is excessive in itself. This excess violence that constitutes a productive element in Europe's border regime does not simply vanish with the physical overcoming of material borders but lingers on, as trauma, depression, and a constant state and fear of deportability (De Genova 2002:438). The family's many collisions with Greek–EU-ropean border forces—but also, and importantly, times in hiding—entail forms of violence that prompt us to reflect on and reconceive the relationship of (border) control and (migration's) excess, thereby complicating assumptions of migration's autonomy or (ontological) primacy. How can we better understand the relationship between excess and control in contemporary forms of migration governance?

This section explores this relationship through Foucault's "Lives of Infamous Men" before returning to the experiences of Jaser's family. In this short but significant piece, Foucault compiles an "anthology of existences," from books and documents that tell the stories of "lives of a few lines or a few pages, nameless misfortunes and adventures gathered into a handful of words" (1994:157). It is in his exploration of these lives that he finds not only unfortunate fates that collided with authority and were subsequently punished but also "excessive fates," those who remained anonymous and hence seemingly autonomously free. These hardly perceptible, even imperceptible, subjects can be thought to be the protagonists of migration understood as an autonomous force. Importantly, however, Foucault draws our attention to changing patterns of authority and governance that necessitate a shift in our understanding of (migration's) excess.

In his short essay, written in 1977 as a preface to a project that would never materialize, Foucault suggests: "I was determined that these texts always be in a relation or, rather, in the greatest possible number of relations with reality:

not only that they refer to it, but they be operative within it; that they form part of the dramaturgy of the real; that they constitute the instrument of a retaliation, the weapon of a hatred, an episode in a battle, the gesticulation of a despair or a jealousy, an entreaty or an order" (1994:160). The lives unearthed by Foucault were "destined to pass away without a trace" had they not been "snatched ... from the darkness in which they could, perhaps should, have remained" (1994:161). These lives were ordinary, un-famous, never prone by themselves to draw the attention of authority to them. They turned in-famous only due to a "combination of circumstances that ... focused the attention of power and the outburst of its anger on the most obscure individual ... , aimed no doubt at suppressing all disorder" (1994:163). The individual's infamy could stem from an atheist lifestyle, from drunken or violent episodes, even from a "madness ... to hide from his family," that were discovered and revealed only due to an unfortunate collision (1994:158).

It was the individuals' "encounter with power" that illuminated their lives and left a trace. Foucault is certain that "without the collision, it's very unlikely that any word would be there to recall their fleeting trajectory" (1994:158). These collisions always relate to the figure of the king, "the source of all justice and an object of every sort of enticement, both a political principle and a magical authority" (1994:171). They were caught in the nets of his authority that arrested their movements and exposed them, in many cases, to punishment. In his search for the historic texts, Foucault suggests that these "particles [were] endowed with an energy all the greater for their being small and difficult to discern" (1994:171). He found the infamous existences only as they had clashed with "power," and what is known of them are merely the fragments that the collisions had produced. What remains unknown is how their lives unfolded afterward.

Foucault's infamous men were those who could, maybe should, have been among the "billions of existences destined to pass away without a trace" (1994:161). While these infamous wo/men became "describable and transcribable, precisely insofar as they were traversed by the mechanisms of a political power," many more did not (1994:169). These "billions of existences" remained un-famous and fleetingly bypassed the king. It appears that Foucault's short piece is not merely an account of those who were unfortunate enough to collide with the king's authority; it also speaks of those unspeakable ones who never left a trace, who remained in the void of history, never documented or accounted for. These were "excessive subjects" who never entered the purview of sovereign control and who, it seems for Foucault, enjoyed a form of freedom found only in anonymity (Prozorov 2007).

For Foucault, whereas before "in Western society, everyday life could accede to discourse only if it was traversed and transfigured by the legendary . . . , [starting] from the seventeenth century, the West saw the emergence of a whole 'fable' of obscure life, from which the fabulous was banished. The impossible or the ridiculous ceased to be the condition under which the ordinary could be recounted" (1994:173). One day, he suggests, the theatricality of the clashes between authority and infamy subsided, the omnipotent king disappeared, and "[power] would be made up of a fine, differentiated, continuous network, in which the various institutions of the judiciary, the police, medicine, and psychiatry would operate hand in hand . . . [and discourse] would develop in a language that would claim to be that of observation and neutrality" (1994:171–72). This "differentiated network," with which Foucault points to contemporary forms of authority, thought of as governmental regimes or dispositifs, operates without recourse to the exuberant and comical exchanges of the lettres de cachet or the exercise of ceremonious punishments. He suggests that within and through such a network, "[the] commonplace would be analyzed through the efficient but colorless categories of administration, journalism, and science" (1994:172).

The simplicity of the absolute authority of the king to pick out, punish, or eliminate subjects of disorder has long gone. While the king vanished and a more nuanced (biopolitical) administrative system manifested itself, the clash between what could have remained anonymous and a zealous power seeking "to prevent the feebleminded from walking down unknown paths," persists (1994:158). There are parallels between Foucault's figure of the infamous "feebleminded" and the contemporary (policy) figure of the undocumented migrant. It is her very movement and being that require governmental intervention, examination, and identification. Her unknown paths must become knowable, for in her motion and being seems to lie an unpredictability challenging the mechanisms of political power based upon clearly categorizable subjects and rationales.

In contemporary forms of migration control, technologies of infamy are regularly employed to legitimize governmental interventions, ranging from processes of categorization and criminalization of cross-border movements to characterizations of humans on the move as agents of disorder, conflict, and even terror. Through these technologies, migrations' movements and paths are sought to be made "describable and transcribable," with the aim, of course, to also traverse the subjects of migration with a power of (elusive) control. To that end, current border regimes increasingly infiltrate mobile subjects themselves, not merely by harvesting bodily information, but also by creating border obstacles that inscribe themselves as lingering feelings of anxiety, fear, unrest, precariousness, and trauma onto these contemporary subjects of infamy (Amoore 2006:338).

Thinking of migration as an excessive force, as is often done by proponents of the autonomy of migration, seems to fold into Foucault's gestures to the excessive freedom of those remaining untraceably in "darkness" while, at times, not sufficiently acknowledging crucial changes in the role and function of authority, as pointed out by Foucault. The clashes of those in Greek transit with forms of border control require us to rethink the oft-maintained dualisms that seem, at times, more relevant in times of the king than in those of Europe's contemporary border regime. As is argued in the following section, these dualisms of anonymous autonomy and capture, perceptibility and imperceptibility, clash and non-clash, control and excess are put in doubt with the intensification and complexification of border enforcements and the excessive violence that they contain.

Section 4: Border Entanglements

Clearly, the episodes of infamy excavated by Foucault not only tell us about individual fates but also animate the functionality and rationality of a (historical) political power. In similar ways, the struggles of Jaser's family to move throughout Europe, while always specific, point to certain underlying truths, needs, and effects of the European border regime. The experiences of Jaser and his family were saturated by (the effects of) EU-rope's "fine, differentiated, continuous network." For them, the border regime not only severely conditioned their chosen migration paths and their mode of transport, but had also arrested them, for months and years, in an unwanted city where hiding in a run-down flat seemed the only option, in turn further impacting on their immobility and arrested transit. Wherever they turned, borders seemed to appear and materialize. Both their perceptibility and imperceptibility were border effects. Experiences and circulating knowledges of psychological and physical everyday violence against migrants and the always-existing possibility of detention and deportation were productive of lives that sought to remain unnoticed, under the radar.

The urban space of Athens has its own geography of fear, with no-go areas for those who do not seem Greek enough, areas known for police sweeps, as strongholds of fascists or civil patrols who mark their territories by hanging up Greek flags or leaving "Greece for Greeks" messages in public squares. Especially since the Xenios Zeus police operation and its modus operandi of stopping anyone who appears foreign, as well as the rise of Golden Dawn, those who are undocumented seek to remain unseen.[23] For many people in transit, self-confinement comes at great cost. Attempted avoidance of physical border collisions means not leaving one's flat for most of the day, keeping the children inside, not engaging with "Greek people," not accessing the few available medical and legal services if they are not offered in the immediate neighborhood.

For Jaser's family, hiding in such "darkness" did not translate into "anonymous freedom" in the borderscape of Athens. While Foucault's fleeting existences enjoyed the freedom that "darkness" seemingly provided, the same does not hold true for those who remain stuck in European transit. Like thousands of others in this urban borderscape, Jaser's family was not prone to draw the attention of authority to them other than through their physical appearance, which might suggest non-Greek, non-European origins. When border controls target those who are perceived to be nonwhite and/or non-Greek, their imperceptibility, achieved only by hiding physically, is based on pervasive fear, instilled through forms of excessive border violence into the minds and bodies of those such as Jaser's many family members.

The story of Jaser, a resident of Germany who travels to Greece as a tourist and is stopped by the Greek police, beaten, and stripped of his documents and rights, is certainly not the most common border collision in contemporary Europe. It sheds light, nonetheless, on the precarity of those considered Europe's (internal) others. Jaser's racialization as someone not quite German, not quite white, trumped his documented (legal) belonging in EU-rope. The police operation Xenios Zeus as well as the EU-ropean counterpart Mos Maiorum in 2014, with nonwhite others as principal targets of control, demonstrate that European whiteness still functions as one of the most significant markers of difference through which border collisions are enforced.[24] What focused "power's attention" on Jaser and his family was not an episode of infamy but of their racialized perceptibility and othering.

The mechanisms of racial differentiation remain deeply entrenched in (post) colonial imaginaries that indicate who does or does not constitute "European" in any case (De Genova 2016a, 2016b). While certain white European individuals and groups may be abused as supposed threats to national homogeneity, the Syrian-German tourist, the African passenger, or the Roma is always already that. She constitutes the "other other," infamous merely for not belonging to Europe's "transnational white ethnicity," whether "legally" in the space of EU-rope or not (Hansen 2004:50). She is the one stopped on German, Italian, or Greek streets as a target of racial stereotyping and profiling. And it is against her that Europe's inside can be defined as an ordered political and cultural community of predominant whiteness (van Houtum 2010). As David Theo Goldberg holds:

Europe remains … in some awkward sense presumptively European. It remains the fantasized space, the "homeland," of those always ever religiously white, of Christians secularized, of the prophylactically protected inner circle ranging from Anglo-Saxony to the Caucasus, from south of the North Pole to the northern shores of the Mediterranean. As flexible as Europe's cartographic and imagined borders throughout modernity have always been, Europe is thus a theological project, as much of racial as religious conviction. The increasingly brown tinge, oil polluting the water, seeping through and across the map of European whiteness, needs guarding against lest it smudge Europe's long-imagined make-up. (2009:186)

While, in Foucault's piece, the authority of the king was reinforced through the punishment of supposedly infamous behavior (more than the subjects' "being" per se), the possibility of punishment has become a generalized condition for nonwhite "others" in contemporary Greece. The one to be punished need not be singled out, as her racialized otherness and her (potential) movements are sufficient attributes to draw the border regime's attention. It is her very nonwhite presence in a particular space that is at odds with the regime. In diffused border collisions, punishment is exerted in a variety of ways, impinging on subjects throughout and beyond their journeys.

What Jaser's family experienced was the excessive violence of the border regime that sought to make their lives unbearable. It was this regime that not only produced them as infamous and therefore precariously illegalized subjects in the first place, but that continuously exposed them to forms of violence that they then sought to flee. The initial reasons for escape, their persecution in war-torn Syria, prompted their practice of flight, which, in Greek EU-rope, became the reason for further persecution. Ultimately, Europe's border practitioners did not prevent most of Jaser's family members from moving on, which, in many ways, cannot univocally be read as either a failure of the border regime or as the success of migration's inventiveness and uncontrollability, but only as continuous border entanglements.

Jaser's family did not overcome the violence of the border regime once they reached Germany. The productivity of its violence exceeded moments of border collision and spectacle in Greek transit (De Genova 2013a:1183). De Genova suggests that, rather than mere technologies of exclusion, European border practices "serve to sort out the most able-bodied, disproportionately favoring the younger, stronger, and healthier among prospective (labor) migrants" (2015c). As the experiences of Jaser's family show, these ruthless selection practices imply forms of excessive violence that live on as physical and mental scars, as loss, trauma, despair, or depression.

Some of Jaser's extended family members disappeared on their journey. Elderly parents were left behind and contact was lost. Many experienced brutal and abusive police controls and detention. A young disabled relative was sent via plane and with falsified papers to Italy. We searched for him but he remains missing. A young woman was murdered by Greek border guards, right beside her mother. Many of the women and children of the family were subjected to sexual harassment and rape. A close relative died in their small flat and his body was not removed, for days tormenting the family and especially the children. The beating, torturing, raping, killing, and dying does not stop at the gates of "Europe" but continues along the external Greek borderscapes, within the urban space of Athens and elsewhere. "If we had known what happened here in Europe, we would not have come" is a phrase uttered innumerable times. Are, then, people on the move not exposed to an excess of violence that, as horror, "is a matter of what one cannot escape, one is forced to witness, and that haunts one's mind, psyche, and body"? (Debrix and Barder 2012:19).

What occurs in the force field of Europe's border regime is, indeed, horrible. At the same time, while such violence is haunting and deadly for some, this does not mean that it, in the majority of cases, "freezes and stops the body or human action" (Debrix and Barder 2012:19; cf. Kristeva 1982:4). The many border collisions that Jaser's family endured meant, for most members at least, neither exclusion nor extermination, but "subordinate inclusion" (De Genova 2013a). However, their eventual (physical) overcoming of borders did equally not translate into "autonomous" escape. The ones who suffered the most or died were the (physically) weakened, children, and the elderly, or those who were particularly exposed to sexual brutality, children and women. Those who did endure were marked nonetheless by the horrors that others in the family succumbed to. The experiences of Jaser's family animate a productive economy of violence, an endurance test with continuously disciplining and precaritizing effects. Instead of the old king's somewhat theatrically and clumsily reactionary violence, the regime's punishment of unwanted people on the move productively enveloped the family's movement and lingers on in the present and future.

Thinking of migration as primary, independent, or excessively autonomous does not do justice in capturing these border entanglements. The Greek–EUropean border dynamics outlined here indicate that contemporary European migration control is a finely stitched network of population control. The intensification and complexification of the border and those who seek to guard it imply a multiplication of points of encounter of migrant lives with governmental authorities. Contemporary European border politics is productive of despair that is felt and not easily shaken off by subjects who have experienced the effects of a regime that does not function hierarchically and centralistically, but through dispersed networks that (thereby) produce the pervasive potentiality of horrible racialized border collisions—not the king and his selective individual punishment, but a regime and its diffused violence. This capacity of the regime is excessive as it stretches far out, delocalizes and externalizes, while infesting novel spaces, geographically but also within bodies and minds themselves. The inaccessibility of EU-ropean visas conditioned and limited the family's migration routes. Barricaded land borders were only overcome with the aid of smugglers. Being stuck in Athens resulted from variously intersecting EU-ropean–Greek border dynamics, including increasingly sophisticated and communalized (biometric) data systems.

Thinking of migration as a specter that elusively haunts and "creatively subverts" sovereign states, as proposed by some, cannot account for this network of migration governance and its horrible productivity. The idea of autonomy which, for Samaddar, consists of "the supplement that remains after (the task of) government has been achieved" underestimates this excessive capacity that operates without (temporal) finality—nothing is achieved, but everything is in the process of being achieved. The often-evoked critique of alleged romanticizing tendencies within AoM, while expressed in various forms and contesting particular aspects, seems to arise from a discomfort intimately connected to the ascription of ontological primacy to migration, which seems closely bound up with an understanding of migration as excessive per se and of control as reactive per se.[25] In this conception, Foucault's "billions of existences" seem to form the subjects of contemporary migration, who "autonomously" exceed border practitioners and controls.

However, how can one remain imperceptible as a large family of nonwhite others in contemporary Europe, whose multiple children and elderly require constant care? When whiteness becomes or remains a differentiation function in border practices, excess and imperceptibility thought of as potential border subversions can translate into self-constraining immobility and into being stuck where one does not want to remain. In the case of Jaser's family, anonymity and imperceptibility turned into something oppressive. It is the subversive possibility found in anonymity that the border regime seeks to increasingly (and often successfully) subject to control. This is not to suggest, of course, that such oppression can ever be exhaustive.

The family's experiences reveal fragments of migration's entanglement with forms of control and dispense with often-upheld dualisms of control and excess.

Migration and border control form co-constitutive forces, interwoven in complex if conflictual ways. The family's attempted imperceptibility was the result of fear, but also provided for moments of rest and reorientation. In their flat they felt trapped, but it was there that they located ways to flee from their precarious situation. Imperceptibility and momentary anonymity can be violent as well as liberating. Whether or not we can assign primacy to the family's mobility or not seems less significant than the question of how they struggled onward and continuously resisted in order to overcome, in various ways, particular border obstacles and their horrors. What is certain is that their movements were not shadows that fleetingly bypassed the many border practitioners they encountered. They were not the figures of migration's "specter," not Foucault's billions of lives unencumbered by the king, but subjects entangled in the fine and differentiated network of border control. They were able to move on, maybe excessively so, but their movements were also engulfed by an excessive violence that beset their minds and bodies, and continued to do so long after reaching their desired destination.

Conclusion

This chapter is an account of how Greek EU-rope was experienced by those who came from somewhere and sought to settle elsewhere. Without doubt, those for whom this elsewhere is not Greece constitute a particular, though considerable, group of people on the move. The stories of Jaser's family are indicative of how many people in transit experience "being stuck" in Greek EU-rope. Prompted by EU-rope's pressure and the Greek government's will to seal off its borders and to cleanse the streets of Athens, police and border forces enacted Greece and EU-rope every day by (racially) identifying what was considered non-Greek and non-European, thereby enforcing violent encounters and collisions, saturating even moments of imperceptibility and anonymity.

Excess can, indeed, never be measured. It may emerge, however, in the will to struggle against various border configurations that seek to deny futures sought after by people on the move. Excess may thus also emerge in border collisions and the abyssal violence they often contain. Experiences of border horrors infiltrate memories and often linger on. Contemporary migration mobilities and their attempted control require us to reconceive the relationship between excess and control. Rather than seeking to find moments and episodes of hopeful anonymity, autonomous escape, or migration's supposed primacy, beginning with border entanglements allows one to inquire into this relationship more closely, into all its ambiguity, within which protagonists form not figures or specters but complex subjects, subjects able to be traumatized and resistant, scared and hopeful, captured and recalcitrant. Border collisions as well as the will and ability to struggle on and resist, perceptibly or imperceptibly, audibly or inaudibly, form today's "dramaturgies of the real," which, as border entanglements, are "in the greatest possible number of relations with reality."

NOTES

1. See, among others, Bojadžijev and Karakayalı (2007); Mezzadra (2004, 2011); Moulier Boutang (2007); Papadopoulos et al. (2008); Papadopoulos and Tsianos (2013).

2. *Oxford Dictionary* (2016), http://www.oxforddictionaries.com/definition /english/exceed, accessed on March 22, 2016.

3. This chapter speaks of "EU-rope" throughout. In this way it seeks to problematize frequently employed usages that equate the EU with Europe and Europe with the EU and suggests, at the same time, that Europe is not reducible to the institutions of the EU.

4. Interview with Yann Moulier-Boutang, Grundrisse, May 1992, my translation; http://www.grundrisse.net/grundrisse34/interview_mit_yann_moulierbouta.htm, accessed on January 5, 2014.

5. Frontex (2012b:5, 13); see also Human Rights Watch (2011).

6. Frontex (2010b).

7. Concerning Greek–Turkish agreements: "On migration, the two sides signed an agreement that allows Greece to send back migrants who illegally enter Greece from Turkey" (BBC News 2010). Concerning EU–Turkey agreements: "Turkey and the EU have signed a deal enabling EU countries to send back illegal migrants who entered the 28-nation bloc via Turkey" (BBC News 2013); cf. European Commission (2013).

8. Pro Asyl (2013:4); see also Amnesty International, "Greece: Frontier of Hope and Fear" (London: Amnesty International, 2014), 6.

9. Frontex (2012a).

10. Pro Asyl (2013:4); EurActiv (2012).

11. Human Rights Watch (2013).

12. Human Rights Watch (2013), 1, 14.

13. Amnesty International (2013).

14. Jaser assured me that I could use his name as he is not in a precarious legal situation in Germany. I will, however, only use his first name and change the names of his family members.

15. Jaser told me the story twice, first in the café in Exarcheia and then again a few days later when I recorded it.

16. Greek Council for Refugees, http://gcr.gr/index.php/en/about-gcr, accessed November 2, 2013.

17. Doctors with Doctors of the World in Athens confirmed a few days later that the impact of the blow had been severe, needing further professional medical treatment, antibiotics, and possibly surgery.

18. This name has been changed.

19. Doctors of the World Greece, http://www.mdmgreece.gr/en, accessed December 2, 2013.

20. Here I would like to thank Carolina for her linguistic and moral support.

21. ELENA (2013).

22. This name has been changed.

23. UNHCR Racist Violence Recording Network (2013).

24. Council of the European Union (2014).

25. See, for example: Ahmed (1999:333); Benz and Schwenken (2005); McNevin (2013); Mezzadra (2010b); Scheel (2013a:13); Sharma (2009).

9

Dubliners

Unthinking Displacement, Illegality, and Refugeeness
within Europe's Geographies of Asylum

FIORENZA PICOZZA

In recent years there has been a proliferation of categories by which non-European people on the move are labeled (Giudici 2013:62; Zetter 2007). Think about "unreturnable detainees," "failed asylum-seekers," "unaccompanied minors," or "trafficking victims." In all these particular cases, yet also in the broader categories of "refugee" or "illegal migrant," the border gaze is twofold: it is performed by the state and its citizens, but it is also unconsciously internalized by those subjected to that gaze (Khosravi 2010:76). The discursive realm of what we call "migration" is much more ambiguous than the obvious regulatory practices of border control, detention, and deportation. Labels do not merely classify; they establish an order in the life of the other, producing the illusion that their essence is immediately accessible, visible, and recognizable (Benasayag and Schmit 2005:75). Through language, the epistemic violence of the border is extended into the everyday life of migrants: as Khosravi remarks, they are not "seen" as individuals but "read" as types (2010:76).

Among these types, *dublinati* is a familiar word to those involved in migrant relief, reception, or legal aid in Italy. Literally, it means "Dublined"—as if "to Dublin" someone was a verb—in reference to the procedures of the Dublin Regulation.[1] The aim of this European legal framework is to rapidly determine the "competent" state for the assessment of an asylum claim, by establishing a hierarchy of criteria. Although the predominant criterion should be the existence of family links in a member state, asylum-seekers are seldom actively encouraged to disclose such information; therefore, the last criterion often proves to be the most often applied, namely the assignation of responsibility to the state through which the applicant first illegally entered the territory of the EU.[2] Those who attempt to apply elsewhere can be returned to the "competent state," and it is to this kind of "returnees" (i.e., deportees) that the term *dublinati* applies in Italian, and, increasingly, the term *Dubliners* in English (Brekke 2012; CIR 2010; Kivistö 2013; Papadimitriou and Papageorgiou 2005).

The Dublin Regulation is based on a twofold falsehood: that there are equal standards of protection and welfare access in any signatory state; and that it is physically possible to illegally enter any of them, so that the distribution of the asylum "burden" would be equal throughout Europe.

This policy is but one piece of a wider regime of mobility control that allows states not only to deport migrants "back home," but also to a "safe third country," literally bouncing them back from one place to another. Moreover, Europe's imaginative and legal geographies have been shifting and expanding: beyond the EU's member states, the Dublin Regulation has also been adopted by Iceland, Liechtenstein, Norway, and Switzerland. These bilateral agreements reverse migration trajectories, turning them into transnational "flows of expulsion" (Mezzadra and Neilson 2003:8; Rigo 2005:6). The conflicting forces of state deportations and migrants' restless mobilities thus produce multiple ruptures and dislocations, resulting in increasingly "fragmented" migration patterns (Collyer 2007). Throughout these trajectories, the distinction between "legality" and "illegality" gets blurred, as migrants—as well as state practices[3]—easily transit from one condition to the other and back (Giudici 2013; Schuster 2005). Once inside "Europe," asylum-seekers can ultimately be subjected to further displacement by means of the Dublin procedure—the transfer (i.e., deportation) of an applicant from a signatory state to the "competent" one. Once protection is obtained under domestic regulations, refugees cannot work and reside elsewhere but that particular country; thus, both asylum-seekers and recognized refugees who move across Europe are subjected to a specific condition of "deportability" (De Genova 2002). Especially because of this condition, I extend the term *Dubliners* to all asylum-seekers and refugees who move within the space of "Europe" or wish to do so in the future, regardless of whether they are Dublin "returnees" or whether they move autonomously.

By stretching the label of "Dubliner," this chapter endeavors to "unthink" migration categories as epistemological devices, analyzing the role of the law in shaping them. Increasingly, EU legislation itself produces illegality, displacement, and refugeeness. It does so through border surveillance, visa imposition, and bureaucratization of asylum—to put it simply, by significantly reducing the possibilities of legal entry. It is crucial to interrogate this productive process, rather than assuming that policy-informed categories regarding the "root causes" of migration should be discrete analytical domains.

The trajectories of the "new Dubliners" are so much influenced by the law—from the impossibility of meeting visa requirements and the consequent necessity of undertaking illegal journeys, to the obligation to reside in a country they have not chosen—that they cannot be reduced to categories such as "illegals," "asylum-seekers," or "economic migrants." While presented as ontological and moral qualities, these labels are uncritically inherited from legal and administrative discourses, and thus reflect the interests and perspective of the state (De Genova 2002; Karakayali and Rigo 2010; Scalettaris 2007; Scheel and Squire 2014). They are built upon a dichotomous discourse around enemies (terrorists, benefit scroungers, criminals, illegals) and victims (refugees, trafficked people, minors). Othered in a strong socio-legal divide between us (citizens) and them (aliens), migrants' legitimacy to be here must be continuously tested through a hierarchy of desperation and then, perhaps, granted by a benevolent act of the state.

The fieldwork that informs this paper was carried out mainly with Afghan migrants in 2014. The choice, however, was not dictated by "cultural" determinants. My aim is not to explain why they decided to migrate, but rather to question Western discourses of mobility at large, while exposing the lived consequences of the relevant EU policies. Afghan "Dubliners" are among the most mobile[4] and shifting populations in Europe (Schuster 2011a:408), particularly in Italy. They might have just arrived and be heading further north, or they might be Dublin returnees from other European states; yet others have been deported to Afghanistan, and are now on their second illegalized journey (Schuster and Majidi 2014); a few of them have settled permanently in Italy; and a final group come to reapply for asylum after being refused in a Northern European country. This heterogeneity embodies a counternarrative of migration and displacement in opposition to their traditional unidirectional representation (De Genova 2005:56)—the migrant coming from a "home" to a "hosting country" with clear-cut reasons for doing so (and with greater or lesser legitimacy within the purview of the law). Questions of "home" and "belonging" are especially problematic in the case of Afghan refugees (Braakman 2005): in terms of identity politics, although shifting, interethnic and linguistic divisions may be strongly pronounced (Schetter 2005); furthermore, following long-term conflict in the area, many Afghan asylum-seekers have been raised in Iran or Pakistan—which complicates questions of the "authenticity" of their asylum claims. Both factors imply considerable sociocultural and political heterogeneity within the group.

The group of Afghan young men who have been the subjects of my research in Italy and beyond had virtually all been subjected to the Dublin procedure (or to similar ones) at least once—and in most cases several times—especially between Austria and Hungary, or between Italy and Greece.[5] Moreover, at the moment I met them, whether in the status of returnees or while autonomously reapplying for asylum in Italy after being refused elsewhere, their experiences of rupture were very similar.

Italy offers challenging insights into the uneven implementation of EU regulations, and it sheds light on the different kinds of subjects produced by the discursive, legal, and disciplinary regime. Italy, in fact, has a double status: on the one hand, due to its geographical position, it is at the forefront of the southern European frontier, alongside Spain, Greece, and Bulgaria, and is therefore one of the major recipients of Dublin returnees (EUROSTAT 2014). Yet it lacks a satisfactory system of reception, in spite of the Reception Conditions Directive (Directive 2003/9/EC). Italian cities are open-air laboratories for understanding the extension of borders in everyday life through socio-spatial segregation and the reduction of interactions between asylum-seekers and Italians mainly to relations of assistance. On the other hand, Italy sometimes does grant protection to people who have been refused elsewhere in the EU. The fact that this practice is undertaken against EU proscriptions should not be underestimated; as Garelli and Tazzioli (2013a:1005) have noted in the context of the "North Africa emergency," the inconsistencies of the Italian asylum system reveal interstitial spaces in which human mobility can exert a certain autonomy. The Dubliners' spatial and temporal heterogeneity emerges within the encounter of their spatial practices and the uneven implementation and lack of harmonization at the regime level. Their cases not only help in "unthinking" migration categories, but also in nuancing questions of the agency of migrants, exposing both their constrictions and their creativity in participating in the reconfiguration of the European space. Despite the system of differentiated citizenship central to the formation of the Schengen space of free movement, refugees partly benefit from it: although they cannot legally reside and work elsewhere than where they have been granted protection, they still can travel.[6] Due to the casual nature of informal unskilled work, they often leave for a short time and then return, thus somehow partaking in the navigation of a highly connected and relatively shrunken European space, provided by visa-free, low-cost travel, and by transnational social networks.

It will therefore emerge that the Dubliner "experience" manifests itself as an interplay between legality and illegality, whereby obtaining papers in one country while "illegally" living in another, at the very least, provides a guarantee against deportation "back home." Accordingly, I inquire into how the Dubliner condition is both legally produced and subjectively experienced, aiming to show how the law has an impact not only on those subject to its procedures (e.g., deportation) but also on countless others who internalize it in new ways of being persons (Andersson 2014b:16). In fact, disruptive practices such as expulsions and deportations produce existential conditions of precariousness, restlessness, and stuckness at the same time.

Along these lines, Sarah Willen (2007) has suggested three analytical frames that can be useful in approaching both the socio-legal production of migrants' statuses and their lived experiences: the legal, sociopolitical, and existential dimensions. In the Dubliners' case, the importance of the legal realm speaks for itself, due to the inherent presence of the law, courts, detention, expulsions, and deportations in their lives. The sociopolitical dimension is equally pervasive, especially relating to the socio-spatial segregation that Dubliners endure, the multiple administrative identities they assume, and the several ruptures they undergo in moving from one country to the other. Finally, the existential aspect assumes a peculiar character, according to the existential quandary arising from whether better opportunities might be found elsewhere. In the lived experience of the Dubliners, illegality and refugeeness are not merely "anomalous juridical status[es]" but also "practical, materially consequential and deeply interiorized mode[s] of being" (Peutz and De Genova 2010:14), affecting their everyday experiences of time, space, embodiment, sociality, and self.

Caught between Refugeeness and Illegality

Qasim was twenty-six when I met him in Rome in late 2010, in the aftermath of his deportation from Germany. He told me his story one morning in the Questura—the police headquarters—where he was finally obtaining renewal of his subsidiary protection, valid for three years.[7] He had been waiting for a year, meanwhile holding a crumpled slip of paper proving his status. That morning his papers were finally issued, but they would have lasted only two more years. Qasim had been raised in Pakistan and came from a fairly well-off family. His older brothers and cousins were living in Munich and, as a student in his early twenties, he had desired to join them in Europe. Unable to obtain sponsorship for a Schengen visa, he was issued one for Turkey instead, where his actual illegal journey started at the Greek border—a border he would never forget, having carried a sick fellow traveler on his shoulders for five kilometers until the companion died before making it to the other side.

Upon arrival in Crotone, hidden in a lorry on a ship, he was photo-identified and fingerprinted, thus tying his destiny to Italy—a country where he had never before thought he would find himself. When interviewed by the Commissione,[8] he declared he had been living in Afghanistan, and recounted a story that could fit the asylum procedure's requisite victimhood parameters. In fact, apart from regularization programs for particular working-sector migrants (Levinson 2005), targeting those already irregularly present on the territory, there are few chances for migrants to be legally granted entry to Italy. Among these few, there is the possibility of qualifying as a "refugee" (Giordano 2014:20).

As soon as he received his papers, Qasim was off to Germany, his original destination. He managed to live there for two years, while reapplying for asylum. Hoping to improve his chances, he would burn his fingertips before each identification appointment. However, he would soon discover the bitter reality: fingertip skin grows back, and it does so with exactly the same patterns. After a few unsuccessful identifications, he was stopped at the border with Austria, fingerprinted, and, as the match was found, sent back to Italy, where he slept for a few months in an abandoned train along the rails of Rome's Ostiense station.

In Rome, refugees and asylum-seekers can be hosted in reception centers run by private companies; former hospitals or hotels, the vast majority are located in isolated suburban areas. Their capacity is much lower than the number of people applying, and waiting times for allocation are around three or four months, which means that a great number of people actually squat or sleep outdoors for long periods of time. In recent years, Afghan migrants have been the protagonists of the area surrounding Ostiense station, in the south of the city. Similar to the area of Omonia in Athens (Cabot 2014), or the Tenth Arrondissement parks in Paris (Sciurba 2009), Ostiense was a "node" (Khosravi 2010:32), a stopover where undocumented travelers could share "the mobile commons of migration" (Papadopulos and Tsianos 2013): meet fellow travelers, exchange information, find—and give—care and support, build networks, and participate in informal economies. Moreover, the site was the object of several social interventions by Italian NGOs, such as free medical checkups and food delivery. Until 2010, both Afghans in transit and permanent stayers would assemble makeshift beds with cardboard and blankets in the sunken foundations of an abandoned building site, known as La Buca—"the hole." Later on, they would sleep in tents alongside platform 15 until their eviction in 2012. Finally, a tensile structure, known as *Il Tendone*—"the big tent"—was opened by the municipality a little further south, in the suburb of Tor Marancia—a night-only temporary accommodation with a capacity of 150 bed spaces, on the corner of the hosting center San Michele and Casale d'Emerode, a building occupied by a housing-struggle group composed of both migrants and Italians.

In this context, Qasim left for Germany a second time but, after being involved in a fight, was arrested, detained, and, once again, deported to Italy, this time with a reentry ban.[9] In Rome, he found accommodation in a night-only hosting center, where he shared a room with four other people. Working as a cleaner, with a very early morning shift, he faced the emptiness of the rest of the day, strolling about Rome and pondering his last five years lost in transit. Qasim endured further interruptions: after returning to Pakistan[10] for a year to visit his family, he went back to Italy to renew his documents before their expiration date, and, eventually, left for Paris, where a friend would help him find a job and (as of our most recent contact) where he is living his life, who knows for how long.

Qasim's trajectory epitomizes the protracted (seemingly permanent) mid-journey in which many Dubliners live; they seem "stuck in transit," spending between five and ten years struggling to settle—legally, socially, economically, and existentially. As the experiences of rupture and new beginnings are so familiar to many of them, their lived experience in Europe resembles a sort of "limbo" (Schuster 2005:768).

Their example exposes, first of all, the paradoxes of "refugeeness": Qasim could be regarded as a "bogus" refugee, since he was not raised in Afghanistan and did not fear for his life. Nevertheless, he deeply felt the authenticity of his "refugeeness": he often used to blame "the West" for having invaded Afghanistan, consequently forcing his family to seek refuge in Pakistan; otherwise he would have been living in Afghanistan, which he regarded as his home. In addition to this, whatever his sociopolitical condition prior to departure, the experience of the illegal journey had made a refugee out of him by the traumas he had endured: imprisonment, homelessness, assaults, and a brush with death. Whether fleeing persecution or not, those subjected to severe visa impositions are forced underground. They undergo existential experiences that can leave permanent socio-emotional marks, thus confining them to a totally different realm of life from that of "authorized" travelers.

These paradoxes notwithstanding, the category of "refugee" stands out as politically central in the contemporary migration regime. The latter legitimates some sectors of unauthorized mobility, following precise parameters of victimhood. As Giordano puts it: "illness travels better than poverty. So does victimization" (2014:21). Such is the case of asylum-seekers, unaccompanied minors (Vacchiano 2014), seriously ill individuals (Fassin 2012:83), and trafficked victims (Mai 2014:178); like the "illegal" migrant, they are socio-legally produced, yet presented as ontological, moral qualities.

The moral dimension of discourses around asylum migration is a key tool of contemporary border regimes at a global level, and particularly in the European case; as the work of Didier Fassin (2012) and Miriam Ticktin (2011) has powerfully shown in the French context, constructing refugees as "victims" to rescue, "lives" to save, and "human beings" to help is a particular political and social gesture that relegates the other to the receiving end of a "benevolent"— and sovereign—act of the state and, by extension, of its citizens. Framing the relationship through concepts such as "compassion" and "innocence" establishes an unbridgeable gap between European citizens and non-European irregular travelers: "those who can feel and act on their compassion . . . and those who must be the subjects (or objects) of it, . . . those who have the power to protect and those who need protection" (Ticktin 2015). Ultimately, there is a politics of victimhood at stake that reasserts a politics of otherness and exclusion of refugees from the political arena. In this way, the refugee issue is not framed as a matter of rights, social justice, and equality, but rather a matter of feelings, or at best "European values" (Yildiz et al. 2016).

Such a politics of victimhood percolates deeply into the humanitarian "management" of refugees: since their vulnerability must be assessed and certified through specific politics of truth and authenticity (Khosravi 2010:33), they are expected to follow bureaucratically defined trajectories aimed at their "protection" and "integration." A broad series of actors are involved in the process: not only institutional actors such as police and government officials responsible for regularization procedures, but also NGOs' medical and psychological "experts" providing certification of torture, trauma, violence, and abuse (Fassin 2012:110; Giudici 2013:74). Ultimately, the credibility of such proofs and accounts draws "biographical borders" between expulsion and recognition (Mai 2014:175).

On the other end of the spectrum, Qasim's story interrogates the concept of "illegality," both as a lived condition and as a socio-legal production (De Genova 2002). Qasim's life was much happier in Munich than in Rome: he had a house, family, friends, a job, and a girlfriend; a normal life. While illegal migrants are often linked to a condition of "abjectivity" (Willen 2007:11), that might not always be the case; in order to have a fulfilling life, a good network is equally or even more significant than legal status. Moreover, Qasim's trajectory sheds light on the contingency of the "illegal" status: an asylum-seeker entering Europe is first and foremost an "illegal" migrant, since asylum-related channels to migrate "legally" are almost nonexistent. Yet a guest worker whose visa expires because of losing her job automatically also becomes "illegal," although entry into that country might have happened legally. And a refugee who has papers in one EU country but resides in another is also a kind of "illegal." In other words, rather than inhabiting a single condition of being "illegal," people on the move are "illegalized" (De Genova 2002) and "vulnerabilized" (Mai 2014) in a wide variety of ways.

Tracing back the history of the EU space of circulation, Karakayali and Rigo (2010) have shown how these socio-legal categories are a matter of governance. Different figures—"guest workers," "refugees," "illegal migrants"—have emerged in correspondence with the preoccupations of the state. These labels, however, do not represent coherent social groups and, most importantly, they obscure the fact that it is the EU legislative system itself that produces clandestinity, irregularity, displacement, and "refugeeness"—and, ultimately, also renders these conditions profitable (Andersson 2014b; Rodier 2012).

With the deployment of language categories, the border acts metaphorically, influencing the everyday reinforcement of the division between citizens and aliens (Vacchiano 2011b), and between authorized and unauthorized aliens. The specific classification of migrant "types" is used to intervene upon them, for either humanitarian or security purposes, and must be understood within "the proliferation of dematerialized spatial and moral borders" (Mai 2014:175). This vocabulary has so much percolated into the everyday that Eurocentric hegemonic discourses of migration operate even when academics, policy makers, activists, and journalists feel sympathy toward migrants. The legalistic language, in fact, indirectly contributes to shape "the way individuals think and act" (Pécoud 2010:16).

The unwitting complicity of migration studies should not be underestimated: by focusing mostly on the causes of displacement, the conceptualization of "forced" and "labor" migration indirectly fosters a moral division between "good" and "bad" migrants (Anderson 2008:2), while diverting attention from the wider regime of mobility control—in Sharma's words (2005), "the making of a Global Apartheid." Yet, most importantly, the very notion of "migrant" is inherently "nation-state-centric" (Anderson et al. 2010:10); while it is a product of the border, migration studies refetishize it (De Genova 2013b:253), devoting most research only to transnational mobility, thus indirectly reasserting the legitimacy of borders and national sovereignty. However, an increasing effort to disrupt this "methodological nationalism" (Glick Schiller and Wimmer 2002) has emerged within the realm of critical border and migration studies; several contributions, including many in this volume, have been framed from the perspective of contemporary "border struggles" and the relevant reconfigurations of political space, seen as lenses through which to interrogate and denaturalize the state, its discourses, and its practices (Mezzadra and Neilson 2013; De Genova 2015a).

Restlessness and Stuckness: A Temporal Regulation
of Precariousness

In Dubliners' eyes, the Dublin Regulation is an obscure system (Schuster 2011a; Szczepanikova 2013). Besides not having previous experience with the law, the police, courts, and detention, they have gone through a long, unsafe journey to reach Europe; once arrived, it seems inconceivable to be forced to live in a country they have not chosen. The Dublin Regulation epitomizes the mandate for state management to prevail over migrants' self-determination, which starkly reveals the Eurocentric view of refugees and asylum-seekers as objects of control and/or charitable intervention (Jackson 2002:84): their presumed desperation disqualifies them from any entitlement to making autonomous decisions about their present condition or future prospects.

However, the lack of homogeneity among different EU member states in terms of Dublin readmissions, asylum acceptance rates, reception standards, and deportations to the countries of origin breaches the image of a harmonious, tight, and solid EU system, thus leading returnees to attempt to move again, despite possible failure (Schuster 2011a; Brekke and Brochmann 2014). It is because of this determination to pursue their desires and freedom that people arrive at the self-mutilating act of burning their fingerprints, quite a common practice among asylum-seekers. This is portrayed in mainstream media as a suspicious means of concealing one's identity, deployed because of migrants' purported criminality; however, their fingerprints are but an embodiment of national borders. Not only do they testify to the identity declared in the first identification; they also inescapably fix each asylum-seeker's identity to a "competent" country.

No wonder that the EURODAC[11] database, where asylum-seekers' fingerprints are stored together with other personal data, was the first large-scale EU biometric information system (Feldman 2012). In fact, technology has a particularly significant role within EU governmentality, since its borders are both physically militarized and biometrically extended into migrants' bodies. In his account of the development of a global system of identification between the 1880s and the 1910s, Adam McKeown (2008) has stressed the role of photography, fingerprinting, and anthropometric measurement in creating people's "unique" identities. Formerly collected in centralized filing systems, and later internationalized, this information has contributed to a particular understanding of human mobility: migration categories (racial, occupational, kin, political) shift over time and countries, yet "the individualities and nations that are objects and frames of these categories are almost never questioned" (McKeown 2008:14).

After the first identification, the EURODAC database indicates the stage of the asylum claim and its denial or granting. According to the Dublin Regulation, a rejected asylum-seeker cannot apply in another signatory state. If she tries to do so, the second state can either request her transfer to the first member state or carry out a "return" (i.e., deportation) procedure to her country of origin. However, national derogations of EU directives are quite a distinct matter.[12] Some asylum-seekers have scarce or vague knowledge of the different countries' protection standards and acceptance rates; yet others know about Italy's "generosity" in granting asylum—and its reluctance to return applicants to other member states. Hence Italy's double status: it could be a prison for those who have been previously identified there while wishing to go elsewhere—as in Qasim's case. Yet, for others, Italy represents the only chance of being granted asylum (Schuster 2005:768)—as is the case for those who have been refused elsewhere.

Migration is popularly represented as a mere response to poverty, underdevelopment, or conflict—consider, for instance, the various UNHCR or IOM reports on migration and resettlement. Conversely, critical migration scholars have stressed how migrants are active participants in the construction of the larger migratory reality, and a powerful, creative force in dealing with border controls (Papadopulos et. al. 2008:202). As Karakayali and Rigo (2010) show, administrative categories come after migration practices, not before, thanks to people's ability "to confound the established spatial orders" (Gupta and Ferguson 1992).

However, the interplay of structural constraints and autonomy is complex, and, certainly, Dubliners' trajectories are mostly circular or fragmented, marked by temporariness and precariousness, and by the intricacies of achieving stable legal status. "Interruptions and discontinuities such as waiting, hiding [and] unexpected diversions" (Andrijasevic 2010:158) have deep consequences for Dubliners' experiences of time, body, and productivity. The precaritization and clandestinization of migrants' lives carried out through practices of expulsion, detention, and deportation contribute to a temporal, as well as spatial, regulation of migration, a paradigm of "decelerated circulation" (Papadopulos et al. 2008:198). In this "pedagogy of labor" (Vacchiano 2011a:4), characterized by the experience of waiting, the body is often disassociated from "its direct economic utilization" (Karakayali and Rigo 2010:133), yet prepared for its involvement in unskilled casual labor. In particular, the Italian sociopolitical configuration of asylum, and its interminable and obscure bureaucracy, tends to prevent stable settlement while catering to the needs of flexible capitalism by providing sources of unskilled, cheap, exploited labor (Giudici 2013:62). Accordingly, several authors agree that the border regime selects mobility, rather than freezing it; it does so through apparatuses (e.g., detention and hosting centers) which confine, yet do not block, migrants' trajectories (De Genova 2015c; Sciurba 2009:231; Tsianos and Karakayali 2010; Vacchiano 2011b).

It is noteworthy that, in Italy, third-sector workers are subjected to a similar regime: most companies have six-month contracts—ironically called "projects," thus imposing on both their "guests" and workers an endless precariousness. The neoliberal privatization of the "nonprofit" sector delegates the task of enforcing borders in everyday practice to a casual and precarious workforce (Vacchiano 2011a), the "guardians" and "judges" of the veridicality of refugees' claims and life histories. According to the paradigm of the assisted refugee, one should be passive in order to be a true victim, genuinely traumatized and needy (Fassin and Rechtman 2009:252). Any deviance from this established pattern, any autonomous choice on how to spend one's own time out of the prescribed activities, or simply a lack of manifested gratitude can cause suspicion. At the core of this moral economy, this mixture of bureaucratic care and disciplinary control that Didier Fassin (2012) calls "humanitarian reason," there is a paradigm of "scarcity" (Vacchiano 2011b:182): since resources are limited, they are not a fundamental right but a benevolent donation of the state, subject to certain conditions.

The explosion of the "Mafia Capitale" scandal, involving structural corruption within Rome's reception system, brought this purported "scarcity" under significant scrutiny. In December 2014, a police inquiry revealed that a network of high-ranking local politicians, former neofascist militants turned full-fledged criminals, and social cooperatives were rigging public contracts for the management of reception centers. According to one of the main suspects, the founder of the social cooperative "29 Giugno" Salvatore Buzzi, the "racket" in refugees was "much more profitable than drug-trafficking" (Povoledo 2014). These events were presented by the mass media only under the prism of the chronic penetration of organized crime into Italian political and economic life. However, it was the pursuit of profit that drove the interests of these criminal groups and their political patrons, thus highlighting that profitability is inherent in the dynamics of migration management (Andersson 2014b; Gammeltoft-Hansen and Nyberg Sørensen 2013). Thus, the episode of the "Mafia Capitale" scandal points to the need for research to also investigate whether and how deep this corruption has percolated into the mindset of precariously employed social workers, whose need for a job and a livelihood may make them eager to maintain the presence of a captive population of vulnerable (and structurally disempowered) people, not unlike the interests of the centers' profiteering managements (Carsetti 2015:45).

The Dubliners are caught in these complex dynamics of interest that take on the form of care, control, profit, and waiting. In Italy, examples of political self-organization among them are very few, due also to the passivization promoted by the recent humanitarianization—and consequent depoliticization—of the border (Walters 2011a), especially evident in the mushrooming of reception centers for "Dubliners and vulnerable people." We should be careful, however, in judging these migration trajectories as "unsuccessful." For those who travel illegally, settling is a long and difficult task, and "success" can be judged only in the long run. Despair has its counterpart in hope, "the blessing, the sin, and the curse of mankind" (Traven 1991:119). The process of migration, in fact, implies an "ambivalence," whereby creativity, hope for the future, nostalgia, vulnerability, and alienation coexist (Rapport 2013:152). It is precisely this ambivalence that animates Dubliners' "struggle for recognition and residence in Europe" (Schuster 2011a:403), despite the risks of being deported and displaced again and again.

This interplay between hope and despair exposes the Dubliner as an unresolved "self-in-transit." There is a stream in critical migration studies that stresses the question of desertion, escape, and desire to exit (Giordano 2014:65; Jackson 2013:2; Mai 2014:183; Mezzadra 2001; Papadopulos et al. 2008). When life becomes "intolerable" due to any experience that might be felt as a "social death," migration becomes a "way out," although the hopes projected onto the foreign land "may prove illusory" (Jackson 2013:2). As people are separated from their familiar surroundings, social relations, and language—the very medium of consciousness—their self becomes a "self-in-transit," marked by change and movement (Dobson 2004:88). Dubliners can be seen as characterized by an "unresolved" self-in-transit: they are unable to "stay put," constantly facing the dilemma of whether a better life can be found elsewhere—or else*when*—while they are in the desired place, but they wait for their documents, meanwhile living in a reception center. In this displacement in space and time, "real" life seems to be always postponed. Dubliners seem never to fully arrive at their destination. And so they restlessly keep moving.

Restlessness and fragmentation manifest themselves in multiple "modalities of consciousness" (Jackson 2002:81): Dubliners assume—and internalize—different legal/administrative identities in order to enhance their possibility of obtaining regular papers; they transit through different sociocultural spaces and different senses of belonging; and they are simultaneously objects of legal, social, or political discourses and autonomous subjects, authors of their destinies. These shifts are embodied in specific manners. I have alluded to how experiences such as waiting, hiding, and detention disassociate the body from its direct productivity—thus disassociating the self from the body, in what has been called a "schizoid experience of unembodiment" (R. D. Laing, *The Divided Self*, quoted in Dobson 2004:101). My interlocutors often daydreamed—an experience that separates the self "from the flesh of the body" (Dobson 2004:101)—either long-ing for their former life or projecting their desires for a future elsewhere. This disassociation affected their bodily posture, rendering it "closed," timid, and in tension. If not lost in thought, they were in any case "absent," distracted by their mobile phones, through which they constantly communicated with dis-tant friends. In the context of Algerians in France, Sayad (2004) has shown how migrants experience a "double absence," physically absent from their place of origin and psychically absent from the hosting country. However, Dubliners are subjected to further displacement by means of the Dublin Regulation, thus ex-periencing multiple absences. They represent a breach in the linear logic of the migrant who comes from one place and goes to another.

Three Narratives of Desire, Autonomy, and Deportability

Ismail and Farhad had come to Europe at different times and for different rea-sons. Throughout the year before I met them they had been inseparable: they shared the same room in a hosting center and later in another one, and they also attended the same Italian language courses. Of the two, Ismail was the more determined to stay in Rome. He had already been granted full refugee status and spoke Italian well. Although he was already twenty-six years old, he was attend-ing the terza media, the third year of middle school. This stage is compulsory for refugees who want to pursue their studies, unless they are able to provide a certified translation of their qualifications. After the terza media exam, Ismail would have had access to high school and, perhaps, in the future, to university. He was six years older than Farhad, which gave him the appearance of the older brother.

Whereas Ismail had found haven and stability in Rome, Farhad had not. As for many others who had previously lived in Denmark, Sweden, Germany, or the UK, Farhad's rupture from his former life in Norway had left a deep mark on his perception of time, space, and sociability. Apparently shy, not comfort-able speaking Italian, he was silent most of the time, and his attention during language classes was constantly diverted by his nostalgia—until he decided to take flight again. Ismail called me early on a Saturday morning in May to in-form me that Farhad had suddenly left. It did not surprise me, though: Farhad had told me, roughly a month earlier, that I might not find him in Rome upon my return: "You know, we're like birds. We always fly away." Dobson (2004:12) notes the suddenness of the decision to leave, relating it to the Latin etymology of the word *refugee*: *fugis*, to flee, and the prefix *re*, denoting recurrence.

Farhad had entered Norway as a minor in 2011, having been lucky enough not to have his fingerprints taken en route. Upon turning eighteen two years later, he had claimed asylum and waited more than a year for the decision, meanwhile provided by the government with housing and 3,000 kroner per month. He fell in love with a Norwegian girl and taught her the Dari language, while he was learning the local language. When his asylum claim was refused, the little stability he had found was suddenly interrupted. He was given a week's time to voluntarily leave the country; otherwise he would have been deported to Afghanistan. Searching through information on the web and consulting friends, he opted for Italy in the hope of obtaining protection there. His girlfriend came along and slept outdoors with him for a week in Rome; eventually, he convinced her to return home while he found temporary accommodation in the "big tent" of Tor Marancia.

Like Farhad, many others had been refused in Northern European countries and were now applying in Italy. Some had been deported back to Afghanistan—mostly UK applicants—and had later returned to Europe. Farhad was told in the Questura to wait nine months for his fingerprints to be deleted from the EURODAC system. A year and a half later, he was granted full refugee status. Constantly haunted by the urgency of supporting his family back home, but lacking work opportunities in Rome, he surrendered nonetheless to the prospect of leaving—this time to Britain. "The trip's not so bad," a UK-based friend had told him on the phone. "You can make it even on your own, if you can't afford to pay traffickers." Ismail was very upset with the decision: Farhad had left without money and without papers; moreover, he did not speak any English, which meant that he was almost completely lacking the required "capital" (Khosravi 2010:14) for any illegal movement, in terms of both finances and knowledge.

Refugees who receive protection in a Schengen country can partly benefit from the regime of free circulation, since they are not subject to border control between member states; yet the same does not hold for those wishing to travel to the UK, who fall under severe visa impositions, and whose living conditions in the surroundings of Calais are barely tolerable. Farhad spent a month there; several times a day he would try his luck, hiding in a truck. Found, each time, by the UK Border Agency, he would be escorted out of the port.[13] Facing continuous evictions and assaults by the French police in the forest camp where he was sleeping, he eventually hid in a lorry going the wrong way and ended up in Hamburg. This twist of fate resonates with several stories I collected; "an unbearable sequence of sheer happenings" (Hannah Arendt, *Men in Dark Times*, quoted in

Jackson 2002:103), such as losing an important phone number or ending up in the wrong lorry, can determine the whole course of future events.

When caught by the police in Hamburg, Farhad declared himself to be a minor and was allocated to an accommodation center. Again he traveled to Calais and again he faced removals and the threat of deportation. Discouraged by the precarious living conditions and fearing he would never reach England, Farhad returned to Hamburg, where he would reapply for asylum upon reaching "the age of majority." It is crucial to dwell on the liminal spaces that Farhad had been crossing, particularly the Calais "Jungle" and the various hosting centers. They are spaces where only a migrant would find him/herself; moreover, in his pursuing recognition in a place where he could also build a new livelihood, he had no chance but to assume different identities, in order to fit the politically "protected" sectors of unauthorized migration.

Back in London, between my trips to Italy, I shared my preoccupation with Farhad's journey with Khalid, who had made it through the Channel Tunnel from Calais roughly a year before. We used to meet in an Afghan restaurant in south London on Wednesdays, his only day off. Khalid had been working, from his very first day in the UK, in a halal butcher's shop. He did not speak any English at the time, but his Urdu fluency was enough to be accepted for the job, since the owners were Pakistani nationals. He worked six days a week, 9 AM to 8 PM, with a salary of £180 a week (about £2.73 per hour).

"Don't worry so much," he reassured me. "It was a long way from Afghanistan to Europe." Laughing, he continued, "We've gone through so many things. Calais is just a small step." Despite the fact that he had formerly expressed how deeply shocked he was by his own experience in Calais, he now adopted a characteristic irony that he exuded whenever we discussed migrants' lives. Even when a boy who worked in the restaurant where we met was arrested and deported back to Italy, Khalid still laughed. He knew only too well that the same fate might have been waiting for him, and for countless others who reside in the UK while only having Italy's refugee papers. His laughter seemed to affirm the maxim "pessimism of the intellect, optimism of the will."[14] My interlocutors had, effectively, "interrupted lives," but Khalid did not essentialize his or the other migrants' subjectivities with terms such as *liminal, vulnerable,* or *in limbo*, although, as Michael Jackson remarks in a recent ethnography, "there are times when these words ring true" (2013:4). On one hand, the life that Khalid led in England was a deep reflection of the neoliberal regime in which migration is inscribed: working informally six days out of seven for miserable pay; not covered by public health insurance; suspended in the precariousness of a prospective deportation. On the other hand, his arrival in London had meant a radical change for him, existentially, socially, and economically.

In Rome, he had been waiting for his asylum outcome for a year, all the while unable to find employment. He was hosted in the state-run, yet privately managed, reception center for asylum-seekers in Castelnuovo di Porto. Around thirty kilometers from Rome, the center was located in an industrial area, seven kilometers from the nearest town. It consisted of several enormous hangars, and it hosted around eight hundred people. Public transport was about ten kilometers away, accessible only by foot, since the company provided private transport only for transfers that were deemed "necessary," such as trips to the police headquarters, the Territorial Commission, or medical visits. The Prefettura— territorial commission of the Ministry of the Interior—provided the management with €32.50 per person per day, and the "guests" should have been granted a daily allowance of €2.50. However, throughout the succession of managements in recent years, this daily allowance could alternately take the form of cigarettes or telephone cards, in each case contributing to the constitution of an informal economy: the guests would sell the goods received in exchange for cash, in order to manage the money as they considered appropriate.

In autumn 2013, after his papers were issued, Khalid was accepted in the SPRAR program (System for the Protection of Asylum Seekers and Refugees), which was created in 2002 and consists of various reception initiatives undertaken by local authorities. The program aims at an "integrated reception . . . beyond the mere provision of board and lodging," and should include "orientation measures, socio-legal assistance," and personalized support for the "socioeconomic integration of individuals" (SPRAR n.d.). Yet he was settled in a remote countryside town near Avellino, where he had no opportunity for study, no social contacts, and no monthly allowance. This loss of self-sufficiency implied a sort of regression to childhood, barely tolerable for someone accustomed to supporting himself since early adolescence. If he had stayed at least a couple of months, he would have been given some €200 a month.

The assistance and reception system in Italy is based mainly on refugee representations linked to loss and deprivation. Focusing only on material needs, not only does it foster a sense of dependency and passivity, but also completely fails to address their desires—such an important part of life, especially in the case of young migrants. After a short time in Avellino, Khalid thought that those precious two months that the center was asking him to wait would have been sufficient to get to England. And there he was, in early 2014, supporting himself financially, sleeping in a shared flat, with a few friends around and a whole new city to discover.

The positivity of pursuing his desires notwithstanding, in London Khalid was often haunted by the fear of having made the wrong decision. His condition of "deportability"—the legal dimension of being a Dubliner, meant that his life could be severely interrupted at any moment, and thus having to start all over again. This awareness had deep implications on his bodily vigilance, especially since police raids in south London are quite common. While working, he was always watchful, ready to take off his apron and run as soon as he might see a UK Border Agency vehicle approaching.

Meanwhile, Ismail was left in Rome with Farhad's stuff: his documents, clothes, and a computer, all left behind (unpacked) in the room they had been sharing in the San Michele hosting center, a temporary solution provided to them while their permanent accommodation underwent essential renovation. When the allocated time in San Michele was up, not having heard from the former center, Ismail felt helpless: without a place to stay, without his closest friend, and without any certainty about his future. "I fear they'll throw me away," he told me once, as if he were a thing that the center's management could dispose of. "I'll have no other choice but to go back to sleep in the big tent."

The length of stay in the municipal centers is six months; after that, further accommodation arrangements can be made, depending on availability. This "waiting discipline" (Vacchiano 2011a) is combined with the oppressive environment of the centers. More ambiguous than outright detention, for their relative openness and "humanity," they nevertheless regard "guests" as incapable of taking responsibility for themselves. Through the infantilization, medicalization, and bureaucratization of migrants' lives, these spaces produce refugees, rather than receiving them (Andersson 2014b:185; Khosravi 2010:71).

Besides legal insecurity, refugees live by physical concentration, isolation, and material deprivation (Szczepanikova 2013). The environment of the centers has disruptive effects on their privacy, intimacy, affectivity, and sexuality. They live in close proximity to same-gender mates only, and they often deal with mostly female social workers. The question of gender is further complicated in the case of Afghan refugees, since women do not travel alone; thus, unmarried migrant men in Europe share social spaces predominantly with other men. Moreover, they sleep in shared rooms, with precise hours of entrance and exit, and they are not able to receive guests. Entrance permission must be requested from the centers' management and, in the case of the CARA (Centre for Asylum Seekers), it has to be solicited from the Prefettura (territorial office of the Ministry of the Interior).

Ismail was quite skeptical of Italy's assistance system. Having lived in Rome for two years already, he knew very well the several organizations concerned with migrants' aid, reception, and education, and this familiarity made him feel slightly emancipated as compared to those recently arrived, for whom all that world was completely new—although reminiscent of spaces and institutions encountered elsewhere during their journeys. With this spirit, he would take me to visit the spaces of the Afghans' everyday life, engaging with me in conversations about their nature, scope, and methods. Some of these spaces were not part of his life anymore; such is the case with the bleak corridor of Centro Astalli's soup kitchen,[15] where recently arrived refugees form a long line to get lunch, and the "big tent," where he was afraid he might end up again if his center's management failed to provide him with a new accommodation. We went there only once, and stood on the threshold of the gate while another Afghan young man recounted his deportation from the UK—where he had left a daughter—to Afghanistan; he had now come all the way back to Europe. We did not dare to enter, fearing that my research would come across as yet a further disciplinary gaze on the lives of those sleeping there, a mixed group of travelers in transit, residents who had lost their allocation in a reception center, and "Dublin cases"—all Afghans, all young, all men.

Ismail told me once: "I've got the impression that all these people, they just use us, because we're refugees." Not only was he upset with the material assistance, but also with the kind of "symbolic" support provided by NGOs' workshops and social spaces aimed at refugees. The fact that he was meeting and making friends only with people coming from one or another kind of volunteering/professional space very much put at risk his affectivity, facing the impossibility of building real affective relations with peers. The kind of distortion that results is poignantly expressed by Benasayag and Schmit (2005:115) in relation to mental health patients: it seems that those who are "outside the norm" never "really" live life. We "normal people" eat food, play music, or watch films, while "they" do "activities."

By the end of my fieldwork, Ismail seemed completely absent, not participating in school "activities," nor meeting friends. Once, while he was staring into the void, some people thought he was observing them. "You don't understand," he answered. "My body's here, but I'm elsewhere." In Khosravi's (2010:74) words, this is what exile is about: "my soul did not return in time." Farhad's departure had destabilized Ismail's determination to stay in Rome and follow his studies, and he could not think of anything else but leaving again. His unresolved self-in-transit came to the surface, and it is for this existential characteristic that I consider even those who have not yet moved or been deported to be Dubliners.

Throughout the chapter, I have attempted to interrogate and disrupt the Dubliner category itself, highlighting how the process of labeling, as well as regulatory policies, "lie in constant tension with migratory practices" (Scheel and Squire 2014:197). Yet an anecdote taken from my early field notes reminds me that, while we can "unthink" and deconstruct labels—and it is imperative to do so—their everyday currency is often powerfully reasserted by those who have been labeled themselves. During my stay in Rome in the summer of 2014, I was participating in the activities of an Italian language school. One morning, we were discussing the vocabulary of mobility and, as the students attending had all reached Italy irregularly, whether asylum-seekers or not, the word clandestine provoked laughter, familiarity, and shame at the same time. When I asked them which words they would use in their own languages, most answers reflected the same governmental categories with which I was already familiar. Yet one peculiar word was presented by a Somali refugee: *raadin* refers to someone who is seeking but does not know exactly what or where to seek; a "seeker," a "curious" person. This word beautifully encompasses the fact that the journey presents perennial possibilities, in contrast to the repetitive routine at home (Jackson 2013:1). Nonetheless, this powerfully metaphorical word caused a certain irony when, unavoidably, the urgency of reality surfaced in the classroom. Another student provocatively replied: "So, should we now go to the Questura and say: 'No, officer, we're not migrants; we're just curious'?"

This "curiosity," this quest for existential mobility that, according to Ghassan Hage (2009), is intertwined with the practice of physical mobility, has often been a strong feature in the choices of the "Dubliners" I have met. Yet migrant narratives have often been stripped of this subjective and existential dimension, so much so that they themselves too often frame their experiences through the rationalistic lens that ties migration predominantly to the search for economic or political security. Traditional theories of "push and pull factors" especially fail to grasp Dubliners' fragmentation of the self, which can lead to sudden "irrational" choices (Dobson 2004), such as taking flight again despite the probable failure to settle and its related ruptures. In contrast to rationalistic explanations of mobility, the Dubliners' experience sheds light on the existential dimension of migration, a "logic" that renders "the self radically fugitive and the world radically fragmented" (Veena Das, "Composition of the Personal Voice: Violence and Migration," quoted in Jackson 2002:94). Because of this subjective dimension, I have chosen to focus on a range of diverse trajectories that could testify to the power of the law to impact not only on those subjected to its procedures, but on countless others who internalize it in particular modes of "being-in-the-world."

I have offered only a "snapshot" of my interlocutors' lives in Europe. Much more could have been said about their biographies, the global structural inequalities that originally led them to take flight, and the journey they had undertaken to reach "Europe." I believe, nonetheless, that focusing only on their experience in the "Dublin space" can help in understanding how categories such as "economic migrant" and "refugee" get blurred in the lived experience of those embodying them. Such distinctions might be tenable before departure. Nonetheless, once migrants arrive—or while they are still in transit—the distinction does not hold: all of them need to find work in order to sustain themselves and to be granted civil and political rights (Sutcliffe 2001).

Finally, functionalist explanations of the "root causes" of migration indirectly obscure the influence that the law has on mobility, thus reasserting the necessity of the allocation of people to the space of a "competent" authority. Conversely, the lived experience of the Dubliners exposes the way in which political asylum, and thus the conceptualization of the "refugee," is embroiled in the complex dynamics of the European border regime. The new Dubliners perhaps belong to those groups that James Scott (1998:1) has called "people who move around," the perennial spanner in the works of the state project of rendering a population's legibility. Against the spatialization of identity and citizenship, and the underlying isomorphism of people, culture, and space (Gupta and Ferguson 1992:17), the excess of human mobility continuously redraws the contours of citizenship and its bordering practices.

NOTES

1. Regulation No. 604/2013, in effect since 2003 and now in its third revision.

2. This responsibility ceases twelve months after the date of the illegal crossing of that border. The first "country" is usually determined by the first fingerprint record of an applicant; however, the competent authorities can also rely on asylum-seekers' own route-related accounts. For further analysis of the Common European Asylum System and the Dublin regulation, see Brekke and Brochmann (2014); Kivistö (2013); Mouzourakis (2014); Schuster (2011a).

3. Joshua J. Kurz (2012:36) underlines how informal agreements with non-EU states are a preferred practice, due to their poor transparency and greater flexibility in terms of interpretation of the obligation of non-refoulement.

4. For a broader discussion on the history of Afghan mobility see Hanifi (2000); Monsutti (2007, 2013).

5. In 2014, a judgment delivered by the EHCR in the case of Sharifi and Others v. Italy and Greece (application no. 16643/09) ruled against unlawful pushbacks from Italy

to Greece. A 1999 Italian–Greek protocol allows for returns with the migrants' care entrusted to the boat captain (Sciurba 2014).

6. At times, however, internal border controls are reintroduced, targeting undocumented migrants (Garelli et al. 2013).

7. Italy has been progressively more reluctant to grant full refugee status, which allows for a five-year residency permit and for a citizenship application upon renewal.

8. Territorial Commission for recognition of international protection, composed of two members from the Ministry of Internal Affairs, one representative from the municipality, and one representative from UNHCR (SPRAR 2009).

9. That in Germany the enforcement of a Dublin transfer may result in a reentry ban has been highlighted in the European Comparative Report "Lives on Hold" (ECRE 2013).

10. The Italian travel document issued to refugees is not valid to travel back to their country of origin. In order to go home, Afghans use two strategies: either they travel to Pakistan with a visa sponsored by family or friends who live there and stamped on the Italian travel document, or they request their Afghan passport from the embassy in Rome, and then travel to Afghanistan via Germany.

11. European Dactyloscopie, set up in 2003. Asylum-seekers' fingerprints are stored in the system for ten years, while those of undocumented foreigners caught crossing an EU external border are kept for two years (Schuster 2011a).

12. Following a judgment of the European Court of Human Rights, from 2011 all deportations to Greece were suspended in most member states (UNHCR 2010). Subsequently, some courts in Switzerland and Germany halted deportations of families to Italy (European Court of Human Rights 2014).

13. The UK border authorities deploy "juxtaposed controls" in France and Belgium, checking documents before departure instead of upon arrival.

14. Originally by Romain Rolland, the maxim was made a slogan by Antonio Gramsci in the pages of *Ordine Nuovo* (1999:395).

15. The Jesuit refugee service.

10

The "Gran Ghettò"

Migrant Labor and Militant Research in Southern Italy

EVELINA GAMBINO

> The spectre of migration will never become a new working class. It will always be a spectre, which comes in through the backdoor of your nation on a smuggled vessel, by using false papers, by crossing hundreds of miles. . . . A spectre that is much more present though than any of the political ghosts summoned in political thought and political struggle. . . . [M]igrants do not hold the place of a historical or a political subject as such, rather they tend to become imperceptible to history. But the more they do this, the more they change history by undermining the sovereign pillars of contemporary societies.
> —DIMITRIS PAPADOPOULOS AND VASSILIS TSIANOS, "After Citizenship," 187

> To detect is to transform and to be transformed is to feel pain.
> —EYAL WEIZMAN, Introduction, *Forensis*, 30

The "Gran Ghettò"—as it is known by its inhabitants, and by the many people who visit it every day—was created in the Capitanata Plain in the southern Italian province of Puglia at the beginning of the 1990s as a temporary, informal settlement where the many migrant seasonal agricultural workers employed in the neighboring fields could live during the harvest season. In the twenty years of its existence, the ghetto has changed in its composition and size as a consequence of the profound changes in the sociopolitical situation of the region, of Italy, and of Europe.[1] Its fundamental function as recruiting center and dormitory, however, has remained unchanged, making it the largest point of reference for West African migrant workers in the whole region and, with its extending networks, the "biggest reserve of black labour power of Puglia" (Ventura 2011:11).

I first visited the Gran Ghettò in 2012 as part of an intervention led by the political network Campagne in Lotta (Fields of Struggle).[2] This chapter is the result of my direct involvement in Campagne in Lotta and my participation, over the course of the ensuing three years, in a number of projects in the Gran Ghettò and in other parts of Italy. My analysis will be articulated in two sections. The first will be concerned with a description of the existing conditions that led to Campagne in Lotta's intervention. In this section the Gran Ghettò will be analyzed in terms of its importance as a strategic point from which to challenge the governmental management of migration. To demonstrate this, I will outline how the organization of migrant labor employed during the harvest is the result of the direct involvement of the management of migration enforced by the Italian state in the process of making and remaking labor markets (Bauder 2006; Moulier Boutang 1998). The ghetto, I will argue, constitutes the concrete manifestation of a "newly emerging spatial politics of labor, a transnational political economy of production that links, not only to a new scale of the economic, but a new economy of scale, in which mass production and the space of work-residence are extensively reconfigured for capital accumulation on a global scale" (Pun and Smith 2007). The ghetto provides a privileged site from which "to observe how the border plays a decisive role in the production of labor power as a commodity," and to contend "that the ways migratory movements are controlled, filtered, and blocked by border regimes, have more general effects on the political and juridical constitution of labor markets, and thus on the experiences of living labour in general" (Mezzadra and Neilson 2013:20). Furthermore, from this analytical perspective I will discuss the structural conditions of life in the ghetto and the governmental narratives surrounding them in order to make sense of the widespread illegality in labor recruitment and retribution and the lack of institutional intervention. Illegality, I will argue, is not a "crack" in this apparently seamless new economy of scale. On the contrary, it is an added layer of control and coercion, a necessary tassel of the present world economic order, which models itself on and echoes the logic of its predecessor, that great game of geopolitics (cf. Cowen and Smith 2009:35), in which warfare, but also centralized networks of exploitation, were legitimate means of conquering and maintaining power. This logic and its bleak manifestation in the form of the "ghetto" is part and parcel of the current formation of Europe, as described by Tazzioli and De Genova (2016): a neoliberal formation, "fortified by [the] very old and morbid cruelties" (De Genova, this volume) that defined its colonial past.

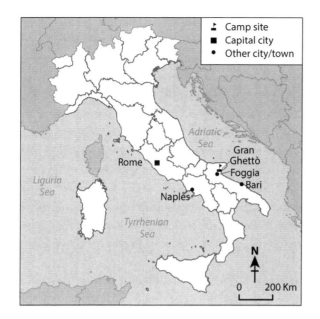

MAP 10.1. The Gran Ghettò (Puglia, southern Italy)

The second section will take a substantially different angle. If this first analysis proposes a multilayered critique of the existing conditions of migrant agricultural work in the region, here I will describe the ways in which the ghetto is the locus of a number of hidden—or, more accurately, "imperceptible" (Papadopoulos and Tsianos 2013)—practices that constitute the fabric onto which Campagne in Lotta has woven its paths of struggle. These practices function as infrastructure to provide the inhabitants of the ghetto with all those services that their cultural, political, and geographical separation render inaccessible. By way of a conclusion, I will argue that those relations, and the virtual global space they trace, are best detected and embraced through the practice of *conricerca*. This practice, literally meaning "co-research," cannot be fixed as the result of any precodified method; on the contrary, I will argue, it is constantly redefined by the participants in a common struggle through collective moments of analysis.

Part I: The "Gran Ghettò"

The "Gran Ghettò" is located approximately twenty kilometers from Foggia, the biggest city in the Capitanata Plain. It lies in the middle of an uncultivated area, unreached by asphalt roads, with no direct access to water except from the tanks installed by the local government. It is serviced by chemical toilets, also provided by the local government. There are no regular buses or other public services that reach the ghetto, and transportation to the field and to the city is self-organized by the migrants. If in the 1990s the Gran Ghettò appeared to visitors as a vast field where a few wrecked farmhouses hosted some hundreds of workers, in the following years the settlement developed into a small town where structures made of cardboard, plastic, and all sorts of other materials have filled the space between the farmhouses, hosting the workers and all the services needed to cater for them, from butchers to tailors to bars—of different sizes and importance—a garage, small shops, and brothels. The establishment of these services has given rise to a solid "informal" economy connecting the ghetto to the rest of Italy, through all sorts of channels, from small commercial ventures to human and drug trafficking, under the control, more or less tight, of the local mafia, Sacra Corona Unita, and its more important counterpart, the Camorra.

The Gran Ghettò is nowadays a small town, which has maintained its temporary character only in its appearance. With the advent of the economic crisis of 2008, a large number of its inhabitants now, in fact, reside there all year long, having lost their jobs in other parts of Italy and preferring to remain in a place where expenses are cut to a minimum and where the presence of a large community of compatriots and fellow migrants guarantees a level of support and security, albeit provisional. The traffic of people and goods crossing the ghetto is constant and embedded in wide networks of social relations, which are sustained and extend themselves on a global level, starting from the seemingly remote and provincial Italian territory where the ghetto is situated.

The Capitanata Plain extends over a large portion of northern Puglia, in southern Italy. One of the most fertile and productive territories in the entire country, the plain is now largely devoted to monocrop cultures of vegetables, the most prominent of which is industrial tomatoes, a large portion of which are processed in the neighboring region of Campania and distributed across Italy and abroad.[3] Unlike other Italian agricultural areas, both southern and northern (such as Rosarno, Piana di Sibari, and Saluzzo), where small and medium-sized agricultural producers still own a large portion of the land, the Capitanata is notably composed of very large estates covering thousands of hectares each and mostly owned by large Italian and, increasingly, foreign corporations. The size of the estates has a crucial meaning for the organization of labor in the fields, as it widens the gap between the worker and the landowner, allowing the emergence of a series of intermediaries who provide their services to both parties, at the expense of the workers. The corporations, thus, are similar to feudal lords sitting at the top of a structure that ends with the workers, working its way down through a series of more of less formalized intermediaries. Most workers, in fact, do not have any contact with landowners: gang-masters receive each labor crew's wages from the employer and then proceed to distribute the wages among the workers, retaining a percentage for their services.

Official estimates (INEA 2014) account for 110,000 agricultural workers employed in the Capitanata, 41,000 of whom are foreign. The majority of nonnative workers—26,875—come from the so-called neocommunitarian countries (the newer EU member states: Romania, Poland, and Bulgaria); the rest are "noncommunitarian" workers, a large number of whom are from West Africa. These estimates, however, do not account for unregulated labor, fake or partial employment contracts, and the numerous other practices of work informalization and exploitation that characterize patterns of employment in the area. In this regard, the data collected by a number of nongovernmental organizations,[4] as well as the direct experience of my own fieldwork, provide a clearer picture of the extent of illegal and semi-illegal (gray) employment of migrant workers in the plain, revealing the official statistics to be a merely approximate number, underestimating the effective extent of the labor market.

The population of the Gran Ghettò has increased exponentially in the past several years. Within the space of two years after my first visit, the number of its inhabitants rose from approximately 900 during the peak of the season of 2012 to more than 1,200 the following year, to a similar number during the low season of early 2014. Such a high density, registered far from the harvest season, is indicative of the shift in the composition of the ghetto's labor force. From being a recruitment center, where most male inhabitants were actively engaged in seasonal agricultural wage labor, the ghetto is increasingly becoming a depository of what Marx referred to as the "reserve army of labour" (Marx 1867:415; cf. Collettivo RicercAzione 2013b:3), a basin of disposable labor power, which exceeds the effective labor demand and becomes its living measure, functional in keeping the price of labor down and increasing the exploitability of the few regularly employed workers.

Labor and Migration

The organization of agricultural labor in the Capitanata Plain is largely built on illegality, in regard to both recruitment methods and labor compensation. Such illegality is directly linked to and fostered by the Italian government's migration policies. In this section I will outline the ways in which the relation between capital and mobile labor is mediated by the Italian state through its strategic deployment of the law, which, as De Genova argues, "ensures the relegation of diverse formations of transnational human mobility to a variegated juridical spectrum of 'legalities' and 'illegalities.' The 'illegality' of 'undesirable' migrants, then, supplies a crucial feature of their distinctive, if disavowed, desirability, as labour for capital" (De Genova 2013a:5).

The links between labor and the control of mobility are explicit in current Italian migration law, specifically in the Bossi-Fini law (Parlamento Italiano 2002); and in the 2009 Security Package (Pacchetto Sicurezza 2009). The legislation, in fact, effectively links migration status to employment, making it impossible to renew one's residence visa—the Permesso di Soggiorno—without a long-term working contract, while at the same time sanctioning the impossibility of obtaining such a contract, in most cases, without a valid residence visa. Being unemployed, therefore, is equated with being illegal, and thus criminal. Furthermore, this Kafkaesque mechanism is supported by a wide range of norms concerning residence, which restrict the possibility for migrants to find regular work or access services outside their first place of residence, effectively criminalizing their mobility within the borders of Italy and depriving them of their most basic rights.

Even if one's status and visa are in order, the bureaucratic process necessary to renew, revise, and obtain one's documents is virtually inaccessible to anyone whose command of Italian is not perfect—a further barrier that is carefully maintained by government officials. This has been directly experienced by many of the militants of Campagne in Lotta, including myself, who have accompanied documented migrant workers to various municipal offices in order to obtain a proof of residence—a document necessary to access local public services, allegedly guaranteed to anyone who requests it if s/he can provide a valid address. During our multiple visits a similar pattern would unfold before our eyes, featuring the refusal of government officials to cooperate with workers or provide translations of the complex bureaucratic documents they are requested to fill out. From our direct experience, it appears clear that most migrant workers are defenseless against the state's bureaucratic machinery, which mixes repressive controls with the workings of racism, sexism, and cultural exclusion as "symbolic—and in some cases less symbolic—boundaries" (Collettivo RicercAzione 2013b), which, far from acting as barriers to "illegal" or "exploited labour," are instead functional in keeping people within the work system (Balibar and Wallerstein 1991:34; Mezzadra and Neilson 2013:74), depriving them of any contractual power and thus effectively producing the perfect exploitable subjects.

Migrant workers are thus forced to accept the most degrading working conditions, allowing producers to employ vast numbers of workers without the necessity of guaranteeing any of the services provided by the collective bargaining agreements. In the Capitanata Plain, and more generally in the agricultural sector in southern Italy, unregulated work is the most common form of employment arrangement. Illegal employment, furthermore, takes many forms: from the complete absence of any form of written agreement between worker and producer to what has been defined as "grey labour" (Rigo and Dines 2014; Peano 2015). This term is deployed to define a number of employment practices that do not completely discard legal forms—contracts, pay slips—but instead deploy them in a partial or distorted way, allowing employers to avoid sanctions while benefiting from untaxed laborers. An example is the phenomenon of "fake contracts." This practice, which is becoming increasingly widespread, entails the registration of a written agreement on which the name of the holder is different from that of the actual worker, a trick that allows Italian friends and relatives of the producer to cash in on the social and unemployment benefits that the state provides after the worker has completed a certain number of working days per year. Some producers, furthermore, employ migrant workers under a partial agreement that officially registers a smaller number of days than those actually worked by the employee, allowing the producer to avoid paying workers' benefits while also preventing the worker from accessing social care. These practices, on the one hand, contribute to enhancing the migrant worker's exploitation and his exclusion from Italian social services; on the other hand, they represent a system of "informal welfare" for Italians, which compensates for the lack of institutional social support, effectively supporting the state in times of crisis (Collettivo RicercAzione 2013b).

In this context, undocumented, or, as we have seen, "precariously documented," non-EU migrants are usually relegated to the lowest-paid and most precarious jobs, not only in agriculture but also in the construction business, logistics, domestic, sexual, and care labor, which are the sectors that register the highest levels of unregulated, informal employment. Even neocommunitarian (EU-citizen) migrants, who have the legal right to stay in the country, are marginalized and exploited. This is due partially to those forms of social discrimination and control mentioned above, but also to the management of "seasonal migration flows," which are controlled by employers and mediators on both sides (Collettivo RicercAzione 2013b). In light of this, "it is immediately apparent how, despite their differences, all productive sectors are permeated by dynamics of exploitation, and how work in general represents the sphere in which capital saves on its production costs" (Collettivo RicercAzione 2013b:3).

"The pivotal encounter" (Mezzadra and Neilson 2013:101) between migration and capital, and the role of the state apparatus in its facilitation, has been a central stake in analyses of migration regimes by a number of critical scholars (Bauder 2006; Collettivo RicercAzione 2013b; De Genova 2002, 2005, 2010b, 2011a, 2013a; Mezzadra 2006, 2011; Mezzadra and Neilson 2012, 2013; Moulier Boutang 1998; Moulier Boutang and Garson 1984; Papadopoulos et al. 2008; Papadopoulos and Tsianos 2013; Varsanyi 2008). An analysis of the organization of labor, and indeed of life, in the ghetto cannot disregard the specific ways in which mechanisms of exclusion effectively work as selective processes to guarantee and enforce forms of "differential inclusion" (Mezzadra 2011; Mezzadra and Neilson 2012), where migrant bodies, rendered docile from the constant threat of "deportability" (De Genova 2002), become disposable tools for the production of surplus value.

Labor Organization during the Tomato Harvest

An account of the organization of labor during the tomato harvest in the Capitanata Plain, as observed during my extensive fieldwork, will provide an example of the mechanism I have just highlighted. The tomato season[5] stretches from mid-July to late September and necessitates a considerable amount of labor, as, unlike other crops, the work has not been fully mechanized.[6] Machines are efficient in picking large quantities of tomatoes in a short time; however, they are not able to distinguish the ripe ones, and without superintendence they would ruin the field. The gangs of workers, therefore, work alongside the machine, driving it and selecting and picking the fruit. The work day usually starts at 6 AM and ends at 4 PM; most fields are distant from the ghetto, and in order to reach them, workers have to wake up as early as 3:30 AM. The work, however, is not subject to an hourly wage, but is paid a piece rate, which in Italy is officially illegal. The pay received for each filled box of tomatoes, weighing 300 kilograms, ranges from three to five euros. In order to arrive at the field some workers deploy their own means, usually bicycles; however, most of them are dependent on transport provided by external figures: the gang-masters.

The presence of gang-masters, individuals who perform the role of mediator between the landowner and the worker, has been a feature of Italian agricultural labor organization for over a century. Italian gang-masters, in the South as well as the North, used to recruit teams of workers, mainly women,[7] and transport them to the fields, charging a price for transport and retaining a percentage from the daily earnings for their mediation services. As Perrotta and Sacchetto (2011, 2012) describe, the advent in the mid-1990s of large numbers of foreign agricultural workers, taking over a large percentage of the agricultural labor in the South, has coincided with the appearance of foreign gang-masters, who organize teams among their compatriots. African gang-masters are called *capo nero* by the workers, and often have a local counterpart, the *capo bianco*—a term that can identify either an Italian gang-master, above the "black" one, or the landowner himself. The role of the gang-master is not fixed, and different gang-masters provide different services. The basic duty of a gang-master, however, is to manage the workers, organizing labor gangs and taking care of their transport to the field. Moreover, gang-masters handle all economic transactions and labor bargaining on behalf of the landowners. The fee for transport ranges from three to five euros, paid by each worker each day; this is a considerable sum to add to the €0.50–1.50 retained by the gang-master from each filled box. The profit an individual worker makes for a day's work ranges, therefore, around forty euros for a ten-hour day. The crisis, however, has exacerbated competition among workers, and prices have consequently fallen, each season reaching new lows.

Each Italian region has specific work regulations that apply to the various sectors of production and are aimed at protecting the labor force from exploitation. These regional collective bargaining agreements establish, among other things, the minimum working wage, which for Puglia amounts to €7.08 per hour. If on one side, the workers' real wages are not even close to the regional minimum, gang-masters can earn thousands of euros per month, providing those necessary services generated by the absence, or inaccessibility, of institutional infrastructure.

The figure of the capo nero is particularly interesting, as it captures, in its complexity, some of the fundamental traits of post-Fordist labor—specifically, the tendency of labor to colonize every realm of life. As Papadopoulos and Tsianos argue, in post-Fordism, "the intensification of exploitation [is] complemented by another mode of surplus value extraction which goes beyond the working day and involves the whole existence of the worker. We are not only dealing with the intensification of the exploitation, but with its extensification" (Papadopoulos and Tsianos 2013:180).[8] Under conditions of post-Fordism, as Paolo Virno contends, "the disproportion between the role of the knowledge objectified in machines and the decreased relevance of labor time has given rise to new and stable forms of domination" (Virno 2001:16). This new form of domination has departed from the rigid division of labor of the Fordist era, giving way to a proliferation of "forms of compulsion no longer mediated by tasks and roles" (Virno 2001:17).

The figure of the gang-master belongs to these new forms of domination, characterized by a "vicious personification of subjection" (Virno 2001:17). His chief skill is, in fact, his capacity to speak and think, and his tasks are fluid and vary from the more or less formal transportation service to a series of informal and ever-changing favors he performs for his relations. In most cases, the gang-masters actually live in the ghettos, thus enabling them to continue to manage their workforce even when they are not working. "Labour-time," therefore, is not adequate to measure his productive role. In his book *A Grammar of the Multitude* (2003), Virno introduces the concept of "the virtuoso" as a proto-type for the contemporary post-Fordist worker. *Virtuosi*, performers, are work-ers whose efforts do not produce any finished product: the fulfillment of their activity rests, in fact, in the presence of "witnesses" (Virno 2003:53). The inher-ent sociality of the virtuoso's performance can be observed in the workings of gang-masters, whose very existence is tied to the constant performance of their hypersociability as "friends of friends" (Boissevain 1974).

Like most performances, the "virtuosity" of gang-masters thrives in an en-closed space. As Perrotta and Sacchetto (2012) have observed, the secluded condi-tion of the ghetto plays a key role in maintaining the supremacy of gang-masters and preventing migrants from working together toward collective alternatives. Seclusion entails a "spatial arrangement that reinforces the overlap of work, lei-sure, rest, and more generally all aspects of the daily reproduction of an individual or a group in one place, from which they are formally free to leave" (Gambino 2003:104–5). Gang-masters thrive on the isolation of the workers and actively reinforce their seclusion. They do so from within: being a part of the secluded world of the ghetto, in which they live, they own businesses and maintain tight networks of social relations that function as tools of control. Gang-masters are complex figures, not completely oppressors, nor purely oppressed; on one side, in fact, they suffer from many of the social, cultural, and political disadvantages to which migrant workers are subject, while on the other, they capitalize on those mechanisms to the detriment of their co-nationals, friends, and in some cases even relatives.

Seclusion, Abjection, and the Spectacle of Migration

> Her workday is never-ending not because she has not machines, but because she is isolated.—MARIAROSA DALLA COSTA AND SELMA JAMES,
> "The Power of Women and the Subversion of Community," 36

Breaking the seclusion of migrant workers should be considered the first nec-essary step toward a process of labor emancipation. As Mariarosa Dalla Costa and Selma James argue, directly addressing capitalist optimism about the devel-opment of machinery: isolation, which in their description is intended as the spatial isolation of women in their homes, but also the discursive isolation of women relegated to their role as housewives, allegedly incomprehensible and distant from men's productive activities, is the fundamental vector of seclusion, allowing the almost complete overlapping of life and labor. Therefore, in order to break seclusion, it is important to understand how it is articulated and maintained through a series of not only material but also discursive practices; breaking spatial seclusion, thus, means allowing workers to take an active part in the myriad of discourses that hold them as "objects." In this section I will outline some of these discursive practices, while proposing an alternative lens of analysis.

The ghetto, like many other similar spatial arrangements, is a self-contained town, catering to the entire range of workers' reproductive and social needs, from food and sex to all kinds of entertainment and commercial ventures. Its self-sufficiency, however, comes with a high level of control, enforced on the workers at various levels, from arrangements for lodging, to work and transport, which results in the ultimate separation from the local native population. Perrotta and Sacchetto (2012:6) describe the multifarious effects of such separation, highlighting four different but interconnected areas of impact: spatial, economic, cultural, and political. The intersection of these four broad areas of the social does not just affect the conditions of migrants; it also influences the way in which they are perceived by the local population. Thus, the multifaceted nature of migrants' separation is reflected in the daily practices of the various institutional and noninstitutional interlocutors who cross the workers' paths on a daily basis. In order to unpack this double-edged separation, it is necessary to understand the role played by discourse in reinforcing such dynamics.

With the terms *border spectacle* and *spectacles of migration*, De Genova (2002, 2005, 2010b, 2013a), following Debord (2009 [1967]), describes what he considers to be the ultimate logic behind governmental narratives of migration. As Debord argues, "Separation is the alpha and omega of the spectacle" (Debord 2009 [1967]:30). Narratives of migration, therefore, build on and reinforce migrants' separation from the rest of society. The spectacle of migration can take different forms, from the "border spectacle"—"a spectacle of enforcement at 'the' border, whereby migrant 'illegality' is rendered spectacularly visible" (De Genova 2013a:1) and the illusion of an invasion of "illegal aliens" is convened—to more subtle forms of spectacle. These can range from the "good spectacle" of the rescue of migrant bodies, dead and alive, from the waters of the Mediterranean by the heroic men of the Italian Coast Guard, to the pietistic spectacle of the destitution of migrants, captured by the camera lens of a "good-hearted" journalist. Spectacular narrations function in a way similar to a holographic machine: "you look into a magic box and a miniature train or horse appears, as you shift your gaze you can see those parts of the object that you were prevented from glimpsing by the laws of perspective.... [I]t is a virtual object in three dimensions that exists even when you don't see it" (Eco 1987:3–4). The hyper-real dimension on which the spectacle thrives is functional to the purposes of control. Through glossy lenses migrants are "dehumanized," while, at the same time, they are rendered constantly visible— their subjectivity harnessed to fit into a fixed category, varying from "victim of a humanitarian crisis" to "illegal alien." A spectacular narrative is, thus, a narrative that fetishizes its subjects, fixing their identity like photographic prints and providing a superficial but nevertheless pervasive interpretation of their actions and lives.[9] The spectacle of migration, moreover, does not just live in the realm of images. On the contrary, it is a concrete relation between subjects under capital, mediated by images (cf. Debord 2009 [1967]:4) As Rigo and Dines argue, "these representations function as a powerful neutralizer of the conflicts produced by contemporary migrations as well as of their political character" (Rigo and Dines 2014:3, my translation). In their short article, Rigo and Dines reflect on the proliferation of accounts concerned with migrant workers' labor conditions in the Italian South. In these narratives, migrant workers, especially Africans, have been portrayed as victims of inhuman labor conditions, often compared to the lives of West African slaves. Reflecting on the broader implication of this widespread victimization, Rigo and Dines argue that these narratives go hand in hand with and are a development of the "emergency" management of migration. Despite describing labor exploitation, in fact, such descriptions effectively result in removing any agency related to the labor relations they are describing, leaving migrant workers as powerless victims of a malign fate.

The logic of separation of the spectacle relegates migrant workers' bodies to the temporally distant dimension of plantation slavery, conferring on them an almost "ghostly" nature. The term *invisible*, increasingly popular in describing the condition of the workers in the Capitanata, offers an example of this logic. A recurrent concern of local press, governmental officials, religious institutions, and mainstream unions has been to liberate the workers from their "invisibility." Images of the "invisibles of the harvest season" (Flai-CGIL 2012), masses of unknown black men, bent under the sun in a tomato field, populate newspapers[10] and penetrate the collective imaginary. Describing the inhabitants of the ghetto as "invisible" engenders a concrete relation between the migrant workers and the Italian/citizen public, one of distance and of justified ignorance, which ultimately precludes an inquiry into the deep causes of the workers' separation, on those levels depicted by Perrotta and Sacchetto. Thus, "invisibility" is a particular mode of describing realty, deemed appropriate for the "residual—and indeed still distinctively colonial—world" (Mbembe and Nuttall 2004:350) of the ghetto.

The colonial dimension is further evoked in the many parallels drawn between these "invisibles" and the enslaved Africans who, after making the voyage across the sea, were subjected to a regime of agricultural labor on American plantations in a previous era. Is this parallel not helpful for highlighting the continuation of the racialized submission at the core of the European project, then as now? It surely is. The Mediterranean, a sea "submerged" by its own cultural myths, which permeate everyday language and political discourses—from a "cradle of civilization" to a mass grave—would indeed benefit from an analytical lens that stresses its grossly unpoetic role in the geoeconomic regime of global labor exploitation today. However, the mainstream accounts that have deployed this comparison have disregarded the legacy of European colonialism as the basis of contemporary formations of domination and labor subordination; on the contrary, and more or less willfully, such discourses have tended to discursively relegate this utterly contemporary form of labor organization to a remote past—an atavistic manifestation in the present of the odd fossil of a bygone era, whose actual contemporary temporality, like its history, is presumed to have never involved Italy, or to somehow no longer implicate Europe, more generally.

This spectacular separation was elevated to a hegemonic discourse in EUrope during the summer of 2015, as De Genova argues in the introduction to this volume. The "refugee crisis" epitomized by the case of Aylan Kurdi, the young boy found dead on a Turkish shore, portrays the crisis of Europe's external borders as a humanitarian crisis "with its root causes always attributed to troubles elsewhere, usually in desperate and chaotic places ostensibly 'outside' of Europe" (De Genova, this volume; New Keywords Collective 2016; cf. De Genova 2013a; Tazzioli 2015a), operating on the basis of a peculiarly EU-ropean form of amnesia that erases the "deeply European (post)colonial histories" (De Genova, this volume). These events emerged from yet obscured the contemporary and ongoing political and economic interests at stake in the maintenance and creation of an ostensible "Fortress Europe," which nonetheless thrives on the existence of places like the Gran Ghettò, where "unwanted" migrant labor may be incubated and exploited. These events are only the tip of the iceberg for an intercontinental postcolonial process that has been at the core of the EU project since its outset: the continuous—and indeed, multifaceted—reconstruction of the borders of "Europe," apparently intended to be coequal to the frontiers of the EU, while also externalizing their reach to geographically distant zones of influence, from the Sahara to the Syrian borders (Bensaad 2007). Moreover—and this is crucial to an understanding of the relevance of this logic for the discursive production around the ghetto and its inhabitants—this reshuffling of the borders of "Europe" is functional to the continuing (re)production and maintenance of the European space as "racial formation of whiteness," shaped by "a global (neoliberal) politics of transnational labor mobility" and the capitalist exploitation of the migrant labor that is the postcolonial harvest of Europe (De Genova, this volume; cf. Cowen and Smith 2009:35).

The tension between the spectacular perception of migrant lives and their concrete separation, within and against the space of the state, arises from governmental discourses and reforms. In the early months of 2014, the region of Puglia approved a resolution called "Capo Free, Ghetto Off."[11] The resolution, which sanctioned the destruction of the ghetto and the eviction and rehousing of all of its inhabitants, was originally scheduled to take place on July 1, 2014, at the beginning of the harvest season. However, after an official launch party, the region quietly decided to postpone its implementation to a later date, possibly during the winter, when a portion of the workers would have left the settlement. Thus, the workers would be divided into "seasonal" and "permanent" categories—as if a clear distinction between the two categories were even remotely possible—and then relocated in different, purposely built, settlements. "Seasonal workers" were to be assigned to tent camps controlled by the Protezione Civile (Civil Defense), "the national body in Italy that deals with the prediction, prevention and management of exceptional events,"[12] while "permanent" workers were to be relocated in a "series of other solutions, such as eco-housing" (Vendola 2014). According to the president of the region, Nicki Vendola, the resolution represented a final effort to "manage the emergency" of migrants in the Capitanata, since the "ghetto represents in some ways a suspension of sovereignty on the part of the state" (Vendola 2014). The need to evict the ghetto, in the president's words, therefore arises from the fact that such a place, and supposedly its "untamed" inhabitants, constitute an "insult," if not a threat, to the state. The presence of the ghetto, especially when highlighted in the national press, exposes an incongruence in the state's monopoly over its territory, which demands to be solved. The solution proposed by the local government, despite being defined as "radical" (Vendola 2014), was merely "cosmetic," however. Furthermore, such a solution was instrumental in its compliance with the increasing treatment of structural and complex conditions as "emergencies"—separate exceptional episodes to be handled expensively, spectacularly, and superficially, avoiding any inquiry into their deep causes. The emergency governance of migration relies on such a strategic displacement: "in place of the palpable social and political relation of migrant labour to the state, border enforcement—whether specifically at the border or within the national space—delivers the public, fetishized and spectacular verification of the migrants' ostensible 'illegality'" (De Genova 2013a:11)—an illegality that, furthermore, becomes an "obscene supplement" to migrants' ostensible exclusion from the sovereign territory of the state.

Discussing the South African township, Mbembe identifies "a peculiar spatial institution scientifically planned for ... the control of urban influx" (Mbembe 2003:26). Township planning reflected Fanon's argument (2001 [1961]) that the division of space into compartments was a central tool of control during colonial occupation. This same logic is at play here. If the operation "Capo Free, Ghetto Off" were to be truly implemented, the old ghetto would be replaced with a series of smaller, prettier, more comprehensively planned (and thus more controllable) new ghettoes, which would reinforce the already existing seclusion of the workers, while extending the state's control over their activities and movements. The logic of the spectacle emerges from this resolution in its infallibility and prevents one from asking the fundamental questions: Why do migrant workers *have* to live in camps? Can they not live in cities like everyone else?

In this regard, De Genova's (2010d) reworking of Kristeva's (1980) notion of "abjection" can provide us with an alternative reading of the worker's condition. Abjection is defined by Kristeva as "something rejected from which one does not part" (Kristeva, quoted in De Genova 2010d:104). Migrant workers, thus, following De Genova, are treated in a similar manner: they are secluded and removed from the social space, but "nevertheless cannot be totally expelled" (De Genova 2010d:104). Migrant workers are pushed to remote areas of the national space. The word *remote* derives from the Latin verb *removeo*: to remove. Remote areas, thus, as Edwin Ardener (1987) argues, do not just gain their descriptor as a consequence of their topographical position; they are remote in the sense that they are removed from something. Remote areas are removed from a center, in a spatial way as much as in a temporal and discursive one: they are the locus of the "other," which is considered to be not quite here, not quite now. Migrant workers in the Capitanata have been removed from the social, cultural, and political life of the region, and institutional reforms are careful to maintain and reinforce their "abjection." However, as Kristeva argues, the abject "from its place of banishment does not cease challenging its master," and its ostensible "exclusion" only draws the subject "toward the place where meaning collapses" (Kristeva, quoted in De Genova 2010d:104). The words of Vendola, quoted above, are enlightening in this regard. The ghetto, despite its functionality and its remoteness, still constitutes a threat to the state's sovereignty: an alien body disrupting it from the inside. Understanding the migrants' condition in terms of abjection, therefore, not only helps us understand the logic behind the state's reforms, but also enables us to appreciate the fundamentally "excessive" character of the migrant workers' position vis-à -vis the state. If, from a governmental viewpoint, such excess demands the deployment of more rigid controls and the enhancement of separation, from a militant perspective, it opens a new terrain of inquiry and intervention.

Part II: Infrastructure, Autonomy, and the Migrant Metropolis

If in the previous section I have outlined the ways in which the thriving illegality of labor organization and the workings of spectacular narratives of migration actively enforce and maintain the exploitation of migrant workers in the Capitanata Plain, in the following section I will focus on how the daily practices of the inhabitants of "the ghetto," through their many long-term and provisional relations—even those that seem to be characterized by sheer oppression—create a network of connections that exceeds the space and controls of the Italian state, linking them to a global space. Tracing the routes of these connections, without fixing them into any static form, I will argue, is a theoretical perspective fundamental for appreciating how autonomous social forms and sociopolitical resistances emerge, are cultivated, and are shared.

This kind of approach implies a critical relation to the analytical method of inquiry. An analysis of life in the ghetto based on these premises exceeds the limits of a sociological inquiry built on the interaction between "order" and "contract." A focus on this "excess" and its autonomy is, therefore, fundamental to creating theoretical scenarios on which a militant inquiry can be constructed. As Mbembe and Nuttall argue: "historical and political scholarship is not combined with fundamental philosophical inquiry, and this has led to a dramatic thinning of 'the social.' The latter is still understood as a matter of order and contract, rather than as the locus of experiment and artifice" (Mbembe and Nuttall 2004:349). This reflection is a call to arms for a radically different type of scholarship, one that positions itself, and the knowledge it seeks to produce, in a relation of radical openness to the world. In the context of an ethnography of the Gran Ghettò, therefore, being able to appreciate the philosophical implications of fieldwork goes hand in hand with the aims and practices of a truly militant investigation.

Previously, I drew a brief parallel between the Gran Ghettò and the South African township, arguing that both arrangements are the result of the unequal compartmentalization of space within both the colony and the contemporary

Italian state. However, as Mbembe and Nuttall argue, it is fundamental to appreciate "the imbrications of city and township" (2004:357) and the role of the latter in the making of the first. If the township is undoubtedly a locus of oppression and separation, an exclusive focus on its "difference" risks undermining the way in which it is part of the making and remaking of the world around it. In a similar way, the Gran Ghettò is a constitutive element not only of the city of Foggia, but also of many other Italian cities and of the larger European space in which it lies, travels, and expands, and from which it is regulated and fostered. An analysis of the relation between the ghetto and its extended urban "outside," however, should not limit itself to picturing the incessant traffic of people and goods traveling to and from the ghetto. People—migrants and nonmigrants alike—cross it every day, conducting all sorts of business. Instead, such an analysis should aim to appreciate how these movements constitute the texture of the ghetto, connecting it to the global space outside it. As I mentioned earlier, the ghetto is both a recruiting center and a place where migrant workers from all around Italy gather to find the protection of a community. The ghetto is a place on a virtual map, the position of which becomes increasingly clear the more people travel to it. Despite being remote, it is incredibly easy to find, following the directions of the many people who have been there. For instance, in his ethnography, Alessandro Ventura (2011) narrates the experience of a group of migrants who, arriving in Italy for the first time from Burkina Faso, managed to reach and settle in the ghetto in less than three days, only following the directions of people they met on their way.

What I aim to highlight, furthermore, is the way in which these relations function as a particular type of "infrastructure, capable of facilitating the intersection of socialities so that expanded spaces of economic and cultural operation become available to residents of limited means" (Simone 2004:408). The term *infrastructure* usually refers to a number of physical appliances such as pipes, bridges, highways, electrical cables, and more, deployed to connect people and resources within geographical territories. However, the urban scholar AbdouMaliq Simone (2004) strategically expands this notion to encompass the activities of people inhabiting urban spaces. In this way, he is able to highlight the extent to which relations between people, as opposed to institutional services and material infrastructure, provide urban dwellers with the necessary services to carry on their daily lives. "People as infrastructure" emphasizes a "relation of non-relation that opens each constituent element onto a multiplicity of relations between forces" (Simone 2004:409), a relation characterized by connectivity rather than affect and which does not imply a moral code but rather functions pragmatically, molding itself according to the immediate needs of the various actors who constitute its strings. Furthermore, Simone's insistence on the materiality of infrastructural connections is aimed at avoiding any possible romanticization of the character of these relations: exploitation and various forms of capital accumulation are, in fact, some of the driving forces of these channels, though which, nevertheless, practices of "commoning" flourish and travel. Analyzing people's connection through the lens of infrastructure thus aims to uncover a "process of conjunction, which is capable of generating social compositions across a range of singular capacities and needs (both enacted and virtual) and which attempts to derive maximal outcomes from a minimal set of elements" (Simone 2004:410). Therefore, to apply this perspective to the ways in which the ghetto's current, past, and future dwellers relate transnationally implies paying attention to the multifarious nature of these connections, as well as recognizing their importance for any attempt to counteract the "toxic" spectacular narratives which oppress them.

When referring to people as infrastructure, therefore, one must understand how "ways of doing and representing things become increasingly 'conversant' with one another. They participate in a diversifying series of reciprocal exchanges, so that positions and identities are not fixed or even, at most times, determinable" (Simone 2004:410–11). In this light, even the figure of the gang-master must be revisited to account for the complex, and sometimes competing, characters who coexist within it. The gang-master, who in the previous section was described as the most direct source of workers' exploitation, is, in fact, the most "institutionalized" form of "person as infrastructure." Through his mediating role, he connects workers with producers, but this is just one of his duties. In different situations gang-masters can act as friends, judges, couriers, or security guards, establishing collaborations and ensuring the necessary conditions for an exchange to take place. In many cases exploitation, camaraderie, and mutual aid mix together in the practices of gang-masters and their interlocutors. This is not to say that gang-masters are not to be condemned; on the contrary, an appreciation of the complexity of their practices and the extent of their relations is fundamental to understanding their role within the production cycle in its local manifestation, as well as on a global scale, and their importance for the maintenance of a structure of oppression in which they are both victim and perpetrator.

If Simone's notion of infrastructure implies a specific urban settlement, a metropolis, at the fringes of which poor dwellers negotiate their living, then the ephemeral but yet ever-present infrastructure built by migrants' relations should also be understood as inserted into an essentially "urban" context. This metropolis constructed through *migrant relations* is thus a relational fact; it takes shape across the ephemeral spaces drawn by the social interactions of migrants across geographical areas. It is not confined to singular geographical spaces and must not be confounded with one particular area inhabited by migrants. Those areas are both part of what De Genova (2015a) has designated *the migrant metropolis*, and also the results of it. The migrant metropolis is "formulated indeed as a peculiar sort of epistemological object, included in the very same hypothesis that sought to comprehend it. Even though this virtual 'object' (or 'place') can be said to be located outside any (empirical) fact, it was and is not at all a fiction" (De Genova 2015a:5). Far from being a merely descriptive term, the migrant metropolis is instead the projection of the human infrastructure described by Simone onto a global texture. It is an imaginative and political stance, based on the appreciation of "the urban" as a pervasive character of contemporary capitalism, where relations emerging from cities encompass and capture the entire globe (see Lefebvre 2003 [1970]). The migrant metropolis is therefore, the privileged space from which to observe the way in which "both capital and territorially defined 'national' states confront transnational labour as the premier manifestation of the sheer restlessness of human life, in its active (productive) relation to the space of the planet" (De Genova 2015a:5).

To detect the migrant metropolis, it is necessary to devote particular attention, as well as a will, to see the "eminently social" (De Genova 2011a:6) character of migrant mobility. As Mbembe and Nuttall argue, a "metropolis is a capitalist formation, closely tied to the money economy and individuality, to calculability and fortuitousness" (Mbembe and Nuttall 2004:365). The space of the migrant metropolis is, thus, produced through the shared knowledge, cooperation, and dissent, mutual support and exploitation, care and deception, that the movements of individuals and groups imprint on the many locations of their travels, signposting them to others and, thus, constantly renegotiating their nature: a production of a space (Lefebvre 1991 [1974]) that rests on "uncertainty and turbulence, instability and unpredictability" (Mbembe and Nuttall 2004:349), set against the gaze of the state, constituting a challenge to its rigor from within its own boundaries.

The particular sensibility necessary to detect and engage with the migrant metropolis is one that shifts its focus from the politics of control to "the subjective practices, the desires, the expectations, and the behaviors of migrants themselves" (Mezzadra 2011:21). The migrant metropolis is visible and becomes productive through what Mezzadra defines as "the gaze of autonomy."[13] "Autonomy of migration," explain Papadopoulos and Tsianos, "is less a discourse about investigating contemporary migration as a social subject against the workings of sovereignty and capital and more an organizing practice for supporting and facilitating freedom of movement" (2013:191). Therefore, what is at stake in the account of the embodied practices of the migrant metropolis is a militant sensibility that positions itself on a plane parallel to that of the migrants, constructing a dialogical relation with their actions while discarding any "spectacularized" discourse. "Training our senses to see movements before capital (but not independent from it) and mobility before control (but not as disconnected from it)" (Papadopoulos and Tsianos 2013:185) is a matter of constituent imagination (see Graeber and Shukaitis 2007) engaged in the production of "alternative ontologies, that is, alternative everyday forms of existence and alternative *forms of life*" (Langdon Winner, *The Whale and the Reactor*, cited in Papadopoulos and Tsianos 2013:191; emphasis in original).

Campagne in Lotta as Conricerca: The Workers' Committee

> Of course there is a growing proximity between migrant labour and precarious labour since migrant labour becomes increasingly precarized (especially after the 2008 economic crisis) and precarious labour becomes increasingly mobile. However if there is a potential for transversal politics between the worlds of migration and precarity, this is not in the form of solidarity or in the creation of a new hybrid political subject. Rather we believe that where migrants and precarious workers meet is in sharing the same urban spaces and that both of them, from their very different positions and with very different aims, participate in the metropolitan uprising of European cities. (Papadopoulos and Tsianos 2013:189)

What is implied by Papadopoulos and Tsianos is that it is in no way possible to merge migrant workers' struggles into a predefined and bounded framework of "native" politics. The recognition of the pervasiveness of precarity which affects migrant noncitizens as well as "native" citizens should be the starting point for the creation of a common struggle which is not unitary but multiple and connected. Here the terrain of reproduction acquires a fundamentally political character, as the locus on which migrant and native subjectivities can be bound in a common struggle through those sometimes imperceptible elements of the human infrastructure that complement and defy institutionalized connections. These, furthermore, are the infinite routes though which "the common" (see Hardt and Negri 2009) is constructed. Thus, what is required is the ability to appreciate a new plane, or new planes, on which the political is created, contested, and actualized. This is not a call for a somewhat mystical approach to politics; it is instead a very specific recognition of the necessity of formulating new forms of struggle, far from the strictly identitarian politics of conventional labor movements. The plane of this struggle is the migrant metropolis, and the instrument of this different form of politics is a militant *conricerca* (Borio et al. 2007). From this perspective it can be argued that the migrant metropolis is a precondition for, and the location of, those acts of resistance that constitute the core of Campagne in Lotta's intervention in the ghetto.

Campagne in Lotta is a network of migrant workers, activists, students, researchers, independent agricultural producers, and more; indeed, one identity does not exclude another in the network, where workers are also activists and vice versa. The network extends across the entire territory of Italy, connecting different subjectivities though a critique of the exploitation of labor and the precaritization and seclusion of migrant, as well as native, workers, starting from the agricultural sector. The idea to create a network that would connect multiple isolated struggles emerging across the country was first formulated in the aftermath of the migrant uprisings in Rosarno (Calabria) in January 2010. The uprisings were a reaction to the numerous violent attacks directed at West African workers by the local population, violence effectively condoned, if not encouraged, by the government, which reacted to the "riots" by forcing the workers to evacuate the region and deporting many of them, while leaving the local aggressors unpunished. After being forcibly dispersed around the country, many of the workers gathered in Rome and gave rise to the first Rosarno African Workers' Assembly in Rome. From the assembly, in which many Italian activists have taken part, emerged the necessity of creating a network able to articulate demands for the regularization of illegal labor and the protection of undocumented migrants in the face of landowner abuse and institutional disregard. In the space of two years an increasing number of people "coalesced around this experience, giving rise to a progressively expanding and morphing network that gives voice to different demands, connecting the exploitation of farm labor to the stifling of small producers by distribution networks, and also to consumers' rights to high-quality and fairly priced products" (Collettivo RicercAzione 2013a:1). Connecting the different instances of African migrants scattered around Italy, the network's work highlights the role of racism, in both its personal and institutional manifestations, in creating and maintaining labor exploitation and seclusion. Racially subordinated migrant workers are relegated to the bottom of the labor ladder, where the looseness of institutional control directly enhances their condition of formal exclusion and subordinate inclusion.

In the course of the three years of its existence, Campagne in Lotta has established a number of projects in key localities where migrant workers convene during the major harvest seasons. The first was the Gran Ghettò, followed by

Boreano in Basilicata, and Saluzzo in Piedmont and Rosarno. These projects, despite remaining distinct, share a cross-territorial outlook. During the course of each intervention, militants visit, and in some cases live in, the settlements that migrant workers inhabit. These settlements vary from spontaneous shantytowns at the edges of cultivated lands, such as the Gran Ghettò, to wretched farmhouses scattered around large territories, to state-built tent camps, to squatted and, in some rare cases, rented buildings. Practices such as the establishment of a self-organized Italian language school, a legal advice service, a pirate radio run by the workers, and a traveling bike kitchen constitute the daily activities during the projects. As the Collettivo RicercAzione, a group of militant researchers—to which I belong—born from the experience of Campagne in Lotta, argues, these practices are aimed at the "participant and participated observation of the work and living condition of migrant workers" (Collettivo RicercAzione 2013b:2). This is, furthermore, directed toward the creation of a terrain on which processes of political self-organization can be facilitated through the emergence of social moments of discussion, and the establishment of collective "safe" spaces, in which workers' assemblies can be organized.

The territories in which the projects are based differ substantially. Thus, each project has been developed on the ground with the participation, and sometimes the active involvement, of local groups of various kinds that are already active in the area. The network aims to act as a bridge between local realities and the migrant workers, two sides of a similar struggle which too often remain distinct. Though the practices around which each project is built may differ, many members of Campagne in Lotta, both workers and nonworkers, circulate among the different projects, thus maintaining a constant dialogue between the various territories and exporting effective practices across the interventions. "Hence, this militant project works toward the collective elaboration of a methodology of intervention, and therefore also of analytical tools that can help to understand and seek to impact on the contexts in which it finds itself" (Collettivo Ricercazione 2013a).

The first project run by Campagne in Lotta in the ghetto in the summer of 2012 was organized in collaboration with a group of missionaries who had been providing charitable solidarity to its inhabitants for several years. Approaching the space through such a channel allowed us to enter without having to publicize our political aims, and it has provided a platform through which it has been possible to develop our different activities, namely the Italian school, the pirate radio, and the legal advice service. In the course of the project these practices, with the exception of the legal advice project, lost their initial connotation of a service provided by Italian citizens for the migrants. As the relations between workers and militants became stronger, the once-defined spaces of the "services" became increasingly a locus of interaction and sociability, where workers gathered after work independently from their participation in the organized activities. The radio in particular quickly became self-organized, transmitting music, interviews, and information curated by the workers. The three months of the duration of the project, in which a conspicuous number of volunteers participated, have been fundamental in building a network of relations with the inhabitants of the ghetto, as well as in mapping the area in its geographical and sociological nature. This knowledge and these relations have been maintained and implemented over the following years, thanks to the activities of many of its participants, both migrants and activists, in other projects run by Campagne in Lotta and the involvement of many in local struggles around similar themes, and all of this has provided the basis for the following intervention. By summer 2013, the internal composition of the network had changed: some of the migrant workers had joined the struggle and became active parts of the network, while many others showed support and interest in the activities of the group. This time, therefore, besides the previous activities, it was also possible to start promoting an assembly process to discuss some of the issues around the migrants' labor conditions, in order to build a common platform of demands directed at local institutions. The assembly process—which the group supported without ever directing—highlighted the many tensions within the ghetto. On various occasions, gang-masters, threatened in their control, attempted to hijack the meetings, making it necessary to hold secret meetings, breaking the main meetings into smaller discussions held in people's homes. Despite these disruptions and the sometimes explicit threats received by the workers, people continued to meet, finally establishing a committee of workers: La Casa de Lavoratori (The Workers' House). The "Committee" is a juridical entity representing the workers in institutional meetings; it was strategically created at a moment where the end of the harvest implied the dispersal of many of the inhabitants of the ghetto and the risk of dissipating the gains made. The principal role of the Committee is thus to be a point of reference for migrants interested in continuing the assembly process and to provide an interface to guarantee the workers' access to institutional meetings, bypassing all the intermediaries—from unions to local associations—who had spoken for the workers in the past. Despite its fixed juridical structure, however, the committee was not static; on the contrary, it moved with the workers and it was used at the same time by various collectives of migrants across the country.

The assembly process and the workers' committee were the results of two years of constant effort and communal life in the various sites of the migrant metropolis. Their formation, moreover, should not be interpreted only as a further step in a process of political determination, but as a collective moment of learning, driven by the different modalities of existences at stake in the discussions. A pedagogical effort is central to every aspect of Campagne in Lotta's intervention. The term *pedagogical* here refers to a specific mode of radical education similar to that described by Paulo Freire (1972): an open-ended mutual encounter between different knowledges, where discipline and control are replaced by dialogue and where the boundaries between educators and students are blurred. A pedagogy constructed on these premises is explicitly revolutionary as it challenges through communication the symbolic and material barriers that enforce worker's exclusion. "The earlier dialogue begins, the more truly revolutionary will the moment be. The dialogue which is radically necessary to revolution corresponds to another radical need: that of women and men as beings who cannot be truly human apart from communication" (Freire 1972:128).

Freire calls this method "the pedagogy of the oppressed," referring to "the pedagogy of people engaged in the fight for their own liberation" (Freire 1972:53). However, it is not to a pedagogy of the *oppressed* that I would like to compare the efforts of Campagne in Lotta. What I am describing, in fact, should rather be understood as a pedagogy of the *abject*. "The distinctly disruptive force of the abject involves that which "disturbs identity, system, order. What does not respect borders, positions, rules. The in-between, the ambiguous, the composite" (Kristeva, quoted in De Genova 2010d:107). In our earlier discussion of abjection we emphasized how abjection implies a challenge to a system from within. This challenge, furthermore, is articulated at the level of a constant and pervasive dismissal of its borders. In this sense, this pedagogy in its most basic manifestations must be seen as "a specific sabotage of the mechanisms of workers' separation that the state-form has assumed in its material constitution" (Negri 2005 [1977]:261) and should be understood as the expression of a process of *conricerca*. *Conricerca*, an Italian neologism for "research-with," is a political process, based on militant inquiry, which aims toward the concrete elaboration of alternative existences, born within a struggle. *Conricerca* is developed as communication and cooperation, as a process of resubjectification and counter-formation, and as a forum for the autonomous political representation of the organized spontaneity of the workers (Borio et al. 2007:168).

The pedagogy of the abject, therefore, does not take place in one particular moment: it would be wrong, in fact, to describe the Italian school in the ghetto, or the other immediately educational moments of the various projects, as its designated location. On the contrary, it is the method and the form of our fight, and it takes place across all the spaces that make up Campagne in

Lotta's interventions, permeating the relations between people involved in the struggle.

> No, I am not looking for a program or a menu. . . . What is required is an indication, a path, a method. . . . Every time I leap forward, I enlarge my existence as part of the collectivity. Every time I break capital's margins of valorization, I appropriate yet another space for workers' valorization. Every space left empty by the enemy is filled, occupied, appropriated, attacked by an expansive force that has no limits. (Negri 2005 [1977]:260)

What is described by Negri is a fight that advances and expands itself in multiple directions, without a preconceived sequence of goals, but molding itself onto different situations—a struggle that unites people without, however, favoring the constitution of hierarchies or norms with which people are forced to comply. The struggle of Campagne in Lotta has just begun. From the macro perspective of governmental control and its intersection with capital, the successes of the network may be imperceptible. However, it is exactly on the basis of this imperceptibility that Campagne in Lotta's "turbulence" (Papastergiadis 2000) moves and acquires meaning. The biggest achievement of the network in these years has been to become a shared knowledge, a passed connection, living and moving through migrants' mobility—a knowledge that, in small steps and through many obstacles, is finally becoming a *common knowledge*.

With such a perspective it becomes clear how the plane on which Campagne in Lotta's struggle moves is radically different from the one claimed by various forms of political organizing such as mainstream labor unions and political parties. When referring to Campagne in Lotta as a common knowledge, what is being described is a "space of connection which moves in an opposite dimension from the segmentation of metropolitan labor power" (De Nicola and Quattrocchi 2014:6, my translation), a segmentation which, as De Nicola and Quattrocchi argue, marks the operational logic of Italian mainstream unions and political parties, which sacrifice mutualism and conflict for a managerial organization, in exchange for inclusion within the institutional elaboration of the political economy (see De Nicola and Quattrocchi 2014:3–4). Campagne in Lotta's struggle, therefore, from the countryside to the metropolis, starts from a denunciation of labor conditions to undermine "the mechanisms of that extractive machine which [from labor] extends into the reproductive sphere" (De Nicola and Quattrocchi 2014:5, my translation). De Nicola and Quattrocchi define this form of political organization as "social unionism" (De Nicola and Quattrocchi 2014:1), purposefully recovering the connection between mutuality and conflict to define a struggle whose boundaries are defined and then renegotiated through a composite of experiences, which, as the Colectivo Situaciones suggests, "defines a relation between bodies" (Colectivo Situaciones 2007:76), leading to the affirmation of new subjectivities, modes of self organization, and valorization (De Nicola and Quattrocchi 2014:3, my translation).

Conclusion

This chapter has been the result of my direct involvement in the political practices of Campagne in Lotta. I have here retraced my own political path, in its two distinct but intertwined moments of observation and participation. Mirroring this field experience, therefore, I have aimed to highlight the multiple dimensions, theoretical and practical, to which an analysis of the ghetto speaks. The first section was devoted to a material description of the locus of most of my fieldwork, the Gran Ghettò, one of the many border zones of Europe, a spontaneous and ever-expanding settlement, which stands in an almost continuous line with the many other similar places—whether actual frontiers or vast, yet contained, territories—which dot and define the wider European space. Governed through strict though often invisible rules, this border/container (cf. Holmes 2007) is one of the nodes of the transnational commodity chain of tomatoes which extends from the Capitanata Plain to supermarket shelves across Europe. Central to this geoeconomic function is the mediating role of the Italian state, which, through the management of migrants' mobility and the creation of a wide range of illegalities, disciplines living labor, thereby creating the most profitable conditions for its exploitation by capital. The degrading labor conditions of migrant workers living in the ghetto are the direct result of this intersection. Seclusion and extreme separation—which encompasses all levels of workers' lives—are, moreover, actively maintained by the "spectacularized" regime of narratives proliferating around the ghetto.

The gaze of control, however, cannot account for the multiple series of actions, networks, and relations, which, starting from, traversing, or ending at the Gran Ghettò, connect its inhabitants to countless places, establishing an alternative cartography intelligible only through participation in these networks. These connections were the focus of the second section of the chapter, in which the work of Campagne in Lotta was introduced and framed. The eminently social character of Campagne in Lotta, characterized by both mutuality and conflict, is what shapes its struggle in opposition to the spectacular logic that informs not only mainstream narratives of migration but also the institutional forms of political organization that fragment workers, fixing their fluid subjectivities into normative forms and ignoring their existing infrastructural connections. This is the logic of a new form of organization, one that privileges relational commoning based on radical pedagogy, *conricerca*, and composition, over party pamphlets and rigid political programs and penetrates the global space of the ever-expanding abject "migrant metropolis," growing within and despite the borders of Europe. Through the virtual, and indeed autonomous, spatiality of the migrant metropolis, the human infrastructure designed by migrants' interactions creates spaces in which practices of commoning and modes of resistance travel and can be shared. It is in this light that Campagne in Lotta's intervention becomes a shared knowledge, which travels on these networks and is constructed through an alternative pedagogical practice of transformation. This common knowledge is invisible to official narrations and adverse to mainstream political organizing. However, it is exactly from its abject but autonomous position within and against the space of the state that this traveling knowledge is poised to constitute a critical challenge to the established configurations of the official space of the European public and the subjects allowed to take part in it.

NOTES

1. The economic crisis that has hit Europe since 2008 has affected migrant as well as native workers: the loss of employment of thousands of migrant workers has resulted in internal migrations from cities to informal rural settlements such as the ghetto. Moreover, the stricter migration policies enforced by European states have generated the necessity to create "safe spaces" where communities of undocumented as well as documented migrants can gather, building communities capable of providing support against the state's controls and destitution. (I will expand on these issues in the following section.)

2. The name Campagne in Lotta has the double meaning of "struggling countrysides" and "fields of struggle"; this double entendre cannot be rendered in an English translation. Here I opt for the latter translation, which has been previously used by other members of the group (Peano 2015).

3. For a detailed account of the commodity chain of industrial tomatoes produced in the Capitanata, with particular reference to its implications for the UK, see Wasley (2011).

4. Medici Senza Frontiere (2005, 2008); Brigate di Solidarietá Attiva et al. (2011).

5. In the course of my analysis I will focus only on the tomato harvest and its composition, leaving aside the other minor harvests taking place on the plain—peppers, grapes, and fennel being the most important—which follow somewhat different patterns, maintaining nevertheless similar conditions of exploitation.

6. In the north of Italy, however, tomato picking has largely been mechanized.

7. The condition of women, and their exploitation as the weakest element of society, is strikingly similar to the current condition of migrant workers—exploited, discriminated against, and abused by institutions and individuals (see Curci 2008).

8. This tendency has been analyzed by a number of theorists (Fumagally 2007; Hardt and Negri 2000, 2004; Hochschild 1983; Papadopoulos et al. 2008; Virno 2003; Weeks 2007), following and elaborating upon Marx's account of automated labor in the *Grundrisse* (1971 [1858]).

9. Spectacular narratives have a central role in the description of subjects perceived as "others." This role can also be understood with reference to Homi Bhabha's work on the "colonial fetish" (see Bhabha 1994:66–85).

10. Some examples: http://archivi.articolo21.org/4593/notizia/dal-gran-ghetto-a-roma-storie-di-invisibili; http://cetri-tires.org/press/2012/video-sugli-invisibili-delle-campagne-di-raccolta-flai-cgil/?lang=it.

11. "Capo Free, Ghetto Off," a quirky mixture of English and Italian, is the original title used by the region.

12. http://en.wikipedia.org/wiki/Protezione_Civile.

13. For a deeper engagement with the autonomy of migration thesis, see Bojadžijev and Karakayali (2007); Mezzadra (2011); Papadopoulos et al. (2008); Papadopoulos and Tsianos (2013).

11

"We Want to Hear from You"
Reporting as Bordering in the Political Space of Europe
DACE DZENOVSKA

Reporting, Securitized Freedom, and Europeanization

In 2013 I learned that the United Kingdom Border Agency (UKBA)—subsequently split into Immigration and Immigration Enforcementand UK Visas—publishes news feeds, which include regular reports on successful raids on restaurants or workplaces, namely raids that result in arrests of workers or persons deemed "illegal." What struck me as I was reviewing these news feeds was that all of them included remarks that the UK Border Agency had been acting on either "intelligence" or information received from the public. Upon further investigation, I found a 2011 report by John Vine, the UK independent chief inspector of borders and immigration, which stated that the UK Border Agency receives intelligence from "members of the public, frontline staff and community organizations" and that "over 100,000 allegations are received per year from members of the public" by "letter, email or telephone" about "individuals living in their community" (Vine 2010:3). In turn, the reporting facility on the UK Home Office's website addressed the public as follows: "If you suspect that someone is working illegally, has no right to be in the UK or is involved in smuggling, we want to hear from you." This appeal to members of the public to report—or denounce—appeared to be part of a broader campaign to involve ordinary people in border practices and other forms of policing. For example, the Intelligence Management System, previously known as the Allegations Management System, of what at the time was the UK Border Agency was launched after Prime Minister David Cameron called upon "'everyone in the country' to help 'reclaim our borders' by reporting on suspected illegal immigrants" (BBC News 2011). Almost in the same breath as he called for "everyone in the country" to report on "suspected illegal immigrants," David Cameron had also called upon the British people to help fight "benefit scroungers," following which the newspaper *The Sun* invited its readership to report on those who were endangering the well-being of ordinary British people by abusing the British welfare system (Aitchison 2010; Talsania 2012). This suggested that reporting was not limited to the governance of migration, but was rather an increasingly prevalent instrument of governance in the United Kingdom and, as I argue in this chapter, within (neo)liberal regimes of governance more broadly.

In the Western political imaginary, reporting—as both one-time acts of denunciation and more continuous "informing"—tends to be associated with the political repertoire of totalitarian states—the historical other of Western liberal democracies embodied by Eastern European and Soviet socialist states for much of the twentieth century (Boyer and Yurchak 2010).[1] Yet liberal democratic states, including the United Kingdom, also rely on reporting in their governance and encourage it as an expression of civic duty. This is done in multiple ways, ranging from general calls to the public to report suspicious activity, to the establishment of hotlines for violations of law or suspicious activity, to requiring that specific social and professional groups report on their family members, peers, or clients. For example, in the UK, Muslim women are encouraged to report on family members perceived to be "at risk" of joining radical political or military formations (Saul 2014), primary school teachers as well as university academics are legally required to report suspicions of "radicalization" among Muslim students (Open Society Foundation 2016), teachers and medical staff are mandated to report on citizens and migrants alike for suspected child neglect (Goebbels et al. 2008), and landlords are required to check their potential tenants' "right to rent."[2]

How does one make sense of this proliferation of calls and requirements to report in a Western liberal democracy? Is it similar to or different from other historical instances of reporting, most notably those of the twentieth-century authoritarian regimes? I suggest that the liberal democratic practices of reporting are both—more similar to the authoritarian ones than it may seem, but also crucially different. First, the increasingly common presence of reporting and calls for reporting in Western liberal democracies such as the United Kingdom suggest that the crass distinction between totalitarian and democratic societies and regimes of governance common to the Western political imaginary is itself a "state effect"; that is, it is a distinction that has emerged as a result of statecraft

(Mitchell 1999). It is as much a tool of self-definition for Western liberal democracies as it corresponds to any material reality. Moreover, when considering reporting from a historical perspective, it becomes apparent that reporting to authorities is neither new nor an exclusive feature of totalitarian states. Historians have traced the role of denunciations—that is, "spontaneous communications from individual citizens to the state (or to another authority such as church) containing accusations of wrongdoing by other citizens or officials and implicitly or explicitly calling for punishment" (Fitzpatrick and Gellately 1996:747)— in community governance in imperial Russia (Burds 1996), in revolutionary France (Lucas 1996), in the late nineteenth-century Roman Catholic Church (Lease 1996), in Nazi and state socialist Germany (Connolly 1996; Gellately 1996), and, of course, in the Soviet Union (Fitzpatrick 2005, 1996; Fitzpatrick and Gellately 1996; Kozlov 1996).

In most historical instances of reporting, there is an assumed external authority—a dictator, revolutionary vanguard, or God—that compels subjects to report. Projects of total social transformation (e.g., nationalist, socialist, or republican revolutions and their subsequent institutionalization), or times of social and moral upheaval (Burds 1996), are particularly conducive to the emergence of a "denunciatory atmosphere" (Gellately 1996:967). In all instances, people are both forced to report and report voluntarily, either because they subscribe to the governing ideology or because they seek to use the system for personal ends (Gellately 1996). There is always an element of freedom in practices of reporting, yet regimes that rely on reporting as a crucial instrument of governance are generally thought of as invasive and repressive (Gellately 1996).

As I show in this chapter, reporting in liberal regimes of governance shares some of these features, especially with regard to how ordinary people take up the call to report and thus contribute to the formation of a "denunciatory atmosphere." At the same time, liberal regimes of governance have their distinctive features. Liberal regimes of governance are not based on revolutionary visions of total social transformation and are not usually thought of as repressive and invasive, at least not when juxtaposed to totalitarian regimes. Their defining ideology is that of personal and political freedom, democracy, and human rights. Projects of governance—micro and macro alike—are articulated as contributions to furthering freedom. It is thus the imaginary of freedom and its valuation as a morally and politically superior end of governance that distinguishes reporting in liberal regimes of governance from other historical instances of reporting. This is why, from a liberal perspective, citizen involvement in governance through denunciation in fascist or socialist regimes is thought of as complicity and castigated as morally wrong, whereas citizen involvement in governance through reporting in liberal regimes is thought of as simply a manifestation of "good citizenship."

There is, however, an added dimension to contemporary liberal regimes of governance, and that is security. In contemporary liberal regimes of governance, reporting takes place not only in conditions of freedom, but also in the context of the emergence of security and surveillance as defining elements of governance (Ball et al. 2012; De Genova 2011b, 2013a; Goldstein 2010; Maguire et al. 2014). Freedom is thus securitized but not abandoned altogether, while security becomes a widely accepted public good.[3] It could thus be argued that contemporary liberal regimes of governance can be thought of as regimes of *securitized freedom*. Within such regimes, surveillance, bordering, and policing are not the sole responsibility of specialized institutions, but of society at large. Ordinary people are called upon to share the responsibility for public security by reporting on suspicious strangers, as well as on misbehaving family members, neighbors, or tenants. Security as a public good is not only about reporting on specific actions or behavior. Contemporary regimes of securitized freedom also seek to normalize reporting as an integral part of civic life and public culture. Public space is saturated with messages—for example, posters on the walls of London Tube stations—that do not invite reporting on particular acts, but rather work to create a general public atmosphere of vigilance by suggesting that people should trust their intuitions and report if they see anything suspicious. Reporting and other practices of citizen involvement in surveillance, bordering, and policing, such as vigilantism and activism (Doty 2001; Shapira 2013) illustrate particularly clearly that the distinction between the state and society is, as Timothy Mitchell (1999) has suggested, a "state effect."

In this chapter, I argue for the need to analyze practices of reporting in order to understand the subjects and socialities that contemporary regimes of securitized freedom assume, deploy, and produce, and thus for understanding the polities and politics that they make possible. In order to take some steps toward such analysis, I analyze reporting in the context of European practices of bordering and nation-building. My reflections are based on fieldwork with the Latvian State Border Guard (e.g., Dzenovska 2014), as well as encounters with other state institutions in Latvia as my primary fieldwork site, such as the Latvian State Language Centre. I also draw on what I have been able to gather on the role of reporting in bordering in the UK, which at this point mainly consists of reading policy reports, media articles, and scrutinizing stray reports that have been submitted to the University of Oxford's Migration Observatory by people who evidently thought that the role of the Migration Observatory is to police rather than to research migration.

Admittedly, empirical material on reporting in contemporary liberal democracies is scarce. Historical analyses of reporting benefit from the availability of archives, which contain letters of denunciation and files of informers or their targets. I have not had access to equivalent data on contemporary scenes of reporting. However, my aim here is to argue for the importance of paying attention to reporting as an increasingly salient element of public culture and as an instrument of governance. I am interested in asking what an analysis of reporting can tell us about how power works in liberal democracies in the current historical moment. How is reporting accommodated in conceptions of good European or national citizenship? What kind of subjects are assumed and produced in the process? How do concrete practices of reporting, as well as the establishment of a "denunciatory atmosphere," constitute particular public socialities and therefore also political futures?

In this chapter, I use a historical analytical lens—that of state socialism—to bring into focus the specificities of reporting as an instrument of governance in Europe after socialism. For example, I ask: How is it that the informing machinery that socialist states deployed is thought of as a feature of totalitarianism, whereas the Intelligence Management System crafted by the UK Home Office is an acceptable, even commendable, technology of government? How is it that the former socialist informers are thought of as victims, collaborators, or cowards, whereas "members of the public" in liberal democratic contexts who report on "individuals living in their community" are virtuous citizens?

By using former socialist contexts as a lens through which to reflect on reporting in liberal regimes of governance I do not mean to suggest that they are the same. I do mean to suggest, however, that historical and anthropological analyses of socialism and postsocialist transformations are helpful in thinking about the specificities of contemporary modes of power (e.g., Boyer and Yurchak 2010). Moreover, analysis of the bordering practices of the Latvian State Border Guard, as it was undergoing integration into EU-ropean structures and a more general Europeanization of its practices and attitudes, provides a link between the socialist past and the EU-ropean present. Thus, while reporting is a feature shared by liberal democratic regimes of governance beyond Europe, this chapter draws on material that shows how reporting emerges as an important instrument of governance in the process of postsocialist transformations and European integration. Latvian border guards are learning both—to erect and guard borders in conditions of freedom and to become "European." This means embracing values of freedom, democracy, and human rights, while also upholding European-ness as a racialized civilizational space. As part of this project of Europeanization, reporting in European regimes of securitized freedom is linked with racialized imaginaries and practices of European-ness.

Becoming European, or Reporting in Conditions of Freedom

The collapse of the Soviet Union in 1991 set in motion myriad practices of re-bordering, which, in the context of Eastern Europe, were also practices of Europeanization. Former internal boundaries between Soviet republics became external borders between new nation-states, and for some, such as Latvia, they became borders between the European Union and Russia. The interests of the renewed Latvian state converged with those of the European Union, as both aimed to strengthen the eastern border in order to regulate the movement of variously defined foreigners. In fact, Latvia's ability to guard the new external border of the European Union became a crucial marker of its European-ness (see Follis 2011 for a similar discussion on Poland). However, the initial period of transformation was somewhat chaotic, as border control procedures and technologies were not yet standardized. The Latvian border guards did what they thought appropriate in order to meet the goal of strengthening the border. A high-ranking official of the Latvian border guard told me that, despite the chaos, "immigration control was successfully devised in the beginning," as measured by the minimal presence of migrants and asylum-seekers in Latvia. Border guard officers explained to me that one of the techniques used to reach this goal was to approach people on the street if they looked as though they did not belong. Indeed, an acquaintance of mine, whose husband is African American, often had to pick him up from various police stations where he had been detained on suspicion that he might be an "illegal" migrant. Immigration police simply detained him on the street until his persona and legal status could be clarified. In the early post-Soviet days, Latvian immigration authorities thus relied on a commonsense understanding of who did and who did not belong. In the process, the proper "European" subject emerged as racially white. Subjects racialized as nonwhite were the presumed targets rather than the beneficiaries of the European practices of bordering and surveillance (Maguire 2012).

Subsequently, in the process of EU integration and border standardization, the Latvian border guard was tasked not only with strengthening the external EU border, but also with becoming civilized, that is, with protecting borders while observing the basic human rights of border-crossers. Approaching people on the street on the basis of their looks could be deemed discriminatory, though, as one officer put it, "we could still do it if we wanted to, but our attitudes have changed." Europeanization as civilization, then, meant keeping a variety of mutually reinforcing policing techniques at one's disposal, while having the "good sense" to use those appropriate for a properly European border force. This process of Europeanization also entailed the institutionalization of alternative policing strategies: for example, as part of the new bordering strategy, border guards received intelligence from individuals who reported their paperless partners in bouts of anger. The Latvian border guard also reoriented its activities toward sustained collaboration with the police, employment agencies, and hotels, which included asking the staff of these institutions to report on suspicious persons or activities. Not being able to racially profile people on the street, the border guard delegated this task to the public, where racialized imaginaries of belonging were common. For the border guard, reporting therefore turned out to be a crucial strategy for controlling the territory in conditions of freedom and within a EU-ropean political and institutional framework. The Europeanization of border practices, thus, entailed an institutional commitment to an inclusive vision of society and human rights, as well as informal practices of racialized categorization.

Reporting was also used by other institutions of governance—for example, by the Latvian State Language Centre, an institution charged with the task of policing language use in the public arena. The role of the center is to implement the Latvian Language Law, which stipulates that individuals occupying jobs in which they might come into contact with the public must demonstrate a certain level of Latvian language skill. In order to enforce this, the center conducts inspections, most of which are initiated by *sūdzības* (complaints) from members of the public. The activities of the center are mostly geared toward counteracting the Russification efforts of the Soviet state, as a result of which Russian became the public lingua franca during the Soviet period. In independent Latvia, Latvian is the state language, and all individuals occupying public positions, whether in public or private sectors, are required to be able to communicate with the public in Latvian. Thus sūdzības in this context are usually assumed to play out tensions between Latvian and Russian speakers. However, as observed by language inspectors, scenes of reporting suggest a more complex theater of tensions than the public and political conflict between Latvians and Russian speakers.

Moreover, despite an ideological commitment to the nationalist task of the State Language Centre and reliance on reporting in carrying out this work, staff members of the Latvian State Language Centre do not necessarily idealize those who submit complaints as virtuous or good citizens. For example, one inspector of the Latvian State Language Centre acknowledged the value of reporting in the center's work, but noted that members of the public mostly report in anger or, in some cases, as part of an act of revenge against their former employer: "I mean, she worked there for all those years and did not have a problem with the language used at work, and then reported on them as soon as she was fired." Other examples mentioned by the language inspector included members of an apartment cooperative reporting on other members for not speaking Latvian in their meetings. This was a private setting where individuals did not seem to be able to resolve communication with each other and turned to the state as a repressive arbitrator. As the language inspector noted, they could have each spoken their own language as long as the other party understood it, but there were other underlying conflicts—for example, debt—that prevented members of the cooperative from resolving the matter themselves. Rather than finding some more neutral means of mediation, they chose the State Language Centre as a punitive state agency to intervene in the conflict. The language inspector concluded that language problems were often entangled with conflicts of a material nature and that most people reported when their material interests were at stake.

This is the lens through which the language inspector evaluated most complaints he received. When prison inmates complained about nurses not speaking the Latvian language, he concluded that the nurses probably did not provide the inmates with desired drugs. He also noted that there are more and more cases where Russian speakers report on other Russian speakers to sort out their economic disputes. Sometimes it is lawyers who report on behalf of their clients. If someone registers a complaint that the Russian language is being imposed in a kindergarten, then it is probably the case that a parent has been reprimanded for their child being late. "Nobody complains just like that," observed the language inspector, as he recounted another case where a teacher who was seventy years old and had worked in a school for most of her working life was reported as not speaking Latvian. "They just needed her to leave," the inspector concluded.

Not all cases, however, were materially motivated. Some people reacted to a humiliating or enraging encounter they experienced in a taxi or in a shop. Reporting activity also intensified in moments of political tension, such as the 2013 referendum on whether to make the Russian language the second state language in Latvia. The inspector also noted that some people are "professional reporters"; that is, they monitor affairs in multiple spheres of public life and report to a variety of state institutions. Perhaps most unexpectedly, multiple inspectors noted that the frequency of reporting is significantly influenced by lunar phases—the number of reports increases substantially around the full moon. Ultimately, the inspector concluded, "we protect the interests of physical persons. It is a small minority of people who report, but, by protecting them, we protect all others." Thus the inspector navigated a murky ethical terrain. On the one hand, he did not have much faith in the moral compass or civic consciousness of the individuals on whose reports his work relied. On the other hand, he reasoned that those people who strive to sort out their private feuds and interests nevertheless contribute to the public good by enabling the State Language Agency to make the public space more Latvian. Insofar as this is a publicly endorsed goal of the institution, relying on reporting was justifiable even as the availability of the mechanism of reporting brought out the worst in those who took it up. In post-Soviet Latvia, then, the institutionalization of reporting in governance is not necessarily thought of as a morally dubious technique of governance even as the virtue of reporters themselves occasionally comes into question. The Latvian case confirms that in situations where the ends of governance and the regime of governance itself are thought to be good, the use of reporting tends to be justified even as the act of reporting itself might not be celebrated.

In the United Kingdom, the few reports mistakenly addressed to Oxford's Migration Observatory also suggest that complex personal relations animate scenes of reporting. Of the five denunciations I have seen, four pertained to the same two asylum-seekers—an Iranian man and woman, allegedly cousins, but, according to the reporters, posing as a couple in the United Kingdom. The reporters—possibly four different individuals, possibly one person writing from four different addresses—reported that both asylum-seekers are well situated back in Iran, but are claiming asylum in the UK because they want to get benefits. In appealing to authorities, the reporters wrote that it was not fair that these two individuals should claim asylum and the associated benefits, especially when foreign students struggle so much to survive "in that crazy land" [the UK] where "life is horrible." The fifth report pertained to a Bangladeshi woman who was also allegedly well situated in Bangladesh—the report included considerable detail as to her family's properties—but had lied in order to obtain asylum because "she is greedy for pound and glittering of London." The reporters suggested that the individuals they reported on deserved to be punished because they had lied out of greed, a desire for benefits and a cosmopolitan lifestyle, and were not in dire economic need at all. The reporters thought that this was especially unfair in relation to other Iranians or Bangladeshis who are struggling to survive in London. While the moralizing overtones of the reports play into prevalent stereotypes about asylum-seekers as benefit-seekers, it is hardly possible to know how these reports came about. It remains unclear to what extent they were animated by a genuine sense of unfairness and to what extent they were animated by other factors, such as anger arising out of personal conflict with the reported individuals, whether in the UK, Iran, or Bangladesh.

Some of the case studies described in a 2014 report of the UK independent chief inspector of borders and immigration on the workings of the Home Office's Intelligence Management System also suggest deeply personal and socially embedded contexts of reporting. One case study described in the evaluation report pertains to an instance of reporting where the reporter informed the authorities about the breakdown of another person's marriage, which effectively eliminated that person's only legal reason for staying in the UK. It is not clear whether the reporter was the partner of the broken marriage or someone else, but the knowledge of marital affairs suggests a degree of intimacy that goes beyond superficial suspicion. Another case study pertained to a report that an individual had overstayed their expired UK visa for six years. Yet another allegation suggested that an individual had applied for a visitor's visa from India, but that their intention was actually to stay in the UK. The authors of the evaluation report lamented that the Home Office did not react in time, thus failing to prevent the issuance of the visa to the said individual (see also Barrett 2013).

All of these cases suggest that reporting is not only about governance, but also, if not most importantly, about intimacy and the constitution of social relations through reporting as an increasingly prominent tool of governance in liberal regimes of securitized freedom. It is therefore crucial to study the socialities assumed and produced by contemporary security regimes in order to understand what collective futures inhere in the present.

Surveillance and Social Relations in the Political Space of Europe

In the course of rebordering Latvia as part of rebordering Europe, bordering is distributed in the political space (Balibar 1993a/2002, 1993b/2002). The emergence of reporting as a mechanism for migration control is part of this redistribution of bordering. However, reporting is not just a technology of surveillance through which the state regulates migration. It is a practice embedded in and productive of social relations, thereby complicating the juxtaposition between the state's mechanisms of surveillance and "ordinary people." For example, in his call for fostering a critical "security anthropology," Daniel Goldstein (2010) invites attention to how nonstate actors understand and inhabit the security turn. Drawing on his own work in Latin America, Goldstein illustrates how people are taking up wartime security by forming vigilante groups. In a similar vein, Harel Shapira (2013) has written an ethnography of the Minutemen—a group of men, mostly military veterans, who have become citizen vigilantes "waiting for José" on the U.S.-Mexico border. Furthermore, in his analysis of policing methamphetamine production and use in a Virginia locality, William

Garriott (2013) shows how policing is distributed within the local community. People are asked to contact police when they encounter suspicious objects or behavior. On many occasions, it turns out that socially embedded knowledge is more effective for policing than intelligence produced by the state bureaucracy. On some occasions, community involvement leads to lethal violence, as was the case in a Florida neighborhood watch. In 2012, George Zimmerman—a neighborhood watch coordinator of The Retreat at Twin Lakes, a gated community in Sanford, Florida—shot Trayvon Martin, an African American teenager, during an altercation between the two. Zimmerman had initially approached Martin, thinking that the boy looked suspicious because he was wearing a hoodie (and because he was black). This and similar instances of community vigilance suggest that the poor, the racially marginalized, and migrants—actual or suspected—are primary targets of policing in polities where responsibility for security is distributed within the population. It is not the state as a clearly delineated entity that exercises power upon bodies. Rather, power in regimes of "securitized freedom" is exercised through socialities of surveillance, where individuals and communities are engaged in watching each other for signs of threat, which more often than not take the form of racialized poverty or foreignness. In other words, there is a social dynamic to surveillance that is entangled with the state, but not single-handedly produced by it. The act of reporting, thus, can serve as a lens through which to examine socialities of liberal security regimes and the political openings or closures they entail.

The Latvian and UK institutions that invite reporting by members of the public, such as the Latvian State Border Guard and the UK Home Office, assume that individuals who report are socially embedded, have friends, family, partake in community life, love, hate, and argue, all of which can become fruitful grounds for reporting. These social relations, however, are not of explicit concern to the institutions. In contrast, as suggested by Katherine Verdery (2014), the Romanian socialist security apparatus was very much concerned not only with the information received, but also with the social relations disrupted or cultivated through reporting. On the basis of analysis of her Securitate file created during her fieldwork in Romania since the 1970s, which she retrieved from the archives of the Romanian security agency, Verdery suggests that the Securitate not only aimed to obtain useful information for the state, but also worked upon social relations through the mechanism of reporting. Verdery argues that, contrary to Western conceptions of liberal autonomous subjects, the Romanian security apparatus worked with conceptions of socially embedded subjects. She describes the case of her friend Mariana, who had been recruited by Securitate to inform on her. Mariana had reluctantly agreed when approached, thinking that she would at least be able to protect Verdery by providing what she thought was irrelevant information to Securitate officers. However, Mariana also suffered, for she could not talk about this with anyone. Verdery writes: "Her relation with her officer introduced a deceitful relation to herself, one she has trouble acknowledging even now, telling me: 'I simply cannot think of myself as an informer.' In a sense, being an informer obscured her from herself" (2014:179).

The use of informers in Romania, Verdery goes on to argue, was parasitic on basic forms of social life, while pushing those forms in new directions to create socialist persons (2014:196). The security apparatus took people's sociality to be dangerous and thus worked to disrupt it. Verdery suggests that the security apparatus intervened by changing persons through their relationships—if persons were the sum of their relationships, then changing their relationships changed them as well. For example, Verdery's file revealed that the security apparatus had tried to prevent her from seeing some people, while inserting others into her social circles. Security officers thus tried to disrupt her social relations by making her "the sum of theirs and not her relations."

Verdery's analysis illuminates an important distinction between modes of power in state socialism and liberalism. Whereas the Romanian socialist regime considered that reformation of social relations was crucial for the making of proper socialist subjects, contemporary liberal regimes do not work on social relations in the same way. That is, liberal regimes of securitized freedom do not aim to remake people's social networks in an invasive manner to create different future men and women, but this does not mean that they do not rely on social relations in governance. In other words, while liberal regimes of securitized freedom do not explicitly work on sociality, they do assume socially embedded persons by introducing the possibility of resolving personal grievances or furthering self-interest using a punitive state apparatus. The UK government's Prevent Programme is a good illustration of the assumed social embeddedness of reporting individuals in that it invites Muslim women to report on male family members planning to go and fight with "jihadists" (Saul 2014). The state is appealing to women to prevent their family members from exposing themselves to danger by reporting to the state. The state furthers its antiterrorism agenda, while the family prevents a possible loss of a family member. This scheme is based on the recognition that people will report for personal reasons rather than as disinterested good citizens in the name of public security. The women are assumed to be family and community members. They are asked to act as socially embedded individuals who know of the plans and intentions of their family members, but also as individuals who have a direct relationship to the state as citizens regardless of their legal status. In this case, the state–citizen relation is constituted through reporting. The assumed subject is thus socially embedded, but unable or unwilling to handle the issue at hand through social relations and networks, and is therefore in need of state intervention. Contemporary security regimes thus are not top-down machines of violence, but crucially depend on the subject who is socially embedded, yet able to distance herself from social relations and enter into a direct relationship with the state, even if for personal benefit.

There is too little data on the social relations assumed and constituted by contemporary practices of reporting, and thus it is premature to authoritatively discuss the effects of socialities of surveillance on individuals and collectivities. However, in the concluding part of this chapter, as I reflect on modes of power at play in contemporary scenes of reporting, I do suggest some avenues for thinking about what such effects may be.

Power, Sociality, and Political Futures

Katherine Verdery places the mode of power at work in socialist security regimes in a line of historical sequence that "runs from the very visible public executions witnessed by large crowds with which Foucault opened *Discipline and Punish*, on to the panopticon popularized by Bentham—where vision is concentrated in a single invisible observer at the center, with the observed citizen arrayed visibly around him—and hence to the socialist power, which places the observed citizen at the center, with multiple kinds of vigilant observers arrayed invisibly around him" (2014:209). The questions that I have tried to open in this chapter are: What modes of power and associated socialities are conjured up by practices of co-surveillance and reporting in contemporary liberal democracies? How do such practices illuminate the current historical moment? What kind of power is at work when individuals are called upon not only to be responsible neoliberal subjects, but also to be responsible subjects of surveillance?

The aim of this chapter has been to suggest that it is worth paying attention to scenes of reporting to push further in thinking about contemporary modes of power in Europe and in (neo)liberal regimes of governance more broadly. I have provisionally described this mode of power as "securitized freedom." I have tacked back and forth between historical analysis of former socialist regimes and reflections on scenes of reporting in the political space of Europe to cast light on some of the ways in which reporting matters today. There are, of course, important differences between the informing apparatus of socialist and liberal states. In addition to the assumption that liberal states govern in the name of freedom, whereas socialist states govern in the name of total (and violent) social transformation of society, there are also differences between the assumed subjects and objects of reporting. For example, whereas in the Soviet Union *everyone* could be considered under suspicion as a potential enemy of the state, in contemporary Latvia and Britain it is mostly those who are perceived to be *foreigners* or *failed citizens* that are targeted by informing practices. Thus, even as everyone is supposed to watch everyone else, or the public space in general, for the sake of the common good, contemporary regimes of securitized freedom mobilize a distinction between beneficiaries and objects of surveillance, which maps onto familiar and racialized distinctions between Europeans and their others. Moreover, European-ness is not mapped solely onto foreigners, but also onto citizens who can gain or lose "goodness" or European-ness depending on their conduct in particular circumstances.

Importantly, the subject of reporting—that is, the person who reports—is not necessarily the beneficiary of regimes of securitized freedom. Despite the implicit appeal to "good citizens" in the state agencies' invitation to report, the reporters are not seen as "good citizens" in the actual scenes of reporting. In fact, as the cases reviewed suggest, it may not even be formal citizens who report on noncitizens. It could very well be migrants reporting on other migrants, because they find their situation unfair in comparison to the life of the people they are reporting. On the basis of insights from preliminary conversations with the authorities in Latvia, and from a review of the few reports received by the Migration Observatory, it seems that the reporter emerges as a marginal subject, seen by the authorities as possibly a poor, not very well-educated person, and someone easily swayed by emotion or even lunar phases. It might be the case, then, that the state does not actually intend for the "good citizens" to report on noncitizens, but rather for the "failed citizens" or noncitizens to report on others like them (Anderson 2013). The effect is that denunciations are state-based tools through which the marginalized help to police themselves for the sake of the security of the normative (neo)liberal subject—the beneficiary par excellence of securitized freedom. The normative (neo)liberal subject may or may not report, but this subject is most often complicit with regimes of securitized freedom by simply going on with life and by taking surveillance to be a "fundamental social institution" that exists for his or her benefit (Graeber 2014:76).

Reporting is about modes of power and regimes of governance. Its distinctive feature as a tool of governance is that it simultaneously constitutes and undermines categorical distinctions. On the one hand, reporting often draws racialized lines between citizens and foreigners, good citizens and failed citizens, and Europeans and non-Europeans. On the other hand, reporting undermines these categories insofar as those who report and those who are reported on cannot be easily categorized. While the calls for citizens to report and thus to protect borders or benefits resound as apparently being aimed at "good citizens," in reality it is "good citizens" reporting on other "good citizens," asylum-seekers reporting on asylum-seekers, migrants on migrants, and "failed citizens" on "failed citizens," as well as any combination thereof. It thus suggests that bordering and policing is done by everyone, while the beneficiaries of regimes of securitized freedom are few.

Reporting is also about sociality and political futures. If the social fabric cultivated in regimes of securitized freedom is one of co-surveillance and reporting, what kind of social and political formations is this producing? Where does one locate one's political interventions in conditions when policing is distributed throughout the population? For example, the raids undertaken by the UK Home Office, which called my attention to practices of reporting in the first place, are often targeted by anti-raid activism. In a blog report on anger over raids in Brixton (London), Tim Dickens quotes a woman saying that "the Border Agency needs to know that if they are going to be conducting these kind of arrests in the community then the community will be watching." However, it seems important to recognize that the community had already been watching. Given that the Home Office cannot conduct speculative immigration checks but must have a reason to act, they must have received or produced "intelligence." This raises the question of how one might conceive of a politics that takes into account the pervasive presence of the reporting subject who makes that phone call or writes that email to inform on "individuals living in their community." The question is consequential indeed: What would it take to rework social relations in a way that would not propel people to sort out their personal or collective grievances by turning acquaintances, neighbors, strangers, and family members over to the punitive agencies of the state? Most importantly, how do we connect scholarly and political interventions that examine or target regimes of governance increasingly based on reporting with interventions that examine and work upon the sociality produced by the emergence of a "denunciatory atmosphere"?

NOTES

1. Sheila Fitzpatrick and Robert Gellately (1996) distinguish informing as a sustained relationship of reporting with the state from denunciations as spontaneous acts of reporting.

2. https://www.gov.uk/government/publications/right-to-rent-landlords-code-of-practice.

3. Some scholars link this "security turn" to a post–September 11, 2001 world (e.g., Schwell 2014). Others point to a more gradual consolidation of racial neoliberal

regimes in Euro-American political spaces that criminalize the poor, migrants, and otherwise marginalized subjects, thus dismantling the difference between internal and external threats (Bigo 2001; Fassin 2011a; Goldberg 2009; Wacquant 2009; Walters 2010). Still others argue that neoliberalism is retreating and giving way "to a darker vision of society harnessed to the valorisation of policing as the primary mechanism of governance" (Susan Brin Hyatt, "What Was Neoliberalism and What Comes Next?" quoted in Riles 2013:560). Importantly, in contemporary security regimes, the threat lies not only outside the polity, but also within it in the form of a variety of racialized denizens. Contemporary security regimes blur the distinction between migrants and "failed citizens" (Anderson 2012, 2013)—for example, ex-prisoners and welfare dependents—and juxtapose both to the figure of the "good citizen."

REFERENCES

Abdulla, Ameer, and Olof Linden, eds. 2008. *Maritime Traffic Effects on Biodiversity in the Mediterranean Sea*. Malaga: IUCN Centre for Mediterranean Cooperation.

Adamson, Fiona. 2006. "Crossing Borders: International Migration and National Security." *International Security* 31 (1): 165–99.

Afet ve Acil Durum Yönetimi Başkanlığı (AFAD) [Prime Ministry Disaster and Emergency Management Presidency] (Turkey). 2013. Syrian Guests Circular on Health and Other Services. Circular No. 8 (September 9). Accessed September 10, 2013. https://www.afad.gov.tr/TR/IcerikDetay.aspx?ID=44.

Agamben, Giorgio. 2005. *State of Exception*. Chicago: University of Chicago Press.

Agier, Michel. 2002. *Aux bords du monde, les réfugiés*. Paris: Flammarion.

———. 2003. "La main gauche de l'Empire: Ordre et désordres de l'humanitaire." *Multitudes*, no. 11.

———. 2006. "The Chaos and the Camps: Fragments of a Humanitarian Government." In *The Maghreb Connection: Movements of Life across North Africa*, ed. Ursula Biemann and Brian Holmes, 260–82. Barcelona: Actar.

———. 2011. *Managing the Undesirables: Refugee Camps and Humanitarian Government*. Cambridge: Polity.

Agier, Michel, and Clara Lecadet, eds. 2014. *Un monde de camps*. Paris: La Découverte.

Ahearn, Laura. 2001. "Language and Agency." *Annual Review of Anthropology* 30:109–37.

Ahmed, Sara. 1999. "Home and Away." *International Journal of Cultural Studies* 2:329–47.

Aitchison, Guy. 2010. "Help Us Stop 1,000 Billion Benefit Scroungers." openDemocracy. https://www.opendemocracy.net/ourkingdom/guy-aitchison/help-us-stop-£1000-billion-benefit-scroungers.

Alioua, Mehdi, and Charles Heller. 2013. "Transnational Migration, Clandestinity and Globalization—Sub Saharan Transmigrants in Morocco." In *New Mobilities Regimes in Art and Social Sciences*, ed. Sven Kesselring and Gerlinde Vogl. London: Ashgate.

Allou, Olivier. 2011. "Trafic de visas au sein des consulats et ambassades (Acte 1): Voici la stratégie des faussaires." *Parole d'Afrique* (Abidjan) (December 5, 2011).

Alpes, Maybritt Jill. 2011. "Bushfalling: How Young Cameroonians Dare to Migrate." Faculty of Social and Behavioural Sciences. Amsterdam: Free University of Amsterdam.

Alpes, Maybritt Jill, and Alexis Spire. 2014. "Dealing with Law in Migration Control: The Powers of Street-Level Bureaucrats at French Consulates." *Social and Legal Studies* 23 (2): 261–74.

Álvarez, Robert. 1995. "The Mexican-US Border: The Making of an Anthropology of Borderlands." *Annual Review of Anthropology* 24:447–70.

———. 2012. "Reconceptualizing the Space of the Mexico-US Borderline." In *A Companion to Border Studies*, ed. Thomas M. Wilson and Hastings Donnan, 538–56. Oxford: Wiley-Blackwell.

Amnesty International. 2013. "Press Release 19th of December 2013." Accessed December 20, 2013. https://www.amnesty.org/en/for-media/press-releases/greece-investigate-police-chief-s-alleged-call-targeting-migrants-2013-12-1.

———. 2014. "Lives Adrift: Refugees and Migrants in Peril in the Central Mediterranean." https://www.amnesty.org/en/documents/EUR05/006/2014/en/.

———. 2015. " 'Libya Is Full of Cruelty': Stories of Abduction, Sexual Violence and Abuse from Migrants and Refugees." https://www.amnesty.org/en/documents/mde19/1578/2015/en/.

Amoore, Louise. 2006. "Biometric Borders: Governing Mobilities in the War on Terror." *Political Geography* 25:336–51.

Anderson, Bridget. 2008. "Illegal Immigrant: Victim or Villain?" Centre on Migration, Policy and Society Working Paper WP-08-64.

———. 2012. "What Does the 'Migrant' Tell Us about the (Good) Citizen?" Centre on Migration, Policy and Society Working Paper No. 94. https://www.compas.ox.ac.uk/fileadmin/files/Publications/working_papers/WP_2012/WP1294_Anderson.pdf.

———. 2013. *Us and Them? The Dangerous Politics of Immigration*. Oxford: Oxford University Press.

Anderson, Bridget, Nandita Sharma, and Cynthia Wright. 2010. "Editorial: Why No Borders?" *Refuge* 26 (2): 5–18.

Andersson, Ruben. 2012. "A Game of Risk: Boat Migration and the Business of Bordering Europe." *Anthropology Today* 28 (6): 7–11.

———. 2014a. "Hunter and Prey: Patrolling Clandestine Migration in the Euro-African Borderlands." *Anthropological Quarterly* 87 (1): 119–49.

———. 2014b. *Illegality, Inc.: Clandestine Migration and the Business of Bordering Europe*. Berkeley: University of California Press.

———. 2016. "The Global Front against Migration." *Anthropology of This Century* 15 (January).

Andreas, Peter. 1998. "The U.S. Immigration Control Offensive: Constructing an Image of Order on the Southwest Border." In *Crossings: Mexican Immigration in Interdisciplinary Perspectives*, ed. Macelo M. Suarez-Orozoco, 341–56. Cambridge, MA: Harvard University Press.

———. 2000. *Border Games: Policing the U.S.-Mexico Divide*. Ithaca, NY: Cornell University Press.

Andreone, Gemma. 2004. "Observations sur la 'Juridictionnalisation' de la Mediterranée." *Annuaire Du Droit de La Mer* 9:7–25.

Andrijasevic, Rutvica. 2010. "From Exception to Excess: Detention and Deportations across the Mediterranean Space." In *The Deportation Regime: Sovereignty, Space, and the Freedom of Movement*, ed. Nicholas De Genova and Nathalie Peutz, 147–65. Durham, NC: Duke University Press.

Andrijasevic, Rutvic, Manuela Bojadžijev, Sabine Hess, Serhat Karakayali, Afthimia Panagiotidis, and Vassilis Tsianos. 2005. "Turbulente Ränder: Konturen eines neuen Migrationsregimes im Südosten Europas." *PROKLA—Zeitschrift für kritische Sozialwissenschaften* 35:345–62.

Appel, H. 2015. "On Simultaneity." *Cultural Anthropology Online* (March 30, 2015). http://culanth.org/fieldsights/658-on-simultaneity.

Aradau, Claudia, and Jef Huysmans. 2009. "Mobilising (Global) Democracy: A Political Reading of Mobility between Universal Rights and the Mob." *Millennium: Journal of International Studies* 37 (3): 583–604.

Ardener, Edward. 1987. "Remote Areas: Some Theoretical Considerations." In *Anthropology at Home*, ed. Anthony Jackson. London: Tavistock. Reprinted (2012) in *HAU: Journal of Ethnographic Theory* 2(1): 519–33.

Asad, Talal. 2002. "Muslims and European Identity: Can Europe Represent Islam?" In *The Idea of Europe from Antiquity to the European Union*, ed. Anthony Pagden, 209–27. New York: Woodrow Wilson Center Press/Cambridge University Press.

Associated Press. 2015. "European Nations Shut Their Borders to Economic Migrants." *New York Times*, November 19, 2015. http://www.nytimes.com/aponline/2015/11/19/world/europe/ap-eu-europe-migrants.html.

Ataç, Ilker, Stefanie Kron, Sarah Schilliger, Helge Schwiertz, and Maurice Stierl. 2015. "Struggles of Migration as In-/Visible Politics." *Movements: Journal für kritische Migrations- und Grenzregimeforschung* [Journal for Critical Migration and Border Regime Research] 1 (2). http://movements-journal.org/issues/02.kaempfe/01.ataç,kron,schilliger,schwiertz,stierl—einleitung~en.html.

Aziza, M. 2008. "Entre Nador et Melilla, une frontière européenne en terre marocaine: Analyse des relations transfrontalières." *Vivre et tracer les frontières dans les mondes contemporains* (Tangiers).

Baeza, C., L. Bonnefoy, and H. Thiollet. 2005. "L'invention de la contestation transnationale par les forums et sommets: La naissance d'un 'espace public mondial'?" *Raisons politiques* 19:25–43.

Bailey, R. 2009. "Up against the Wall: Bare Life and Resistance in Australian Immigration Detention." *Law and Critique* 20 (2): 113–32.

Balibar, Étienne. 1991a. "Es Gibt keinen Staat in Europa: Racism and Politics in Europe Today." *New Left Review* 186:5–19.

———. 1991b. "Is There a 'Neo-Racism'?" In Balibar and Wallerstein (1991), *Race, Nation, Class: Ambiguous Identities*, 17–28. New York: Verso.

———. 1991c. "Racism and Crisis." In Balibar and Wallerstein (1991), *Race, Nation, Class: Ambiguous Identities*, 217–27. New York: Verso.

———. 1992/2002. "Is There Such a Thing as European Racism?" In Balibar (2002), *Politics and the Other Scene*, 40–55. New York: Verso.

———. 1993a/2002. "The Borders of Europe." In Balibar (2002), *Politics and the Other Scene*, 87–103). New York: Verso.

———. 1993b/2002. "What Is a Border?" In Balibar (2002), *Politics and the Other Scene*, 75–86. New York: Verso.

———. 1998. "Ce que nous devons aux 'Sans-Papiers.'" In Balibar, *Droit de cite*, 23–25. Paris: PUF.

———. 1999a. "At the Borders of Europe." In Balibar (2004), *We, the People of Europe? Reflections on Transnational Citizenship*, 1–10. Princeton, NJ: Princeton University Press.

———. 1999b. "*Droit de Cité* or Apartheid?" In Balibar (2004), *We, the People of Europe? Reflections on Transnational Citizenship*, 31–50. Princeton, NJ: Princeton University Press.

———. 2004. *We, the People of Europe? Reflections on Transnational Citizenship*. Princeton, NJ: Princeton University Press.

———. 2004/2009. "Europe as Borderland." *Environment and Planning D: Society and Space* 27 (2) (2009): 190–215.

Balibar, Étienne, and Immanuel Wallerstein. 1991. *Race, Nation Class: Ambiguous Identities*. London:Verso.

Ball, Kirstie, Kevin Haggerty, and David Lyon, eds. 2012. *Routledge Handbook of Surveillance Studies*. London: Routledge.

Barnett, Michael N., and Thomas George Weiss. 2008. *Humanitarianism in Question: Politics, Power, Ethics*. Ithaca, NY: Cornell University Press.

———. Weiss. 2011. *Humanitarianism Contested: Where Angels Fear to Tread*. Oxon: Routledge.

Barrett, David. 2013. "Home Office Fails to Investigate Vast Majority of Tip-Offs about Illegal Immigrants." *The Telegraph*, November 8. http://www.telegraph.co.uk/news/uknews/immigration/10434062/Home-Office-fails-to-investigate-vast-majority-of-tip-offs-about-illegal-immigrants.html.

Barthes, Roland. 1972. *Mythologies*. Ed. and trans. Annette Lavers. New York: Hill and Wang.

Basaran, A., and H.-G. Eberl. 2009. "Im Land der Abgeschobenen: Soziale Realitäten und Selbstorganisierung von unten in Togo." *Hinterland Magazin* 10:5–15.

Bauder, Harald. 2006. *Labour Movement: How Migration Regulates Labour Markets*. New York: Oxford University Press

———. 2013. "Why We Should Use the Term Illegalized Immigrant." RCIS Research Brief No. 2013/1:1–7. Toronto: Ryerson Centre for Immigration and Settlement.

Baumann, Zigmunt. 1995. "Making and Unmaking of Strangers." *Thesis Eleven* 43:1–16.

BBC News. 2010. 'Turkish Leader Erdogan Makes 'Historic' Greek Visit." Accessed 10/01/2013. http://news.bbc.co.uk/1/hi/world/europe/8682390.stm.

———. 2011. "David Cameron Urges People to Report Illegal Immigrants." October 10, 2011. http://www.bbc.co.uk/news/uk-15235649.

———. 2013. "EU and Turkey Agreement on Deporting Migrants and Visas." Accessed October 10, 2013. http://www.bbc.co.uk/news/world-europe-25398872.

———. 2015. "Mediterranean Migrants: Hundreds Feared Dead after Boat Capsizes." April 19, 2015. http://www.bbc.co.uk/news/world-europe-32371348.

Bensaad, A. 2007. "The Mediterranean Divide and Its Echo in the Sahara: New Migratory Routes and New Barriers on the Path to the Mediterranean." In *Between Europe and the Mediterranean: The Challenges and the Fears*, ed. Thierry Fabre and Paul Sant-Cassia. New York: Palgrave Macmillan.

Benasayag, Miguel, and Gérard Schmit. 2005. *L'epoca delle Passioni Tristi*. Milan: Feltrinelli.

Benton, Lauren. 2010. *A Search for Sovereignty: Law and Geography in European Empires, 1400–1900*. Cambridge: Cambridge University Press.

Benz, Martina, and Helen Schwenken. 2005. "Jenseits von Autonomie und Kontrolle: Migration als eigensinnige Praxis." *PROKLA—Zeitschrift für kritische Sozialwissenschaften* 35:363–78.

Bhabha, Homi. 1994. *The Location of Culture*. London: Routledge.

Bialasiewicz, Luiza. 2012. "Off-Shoring and Out-Sourcing the Borders of Europe: Libya and EU Border Work in the Mediterranean." *Geopolitics* 17 (4): 843–66.

Biehl, Kristen. 2015. "Spatializing Diversities, Diversifying Spaces: Housing Experiences in a Migration Hub of Istanbul." *Ethnic and Racial Studies* 38 (4).

Bigo, Didier. 2000. "When Two Become One: Internal and External Securitisations in Europe." In *International Relations Theory and the Politics of European Integration: Power, Security and Community*, ed. Morten Kelstrup and Michael C. Williams. London: Routledge.

———. 2001. "Migration and Security." In *Controlling a New Migration World*, ed. Virginie Guiraudon and Christian Joppke. London: Routledge.

———. 2002. "Security and Immigration: Toward a Critique of the Governmentality Unease." *Alternatives: Global, Local, Political* 27 (1): 63–92.

———. 2007. "Detention of Foreigners, States of Exception, and the Social Practices of Control of the Banopticon." In *Borderscapes. Hidden Geographies and Politics at Territory's Edge*, ed. Prem Kumar Rajaram and Carl Grundy-Warr. Minneapolis: University of Minnesota Press.

———. 2014. "The (In)securitization Practices of the Three Universes of EU Border Control: Military/Navy—Border Guards/Police—Database Analysts." *Security Dialogue* 45 (3): 209–25.

Bigo, Didier, and Elspeth Guild. 2003. "La logique du visa Schengen: Police à distance." *Cultures et Conflits* 49:5–147.

Blanchard, E. 2006. "Qu'est-ce que l'externalisation?" http://lmsi.net/Qu-est-ce-que-1 -externalisation.

Blin, T. 2005. *Les sans-papiers de Saint-Bernard: Mouvement social et action organisée*. Paris: L'Harmattan.

Boissevain, Jeremy. 1974. *Friends of Friends*. Oxford: Basil.

Bojadžijev, Manuela, and Serhat Karakayali. 2007. "Autonomie der Migration: 10 Thesen zu einer Methode." In *Turbulente Ränder. Neue Perspektiven auf Migration an den Grenzen Europas*, ed. Forschungsgruppe Transit Migration, 209–15. Bielefeld: Transcript.

———. 2010. "Recuperating the Sideshows of Capitalism: The Autonomy of Migration Today." *e-flux* 17.

Bojadžijev, Manuela, and Isabelle Saint-Saëns. 2006. "Borders, Citizenship, War, Class: A Discussion with Étienne Balibar and Sandro Mezzadra." *New Formations* 58:10–30.

Bologna, Sergio. 2013 [1972]. "Class Composition and the Theory of the Party at the Origins of Workers' Councils Movement." *Viewpoint* 3. Accessed May 14, 2014. http://viewpointmag.com/2013/09/30/issue-3-workers-inquiry/.

Borio, G., F. Pozzi, and G. Roggero. 2007. "Conricerca as Political Action." In *Utopian Pedagogy: Radical Experiments against Neoliberal Globalization*, ed. M. Coté, R. Day, and G. de Peuter, 163–85. Toronto: University of Toronto Press.

Bouchard, Geneviève, and Barbara Wake Carroll. 2002. "Policy-Making and Administrative Discretion: The Case of Immigration in Canada." *Canadian Public Administration* 45 (2): 239–57.

Bourdieu, Pierre. 1977. *Outline of a Theory of Practice*. Cambridge: Cambridge University Press.

Boyer, Dominic, and Alexei Yurchak. 2010. "American Stiob: Or, What Late-Socialist Aesthetics of Parody Reveal about Contemporary Political Culture in the West." *Cultural Anthropology* 25 (2): 179–222.

Braakman, M. 2005. *Roots and Routes: Questions of Home, Belonging and Return in an Afghan Diaspora*. Leiden University, Department of Cultural Anthropology and Sociology of Non-Western Societies. Leiden: Leiden University.

Brachet, J. 2009. *Migrations transsahariennes: Vers un désert cosmopolite et morcelé (Niger)*. Paris: Éditions du Croquant.

Braudel, Fernand. 1976. *The Mediterranean and the Mediterranean World in the Age of Philip II*, 2nd ed., 2 vols. Sian Reynolds, trans. New York: Harper and Row.

Bravo Nieto, A. 1996. *La construcción de una ciudad europea en el contexto norteafricano: Arquitectos e ingenieros en la Melilla contemporánea*. Melilla: Universidad de Málaga, Servicio de Publicaciones e Intercambio Científico.

Bredeloup, Sylvie. 2012. "Sahara Transit: Times, Spaces, People." *Population, Space and Place* 18 (4): 457–67.

Brekke, J. 2012. "Stuck in Transit? Reception Conditions for Asylum Seekers in Italy." *VAMMIG—Migration to Norway, Flows and Regulations*, Working Paper.

Brekke, J., and G. Brochmann. 2014. "Stuck in Transit: Secondary Migration of Asylum Seekers in Europe, National Differences, and the Dublin Regulation." *Journal of Refugee Studies*. doi: 10.1093/jrs/feu028.

Brewer, K., and D. Yükseker. 2009. "A Survey of African Migrants and Asylum Seekers in Istanbul." In *Land of Diverse Migrations*, ed. A. İçduygu and K. Kirişçi, 637–718. Istanbul: Istanbul Bilgi University Press.

Brigate di Solidarietá Attiva, Devi Sacchetto, D. Perrotta, M. Nigro, G. 2011. *Sulla Pelle Viva*. Rome: Derive Approdi.

Broeders, Dennis. 2007. "The New Digital Borders of Europe: EU Databases and the Surveillance of Irregular Migrants." *International Sociology* 22 (1): 71–92.

———. 2011. "A European 'Border' Surveillance System under Construction." In *Migration and the New Technological Borders of Europe*, ed. Huub Dijstelbloem and Albert Meijer. Basingstoke: Palgrave Macmillan.

Burds, Jeffrey. 1996. "A Culture of Denunciation: Peasant Labor Migration and Religious Anathemization in Rural Russia, 1860–1905." *Journal of Modern History* 68 (4): 786–818.

Burnett, Graham. 2009. "Hydrographic Discipline among the Navigators." In *The Imperial Map: Cartography and the Mastery of Empire*, ed. James Ackerman. Chicago: University of Chicago Press.

Cabot, H. 2014. *On the Doorstep of Europe: Asylum and Citizenship in Greece*. Philadelphia: University of Pennsylvania Press.

Calderón Vázquez, F. J. 2008. "Fronteras, identidad, conflicto e interacción: Los presidios españoles en el norte africano." www.eumed.net/libros/2008c/433/.

Campagne in Lotta. 2012. "Radio Ghetto e I Raccoglitori di Pomodoro." *Gli Asini: Educazione ed Intervento Sociale* 10.

Campbell, Scott. 2015. "Calais Jungle Migrant Camp 'Set on Fire' after Hundreds Killed in Terror Attacks." *Daily Express*, November 14, 2015. http://www.express .co.uk/news/world/619361/Calais-Jungle-migrant-camp-fire-Paris-terror-attacks ?utm_content=buffer4b0c3&utm_medium=social&utm_source=twitter.com &utm_campaign=buffer.

Carlier, J.-Y. 2007. "L'Europe et les étrangers." In *Mondialisation, migration et droits de l'homme: Le droit international en question*, vol. 2, ed. V. Chetail, 239–78. Bruxelles: Bruylant.

Carling, Jørgen. 2007a. "Migration Control and Migrant Fatalities at the Spanish-African Borders." *International Migration Review* 41 (2): 316–43.

———. 2007b. "Unauthorized Migration from Africa to Spain." *International Migration* 45 (4): 3–37.

Carr, Matthew. 2012. *Fortress Europe: Dispatches from a Gated Continent*. London: C. Hurst.

Carr, R. 1982. *Spain, 1808–1975*. Oxford: Clarendon Press.

Carrera, Sergio. 2007. The EU Border Management Strategy: FRONTEX and the Challenges of Irregular Immigration in the Canary Islands. CEPS Working Document No. 261 (March 2007).

Carsetti, M. 2015. "Senza Scampo: Racconti Romani." *Gli Asini: Educazione ed Intervento Sociale* 25:29–45.

Carter, Donald, and Heather Merrill. 2007. "Bordering Humanism: Life and Death on the Margins of Europe." *Geopolitics* 12 (2): 248–64.

Casas-Cortes, Maribel, Sebastián Cobarrubias, and John Pickles. 2011. "Stretching Borders beyond Sovereign Territories? Mapping EU and Spain's Border Externalization Policies." *Geopolitica(s)* 2 (1): 71–90.

———. 2013. "Re-Bordering the Neighbourhood: Europe's Emerging Geographies of Non-Accession Integration." *European Urban and Regional Studies* 20 (1): 37–58.

Cassarino, Jean-Pierre. 2013. "Tunisia's New Drivers in Migration Governance." Paper presented at the International Studies Association Conference, San Francisco, April 3–6.

Castañeda, Heide. 2010. "Deportation Deferred: 'Illegality,' Visibility, and Recognition in Contemporary Germany." In *The Deportation Regime: Sovereignty, Space, and the Freedom of Movement*, eds. Nicholas De Genova and Nathalie Peutz, 245–61. Durham, NC: Duke University Press.

Castles, Stephen. 2004. "Why Migration Policies Fail." *Ethnic and Racial Studies* 27 (2): 205–27.

Castro, A. 1987. *La Realidad Histórica de España*. Mexico: Porrúa.

Catudal, H. M. 1974. "Exclaves." *Cahiers de Geographie de Quebec* 18 (43): 107–36.

Cembrero, I. 2009. "La muerte de Safia, la porteadora." *El País*, January 4, 2009.

Chalfin, B. 2012. "Border Security as a Late-Capitalist Fix." In *A Companion to Border Studies*, ed. T. M. Wilson and H. Donnan. London: Wiley-Blackwell.

Chebel d'Appollonia, Ariane. 2012. *Frontiers of Fear: Immigration and Insecurity in the United States and Europe*. Ithaca, NY: Cornell University Press.

CIMADE. 2010. "Visa refusé: Enquête sur les practiques des consulats de France en matière de delivrance des visas." Paris: CIMADE.

CIR. 2010. *Dubliners Project Report*. Accessed September 8, 2014. http://helsinki.hu /wp-content/uploads/dublinerCORRETTO-definitivo.pdf.

Cisse, Madjiguène. 1999. *Parole de sans-papiers*. Paris: La Dispute.

Civipol. 2003. "Feasibility Study on the Control of the European Union's Maritime Borders." European Commission (JHA). Accessed May 4, 2015. http://www.ifmer .org/assets/documents/files/documents_ifm/st11490-re01en03.pdf.

Clayton, Gina. 2011. "Asylum Seekers in Europe: M.S.S. v Belgium and Greece." *Human Rights Law Review* 11.

Cohen, S. 2011. *Folk Devils and Moral Panics*. London: Routledge.

Colectivo Situaciones. 2007. "Something More on Research Militancy: Footnotes on Procedures and (in)Decisions." In *Constituent Imagination: Militant Investigation, Collective Theorization*, ed. David Graeber and Stevphen Shukhaitis. Oakland, CA: AK Press.

Collett, Elizabeth. 2016. "The Paradox of the EU-Turkey Refugee Deal." Migration Policy Institute. http://www.migrationpolicy.org/news/paradox-eu-turkey -refugee-deal.

Collettivo RicercAzione. 2013a. "Collective Militant Research: Building on the Experience of a Volunteers Workers Camp with Migrant Workers in Southern Italy." Accessed September 9, 2014. http://collettivoricercazione.noblogs.org/post/2013/01/30 /collective-militant-rcollective-militant-research-building-on-the-experience-of-a-volun teer-camp-with-migrant-workers-in-southern-italy/.

———. 2013b. "Migrant Farm Workers' Struggles and Their Composition and Facilitation in Italy." Accessed September 15, 2014. http://collettivoricercazione.noblogs.org /post/author/cra3/.

Collyer, Michael. 2007. "In Between Places: Undocumented Sub-Saharan Transit Migrants in Morocco." *Antipode* 39 (4): 620–35.

———. 2010. "Stranded Migrants and the Fragmented Journey." *Journal of Refugee Studies* 23 (3): 273–93.

Collyer, Michael, and Hein de Haas. 2010. "Developing Dynamic Categorisations of Transit Migration." *Population, Space and Place* 18:468–81.

Collyer, Michael, Hein de Haas, and Franck Düvell. 2012. "Critical Approaches to Transit Migration." *Population, Space and Place* 18:407–14.

Connolly, John. 1996. "The Uses of Volksgemeinschaft: Letters to the NSDAP Kreisleitung Eisanach, 1939–1940." *Journal of Modern History* 68 (4): 899–930.

Cooper, Frederick. 2005. *Colonialism in Question: Theory, Knowledge, History.* Berkeley: University of California Press.

Corbin, J. 1989. "The Myth of Primitive Spain." *Anthropology Today* 5 (4): 25–27.

Costa-Lascoux, J. 1992. "Vers une Europe des citoyens." In *Logiques d'Etats et immigrations,* ed. J. Costa-Lascoux and P. Weil, 281–93. Paris: Editions Kimé.

Coté, Mark. 2010. "Technics and the Human Sensorium: Rethinking Media Theory through the Body." *Theory and Event* 13 (4): 1092–311.

Council of the European Union. 2001. "Council Regulation (EC) No. 539/2001 of 15 March 2001 Listing the Third Countries Whose Nationals Must Be in Possession of Visas when Crossing the External Borders and Those Whose Nationals Are Exempt from That Requirement." http://eur-lex.europa.eu/legal-content/EN/TXT /?uri=CELEX%3A32001R0539.

———. 2014. "Joint Operations 'Mos Maiorum.'" Accessed October 28, 2014. http:// www.statewatch.org/news/2014/sep/eu-council-2014-07-10-11671-mos -maioum-jpo.pdf.

Coutin, Susan B. 2005. "Being en Route." *American Anthropologist* 107 (2): 195–206.

———. 2010. "Confined Within: National Territories as Zones of Confinement." *Political Geography* 29 (4): 200–208.

Cowburn, Ashley. 2016a. "Syrian Refugee Shot by Border Guards Trying to Enter Slovakia from Hungary." *The Independent,* May 9, 2016. http://www.independent .co.uk/news/world/europe/syrian-refugee-shot-by-border-guards-trying-to-enter -slovakia-a7020846.html.

———. 2016b. "Turkish Border Forces 'Fire Live Rounds at Syrian Refugees' Fleeing Isis Fighting." *The Independent,* April 15, 2016. http://www.independent.co.uk/news /world/middle-east/turkish-border-forces-fire-live-rounds-at-syrian-refugees-fleeing -isis-fighting-a6986771.html.

Cowen, Deb, and Neil Smith. 2009. "After Geopolitics? From the Geopolitical Social to Geoeconomics." *Antipode* 41 (1): 22–48.

Crampton, Jeremy. 2010. *Mapping: A Critical Introduction to Cartography and GIS.* Oxford: Wiley-Blackwell.

Cruikshank, J. 1998. *The Social Life of Stories: Narrative and Knowledge in the Yukon Territory.* Lincoln: University of Nebraska Press.

Cunningham, Hilary, and Josiah Heyman. 2004. "Introduction: Mobilities and Enclosures at Borders." *Identities: Global Studies in Culture and Power* 11 (3): 289–302.

Curci, S. 2008. *Nero, Invisibile, Normale: Lavoro Migrante e Caporalato in Capitanata.* Roma: Edizioni del Rosone.

Curry, M. 1996. *The Work in the World: Geographical Practice and the Written Word.* Minneapolis: University of Minnesota Press.

Cuttitta, Paolo. 2007. "Le monde-frontière: Le contrôle de l'immigration dans l'espace globalise." *Cultures & Conflits* 68:61–84.

———. 2012. *Lo spettacolo del confine: Lampedusa tra produzione e messa in scena della frontiera.* Milan: Mimesis.

———. 2014. "'Borderizing' the Island: Setting and Narratives of the Lampedusa 'Border Play.'" *CME: An International E-Journal for Critical Geographies* 13 (2): 196–219.

Dalla Costa, Mariarosa, and Selma James. 1972. "The Power of Women and the Subversion of Community." Accessed September 15, 2014. https://libcom.org/library /power-women-subversion-community-della-costa-selma-james.

Danış, D. 2007. "A Faith That Binds: Iraqi Christian Women on the Domestic Service Ladder." *Journal of Ethnic and Migration Studies* 33 (4): 601–15.

Daum, Christophe. 1997. "La coopération, alibi de l'exclusion des immigrés?" In *Les lois de l'inhospitalité: Les politiques de l'immigration à l'épreuve des sans-papiers*, ed. D. Fassin, A. Morice, and C. Quiminal, 197–216. Paris: La Découverte.

Daum, Christophe, and C. Le Guay. 2005. "Le Mali, sa démocratisation et ses émigrés." "Les migrants et la démocratie dans les pays d'origine," dossier coordonné par Christophe Daum. *Hommes et Migrations* 1256.

Davies, N. 2010. "Melilla: Europe's Dirty Secret." *The Guardian*, April 17, 2010.

Dearden, L. 2016. "Denmark Approves Controversial Refugee Bill Allowing Police to Seize Asylum Seekers' Cash and Valuables." *The Independent*. Accessed April 4, 2016. http://www.independent.co.uk/news/world/europe/denmark-approves -controversial-refugee-bill-allowing-police-to-seize-asylum-seekers-cash-and-a6834 581.html.

DeBono, Daniela. 2013. "'Less Than Human': The Detention of Irregular Immigrants in Malta." *Race and Class* 55 (2): 60–81.

Debord, Guy. 2009 [1967]. *The Society of the Spectacle*. Eastbourne: Soul Bay Press.

Debrix, François, and Alexander D. Barder. 2012. *Beyond Biopolitics*. Oxon: Routledge.

de Certeau, Michel. 1984. *The Practice of Everyday Life*. Berkeley: University of California Press.

———. 2008. "Pour une nouvelle culture: Le pouvoir de parler." *Etudes* 408:628–35.

De Genova, Nicholas. 2002. "Migrant 'Illegality' and Deportability in Everyday Life." *Annual Review of Anthropology* 31:419–47.

———. 2005. *Working the Boundaries: Race, Space, and "Illegality" in Mexican Chicago*. Durham, NC: Duke University Press.

———. 2007. "The Production of Culprits: From Deportability to Detainability in the Aftermath of 'Homeland Security.'" *Citizenship Studies* 11 (5): 421–48.

———. 2008. "Inclusion through Exclusion: Explosion or Implosion?" *Amsterdam Law Forum* 1 (1). www.amsterdamlawforum.org.

———. 2009. "Conflicts of Mobility and the Mobility of Conflict: Rightlessness, Presence, Subjectivity, Freedom." *Subjectivity* 29 (1): 445–66.

———. 2010a. "Antiterrorism, Race, and the New Frontier: American Exceptionalism, Imperial Multiculturalism, and the Global Security State." *Identities* 17 (6): 613–40.

———. 2010b. "The Deportation Regime: Sovereignty, Space, and the Freedom of Movement." In *The Deportation Regime: Sovereignty, Space, and the Freedom of Movement*, ed. Nicholas De Genova and Nathalie Peutz, 33–65. Durham, NC: Duke University Press.

———. 2010c. "Migration and Race in Europe: The Trans-Atlantic Metastases of a Post-Colonial Cancer." *European Journal of Social Theory* 13 (3): 405–19.

———. 2010d. "The Queer Politics of Migration: Reflections on 'Illegality' and Incorrigibility." *Studies in Social Justice* 4 (2): 101–26.

————. 2011a. "Alien Powers: Deportable Labour and the Spectacle of Security." In *The Contested Politics of Mobility: Borderzones and Irregularity*, ed. Vicki Squire, 91–115. London: Routledge.

————. 2011b. "Spectacle of Security, Spectacle of Terror." In *Accumulating Insecurity: Violence and Dispossession in the Making of Everyday Life*, ed. Shelley Feldman, Charles Geisler, and Gayatri Menon. Athens: University of Georgia Press.

————. 2013a. "Spectacles of Migrant 'Illegality': The Scene of Exclusion, the Obscene of Inclusion." *Ethnic and Racial Studies* 36 (7): 1180–98.

————. 2013b. " 'We Are of the Connections': Migration, Methodological Nationalism, and 'Militant Research.' " *Postcolonial Studies* 16 (3): 250–58.

————. 2015a. "Border Struggles in the Migrant Metropolis." *Nordic Journal of Migration Research* 5 (1): 3–10.

————. 2015b. "Denizens All: The Otherness of Citizenship." In *Citizenship and Its Others*, ed. Bridget Anderson and Vanessa Hughes. Basingstoke: Palgrave Macmillan.

————. 2015c. "Extremities and Regularities: Regulatory Regimes and the Spectacle of Immigration Enforcement." In *The Irregularization of Migration in Contemporary Europe: Detention, Deportation, Drowning*, ed. Yolande Jansen, Robin Celikates, and Joost de Bloois. London: Rowman and Littlefield.

————. 2015d. "In the Land of the Setting Sun: Reflections on 'Islamization' and 'Patriotic Europeanism.' " *Movements: Journal für kritische Migrations- und Grenzregimeforschung* [Journal for Critical Migration and Border Regime Research] 1 (2). http://movements-journal.org/issues/02.kaempfe/15.de-genova—pegida-islamization-patriotic-europeanism.html.

————. 2016a. "The 'European' Question: Migration, Race, and Post-Coloniality in 'Europe.' " In *An Anthology of Migration and Social Transformation: European Perspectives*, ed. Anna Amelina, Kenneth Horvath, and Bruno Meeus, 343–56. New York: IMISCOE Research Series/Springer.

————. 2016b. "The European Question: Migration, Race, and Postcoloniality in Europe." *Social Text* 34 (3): 75–102.

————. 2017. "The Whiteness of Innocence: *Charlie Hebdo* and the Metaphysics of Antiterrorism in Europe." In *Suis-je Charlie? Politics and Media after the Paris Attacks*, ed. Gavan Titley, Des Freedman, Gholam Khiabany, and Aurélian Mondon. London: Pluto Press.

De Genova, Nicholas, Sandro Mezzadra, and John Pickles. 2015. "New Keywords: Migration and Borders: Introduction." In Maribel Casas-Cortes, Sebastian Cobarrubias, Nicholas De Genova, Glenda Garelli, Giorgio Grappi, Charles Heller, Sabine Hess, Bernd Kasparek, Sandro Mezzadra, Brett Neilson, Irene Peano, Lorenzo Pezzani, John Pickles, Federico Rahola, Lisa Riedner, Stephan Scheel, and Martina Tazzioli, "New Keywords: Migration and Borders." *Cultural Studies* 29 (1): 55–87.

De Genova, Nicholas, and Nathalie Peutz, eds. 2010. *The Deportation Regime: Sovereignty, Space, and the Freedom of Movement*. Durham, NC: Duke University Press.

De Genova, Nicholas, and Martina Tazzioli. 2015. "The 'European' Question after Charlie Hebdo: An Interview with Nicholas De Genova by Martina Tazzioli." *Darkmatter: International Peer-Reviewed Online Journal of Postcolonial Critique* 12. http://www.darkmatter101.org/site/category/issues/12-border-struggles/.

De Guchteneire, Paul, and Antoine Pécoud. 2006. "International Migration, Border Controls and Human Rights: Assessing the Relevance of a Right to Mobility." *Journal of Borderlands Studies* 21 (1): 69–86.

de Haas, Hein. 2008. "The Myth of Invasion: The Inconvenient Realities of African Migration to Europe." *Third World Quarterly* 29 (7): 1305–22.

De León, Jason. 2015. *The Land of Open Graves: Living and Dying on the Migrant Trail.* Berkeley: University of California Press.

De Nicola, A., and B. Quattrocchi. 2014. "La Torsione Neoliberale del Sindacato Tradizionale e l'Immaginazione del 'Sindacalismo Sociale': Appunti per una Discussione." Euronomade. Accessed November 16, 2014. http://www.euronomade.info/?p=2482.

Depledge, Duncan. 2013. "Geopolitical Material: Assemblages of Geopower and the Constitution of the Geopolitical Stage." *Political Geography* 1–2.

Di Cintio, M. 2013. *Walls: Travels along the Barricades.* Berkeley, CA: Soft Skull Press.

Dickens, Tim. 2012. "Anger over Border Agency Raids in Brixton." BrixtonBlog. http://www.brixtonblog.com/concerns-raised-over-brixton-border-agency-raids/6574.

Dickson, Andonea. 2015. "Distancing Asylum Seekers from the State: Australia's Evolving Political Geography of Immigration and Border Control." *Australian Geographer* 46 (4): 437–54.

Di Filippo, Marcello. 2013. "Irregular Migration across the Mediterranean Sea: Problematic Issues Concerning the International Rules on Safeguard of Life at Sea." *Paix et Sécurité Internationales* 1:53–76.

Diop, A. 1997. *Dans la peau d'un sans-papiers.* Paris: Seuil.

Dobson, S. 2004. *Cultures of Exile and the Experience of Refugeeness.* Bern: Peter Lang.

Donato, Katharine M., Brandon Wagner, and Evelyn Patterson. 2008. "The Cat and Mouse Game at the Mexico-U.S. Border: Gendered Patterns and Recent Shifts." *International Migration Review* 42 (2): 330–59.

Doppler, Lisa. 2015. " 'A Feeling of Doing the Right Thing': Forming a Successful Alliance against Dublin-Deportations." *Movements: Journal für kritische Migrations-und Grenzregimeforschung* [Journal for Critical Migration and Border Regime Research] 1 (2). http://movements-journal.org/issues/02.kaempfe/12.doppler–successful-alliance-against-dublin-deportations.html.

Doty, Roxanne Lynn. 2001. "Desert Tracts: Statecraft in Remote Places." *Alternatives: Global, Local, Political* 26 (4): 523–43.

Douglas, Mary. 1966. *Purity and Danger: An Analysis of the Concepts of Pollution and Taboo.* London: Routledge.

Dowd, Rebecca. 2008. "Trapped in Transit: The Plight and Human Rights of Stranded Migrants." UNHCR Research Paper No. 156. Vienna: UNHCR.

Dresch, P. 1988. "Segmentation: Its Roots in Arabia and Its Flowering Elsewhere." *Cultural Anthropology* 3 (1): 50–67.

Driessen, H. 1992. *On the Spanish-Moroccan Frontier: A Study in Ritual, Power and Ethnicity.* Oxford: Berg.

———. 1999. "Smuggling as a Border Way of Life: A Mediterranean Case." In *Frontiers and Borderlands: Anthropological Perspectives*, ed. Michael Rösler and Tobias Wend. Frankfurt: Peter Lang.

Dunn, Timothy J. 2009. *Blockading the Border and Human Rights: The El Paso Operation That Remade Immigration Enforcement*. Austin: University of Texas Press.

Dünnwald, S. 2010. "Destination Bamako: Die Arbeit der Association Malienne des Expulsés am Flughafen." *Hinterland Magazin* 15:22–23.

Düvell, Franck. 2008. "Clandestine Migration in Europe." *Social Science 16 Information* 47 (4): 479–97.

———. 2010. "Transit Migration: A Blurred and Politicized Concept." *Population, Space and Place* 18:415–27.

———. 2011. "Paths into Irregularity: The Legal and Political Construction of Irregular Migration." *European Journal of Migration and Law* 13 (3): 275–95.

Dzenovska, Dace. 2013a. "The Great Departure: Rethinking National(ist) Common Sense." *Journal of Ethnic and Migration Studies* 39 (2): 201–18.

———. 2013b. " 'We Want to Hear from You' (or How Informing Works in a Liberal Democracy)." COMPAS. http://compasoxfordblog.co.uk/2013/04/we-want-to-hear-from-you-or-how-informing-works-in-a-liberal-democracy/.

———. 2014. "Bordering Encounters, Sociality, and Distribution of the Ability to Live a 'Normal Life.' " *Social Anthropology* 22 (3): 271–87.

Eco, Umberto. 1987. *Travels in Hyperreality: Essays*. London: Pan Books.

ECRE. 2013. "Dublin II Regulation: Lives on Hold." Accessed May 30, 2015. http://www.ecre.org.

Edkins, J. 2000. "Sovereign Power, Zones of Indistinction and the Camp." *Alternatives* 25:3–25.

ELENA. 2013. "Information Note on Syrian Asylum Seekers and Refugees in Europe." November 2013.

Elgot, Jessica, and Matthew Taylor. 2015. "Calais Crisis: Cameron Condemned for 'Dehumanising' Description of Migrants." *The Guardian*, July 30, 2015. http://www.theguardian.com/uk-news/2015/jul/30/david-cameron-migrant-swarm-language-condemned.

Ellermann, Antje. 2008. "The Limits of Unilateral Migration Control: Deportation and Inter-State Cooperation." *Government and Opposition* 43 (2): 168–89.

EurActiv. 2012. "Facing Schengen Expulsion, Greece Locks Up Immigrants." Accessed February 1, 2014. http://www.euractiv.com/justice/facing-schengen-expulsion-greece-news-511834.

European Commission (EC). 2003. "Communication from the Commission to the Council and the European Parliament: Development of the Schengen Information System II and Possible Synergies with a Future Visa Information System (VIS). COM(2003) 771 Final, Brussels, 11.12.2003."

———. 2006. "Communication of the Commission on Policy Priorities in the Fight against Illegal Immigration of Third-Country Nationals. COM (2006) 402 Final, Brussels, 19.7.2006."

———. 2010. "Commission Decision of 19.3.2010 on Establishing the Handbook for the Processing of Visa Applications and the Modification of Issued Visas. Brussels, 19.3.2010, C (2010) 1620 Final."

———. 2013. "Cecilia Malmström Signs the Readmission Agreement and Launches the Visa Liberalisation Dialogue with Turkey." Accessed November 5, 2014. http:// europa.eu/rapid/press-release_IP-13–1259_en.htm.

European Commission/Joint Research Centre. 2008. "Integrated Maritime Policy for the EU." Working Document III on Maritime Surveillance Systems. ISPRA: European Commission/Joint Research Centre. Accessed December 10, 2013. http://ec .europa.eu/maritimeaffairs/policy/integrated_maritime_surveillance/documents /maritime-surveillance_en.pdf.

———. 2011. "Space-Borne SAR Small Boat Detection Campaign: Italy and Spain." Luxembourg: Publications Office of the European Union. Accessed September 5, 2013. http://publications.jrc.ec.europa.eu/repository/bitstream/111111111/24183/1 /lbna25065enn.pdf.

European Court of Human Rights. 2014. " 'Dublin' Cases Factsheet." Accessed December 1, 2014. http://www.echr.coe.int/Documents/FS_Dublin_ENG.pdf.

European Parliament (EP) and Council of the European Union. 2008. "Regulation (EC) No. 767/2008 of the European Parliament and Council of 9 July 2008 Concerning the Visa Information System (VIS) and the Exchange of Data between Member States on Short-stay Visas (VIS Regulation)." *Official Journal of European Union* 218:60–81.

———. 2009a. "Regulation (EC) No. 81/2009 of the European Parliament and of the Council of 14 January 2009 Amending Regulation (EC) No. 562/2006 as Regards the Use of the Visa Information System (VIS) under the Schengen Borders Code." *Official Journal of European Union* 56–58.

———. 2009b. "Regulation (EC) No. 810/2009 of the European Parliament and the Council of 13 July 2009 Establishing a Community Code on Visas (Visa Code)." *Official Journal of the European Union* 243.

European Union Press Office. 2016. "European Union-Turkey Agreement." Press Release 144/16 (April 1, 2016). Accessed January 16, 2017. http://turabder.org/en /news-section.

EUROSTAT. 2014. "Dublin Statistics on Countries Responsible for Asylum Application." March 2014. http://ec.europa.eu/eurostat/statistics-explained/index.php /Dublin_statistics_on_countries_responsible_for_asylum_application#.

Eyezo'o, O. 2015. *Et je fus expulsé. . . .* Les éditions du Kamerun.

Fanon, Frantz. 2001 [1961]. *The Wretched of the Earth.* London: Penguin.

Fassin, Didier. 2005. "Compassion and Repression: The Moral Economy of Immigration Policies in France." *Cultural Anthropology* 20 (3): 362–87.

———. 2011a. *Enforcing Order: An Ethnography of Urban Policing.* Cambridge: Polity.

———. 2011b. "Policing Borders, Producing Boundaries: The Governmentality of Immigration in Dark Times." *Annual Review of Anthropology* 40:213–26.

———. 2012. *Humanitarian Reason: A Moral History of the Present Times.* Berkeley: University of California Press.

———. 2014. *Ripoliticizzare il mondo: Studi antropologici sulla vita, il corpo e la morale.* Verona: Ombre Corte.

Fassin, Didier, and Mariella Pandolfi, eds. 2010. *Contemporary States of Emergency: The Politics of Military and Humanitarian Interventions.* New York: Zone Books.

Fassin, Didier, and Richard Rechtman. 2009. *The Empire of Trauma*. Princeton, NJ: Princeton University Press.

Fekete, Liz. 2006. "The Deportation Machine: Europe, Asylum and Human Rights." *European Race Bulletin* 51.

———. 2014. "Europe against the Roma." *Race and Class* 55 (3): 60–70.

Feldman, Gregory. 2012. *The Migration Apparatus: Security, Labor, and Policymaking in the European Union*. Stanford, CA: Stanford University Press.

Feldman, Ilana, and Miriam Iris Ticktin. 2010. *In the Name of Humanity: The Government of Threat and Care*. Durham, NC: Duke University Press.

Ferguson, James. 2005. "Seeing Like an Oil Company: Space, Security, and Global Capital in Neoliberal Africa." *American Anthropologist* 107 (3): 377–82.

Ferrer-Gallardo, Xavier. 2007. "Border Acrobatics between the European Union and Africa: The Management of Sealed-Off Permeability on the Borders of Ceuta and Melilla." In *Borderlands: Comparing Border Security in North America and Europe*, ed. E. Brunet-Jailly. Ottawa: University of Ottawa Press.

Ferrer-Gallardo, Xavier, and Abel Albet-Mas. 2014. "EU-Limboscapes: Ceuta and the Proliferation of Migrant Detention Spaces across the European Union." *European Urban and Regional Studies* (November 11, 2013). doi: 10.1177/0969776413508766.

Fischer, Nicholas. 2013. "Negotiating Deportations: An Ethnography of the Legal Challenge of Deportation Orders in a French Immigration Detention Centre." In *The Social, Political and Historical Contours of Deportation*, ed. Bridget Anderson, Matthew Gibney, and Emanuela Paoletti. New York: Springer.

Fischer-Lescano, Andreas, and Gunther Teubner. 2004. "Regime-Collisions: The Vain Search for Legal Unity in the Fragmentation of Global Law." *Michigan Journal of International Law* 25:999–1046.

Fitzpatrick, Sheila. 2005. "A Little Swine." *London Review of Books* 27 (21): 3–6.

———. 1996. "Letters from Below: Soviet Letters of Denunciation of the 1930s." *Journal of Modern History* 68 (4): 831–66.

Fitzpatrick, Sheila, and Robert Gellately. 1996. "Introduction to Practices of Denunciation in Modern European History." *Journal of Modern History* 68 (4): 747–67.

Flai-CGIL. 2012. "Video sugli invisibili delle campagne di raccolta" (September 16, 2012). Accessed January 16, 2017. http://cetri-tires.org/press/2012/video-sugli-invisibili-delle-campagne-di-raccolta-flai-cgil/?lang=it.

Flynn, Michael, and Cecilia Cannon. 2010. "Detention at the Borders of Europe: Report on the Joint Global Detention Project—International Detention Coalition Workshop in Geneva, Switzerland, 2–3 October 2010." Geneva: Global Detention Project. http://www.globaldetentionproject.org/fileadmin/publications/GDP_Workshop_Report_2010.pdf.

Follis, Karolina S. 2011. *Building Fortress Europe: The Polish-Ukrainian Frontier*. Philadelphia: University of Pennsylvania Press.

Forensic Architecture. 2014. *Forensis: The Architecture of Public Truth*. Berlin: Sternberg Press.

Forsythe, David P. 2009. "Contemporary Humanitarianism: The Global and the Local Contemporary." In *Humanitarianism and Suffering: The Mobilization of Empathy*, ed. R. Wilson and R. D. Brown. Cambridge: Cambridge University Press.

Foucault, Michel. 1980 [1977]. "The Confession of the Flesh: Interview." In *Power/Knowledge: Selected Interviews and Other Writings*, ed. Colin Gordon. New York: Pantheon.

———. 1994. "Le sujet et le pouvoir." *Dits et écrits* 4:222–43.

———. 1994 [1977]. "Lives of Infamous Men." In Foucault, *Power: Essential Works of Foucault, 1954–1984*, ed. James D. Faubion, 157–75. London: Penguin.

———. 2003. *"Society Must Be Defended": Lectures at the Collège de France, 1975–1976*. David Macey, trans. New York: Picador.

———. 2007. *Security, Territory, Population: Lectures at the Collège de France, 1977–78*. New York: Palgrave Macmillian.

Fox, Jon E. 2012. "The Uses of Racism: Whitewashing New Europeans in the UK." *Ethnic and Racial Studies* 36 (11): 1871–89.

Fox, Jon E., Laura Moroşanu, and Ezster Szilassy. 2012. "The Racialization of the New European Migration to the UK." *Sociology* 46 (4): 680–95.

Freire, Paulo. 1972. *Pedagogy of the Oppressed*. Middlesex: Penguin.

Frontex. 2010a. *Beyond the Frontiers: Frontex—The First Five Years*. Warsaw: Frontex.

———. 2010b. "Frontex Signs Seat Agreement with Greece." Accessed November 2, 2014. http://frontex.europa.eu/news/frontex-signs-seat-agreement-with-greece-9DrT7S.

———. 2012a. "FRAN Quarterly, Q2 2012." Accessed February 2, 2014. http://frontex.europa.eu/publications/.

———. 2012b. "FRAN Quarterly, Q3 2012." Accessed February 1, 2014. http://frontex.europa.eu/publications/.

Fumagalli, A. 2007. *Bioeconomia e Capitalismo Cognitivo: Verso un Nuovo Paradigma di Accumulazione*. Roma: Carocci.

Gambino, F. 2003. *Migranti nella tempesta: Avvistamenti per l'inizio del nuovo millennio*. Verona: Ombre Corte.

Gammeltoft-Hansen, Thomas, and Tanja E. Aalberts. 2010. "Sovereignty at Sea: The Law and Politics of Saving Lives in the Mare Liberum." DIIS Working Paper 2010–18.

Gammeltoft-Hansen, Thomas, and Nina Nyberg Sørensen, eds. 2013. *The Migration Industry and the Commercialization of International Migration*. London: Routledge.

Garcia, Sandrine. 1997. "La fraude forcée." *Actes de la Recherche en Science Sociales* 118:81–91.

García Velasco, Marcos Miguel, Guillermo Sarmiento Zea, andAlejandro del Canto Bossini. 1985. "Análisis Estructural del Comercio en Melilla." *Aldaba: Revista del Centro Asociado de la UNED de Melilla* 5:83–95.

Garelli, Glenda, Federica Sossi, and Martina Tazzioli, eds. 2013. *Spaces in Migration: Postcards of a Revolution*. London: Pavement Books.

Garelli, Glenda, and Martina Tazzioli. 2013a. "Arab Springs Making Space: Territoriality and Moral Geographies for Asylum Seekers in Italy." *Environment and Planning D: Society and Space* 31 (6): 1004–21.

———. 2013b. "Migration Discipline Hijacked: Distances and Interruptions of a Research Militancy." *Postcolonial Studies* 16 (3): 299–308.

———. 2014. "Crisis as Border: Choucha Refugee Camp and Migration in Crisis." *Etnografia e Ricerca Qualitativa* 1:15–26.

———. 2016a. "The EU Hotspot Approach at Lampedusa." openDemocracy, February 26, 2016. https://www.opendemocracy.net/can-europe-make-it/glenda-garelli-martina-tazzioli/eu-hotspot-approach-at-lampedusa.

———. 2016b. *Tunisia as a Revolutionized Space of Migration.* Basingstoke: Palgrave Macmillan.

———. 2017. "The EU Humanitarian War against Migrant Smugglers at Sea." *Antipode*: forthcoming.

Garriott, William. 2013. "Policing Methamphetamine: Police Power and the War on Drugs in a Rural US Community." In *Policing and Contemporary Governance: The Anthropology of Police in Practice*, ed. William Garriott. New York: Palgrave Macmillan.

Garrison, Tom. 2009. *Essentials of Oceanography*, 5th ed. Belmont, CA: Brooks/Cole Cengage Learning.

Gary-Tounkara, D. 2013. "La gestion des migrations de retour: Un paramètre négligé de la grille d'analyse de la crise malienne." *Politique africaine* 130:47–68.

Gellately, Robert. 1996. "Denunciations in Twentieth-Century Germany: Aspects of Self-Policing in the Third Reich and the German Democratic Republic." *Journal of Modern History* 68 (4): 931–67.

Gifra-Adroher, P. 2000. *Between History and Romance: Travel Writing on Spain in the Early Nineteenth-Century United States.* Cranbury, NJ: Associated University Presses.

Giordano, C. 2014. *Migrants in Translation: Caring and the Logics of Difference in Contemporary Italy.* Berkeley: University of California Press.

Giudici, D. 2013. "From 'Irregular Migrants' to Refugees and Back: Asylum Seekers' Struggle for Recognition in Contemporary Italy." *Journal of Mediterranean Studies* 22 (1): 61–86.

Glaeser, Andreas. 2009. *Political Epistemics: The Secret Police, the Opposition, and the End of East German Socialism.* Chicago: University of Chicago Press.

Glick Schiller, Nina, and Andreas Wimmer. 2002. "Methodological Nationalism and Beyond: Nation-State Building, Migration and the Social Sciences." *Global Networks* 2 (4): 301–34.

Goebbels, A. F. G., J. M. Nicholson, K. Walsh, and H. De Vries. 2008. "Teachers Reporting on Suspected Child Abuse and Neglect: Behavior and Determinants." *Health Education Research* 23 (6): 941–51.

Goffman, Erving. 1959. *The Presentation of Self in Everyday Life.* New York: Anchor.

Gold, Steve. 2012. "Border Control Biometrics and Surveillance." *Biometric Technology Today* 12 (7): 9–11.

Goldberg, David Theo. 2006. "Racial Europeanization." *Ethnic and Racial Studies* 29 (2): 331–64.

———. 2009. *The Threat of Race: Reflections on Racial Neoliberalism.* Malden, MA: Wiley-Blackwell.

Goldstein, Daniel. 2010. "Towards a Critical Anthropology of Security." *Current Anthropology* 51 (4): 487–517.

Graeber, David. 2013. "Culture as Creative Refusal." *Cambridge Anthropology* 31 (2): 1–19.

———. 2014. "Anthropology and the Rise of the Professional-Managerial Class." *HAU: The Journal of Ethnographic Theory* 4 (3): 73–88.

Graeber, David, and Stevphen Shukhaitis. 2007. "Introduction." In *Constituent Imagination: Militant Investigation, Collective Theorization*, ed. David Graeber and Stevphen Shukhaitis. Oakland, CA: AK Press.

Gramsci, Antonio. 1999. *Selections from the Prison Notebooks*. London: Elecbook.

Grbac, P. 2013. "Civitas, Polis, and Urbs: Reimagining the Refugee Camp as the City." Refugee Studies Centre, Working Paper Series No. 96. Accessed April 30, 2015. http://www.rsc.ox.ac.uk/files/publications/working-paper-series/wp96-civitas -polis-urbs-2013.pdf.

Green, Sarah. 2010. "Performing Border in the Aegean: On Relocating Political, Economic and Social Relations." *Journal of Cultural Economy* 3:261–78.

———. 2013. "Borders and the Relocation of Europe." *Annual Review of Anthropology* 42:345–61.

Gregory, Derek. 2004. *The Colonial Present*. Oxford: Blackwell.

Griffiths, Melanie. 2012. " 'Vile Liars and Truth Distorters': Truth, Trust and the Asylum System." *Anthropology Today* 28 (5): 8–12.

Grill, Jan. 2012a. " 'It's Building Up to Something and It Won't Be Nice When It Erupts': Making of Roma Migrants in a 'Multicultural' Scottish Neighborhood." *Focaal: Journal of Global and Historical Anthropology* 62:42–54.

———. 2012b. " 'Going Up to England': Exploring Mobilities among Roma from Eastern Slovakia." *Journal of Ethnic and Migration Studies* 38 (8): 1269–87.

Groebner, Valentin. 2004. *Der Schein der Person*. Munich: Beck.

Grosz, Elizabeth. 2012. "Geopower." *Environment and Planning D: Society and Space* 30:971–88.

Groupe Antiraciste d'Accompagnement et de Défense des Étrangers et Migrants (GADEM). 2010. "The Human Rights of Sub-Saharan Migrants in Morocco." Justice Without Borders Project.

Guardia Civil (Spain). 2008. *SIVE: Cinco años vigilando la frontera*. Madrid: Guardia Civil.

Guild, Elspeth, and Didier Bigo. 2010. "The Transformation of European Border Controls." In *Extraterritorial Immigration Control: Legal Challenges*, eds. B. Ryan and V. Mitsilegas. Leiden: Brill.

Gupta, Akhil, and James Ferguson. 1992. "Beyond 'Culture': Space, Identity, and the Politics of Difference." *Cultural Anthropology* 7 (1): 6–23.

Guyer, J. 2007. "Prophecy and the Near Future: Thoughts on Macroeconomics, Evangelical, and Punctuated Time." *American Ethnologist* 34 (3): 409–21.

Haddad, E. 2008. "The External Dimension of EU Refugee Policy: A New Approach to Asylum?" *Government and Opposition* 43 (2): 190–205.

Hage, Ghassan. 2005. "A Not So Multi-Sited Ethnography of a Not So Imagined Community." *Anthropological Theory* 5:463–75.

———. 2009. "Waiting Out the Crisis: On Stuckedness and Governmentality." In *Waiting*, ed. Ghassan Hage. Carlton, Victoria: Melbourne University Publishing.

Haggerty, Kevin D. 2012. "Surveillance, Crime and the Police." In *Routledge Handbook of Surveillance Studies*, ed. Kirstie Ball, Kevin Haggerty, and David Lyon, 235–43. London: Routledge.

Hall, A., and J. Leichfield. 2015. "Germany Opens Its Gates: Berlin Says All Syrian Asylum-Seekers Are Welcome to Remain, as Britain Is Urged to Make a 'Similar Statement.'" *The Independent*. Accessed April 5, 2016. http://www.independent.co.uk/news/world/europe/germany-opens-its-gates-berlin-says-all-syrian-asylum-seekers-are-welcome-to-remain-as-britain-is-10470062.html.

Hanafi, Sari. 2009. "Spacio-cide: colonial politics, invisibility and rezoning in Palestinian territory." *Contemporary Arab Affairs* 2 (1): 106–21.

Hanafi, Sari, and Taylor Long. 2010. "Governance, Governmentalities, and the State of Exception in the Palestinian Refugee Camps of Lebanon." *Journal of Refugee Studies* 23 (2): 134–59.

Hanifi, M. J. 2000. "Anthropology and the Representations of Recent Migrations from Afghanistan." In *Rethinking Refuge and Displacement: Selected Papers on Refugees and Immigrants*, vol. 8, ed. E. M. Godziak and D. J. Shandy. Arlington, VA: American Anthropological Association.

Hansen, Peo. 2004. "In the Name of Europe." *Race and Class* 45:49–62.

Hansen, Peo, and Stefan Jonsson. 2011. "Demographic Colonialism: EU–African Migration Management and the Legacy of Eurafrica." *Globalizations* 8 (3): 261–76.

Hansen, R. 1999. "Migration, Citizenship and Race in Europe: Between Incorporation and Exclusion." *European Journal of Political Research* 35 (4): 415–44.

Hardt, Michael, and Antonio Negri. 2000. *Empire*. Cambridge, MA: Harvard University Press.

———. 2004. *Multitude: War and Democracy in the Age of Empire*. New York: Penguin.

———. 2009. *Commonwealth*. Cambridge, MA: Harvard University Press.

Hartocollis, Anemona. 2015. "Traveling in Europe's River of Migrants." *New York Times*, August 27–September 7, 2015. http://www.nytimes.com/interactive/projects/cp/reporters-notebook/migrants/syrian-migrants-in-austria.

Harvey, David. 1989. *The Condition of Postmodernity: An Enquiry into the Origins of Cultural Change*. Oxford: Blackwell.

———. 1996. *Justice, Nature and the Geography of Difference*. Oxford: Blackwell.

———. 2001. "Globalization and the Spatial Fix." *Geographische Revue* 2 (3): 23–31.

Hayes, Ben. 2012. "The Surveillance-Industrial Complex." In *Routledge Handbook of Surveillance Studies*, ed. Kirstie Ball, Kevin Haggerty, and David Lyon. London: Routledge.

Hayes, Ben, and Mathias Vermeulen. 2012. *Borderline: EU Border Surveillance Initiatives*. Heinrich Böll Stiftung report.

Heller, Charles, Lorenzo Pezzani, and Situ Research. 2012. "Report on the Left-to-Die Boat." London: Forensic Architecture. Accessed December 10, 2013. http://www.forensic-architecture.org/wp-content/uploads/2014/05/FO-report.pdf.

Helmreich, Stefan. 2011. "Nature/Culture/Seawater." *American Anthropologist* 113 (1): 132–44.

Hepworth, Katherine. 2012. "Abject Citizens: Italian 'Nomad Emergencies' and the Deportability of Romanian Roma." *Citizenship Studies* 16 (3–4): 431–49.

———. 2014. "Encounters with the Clandestino/a and the Nomad: The Emplaced and Embodied Constitution of (Non-)Citizenship." *Citizenship Studies* 18 (1): 1–14.

———. 2015. *At the Edges of Citizenship: Security and the Constitution of Non-Citizen Subjects*. Farnham, UK: Ashgate.

Herzfeld, Michael. 1987. *Anthropology through the Looking Glass: Critical Ethnography in the Margins of Europe*, Cambridge: Cambridge University Press.

———. 2005. *Cultural Intimacy: Social Poetics in the Nation-State*. London: Routledge.

Hess, Sabine. 2010. "De-Naturalizing Transit Migration: Theory and Methods of an Ethnographic Regime Analysis." *Population, Space and Place* 18:428–40.

Heyman, Josiah. 1995. "Putting Power in the Anthropology of Bureaucracy: The Immigration and Naturalization Service at the Mexico-United States Border." *Current Anthropology* 36 (2): 261–87.

———. 2012. "Capitalism and US Policy at the Mexican Border." *Dialectical Anthropology* 36 (3–4): 263–77.

Hochschild, A. 1983. *The Managed Heart: Commercialization of Human Feeling*. Berkeley: University of California Press.

Holmes, B. 2007. "Continental Drift: Activist Research from Geopolitics to Geopoetics." In *Constituent Imagination: Militant Investigation, Collective Theorization*, ed. David Graeber and Stevphen Shukaitis. Oakland, CA: AK Press.

Hontanilla, A. 2008. "Images of Barbaric Spain in Eighteenth-Century British Travel Writing." *Studies in Eighteenth-Century Culture* 37:119–43.

Human Rights Watch (HRW). 2011. "The EU's Dirty Hands: Frontex Involvement in Ill-Treatment of Migrant Detainees in Greece." New York: Human Rights Watch.

———. 2012. "Hidden Emergency: Migrant Deaths in the Mediterranean." New York: Human Rights Watch.

———. 2013. "Unwelcome Guests, Greek Police Abuses of Migrants in Athens." New York: Human Rights Watch.

———. 2014. "Abused and Expelled: Ill-Treatment of Sub-Saharan African Migrants in Morocco." New York: Human Rights Watch.

Hyndman, Jennifer, and Alison Mountz. 2008. "Another Brick in the Wall? Neo-Refoulement and the Externalization of Asylum by Australia and Europe." *Government and Opposition* 43 (2): 249–69.

İçduygu, A. 2004. "Transborder Crime between Turkey and Greece: Human Smuggling and Its Regional Consequences." *Southeast European and Black Sea Studies* 4 (2): 294–314.

İçduygu, A., and Yükşeker. 2010. "Rethinking Transit Migration in Turkey: Reality and Representation in the Creation of a Migration Phenomenon." *Population, Space, and Place* 18:441–56.

İneli-Ciğer, M. 2014. "Implications of the New Turkish Law on Foreigners and International Protection and Regulation no. 29153 on Temporary Protection for Syrians." *Oxford Monitor of Forced Migration* 4 (2): 28–36.

Infantino, Federica. 2013. "Bordering at the Window: The Allocation of Schengen Visa at the Italian Embassy and Consulate in Morocco." In *Foreigners, Refugees or Minorities? Rethinking People in the Context of Border Controls and Visas*, ed. Didier Bigo, Sergio Carrera, and Elspeth Guild. Farnham: Ashgate.

Infantino, Federica, and Andrea Rea. 2012. "La mobilisation d'un savoir pratique local: Attribution des visas Schengen au Consulat général de Belgique à Casablanca." *Sociologies Pratiques* 24:67–78.

Instituto Nazionale D'Economia Agraria (INEA). 2014. "Indagine sull'impiego in Agricoltura dei Migranti nel 2012." Rome: INEA.

International Organization of Migration (IOM). 2010. "World Migration Report 2010: The Future of Migration: Building Capacities for Change." Geneva: IOM. Accessed April 29, 2016. http://www.migration4development.org/sites/default/files/wmr _2010_english.pdf.

——. 2014. *Fatal Journeys: Tracking Lives Lost during Migration*, ed. Tara Brian and Frank Laczko. Geneva: IOM. https://publications.iom.int/system/files/pdf /fataljourneys_countingtheuncounted.pdf.

Irving, Washington. 1998 [1861]. *The Complete Tales of Washington Irving*. New York: Da Capo Press.

Jackson, Michael. 2002. *The Politics of Storytelling: Violence, Transgression and Intersubjectivity*. Copenhagen: Museum Tusculanum Press, University of Copenhagen.

——. 2013. *The Wherewithal of Life: Ethics, Migration, and the Question of Well-Being*. Berkeley: University of California Press.

Jansen, Yolande, Robin Celikates, and Joost de Bloois, eds. 2015. *The Irregularization of Migration in Contemporary Europe: Detention, Deportation, Drowning*. London: Rowman and Littlefield.

Jiménez, A. C. 2003. "On Space as Capacity." *Journal of Royal Anthropological Institute* 9:137–53.

Jiménez Lozano, J. 1966. *Meditación española sobre la libertad religiosa*. Barcelona: Ediciones Destino.

Johnson, Heather L. 2014. *Borders, Asylum and Global Non-Citizenship: The Other Side of the Fence*. Cambridge: Cambridge University Press.

Jones, Reece. 2012. *Border Walls: Security and the War on Terror in the United States, India, and Israel*. London: Zed Books.

Juris, J. S. 2007. "Practicing Militant Ethnography with the Movement of Global Resistance in Barcelona." In *Constituent Imagination: Militant Investigation, Collective Theorization*, ed. David Graeber and Stevphen Shukhaitis. Oakland, CA: AK Press.

Kallius, Annastiina, Daniel Monterescu, and Prem Kumar Rajaram. 2016. "Immobilizing Mobility: Border Ethnography, Illiberal Democracy, and the Politics of the 'Refugee Crisis' in Hungary." *American Ethnologist* 43 (1): 25–37.

Kanstroom, Daniel. 2007. *Deportation Nation: Outsiders in American History*. Cambridge, MA: Harvard University Press.

——. 2012. *Aftermath: Deportation Law and the New American Diaspora*. New York: Oxford University Press.

Kanter, James, and Andrew Higgins. 2015. "E.U. Offers Turkey 3 Billion Euros to Stem Migrant Flow." *New York Times*, November 29, 2015. http://www.nytimes.com/2015/11/30/world/europe/eu-offers-turkey-3-billion-euros-to-stem-migrant-flow.html?emc=edit_th_20151130&nl=todaysheadlines&nlid=44765954&_r=0.

Karakayali, Serhat. 2008. *Gespenster der Migration: Zur Genealogie illegaler Einwanderung in der Bundesrepublik Deutschland.* Bielefeld: transcript.

Karakayali, Serhat, and Enrica Rigo. 2010. "Mapping the European Space of Circulation." In *The Deportation Regime: Sovereignty, Space, and the Freedom of Movement*, ed. Nicholas De Genova and Nathalie Peutz, 123–44. Durham, NC: Duke University Press.

Karakayali, Serhat, and Vassilis Tsianos. 2005. "Mapping the Order of New Migration: Undokumentierte Arbeit und die Autonomie der Migration." *Peripherie* 25 (97/98): 35–64.

Kasparek, Bernd, and Marc Speer. 2015. "Of Hope: Hungary and the Long Summer of Migration." bordermonitoring.eu, September 9, 2015. http://bordermonitoring.eu/ungarn/2015/09/of-hope-en/.

Khosravi, Shahram. 2010. *"Illegal" Traveller: An Auto-Ethnography of Borders.* Basingstoke: Palgrave Macmillan.

Kivistö, Hanna-Mari. 2013. " 'Dubliners' in the European Union: A Perspective on the Politics of Asylum-Seeking." In *The Distant Present*, ed. T. Vaarakallio and T. Haapala, 106–25. Jyväskylä: University of Jyväskylä, SoPhi. Accessed December 3, 2014. https://jyx.jyu.fi/dspace/bitstream/handle/123456789/41748/978-951-39-5102-3.pdf?sequence=1.

Knorr Cetina, Karin. 2009. "The Synthetic Situation: Interactionism for a Global World." *Symbolic Interaction* 32 (1): 61–87.

Kozlov, Vladimir K. 1996. "Denunciation and Its Functions in Soviet Governance: A Study of Denunciations and Their Bureaucratic Handling from Soviet Police Archives, 1944–1953." *Journal of Modern History* 68 (4): 867–98.

Kristeva, Julia. 1982. *Powers of Horror: An Essay on Abjection.* New York: Columbia University Press.

Kurgan, Laura. 2013. *Close Up at a Distance: Mapping, Technology, and Politics.* New York: Zone Books.

Kurz, Joshua. 2012. "(Dis)locating Control: Transmigration, Precarity and the Governmentality of Control." *Behemoth: A Journal on Civilisation* 5 (1): 30–51.

Latour, Bruno. 1993. *We Have Never Been Modern.* Hemel Hempstead: Harvester Wheatsheaf.

———. 2006. "Air." In *Sensorium*, ed. Caroline A. Jones. Cambridge, MA: MIT Press.

———. 2013. "The Anthropocene and the Destruction of the Image of the Globe." Latour's Fourth Gifford Lecture, Edinburgh. Accessed September 30, 2014. http://www.ed.ac.uk/schools-departments/humanities-soc-sci/news-events/lectures/gifford-lectures/archive/series-2012-2013/bruno-latour/lecture-four.

Lavenex, Sandra, and Emek M. Uçarer. 2004. "The External Dimension of Europeanization: The Case of Immigration Policies." *Cooperation and Conflict* 39 (4): 417–43.

Lease, Gary. 1996. "Denunciation as a Tool of Ecclesiastical Control: The Case of Roman Catholic Modernism." *Journal of Modern History* 68 (4): 819–30.

Lecadet, Clara. 2012a. "Expulsions et prises de parole au Mali: Quand le politique se récrie en ses marges." In *Politiques de l'exception: Réfugiés, sinistrés, sans-papiers*, ed. Michel Agier. Paris: Editions Téraèdre.

———. 2012b. " 'Tinzawaten, c'est le grand danger pour nous les immigrés!' " *Hermès* 63:95–100.

———. 2013a. "From Migrant Destitution to Self-Organization into Transitory National Communities: The Revival of Citizenship in Post-Deportation Experience in Mali." In *The Social, Political and Historical Contours of Deportation*, ed. Bridget Anderson, Matthew Gibney, and Emanuela Paoletti. New York: Springer.

———. 2013b. "Le droit, la politique et les expulsés: Scènes maliennes." *Le sujet dans la cité* 3:183–94.

———. 2014a. "De Tinzawaten à Bamako (Mali): Les ghettos de l'expulsion." In *Un monde de camps*, ed. M. Agier and C. Lecadet, 364–74. Paris: Editions de la Découverte.

———. 2014b. "Ghettos: Deportation without a Voice." In *Migration: The COMPAS Anthology*, ed. B. Anderson and M. Keith, 157–59. Oxford: COMPAS. http://compasanthology.co.uk/ghettos-deportation-without-voice/.

Lefebvre, Henri. 2003 [1970]. *The Urban Revolution*. Minneapolis: University of Minnesota Press.

———. 1991 [1974]. *The Production of Space*. Cambridge, MA: Blackwell.

Levinson, A. 2005. "Regularisation Programmes in Italy." In *The Regularisation of Unauthorised Migrants: Literature Survey and Country Case Studies*. Oxford: COMPAS. Accessed December 5, 2014. https://www.compas.ox.ac.uk/fileadmin/files/Publications/Reports/Country%20Case%20Italy.pdf.

Lipsky, Michael. 1980. *Street-Level Bureaucracy: Dilemmas of the Individual in Public Services*. New York: Russell Sage Foundation.

López-Guzmán, T., and V. González Fernández. 2009. "Melilla: Fiscalidad local y actividad comercial. Una reflexión." *Boletín Económico de ICE* 2958.

Lucas, Colin. 1996. "The Theory and Practice in Denunciation in Revolutionary France." *Journal of Modern History* 68 (4): 768–85.

Lucht, Hans. 2012. *Darkness before Daybreak: African Migrants Living on the Margins in Southern Italy Today*. Berkeley: University of California Press.

Lyman, Rick. 2015. "Regulating Flow of Refugees Gains Urgency in Greece and Rest of Europe." *New York Times*, November 25, 2015. http://www.nytimes.com/2015/11/26/world/europe/regulating-flow-of-refugees-gains-urgency-in-greece-and-rest-of-europe.html?emc=edit_th_20151126&nl=todaysheadlines&nlid=44765954.

Maguire, Mark. 2009. "The Birth of Biometric Security." *Anthropology Today* 25 (2): 9–14.

———. 2012. "Biopower, Racialization and New Security Technology." *Social Identities* 18 (5): 593–607.

Maguire, Mark, Catarina Frois, and Nils Zurawski, eds. 2014. *The Anthropology of Security: Perspectives from the Frontline of Policing, Counter-Terrorism and Border Control*. London: Pluto Press.

Mai, Nicola. 2014. "Between Embodied Cosmopolitism and Sexual Humanitarianism: The Fractal Mobilities and Subjectivities of Migrants Working in the Sex Industry." In *Borders, Mobilities and Migrations: Perspectives from the Mediterranean, 19–21st Century,* ed. V. Baby-Collins and L. Anteby, 175–92. Brussels: Peter Lang.

Malkki, Liisa H. 1995. *Purity and Exile: Violence, Memory, and National Cosmology among Hutu Refugees in Tanzania.* Chicago: Chicago University Press.

Mancke, Elizabeth. 1999. "Early Modern Expansion and the Politicisation of Oceanic Space." *Geographical Review* 89 (2): 225–36.

Mann, G. 2003. "Immigrants and Arguments in France and West Africa." *Comparative Studies in Society and History* 45 (2): 362–85.

Martin, Lauren, and Matthew L. Mitchelson. 2009. "Geographies of Detention and Imprisonment: Interrogating Spatial Practices of Confinement, Discipline, Law, and State Power." *Geography Compass* 3 (1): 458–77.

Martín Corrales, E. 1988. "El Puerto Malagueño y el Aprovisionamiento de Melilla (1797–1808)." *Trápana: Revista de la Asociación de Estudios Melillenses* 2.

Marx, Karl. 1858 [1971]. "The Fragment on Machines." In *Grundrisse: Foundations of the Critique of Political Economy.* London: Penguin/New Left Review.

———. 1867 [1976]. *Capital: A Critique of Political Economy,* vol. 1. New York: Vintage/Random House.

Maschino, Maurice T. 2008. "Hauptgewinn: Ein Visum für Frankreich." *Edition Le Monde Diplomatique* 4:43–47.

Massey, Doreen. 2005. *For Space.* London: Sage.

Mastnak, Tomaž. 2003. "Europe and the Muslims: The Permanent Crusade?" In *The New Crusades: Constructing the Muslim Enemy,* ed. Emran Qureshi and Michael A. Sells. New York: Columbia University Press.

Mayoral del Amo, Juan Francisco. 2005. "El Mosaico de Melilla." In *Experiencias Interculturales en Melilla.* Melilla: STATE-STES and Facultad de Educación y Humanidades de Melilla (UGR).

Mbembe, Achille. 2000. *De La Postcolonie: Essai Sur L'imagination Politique Dans l'Afrique Contemporaine.* Les Afriques. Paris: Karthala.

———. 2003. "Necropolitics." *Public Culture* 15 (1): 11–40.

Mbembe, Achille, and Sarah Nuttall. 2004. "Writing the World from an African Metropolis." *Public Culture* 16 (3): 347–72.

McKeown, Adam. 2008. *Melancholy Order: Asian Migration and the Globalization of Borders.* New York: Columbia University Press.

McMurray, D. A. 2001. *In and Out of Morocco: Smuggling and Migration in a Frontier Boomtown.* Minneapolis: University of Minnesota Press.

McNevin, Anne. 2013. "Ambivalence and Citizenship: Theorising the Political Claims of Irregular Migrants." *Millennium* 41:182–200.

Médecins Sans Frontières. 2005. "Violence and Immigration: Report on Illegal Sub-Saharan Immigrants (ISSs) in Morocco." http://www.statewatch.org/news/2005/oct/MSF-morocco-2005.pdf.

Medici Senza Frontiere. 2005. "Indagine sulle condizioni di vita e salute dei lavoratori stranieri impiegati nell'agricoltura." Accessed September 5, 2014. www.medici-senzfrontiere.it.

———. 2008. "Una stagione all'inferno: Rapporto sulle condizioni degli immigrati impiegati in agricoltura nelle regioni del Sud Italia." Accessed September 15, 2014. www.medici-senzafrontiere.it.

Mezzadra, Sandro. 2001. *Diritto di fuga: Migrazioni, cittadinanza, globalizzazione.* Verona, Italy: Ombre Corte.

———. 2004. "The Right to Escape." *Ephemera* 4 (3): 267–75. www.ephemeraweb.org /journal/4-3/4-3mezzadra.pdf.

———. 2006. "Citizen and Subject: A Postcolonial Constitution for the European Union?" *Situations* 1 (2): 31–42.

———. 2010a. "Anti-Racist Research and Practice in Italy." *Darkmatter*, October 10, 2010. http://www.darkmatter101.org/site/category/issues/6-challenging -italian-racism/.

———. 2010b. "Autonomie der Migration—Kritik und Ausblick." *Grundrisse.* Accessed July 6, 2014. http://www.grundrisse.net/grundrisse34/Autonomie_der_Migration .htm.

———. 2011. "The Gaze of Autonomy: Capitalism, Migration, and Social Struggles." In *The Contested Politics of Mobility: Borderzones and Irregularity*, ed. Vicki Squire. London: Routledge.

Mezzadra, Sandro, and Brett Neilson. 2003. "Né qui, né altrove—Migration, Detention, Desertion: A Dialogue." *borderlands e-journal* 2 (1). www.borderlandsejournal .adelaide.edu.au/vol2no1_2003/mezzadra_neilson.html.

———. 2012. "Borderscapes of Differential Inclusion: Subjectivity and Struggles on the Threshold of Justice's Excess." In *The Borders of Justice*, ed. Étienne Balibar, Sandro Mezzadra, and Ranabir Samaddar. Philadelphia: Temple University Press.

———. 2013. *Border as Method, or, The Multiplication of Labor.* Durham, NC: Duke University Press.

Miéville, China. 2006. *Between Equal Rights: A Marxist Theory of International Law.* London: Haymarket.

Migreurop. 2013. *Atlas of Migration in Europe: A Critical Geography of Migration Policies.* London: New Internationalist Publications.

Millner, Naomi. 2011. "From 'Refugee' to 'Migrant' in Calais Solidarity Activism: Re-Staging Undocumented Migration for a Future Politics of Asylum." *Political Geography* 30:320–28.

Mitchell, Timothy. 1999. "Society, Economy, and the State Effect." In *State/Culture: State-Formation after the Cultural Turn*, ed. George Steinmetz, 76–97. Ithaca, NY: Cornell University Press.

Mitropoulos, Angela. 2006. "Autonomy, Recognition, Movement." *The Commoner* 11:5–14. Reprinted in *Constituent Imagination: Militant Investigation, Collective Theorization*, ed. David Graeber and Stevphen Shukaitis, 127–36. Edinburgh: AK Press, 2007.

Monsutti, A. 2007. "Migration as a Rite of Passage: Young Afghans Building Masculinity and Adulthood in Iran." *Iranian Studies* 40 (2): 167–85.

———. 2013. "Anthropologizing Afghanistan: Colonial and Postcolonial Encounters." *Annual Review of Anthropology* 42:269–85.

Morales Lezcano, V. 1988. *Africanismo y orientalismo español en el siglo XIX*. Madrid: Universidad Nacional de Educación a Distancia.

Moulier Boutang, Yann. 1992. "Interview." *Grundrisse*, May 1992. Accessed January 1, 2014. http://www.grundrisse.net/grundrisse34/interview_mit_yann_moulierbouta.htm.

———. 1993. "Interview." In *Materialien für einen neuen Antiimperialismus* Nr. 5, ed. N. N. Berlin. Göttingen: Schwarze Risse/Rote Straße.

———. 1998. *De l'esclavage au salariat: Economie historique du salariat bridé*. Paris: Presses Universitaires de France.

———. 2001. "Between the Hatred of All Walls and the Walls of Hate: The Minoritarian Diagonal of Mobility." In *"Race" Panic and the Memory of Migration*, ed. Meaghan Morris and Brett de Bary, 105–30. Hong Kong: Hong Kong University Press.

———. 2007. "Europa, Autonomie der Migration, Biopolitik." In *Empire und die biopolitische Wende: Die Internationale Diskussion im Anschluss an Negri und Hardt*, ed. Marianne Pieper, Thomas Atzert, Serhat Karakayali, and Vassilis Tsianos. Frankfurt am Main: Campus.

Moulier Boutang, Yann, and Jean-Pierre Garson. 1984. "Major Obstacles to Control of Irregular Migrations: Prerequisites to Policy." *International Migration Review* 18 (3): 579–92.

Moulier-Boutang, Yann, and Stany Grelet. 2001. "The Art of Flight: An Interview with Yann Moulier-Boutang." *Rethinking Marxism* 13 (3/4): 227–35.

Mountz, Alison. 2011. "The Enforcement Archipelago: Detention, Haunting, and Asylum on Islands." *Political Geography* 30:118–28.

Mountz, Alison, Richard Wright, Ines Miyares, and Adrian J. Bailey. 2002. "Lives in Limbo: Temporary Protected Status and Immigrant Identities." *Global Networks* 2 (4): 335–56.

Mouzourakis, M. 2014. "'We Need to Talk about Dublin': Responsibility under the Dublin System as a Blockage to Asylum Burden-Sharing in the European Union." *RSC* Working Paper No.105.

Mufti, Amir. 2014. "Stathis Gourgouris Interviews Aamir Mufti." *Greek Left Review*, July 14, 2014. http://greekleftreview.wordpress.com/2014/07/14/stathis-gourgouris-interviews-aamir-mufti/.

Muller, Benjamin. 2010. *Security, Risk and the Biometric State*. New York: Routledge.

Multiplicity. 2002. "Materials for a Research Programme on Contemporary Flows through the Mediterranean." *Archis* (September).

Musarò, Pierluigi. 2016. "Mare Nostrum: The Visual Politics of a Military-Humanitarian Operation in the Mediterranean Sea." *Media, Culture and Society* 6:1–18.

Natter, Katharina. 2013. "The Formation of Morocco's Policy towards Irregular Migration (2000–2007): Political Rationale and Policy Processes." *International Migration*. doi: 10.1111/imig.12114.

Ndiaye, G. 1980. *L'échec de la Fédération du Mali*. Dakar: Les nouvelles éditions africaines.

Negri, Antonio. 2005 [1977]. "Domination and Sabotage: On the Marxist Method of Social Transformation." In Negri, *Books for Burning: Between Civil War and Democracy in 1970's Italy*. London: Verso.

———. 2005 [1982]. "Archaeology and Project: The Mass Worker and the Social Worker." libcom.org.

———. 2007. "Logic and Theory of Inquiry: Militant Praxis as Subject and Episteme." In *Constituent Imagination: Militant Investigation, Collective Theorization*, ed. David Graeber and Stevphen Shukhaitis. Oakland, CA: AK Press.

Nevins, Joseph. 2002. *Operation Gatekeeper: The Rise of the "Illegal Alien" and the Making of the U.S.-Mexico Boundary*. New York: Routledge.

———. 2008. *Dying to Live: A Story of U.S. Immigration in an Age of Global Apartheid*. San Francisco: Open Media/City Lights Books.

———. 2010. *Operation Gatekeeper and Beyond: The War on "Illegals" and the Remaking of the U.S.-Mexico Boundary*, 2nd ed. New York: Routledge.

New Keywords Collective. 2016. "Europe/Crisis: New Keywords of 'the Crisis' in and of 'Europe,'" ed. Nicholas De Genova and Martina Tazzioli. *Near Futures Online* 1. New York: Zone Books. http://nearfuturesonline.org/europe crisis-new-keywords-of-crisis-in-and-of-europe/.

Newman, David. 2006. "Borders and Bordering: Towards an Interdisciplinary Dialogue." *European Journal of Social Theory* 9 (2): 171–86.

Ngai, Mae M. 2004. *Impossible Subjects: Illegal Aliens and the Making of Modern America*. Princeton, NJ: Princeton University Press.

Noiriel, G. 1991. *Réfugiés et sans-papiers: La République face au droit d'asile XIXe–XXe*. Paris: Calmann-Lévy.

Noll, Gregor. 2003. "Visions of the Exceptional: Legal and Theoretical Issues Raised by Transit Processing Centres and Protection Zones." *European Journal of Migration and Law*. www.opendemocracy.net/content/articles/PDF/1322.pdf.

Nugent, P., and A. I. Asiwaju, eds. 1996. *African Boundaries: Barriers, Conduits, and Opportunities*. London: Pinter.

Nyers, Peter. 2003. "Abject Cosmopolitanism: The Politics of Protection in the Anti-Deportation Movement." *Third World Quarterly* 24 (6): 1069–93. Reprinted in *The Deportation Regime: Sovereignty, Space, and the Freedom of Movement*, ed. Nicholas De Genova and Nathalie Peutz, 413–41. Durham, NC: Duke University Press, 2010.

Oelgemöller, O. 2011. "'Transit' and 'Suspension': Migration Management or the Metamorphosis of Asylum-Seekers into 'Illegal' Immigrants." *Journal of Ethnic and Migration Studies* 37 (3): 407–24.

O'Malley, Pat, Lorna Weir, and Shearing Clifford. 1997. "Governmentality, Criticism, Politics." *Economy and Society* 26 (4): 501–17.

Open Society Foundation. 2016. "Eroding Trust: The UK's Prevent Counter-Extremism Strategy in Health and Education." Open Society Justice Initiative (October 2016). https://www.opensocietyfoundations.org/sites/default/files/eroding-trust-20161017 _0.pdf.

Pacchetto Sicurezza. 2009. Legge 15 Luglio 2009 n94. Accessed January 16, 2017. http://www1.interno.gov.it/mininterno/site/it/sezioni/servizi/old_servizi/legislazione /sicurezza/0979_2009_07_27_legge_sicurezza.html.

Pagden, Anthony, ed. 2002. *The Idea of Europe: From Antiquity to the European Union*. Cambridge: Cambridge University Press.

Palan, R. 1998. "The Emergence of an Offshore Economy." *Futures* 30 (1): 63–73.

———. 2003. *The Offshore World: Sovereign Markets, Virtual Places and Nomad Millionaires*. Ithaca, NY: Cornell University Press.

Pallister-Wilkins, Polly. 2015. "The Humanitarian Politics of European Border Policing: Frontex and Border Police in Evros." *International Political Sociology* 9:53–69.

Pandolfi, Mariella. 2010. "Humanitarianism and Its Discontents." In *Forces of Compassion: Humanitarianism between Ethics and Politics*, ed. E. Bornstein and P. Redfield, 227–48. Santa Fe, NM: School for Advanced Research Press.

Papadimitriou, P. N., and I. F. Papageorgiou. 2005. "The New 'Dubliners': Implementation of European Council Regulation 343/2003 (Dublin-II) by the Greek Authorities." *Journal of Refugee Studies* 18 (3): 299–318.

Papadopoulos, Dimitris, Niamh Stephenson, and Vassilis Tsianos. 2008. *Escape Routes: Control and Subversion in the 21st Century*. London: Pluto Press.

Papadopoulos, Dimitis, and Vassilis Tsianos. 2013. "After Citizenship: Autonomy of Migration, Organizational Ontology and Mobile Commons." *Citizenship Studies* 17 (2): 178–96.

Papadopoulou, A. 2004. "Smuggling into Europe: Transit Migrants in Greece." *Journal of Refugee Studies* 17 (2): 167–84.

Papastavridis, Efthymios. 2011a. "Rescuing 'Boat People' in the Mediterranean Sea: The Responsibility of States under the Law of the Sea." *European Journal of International Law* (May 31). Accessed December 5, 2013. http://www.ejiltalk.org /rescuing-boat-people-in-the-mediterranean-sea-the-responsibility-of-states-under -the-law-of-the-sea/.

———. 2011b. "The Right of Visit on the High Seas in a Theoretical Perspective: Mare Liberum versus Mare Clausum Revisited." *Leiden Journal of International Law* 24 (1): 45–69.

Papastergiadis, Nikos. 2000. *The Turbulence of Migration: Globalization, Deterritorialization and Hybridity*. Cambridge: Polity Press.

———. 2005. "Mobility and the Nation: Skins, Machines, and Complex Systems." Willy Brandt Series of Working Papers. School of International Migration and Ethnic Relations, Malmö University, Sweden.

———. 2010. "Wars of Mobility." *European Journal of Social Theory* 13 (3): 343–61.

Parks, Lisa. 2009. "Digging into Google Earth: An Analysis of 'Crisis in Darfur.'" *Geoforum* 40:535–45.

Parks, Lisa, and James Schwoch, eds. 2012. *Down to Earth: Satellite Technologies, Industries, and Cultures*. New Brunswick, NJ: Rutgers University Press.

Parla, Ayşe. 2009. "Remembering across the Border: Postsocialist Nostalgia among Turkish Immigrants from Bulgaria." *American Ethnologist* 36 (4): 750–67.

———. 2011. "Labor Migration, Ethnic Kinship, and the Conundrum of Citizenship in Turkey." *Citizenship Studies* 15 (3–4): 457–70.

Parlamento Italiano. 2002. "Modifica alla Normativa in Materia di Immigrazione e di Asilo." Legge 30 luglio 2002, n. 189. Gazzetta Ufficiale n. 199 (August 26, 2002). Accessed January 16, 2017. http://www.camera.it/parlam/leggi/02189l.htm.

Parliamentary Assembly of Council of Europe (PACE). 2011. "The Interception and Rescue at Sea of Asylum Seekers, Refugees and Irregular Migrants." Document

No. 12628. Accessed September 7, 2013. http://assembly.coe.int/nw/xml/XRef/Xref-XML2HTML-en.asp?fileid=18008&lang=en.

———. 2012. "Lives Lost in the Mediterranean Sea: Who Is Responsible?" Strasbourg: Council of Europe. Accessed May 2015. http://www.assembly.coe.int/Committee Docs/2012/20120329_mig_RPT.EN.pdf.

———. 2014. "The 'Left-to-Die Boat': Actions and Reactions." Strasbourg: Council of Europe. Accessed May 2015. http://assembly.coe.int/nw/xml/XRef/Xref-XML2HTML-en.asp?fileid=20940&lang=en.

Parusel, Bernd, and Jan Schneider. 2012. "Visa Policy as Migration Channel: The Impact of Visa Policy on Migration Control." Study by the German Contact Point of the European Migration Network (EMN). Nuremburg: Federal Office for Migration and Refugees.

Peano, Irene. 2012. "Excesses and Double Standards: Migrant Prostitutes, Sovereignty and Exceptions in Contemporary Italy." *Modern Italy* 74 (4): 419–32.

———. 2015. "Emergenc(i)es in the Fields: Affective Composition and Counter-Camps against the Exploitation of Migrant Farm Labour in Italy." Unpublished manuscripts.

Pécoud, Antoine. 2010. "Informing Migrants to Manage Migration? An Analysis of IOM's Information Campaigns." In *The Politics of International Migration Management*, ed. Martin Geiger and Antoine Pécoud, 184–201. New York: Palgrave Macmillan.

———. 2012. "Informer les migrants: Contrôler les migrations. Les campagnes d'informations de l'Organisation internationale pour les migrations." In *Politiques de l'exception: Réfugiés, sinistrés, sans-papiers*, ed. Michel Agier. Paris: Éditions Téraèdre.

Perrotta, Domenico, and Devi Sacchetto. 2011. "Tomato Harvest in Nardò, Puglia: The First Self-Organised Strike of the Day Labourers." *Wildcat* 91 (autumn). http://www.wildcat-www.de/en/wildcat/91/e_w91_nardo.html.

———. 2012. "Il Ghetto e lo Sciopero: Braccianti Stranieri nell'Italia Meridionale." *Sociologia del Lavoro* 128:152–66.

Peutz, Nathalie, and Nicholas De Genova. 2010. "Introduction." In *The Deportation Regime*, eds. Nicholas De Genova and Nathalie Peutz, 1–29. Durham, NC: Duke University Press.

Pew Hispanic Center. 2006. "Modes of Entry for the Unauthorized Migrant Population." Washington, DC: Pew Research Center. Accessed April 29, 2016. http://www.pewhispanic.org/files/2011/10/19.pdf.

Pezzani, Lorenzo. 2015. "Liquid Traces: Spatial Practices, Aesthetics and Humanitarian Dilemmas at the Maritime Borders of the EU." Ph.D. diss., Centre for Research Architecture, Department of Visual Cultures, Goldsmiths, University of London.

Pezzani, Lorenzo, and Charles Heller. 2013. "A Disobedient Gaze: Strategic Interventions in the Knowledge(s) of Maritime Borders." *Postcolonial Studies* 16 (3): 289–98.

Pickles, John. 2004. *A History of Spaces: Cartographic Reason, Mapping and the Geo-Coded World*. London: Routledge.

———, ed. 1995. *Ground Truth: The Social Implications of Geographical Information Systems*. New York: Guilford.

Pike, R. 1983. *Penal Servitude in Early Modern Spain*. Madison: University of Wisconsin Press. http://libro.uca.edu/pservitude/pservitude.htm.

Piliavsky, Anastasia. 2013. "Borders without Borderlands: On the Social Reproduction of State Demarcation in Western India." In *Borderlands in Northern South Asia*, ed. D. Gellner. Durham, NC: Duke University Press.

Planet Contrevas, A. 1998. *Melilla y Ceuta: Espacios-frontera hispano-marroquíes*. Melilla: UNED-Ciudad Autónoma de Melilla–Ciudad Autónoma de Ceuta.

Povinelli, Elizabeth. 2011. *Economies of Abandonment: Social Belonging and Endurance in Late Liberalism*. Durham, NC: Duke University Press.

Povoledo, E. 2014. "Italy Gasps as Inquiry Reveals Mob's Long Reach." *New York Times*. Accessed February 23, 2015. http://nyti.ms/1zEp41x.

Pro Asyl. 2013. "Pushed Back: Systematic Human Rights Violations against Refugees in the Aegean Sea and at the Greek-Turkish Land Border. November 2013. https://www.proasyl.de/wp-content/uploads/2015/12/PRO_ASYL_Report_Pushed_Back_english_November_2013.pdf.

Prozorov, Sergei. 2007. *Foucault, Freedom and Sovereignty*. Hampshire: Ashgate.

Pun, Ngai, and Chris Smith. 2007. "Putting Transnational Labour Process in Its Place: The Dormitory Labour Regime in Post-Socialist China." *Work, Employment and Society* 21 (1): 27–45.

Rajaram, Prem Kumar, and Carl Grundy-Warr, eds. 2007. *Borderscapes: Hidden Geographies and Politics at Territory's Edge*. Minneapolis: University of Minnesota Press.

Rajkumar, Deepa, Laurel Berkowitz, Leah F. Vosko, Valerie Preston, and Robert Latham. 2012. "At the Temporary-Permanent Divide: How Canada Produces Temporariness and Makes Citizens through Its Security, Work, and Settlement Policies." *Citizenship Studies* 16 (3–4): 483–510.

Ramadan, A. 2013. "Spatialising the Refugee Camp." *Transactions of the Institute of British Geographers* 38 (1): 65–77.

Rancière, Jacques. 2004. *Aux bords du politique*. Paris: Gallimard.

———. 2006. *The Politics of Aesthetics: The Distribution of the Sensible*. London: Continuum.

———. 2007. *La mésentente: Politique et philosophie*. Paris: Galilée.

Rapport, N. 2013. "A Migrant or Circuitous Sensibility." In *Being Human, Being Migrant: Sense of Self and Well-Being*, ed. A. Sigfrid Grønseth. New York: Berghahn.

Regan, Margaret. 2010. *The Death of Josseline: Immigration Stories from the Arizona Borderlands*. Boston: Beacon Press.

Reidy, Michael. 2008. "The Royal Navy and the Rise of Modern Geophysics." *Trafalgar Chronicle* 18:222–37.

Reinisch, Jessica. 2015. "'Forever Temporary': Migrants in Calais, Then and Now." *Political Quarterly* (September 18, 2015). doi:10.1111/1467–923X.12196.

Riedner, Lisa, Soledad Álvarez-Velasco, Nicholas De Genova, Martina Tazzioli, and Huub van Baar. 2016. "Mobility." In *Europe/Crisis: New Keywords of "the Crisis" in and of "Europe,"* by New Keywords Collective, edited by Nicholas De Genova and Martina Tazzioli. New York: Zone Books. http://nearfuturesonline.org/europe crisis-new-keywords-of-crisis-in-and-of-europe-part-6/.

Rigby, Joe, and Raphael Schlembach. 2013. "Impossible Protest: No Borders in Calais." *Citizenship Studies* 17 (2): 157–72.

Rigo, Enrica. 2005. "Implications of EU Enlargement for Border Management and Citizenship in Europe." EUI Working Papers.

———. 2011. "Citizens Despite Borders: Challenges to the Territorial Order of Europe." In *The Contested Politics of Mobility: Borderzones and Irregularity*, ed. Vicki Squire, 199–214. London: Routledge.

Rigo, Enrica, and Nick Dines. 2014. "Oltre la Clandestinità, lo Sfruttamento Umanitario del Lavoro nelle Campagne del Mezzogiorn." Accessed November 16, 2014. http://www.connessioniprecarie.org/2014/11/04/oltre-la-clandestinita-lo-sfrutta mento-umanitario-del-lavoro-nelle-campagne-del-mezzogiorno/.

Riles, Annelise. 2013. "Market Collaboration: Finance, Culture, and Ethnography after Neoliberalism." Cornell Law Faculty Publications. Paper No. 665. http:// scholarship.law.cornell.edu/facpub/665/?utm_source=scholarship.law.cornell .edu%2Ffacpub%2F665&utm_medium=PDF&utm_campaign=PDFCoverPages.

Rodier, Claire. 2012. *Xénophobie Business: À Quoi Servent les Contrôles Migratoires?* Paris: La Découverte.

Rodier, Claire, and Isabelle Saint-Saëns. 2007. "Contrôler et filtrer: Les camps au service des politiques migratoires de l'Europe." In *Mondialisation, migration et droits de l'homme: Le droit international en question*, vol. 2, dir. V. Chetail, 619–63. Bruxelles: Bruylant.

Rosas, Gilberto. 2006. "The Managed Violences of the Borderlands: Treacherous Geographies, Policeability, and the Politics of Race." *Latino Studies* 4 (4): 401–18.

Rose, Mitch. 2002. "The Seductions of Resistance: Power, Politics and a Performative Style of Systems." *Environment and Planning D: Society and Space* 20 (4): 383–400.

Rygiel, Kim. 2011. "Bordering Solidarities: Migrant Activism and the Politics of Movement and Camps at Calais." *Citizenship Studies* 15 (1): 1–19.

———. 2014. "In Life through Death: Transgressive Citizenship at the Border." In *Routledge Handbook of Global Citizenship Studies*, ed. Engin F. Isin and Peter Nyers. New York: Routledge.

Said, Edward W. 1978. *Orientalism*. London: Routledge.

Samaddar, Ranabir. 2005. "The Politics of Autonomy: An Introduction." In *The Politics of Autonomy: Indian Experiences*, ed. Ranabir Samaddar, 9–34. London: Sage.

Sánchez, P. 2013. "Aumentan un 771% las entradas de inmigrantes por la valla de Melilla en 2012." *El Mundo*, January 15, 2013.

Sassen, Saskia. 2006. *Territory, Authority, Rights: From Medieval to Global Assemblages*. Princeton, NJ: Princeton University Press.

———. 2009. "Bordering Capabilities versus Borders: Implications for National Borders." Keynote address at the Michigan Journal of International Law Symposium on "Territory without Boundaries," February 2009.

Saul, Heather. 2014. "Syria Crisis: UK Police Urge Muslim Women to Report Relatives Planning to Join War." *The Independent*, December 30, 2014. http://www.indepen dent.co.uk/news/world/middle-east/syria-crisis-uk-police-urge-muslim-women-to -report-relatives-planning-to-join-war-9281100.html.

Sayad, Abdelmalek. 2004. *The Suffering of the Immigrant*. Cambridge: Polity Press.

Scalettaris, G. 2007. "Refugees or Migrants? The UNHCR's Comprehensive Approach to Afghan Mobility into Iran and Pakistan." In *The Politics of International Migration Management*, ed. M. Geiger and A. Pécoud, 252–70. New York: Palgrave Macmillan.

Scheel, Stephan. 2013a. "Autonomy of Migration Despite Its Securitisation? Facing the Terms and Conditions of Biometric Rebordering." *Millennium: Journal of International Studies* 41 (3): 575–600.

———. 2013b. "Studying Embodied Encounters: Autonomy of Migration beyond Its Romanticization." *Postcolonial Studies* 16 (3): 279–88.

———. 2017. *Autonomy of Migration? On the Appropriation of Mobility within Biometric Border Regimes*. London: Routledge.

Scheel, Stephan, and Vicki Squire. 2014. "Forced Migrants as Illegal Migrants." In *The Oxford Handbook of Refugee and Forced Migration Studies*, ed. Elena Fiddian-Qasmiyeh, Gil Loescher, Kathy Long, and Nando Sigona, 188–99. Oxford: Oxford University Press.

Schetter, C. 2005. "Ethnicity and the Political Reconstruction of Afghanistan." Center for Development Studies (ZEF), University of Bonn, Working Papers No. 3.

Schmitt, Carl. 2003 [1950]. *The Nomos of the Earth in the International Law of the Jus Publicum Europaeum*. New York: Telos Press.

Schoorl, Jeannette, Liesbeth Heering, Ingrid Esveldt, Georg Groenewold, Rob van den Erf, Alinda Bosch, Helga de Valk, and Bart de Bruin. 2000. "Push and Pull Factors of International Migration: A Comparative Report." Luxembourg: Eurostat.

Schuster, Liza. 2005. "The Continuing Mobility of Migrants in Italy: Shifting between Statuses and Places." *Journal of Ethnic and Migration Studies* 31 (4): 757–74.

———. 2011a. "Dublin II and Eurodac: Examining the (Un)intended(?) Consequences." *Gender, Place and Culture: A Journal of Feminist Geography* 18 (3): 401–16.

———. 2011b. "Turning Refugees into 'Illegal Migrants': Afghan Asylum Seekers in Europe." *Ethnic and Racial Studies* 34 (8): 1392–1407.

Schuster, Liza, and Nassim Majidi. 2014. "Deportation Stigma and Re-migration." *Journal of Ethnic and Migration Studies* 41 (4): 635–652.

Schwell, Alexandra. 2014. "Compensating (In)security: Anthropological Perspectives on Internal Security." In *The Anthropology of Security: Perspectives from the Frontline of Policing, Counter-Terrorism and Border Control*, ed. Mark Maguire, Catarina Frois, and Nils Zurawski, 83–103. London: Pluto Press.

Sciortino, Giuseppe. 2004. "Between Phantoms and Necessary Evils: Some Critical Points in the Study of Irregular Migrations to Western Europe." *IMIS-Beiträge* 24:17–43.

Sciurba, Alessandra. 2009. *Campi di Forza: Percorsi Confinati di Migranti in Europa*. Verona: Ombre Corte.

———. 2014. "Sharifi et al. vs. Italy and Greece Case: The Strasbourg Court Finds Italy Guilty. An Appeal from Below Stops Refoulements from the Adriatic Sea Ports." *Melting Pot*, October 24. Accessed December 5, 2014. http://www.melt ingpot.org/Sharifi-et-al-vs-Italy-and-Greece-case-The-Strasbourg-Court.html# .VIGTZYdSbQw.

———. 2016. "Hotspot System as a New Device of Clandestinisation: View from Sicily." openDemocracy, February 25, 2016. https://www.opendemocracy.net /can-europe-make-it/alessandra-sciurba/hotspot-system-as-new-device-of -clandestinisation-view-from-si.

Scott, James C. 1985. *Weapons of the Weak: Everyday Forms of Peasant Resistance.* New Haven, CT: Yale University Press.

———. 1998. *Seeing Like a State: How Certain Schemes to Improve the Human Condition Have Failed.* New Haven, CT: Yale University Press.

Sekula, Allan, and Noël Burch. 2010. *The Forgotten Space.* Documentary film. Amsterdam: Doc.Eye Film, WILDart Film.

Semple, Ellen Churchill. 1911. *Influences of Geographic Environment: On the Basis of Ratzel's System of Anthropo-Geography.* New York: Henry Holt.

Serón, Gema, et al. 2011. *Coherencias de políticas españolas hacia África: Migraciones.* Report by Grupo de Estudios Africanos, Universidad Autónoma de Madrid.

Shapira, Harel. 2013. *Waiting for José: The Minutemen's Pursuit of America.* Princeton, NJ: Princeton University Press.

Sharma, Nandita. 2005. "Anti-Trafficking Rhetoric and the Making of a Global Apartheid." *NWSA Journal* 17 (3): 88–111.

———. 2009. "Escape Artists: Migrants and the Politics of Naming." *Subjectivity* 29:467–76.

Shields, Peter. 2015. "The Human Cost of the European Union's External Border Regime." *Peace Review: A Journal of Social Justice* 27 (1): 82–90.

Shore, Chris. 2000. *Building Europe: The Cultural Politics of European Integration.* London: Routledge.

Shukaitis, Stevphen. 2009. *Imaginal Machines: Autonomy and Self-Organization in the Revolutions of Everyday Life.* New York: Autonomedia.

Shryock, Andrew, ed. 2004. *Off Stage/On Display: Intimacy and Ethnography in the Age of Public Culture.* Stanford, CA: Stanford University Press.

Sigona, Nando. 2015. "Campzenship: Reimagining the Camp as a Social and Political Space." *Citizenship Studies* 19 (1): 1–15.

Sigona, Nando, and Vanessa Hughes. 2012. "No Way Out, No Way In: Irregular Migrant Children and Families in the UK." Oxford: ESRC Centre on Migration, Policy and Society.

Sigona, Nando, and Nidhi Trehan, eds. 2009. *Romani Politics in Contemporary Europe: Poverty, Ethnic Mobilization and the Neoliberal Order.* Basingstoke: Palgrave Macmillan.

Simeant, J. 1998. *La cause des sans-papiers.* Paris: Presses de Science-Po.

Simone, AbdouMaliq. 2004. "People as Infrastructure: Intersecting Fragments in Johannesburg." *Public Culture* 16 (3): 407–29.

Sossi, Federica. 2007. *Migrare: Spazi di confinamento e strateige di esistenza.* Milan: Il Saggiatore.

Soto Bermant, Laia. 2007. "The Myth of Al-Andalus: A Study of Spanish Identity." M.Phil. thesis, Institute of Social and Cultural Anthropology, University of Oxford.

———. 2014. "Consuming Europe: The Moral Significance of Mobility and Exchange at the Spanish–Moroccan Border of Melilla." *Journal of North African Studies* 19 (1): 110–29.

———. 2015. "A Tale of Two Cities: Notes on the Social Production of Difference in a Mediterranean Border Enclave." *Social Anthropology/Anthropologie Sociale* 23 (4): 450–64.

Soukouna, S. 2011. "L'Échec d'une Coopération Franco-Malienne sur les Migrations: Les logiques du refus malien de signer." Mémoire de Master 2 en science politique (relations internationales), Paris 1 Panthéon-Sorbonne, Paris.

Sparke, M. 2006. "A Neoliberal Nexus: Economy, Security and the Biopolitics of Citizenship on the Border." *Political Geography* 25:151–80.

Spijkerboer, Thomas. 2007. "The Human Costs of Border Control." *European Journal of Migration and Law* 9 (2): 127–39.

———. 2013. "Are European States Accountable for Border Deaths?" In *Research Companion to Migration Law and Theory*, ed. Satvinder Juss. Aldershot: Ashgate.

Spijkerboer, Thomas, and Tamara Last. 2014. "Tracking Deaths in the Mediterranean." In *Fatal Journeys: Tracking Lives Lost During Migration*, eds. Tara Brian and Frank Laczko. Geneva: International Organization for Migration.

Spire, Alexis. 2009. *Accueillir ou reconduire: Enquête sur les guichets de l'immigration.* Paris: Raisons d'Agir Éditions.

Squire, Vicki. 2011. "The Contested Politics of Migration: Politicizing Mobility, Mobilizing Politics." In *The Contested Politics of Mobility: Borderzones and Irregularity*, ed. Vicki Squire. London: Routledge.

———. 2014. "Desert 'Trash': Posthumanism, Border Struggles, and Humanitarian Politics." *Political Geography* 39:11–21.

Stallaert, C. 1996. *Etnogénesis y etnicidad en España: Una aproximación histórico-antropológica al casticismo.* Barcelona: Proyecto A Ediciones.

Steinberg, Philip E. 1999. "Lines of Division, Lines of Connection: Stewardship in the World Ocean." *Geographical Review* 89 (2): 254–64.

———. 2001. *The Social Construction of the Ocean.* Cambridge: Cambridge University Press.

———. 2009a. "Oceans." In *International Encyclopedia of Human Geography*, ed. Nigel Thrift. Oxford: Elsevier Science.

———. 2009b. "Sovereignty, Territory, and the Mapping of Mobility: A View from the Outside." *Annals of the Association of American Geographers* 99 (3): 467–95.

———. 2011. "Free Sea." In *Spatiality, Sovereignty and Carl Schmitt: Geographies of the Nomos*, ed. Stephen Legg. London: Routledge.

———. 2013a. "Oceans." Accessed December 2013. http://www.oxfordbibliographies.com/display/id/obo-9780199874002-0052.

———. 2013b. "Of Other Seas: Metaphors and Materialities in Maritime Regions." *Atlantic Studies* 10 (2): 156–69.

———. 2014. "Mediterranean Metaphors: Travel, Translation, and Oceanic Imaginaries in the 'New Mediterraneans' of the Arctic Ocean, the Gulf of Mexico and the

Caribbean." In *Water Worlds: Human Geographies of the Ocean*, ed. Jon Anderson and Kimberley Peters. Farnham: Ashgate.

Stephen, Chris. 2016. "Libya Faces Influx of Migrants Seeking New Routes to Europe." *The Guardian*, April 9, 2016. http://www.theguardian.com/world/2016/apr/09/libya-influx-migrants-europe.

Stephen, Lynn. 2008. "Los Nuevos Desaparecidos: Immigration, Militarization, Death, and Disappearance on Mexico's Borders." In *Security Disarmed: Critical Perspectives on Gender, Race, and Militarization*, ed. Barbara Sutton, Sandra Morgen, and Julie Novkov. New Brunswick, NJ: Rutgers University Press.

Stierl, Maurice. 2015. "The WatchTheMed Alarm Phone: A Disobedient Border-Intervention." *Movements: Journal für kritische Migrations- und Grenzregimeforschung* [Journal for Critical Migration and Border Regime Research] 1 (2). http://movements-journal.org/issues/02.kaempfe/13.stierl–watchthemed-alarmphone.html.

———. 2016. "Contestations in Death: The Role of Grief in Migration Struggles." *Citizenship Studies* 20 (2): 173–91.

Stoler, Ann L. 2006. "On Degrees of Imperial Sovereignty." *Public Culture* 18 (1): 125–46.

Storiemigranti. 2015. "Migrants in Tunisia: Detained and Deported." Accessed April 30, 2015. http://www.storiemigranti.org/spip.php?article1080.

Stuesse, Angela, and Mathew Coleman. 2014. "Automobility, Immobility, Altermobility: Surviving and Resisting the Intensification of Immigrant Policing." *City and Society* 26 (1): 51–72.

Suárez de Vivero, Juan Luis. 2010. *Jurisdictional Waters in the Mediterranean and Black Seas*. Brussels: European Parliament.

Suárez-Navas, Liliana. 2004. *Rebordering the Mediterranean: Boundaries and Citizenship in Southern Europe*. Oxford: Berghahn.

———. 2014. "Imaginarios Etnoculturales y Refronterización Europea: Descolonizando los Espacios de Proyección Ibérica en el Mediterráneo y el Atlántico." In *Periferias, Fronteras y Diálogos: Actas del XIII Congreso de Antropología de la Federación de Asociaciones de Antropología del Estado Español*, Tarragona, 2–5 de Septiembre de 2014. Tarragona: Universitat Rovira i Virgili.

Sundberg, Juanita. 2011. "Diabolic Caminos in the Desert and Cat Fights on the Río: A Posthumanist Political Ecology of Boundary Enforcement in the United States–Mexico Borderlands." *Annals of the Association of American Geographers* 101 (2): 318–36.

Sutcliffe, B. 2001. "Migration and Citizenship: Why Can Birds, Whales, Butterflies and Ants Cross International Frontiers More Easily Than Cows, Dogs and Human Beings?" In *Migration and Mobility*, ed. Subrata Ghatak and Anne Showstack Sassoon, 66–82. Basingstoke: Palgrave Macmillan. Accessed August 26, 2014. http://www.palgraveconnect.com/pc/doifinder/10.1057/9780230523128.

Svantesson, Monica. 2014. *Threat Construction inside Bureaucracy: A Bourdieusian Study of the European Commission and the Framing of Irregular Immigration, 1974–2009*. Stockholm: Stockholm University.

System for the Protection of Asylum Seekers and Refugees (SPRAR). 2009. "Guida Pratica per i Titolari di Protezione Internazionale." Accessed September 13, 2014.

http://www.interno.gov.it/mininterno/export/sites/default/it/assets/files
/18/00914_EN_SPRAR_Vademecum_Protezione.pdf.

———. n.d. "System for the Protection of Asylum Seekers and Refugees *SPRAR*." Accessed September 10, 2014. http://www.serviziocentrale.it/file/server/file/SPRAR%20 Description%20-%20Italy.pdf.

Szczepanikova, A. 2013. "Between Control and Assistance: The Problem of European Accommodation Centres for Asylum Seekers." *International Migration* 51 (4): 130–43.

Talsania, Krishna. 2012. "Are Sun Readers Ready to 'Beat the Cheat' Armed with the Facts?" *The Guardian*, March 7, 2012. http://www.theguardian.com/comment isfree/2012/mar/07/sun-beat-the-cheat-benefits.

Tazzioli, Martina. 2012. "S/confinamenti degli spazi frontiera: Choucha, Ras-Jadir, Tataouine." In *Spazi in migrazione: Cartoline di una rivoluzione*, ed. Federica Sossi. Verona: Ombre Corte.

———. 2013. "Migration (in) Crisis and 'People Who Are Not of Our Concern.'" In *Spaces in Migration: Postcards of a Revolution*, ed. Glenda Garelli, Federica Sossi, and Martina Tazzioli, 87–100. London: Pavement Books.

———. 2014. *Spaces of Governmentality: Autonomous Migration and the Arab Uprisings*. New York: Rowman and Littlefield.

———. 2015a. "The Desultory Politics of Mobility and the Humanitarian-Military Border in the Mediterranean: Mare Nostrum beyond the Sea." *REMHU: Revista Interdisciplinar da Mobilidade Humana* 23 (44). http://www.scielo.br/scielo .php?pid=S1980-85852015000100061&script=sci_arttext&tlng=es.

———. 2015b. "Which Europe? Migrants' Uneven Geographies and Counter-Mapping at the Limits of Representation." *Movements: Journal für kritische Migrations- und Grenzregimeforschung* [Journal for Critical Migration and Border Regime Research] 1 (2). http://movements-journal.org/issues/02.kaempfe/04.tazzioli–europe-migrants -geographies-counter-mapping-representation.html.

Tazzioli, Martina, and Nicholas De Genova. 2016. "Europe/Crisis: Introducing New Keywords of 'the Crisis' in and of 'Europe.'" *Near Futures Online* 1. New York: Zone Books. http://nearfuturesonline.org/europecrisis-new-keywords -of-crisis-in-and-of-europe/.

Terray, E. 2008. "L'Etat nation vu par les sans papiers." *Actuel Marx* 44:41–52.

Thomas, Rebekah. 2005. "Biometrics, Migrants, and Human Rights." *Migration Information Source*. Washington, DC: Migration Policy Institute.

Ticktin, Miriam. 2006. "Where Ethics and Politics Meet: The Violence of Humanitarianism in France." *American Ethnologist* 33 (1): 33–49.

———. 2011. *Casualties of Care: Immigration and the Politics of Humanitarianism in France*. Berkeley: University of California Press.

———. 2015. "The Problem with Humanitarian Borders." Public Seminar. http://www.pub licseminar.org/2015/09/the-problem-with-humanitarian-borders/#.VxagfXBmh4M.

Tofiño-Quesada, I. 2003. "Spanish Orientalism: Uses of the Past in Spain's Colonization in Africa." *Comparative Studies of South Asia, Africa and the Middle East* 23 (1–2): 141–48.

Tondini, Matteo. 2010. "Fishers of Men? The Interception of Migrants in the Mediterranean Sea and Their Return to Libya." *INEX Paper* (October): 1–28.

———. 2012. "The Legality of Intercepting Boat People under Search and Rescue and Border Control Operations." *Journal of International Maritime Law* 18 (1): 59–74.

Tounkara, M. 2013. "Les dimensions socioculturelles de l'échec de la migration: Cas des expulsés maliens de France." Thèse de socio-anthropologie, Université Paris-Est.

Traven, B. 1991 [1934]. *The Death Ship*. New York: L. Hill Books.

Traynor, Ian. 2015a. "Migrant Crisis: EU Plan to Strike Libya Networks Could Include Ground Forces." *The Guardian*, May 13, 2015. http://www.theguardian.com/world/2015/may/13/migrant-crisis-eu-plan-to-strike-libya-networks-could-include-ground-forces.

———. 2015b. "Migration Crisis: Hungary PM Says Europe in Grip of Madness." *The Guardian*, September 3, 2015. http://www.theguardian.com/world/2015/sep/03/migration-crisis-hungary-pm-victor-orban-europe-response-madness.

———. 2015c. "Molenbeek: The Brussels Borough Becoming Known as Europe's Jihadi Central." *The Guardian*, November 15, 2015. http://www.theguardian.com/world/2015/nov/15/molenbeek-the-brussels-borough-in-the-spotlight-after-paris-attacks.

Tsianos, Vassilis, and Serhat Karakayali. 2010. "Transnational Migration and the Emergence of the European Border Regime: An Ethnographic Analysis." *European Journal of Social Theory* 13 (3): 373–87.

UN Office of the High Commissioner for Refugees (UNHCR). 2003. "Conclusion on Protection Safeguards in Interception Measures." Geneva: UNHCR. Accessed December 4, 2013. www.unhcr.org/excom/EXCOM/3f93b2894.html.

———. 2010. "Submission of the Office of the UN High Commissioner for Refugees in the case of Ahmed Ali and Others v. the Netherlands and Greece." Accessed September 13, 2014. http://www.unhcr.org/refworld/docid/4b8d14fb2.html.

UNHCR Racist Violence Recording Network. 2013. "Annual Report." Accessed October 8, 2013. http://www.unhcr.gr/1againstracism/en/2012-annual-report-of-the-racist-violence-recording-network/.

Urrea, Luis Alberto. 2004. *The Devil's Highway: A True Story*. New York: Little, Brown.

U.S. Department of Homeland Security (DHS). 2016. "Entry/Exit Overstay Report for Fiscal Year 2015." January 19, 2016. Accessed April 29, 2016. https://www.dhs.gov/news/2016/01/19/dhs-releases-entryexit-overstay-report-fiscal-year-2015.

Vacchiano, Francesco. 2011a. "Frontiere della Vita Quotidiana: Pratiche di Burocratica Violenza nell'Accoglienza di Richiedenti Asilo e Rifugiati." In *Un Rifugio all'Esclusione: L'Accoglienza Non Istituzionale dei Richiedenti Asilo a Torino*, ed. A. Vailati. Torino: L'Harmattan Italia.

———. 2011b. "Discipline della Scarsità e del Sospetto: Rifugiati e Accoglienza nel Regime di Frontiera." *Lares* 77 (1): 181–98.

———. 2014. "Beyond Borders and Limits: Moroccan Migrating Adolescents between Desire, Vulnerability and Risk." *Saude e Sociedade* 23 (1): 17–29.

van Baar, Huub. 2011a. *The European Roma: Minority Representation, Memory, and the Limits of Transnational Governmentality*. Self-published Ph.D. dissertation, University of Amsterdam.

———. 2011b. "Europe's Romaphobia: Problematization, Securitization, Nomadization." *Environment and Planning D: Society and Space* 29 (2): 203–12.

———. 2015. "The Perpetual Mobile Machine of Forced Mobility." In *The Irregularization of Migration in Contemporary Europe: Detention, Deportation, Drowning*, ed. Yolande Jansen, Joost de Bloois, and Robin Celikates. London: Rowman and Littlefield.

van Houtum, Henk. 2010. "Human Blacklisting: The Global Apartheid of the EU's External Border Regime." *Environment and Planning D: Society and Space* 28 (6): 957–76.

van Houtum, Henk, and Freerk Boedeltje. 2009. "Europe's Shame: Death at the Borders of the EU." *Antipode* 41 (2): 226–30.

van Houtum, Henk, and Roos Pijpers. 2007. "The European Union as a Gated Community: The Two-Faced Border and Immigration Regime of the EU." *Antipode* 39 (2): 291–309.

Varsanyi, Monica. 2008. "Immigration Policy through the Back Door: City Ordinances, the Right to the City and the Exclusion of Undocumented Day Labourers." *Urban Geography* 29 (1): 29–52.

Vaughan-Williams, Nick. 2015. *Europe's Border Crisis: Biopolitical Security and Beyond.* Oxford: Oxford University Press.

Vendola, N. 2014. "Capo Free, Ghetto Off." Accessed September 15, 2014. http://www.giornalediApulia.com/2014/04/capo-freeghetto-off-rignano-garganico.html.

Ventura, A. 2011. "I Ghetti Africani di Puglia." *Etnografia e Ricerca Qualitativa* 2 (6): 9–25.

Verdery, Katherine. 2014. *Secrets and Truths: Ethnography in the Archive of Romania's Secret Police.* Budapest: Central European University Press.

Vigh, H. 2009. "Wayward Migration: On Imagined Futures and Technological Voids." *Ethnos* 74 (1): 91–109.

Vine, John. 2010. "Preventing and Detecting Immigration and Customs Offenses: A Thematic Inspection of How the UK Border Agency Receives and Uses Intelligence." http://icinspector.independent.gov.uk/wp-content/uploads/2011/02/Preventing-and-detecting-immigration-and-customs-offences.pdf.

———. 2014. "An Inspection of the Intelligence Management System." London: Independent Chief Inspector of Borders and Immigration. http://icinspector.independent.gov.uk/wp-content/uploads/2014/10/An-inspection-of-the-Intelligence-Management-System-FINAL-WEB.pdf.

Virno, Paolo. 2001. "General Intellect." in *Lessico Postfordista: Dizionarion delle Idee della Mutazione*, ed. A. Zanini and U. Fadini. Milano: Feltrinelli Editore.

———. 2003. *A Grammar of the Multitude: For an Analysis of Contemporary Forms of Life.* Cambridge: Semiotexte.

von Busekist, A., ed. 2008. "Voice! Identités et mobilisations." *Raisons Politiques* 29.

Wacquant, Loïc. 2009. *Punishing the Poor: The Neoliberal Government of Social Insecurity.* Durham, NC: Duke University Press.

———. 2010. "Crafting the Neoliberal State: Workfare, Prisonfare and Social Insecurity." *Sociological Forum* 25 (2): 197–220.

Walters, William. 2004. "The Frontiers of the European Union: A Geostrategic Perspective." *Geopolitics* 9 (2): 674–98.

———. 2006. "Border/Control." *European Journal of Social Theory* 9 (2): 187–203.

———. 2008. "Putting the Migration-Security Complex in Its Place." In *Risk and the War on Terror*, ed. Louise Amoore and Marieke de Goede. London: Routledge.

———. 2009. "Europe's Borders." In *Sage Handbook of European Studies*, ed. Chris Rumford. London: Sage.

———. 2010. "Migration and Security." In *The Handbook of New Security Studies*, ed. Peter Burgess, 217–28.

———. 2011a. "Foucault and Frontiers: Notes on the Birth of the Humanitarian Border." In *Governmentality: Current Issues and Future Challenges*, ed. Ulrich Bröckling, Susanne Krasmann, and Thomas Lemke. London: Routledge.

———. 2011b. "Where Are the Missing Vehicles? Critical Reflections on Viapolitics." Paper presented at the Summer School on Border Crossing Selves, Hanyang University, Seoul, June 25–29.

———. 2014. "Migration, Vehicles, and Politics: Three Theses on Viapolitics." *European Journal of Social Theory*. doi:10.1177/1368431014554859.

———. 2015a. "On the Road with Michel Foucault: Migration, Deportation, and Viapolitics." In *Foucault and the History of Our Present*, ed. Sophie Fuggle, Yari Lanci, and Martina Tazzioli. Basingstoke: Palgrave Macmillan.

———. 2015b. "Reflections on Migration and Governmentality." *Movements: Journal für kritische Migrations- und Grenzregimeforschung* [Journal for Critical Migration and Border Regime Research] 1 (1). http://movements-journal.org/issues/01.grenz regime/04.walters–migration.governmentality.html.

Walters, William, Charles Heller, Lorenzo Pezzani, and Mathew Coleman. n.d. *Vehicles of Migration, Routes of Power: Essays on Viapolitics*. Unpublished manuscript.

Wasley, A. 2011. "Scandal of the 'Tomato Slaves' Harvesting Crop Exported to UK." *Ecologist* (September 1). Accessed September 15, 2014. http://www.theecologist .org/News/news_analysis/1033179/scandal_of_the_tomato_slaves_harvesting _crop_exported_to_uk.html.

Weber, Leanne. 2006. "The Shifting Frontiers of Migration Control." In *Borders, Mobility and Technologies of Control*, ed. Sharon Pickering and Leanne Weber. Dordrecht: Springer.

Weber, Leanne, and Sharon Pickering. 2011. *Globalization and Borders: Death at the Global Frontier*. London: Palgrave Macmillan.

Weeks, K. 2007. "Life Within and against Work: Affective Labour, Feminist Critique and Post-Fordist Politics." *Ephemera: Theory and Politics in Organization* 7 (1): 233–49.

Weizman, Eyal. 2007. *Hollow Land: Israel's Architecture of Occupation*. London: Verso.

———. 2012. "Forensic Architecture: Notes from Fields and Forums." In *100 Notes— 100 Thoughts*, ed. Documenta 13. Ostfildern: Hatje Cantz Verlag.

———. 2013. "Introduction: Forensis." In *Forensis: The Architecture of Public Truth*, ed. Forensic Architecture. Berlin: Sternberg Press.

Willen, Sarah. 2007. "Toward a Critical Phenomenology of 'Illegality': State Power, Criminalization, and Abjectivity among Undocumented Migrant Workers in Tel Aviv, Israel." *International Migration* 45 (3): 8–38.

Williams, Jill M. 2015. "From Humanitarian Exceptionalism to Contingent Care: Care and Enforcement at the Humanitarian Border." *Political Geography* 47:11–20.

———. 2016. "The Safety/Security Nexus and the Humanitarianisation of Border Enforcement." *Geographical Journal* 182 (1): 27–37.

Yaghmaian, B. 2005. *Embracing the Infidel: Stories of Muslim Migrants on the Journey West.* New York: Delacorte.

Yeung, H. W. C. 1998. "Capital, State and Space: Contesting the Borderless World." *Transactions of the Institute of British Geographers* 23 (3): 291–309.

Yildiz, Can, and Nicholas De Genova. n.d. "Un/Free Mobility: Roma Migrants in the European Union." Unpublished manuscript.

Yildiz, Can, Nicholas De Genova, Yolande Jansen, Laia Soto Bermant, Aila Spathopoulou, Maurice Stierl, and Zakeera Suffee. 2016. "(The Crisis of) 'European Values.'" In *Europe/Crisis: New Keywords of "the Crisis" in and of "Europe,"* by New Keywords Collective, ed. Nicholas De Genova and Martina Tazzioli. New York: Zone Books. http://nearfuturesonline.org/europecrisis-new-keywords-of-crisis-in-and-of-europe-part-7/.

Yınanç, B. 2013. "Poor Transparency Shadows Turkey's Syria Refugee Policy." *Hürriyet Daily News.* Accessed April 5, 2016. http://www.hurriyetdailynews .com/?PageID=238&NID=47639.

Zampagni, Francesca. 2011. "A Visa for Schengen's Europe: Consular Practices and Regular Migration from Senegal to Italy." Florence: Robert Schuman Centre for Advanced Studies, European University Institute.

———. 2013. "Who Moves? Schengen Visa Policies and Implementation in Consulates: A Fieldwork Study from the Embassy of Italy in Senegal." Unpublished dissertation, Department for Political and Social Science, University of Pisa.

Zetter, R. 2007. "More Labels, Fewer Refugees: Remaking the Refugee Label in an Era of Globalization." *Journal of Refugee Studies* 20:172–92.

Žižek, Slavoj. 2015. "We Can't Address the EU Refugee Crisis without Confronting Global Capitalism." *In These Times*, September 9, 2015. http://inthesetimes.com /article/18385/slavoj-zizek-european-refugee-crisis-and-global-capitalism.

———. 2016a. "The Cologne Attacks Were an Obscene Version of Carnival." *New Statesman*, January 13, 2016. http://www.newstatesman.com/world/europe/2016 /01/slavoj-zizek-cologne-attacks.

———. 2016b. "'EU Must Militarize Chaotic Immigration, Identify States behind Middle East Crisis'—Zizek to RT." Interview with RT News, April 22, 2016. https:// www.rt.com/news/340562-eu-refugee-policy-chaos-militarization/.

———. 2016c. "What Our Fear of Refugees Says about Europe." *New Statesman*, February 29, 2016. http://www.newstatesman.com/politics/uk/2016/02/slavoj-zizek -what-our-fear-refugees-says-about-europe.

REGULATIONS

European Union-Turkey Agreement. EU Press Release 144/16, March 18, 2016. Accessed April 1, 2016. http://turabder.org/en/news-section.

Regulation No. 1994/6169 on the Procedures and Principles Related to Possible Population Movements and Aliens Arriving in Turkey Either as Individuals or in Groups Wishing to Seek Asylum Either from Turkey or Requesting Residence Permission in Order to Seek Asylum from Another Country, January 19, 1994. Accessed December 20, 2013. http://www.refworld.org/docid/49746cc62.html.

Regulation No. 29153 on Temporary Protection [Turkey], October 22, 2013. Accessed December 1, 2014. http://www.tkhk.gov.tr/DB/14/1673_gecici-koruma-yonetm.

LAWS

Laws on Foreigners and International Protection Numbered 6458, 04 April 2013. *Official Gazette*, No. 28615, April 11, 2013. Accessed June 13, 2013. http://www.resmigazete.gov.tr/main.aspx?home=http%3A%2F%2Fwww.resmigazete.gov.tr%2Feskiler%2F2013%2F04%2F20130411.htm&main=http%3A%2F%2Fwww.resmigazete.gov.tr%2Feskiler%2F2013%2F04%2F20130411.htm.

EURO STATISTICS

http://appsso.eurostat.ec.europa.eu/nui/show.do?dataset=migr_asyappctza&lang=en.
http://appsso.eurostat.ec.europa.eu/nui/show.do?dataset=migr_asydcfina&lang=en.

CONTRIBUTORS

RUBEN ANDERSSON is an Associate Professor in the Department of International Development at the University of Oxford, and an associated researcher in the Department of Anthropology, Stockholm University. He was previously an AXA postdoctoral research fellow in the Civil Society and Human Security Research Unit of the Department of International Development, London School of Economics and Political Science (LSE). His doctoral thesis in anthropology at the LSE was awarded the 2014 Maria Ioannis Baganha Dissertation Award of the international interdisciplinary research network International Migration, Integration and Social Cohesion in Europe (IMISCOE). His book *Illegality, Inc.: Clandestine Migration and the Business of Bordering Europe* (2014) was the winner of the annual Ethnography Award of the BBC Radio4 program *Thinking Allowed*, in association with the British Sociological Association.

————

NICHOLAS DE GENOVA (www.nicholasdegenova.com) has held academic appointments in Geography at King's College London, where he was also the director of research groups on Cities and then on Spatial Politics, and in Anthropology at Stanford, Columbia, and Goldsmiths, University of London, as well as visiting professorships or research positions at the Universities of Warwick, Bern, Amsterdam, and Chicago. He is the author of *Working the Boundaries: Race, Space, and "Illegality" in Mexican Chicago* (2005), coauthor of *Latino Crossings: Mexicans, Puerto Ricans, and the Politics of Race and Citizenship* (2003), editor of *Racial Transformations: Latinos and Asians Remaking the United States* (2006), and coeditor of *The Deportation Regime: Sovereignty, Space, and the Freedom of Movement* (2010). With Martina Tazzioli, he coordinated and coedited a collaborative writing project involving 15 coauthors (including several of the contributors to this volume), on "Europe/Crisis: New Keywords of 'the Crisis' in and of 'Europe,'" published by *Near Futures Online* (2016). He is currently writing two new books, one on *The Migrant Metropolis* and another on *The "European" Question: Race, Migration, and Postcoloniality*.

————

DACE DZENOVSKA is an Associate Professor in the Anthropology of Migration at the University of Oxford. Previously, she held academic and research positions at the University of Latvia and in the Centre on Migration, Policy and Society (COMPAS) at the

University of Oxford. She holds a doctoral degree in sociocultural anthropology from the University of California, Berkeley. Her research interests include Europe and coloniality, bordering and polity formation, and mobility and governance. Her book *The Great Departure: Staying and Leaving after Postsocialism* is forthcoming from Berghahn Books. She recently completed a new book manuscript, provisionally titled *School of Europeanness: Tolerance and Other Lessons in Political Liberalism*. Her articles have been published in *Comparative Studies in Society and History*, *Anthropological Theory*, *Journal of Ethnic and Migration Studies*, *Ethnos*, and *Social Anthropology*.

———

EVELINA GAMBINO is a Ph.D. student in the Department of Geography at the University of Nottingham. Her current research project, " 'An Outstretched Hand between Europe and Asia': Logistical Infrastructure and National Imaginations in Contemporary Georgia," explores the recent history of infrastructural regeneration in contemporary Georgia, and proposes an original contribution to post-Soviet geographies through an ethnographic attention to "frictions" that shape and inform the expansion of capital on a global scale. She holds an M.A. in anthropology from Goldsmiths, University of London. Her chapter in this volume results from her involvement with the network Campagne in Lotta in migrant agricultural workers' struggles in various regions of Italy. She is also part of the militant research collective Collettivo RicercAzione.

———

GLENDA GARELLI is an urban studies scholar who studies border regimes and migrant struggles in the Mediterranean, contributing to a human geography of the European Union political project and of the Mediterranean policy region. She is coauthor of *Tunisia as a Revolutionized Space of Migration* (2016), and coeditor of *Spaces in Migration: Postcards of a Revolution* (2013). Her single- and coauthored work has appeared in *Environment and Planning D: Society and Space*, *Postcolonial Studies*, *Cultural Studies*, *Materialifoucaultiani*, and *Etnografia*. In 2015, she completed her doctoral dissertation, "Mediterranean Routes: Migrants' Border Deaths, Humanitarian Containment, and Contested Presence," in urban studies at the University of Illinois at Chicago. She also contributes to the web-based archive www.storiemigranti.org.

———

CHARLES HELLER is a filmmaker and researcher whose work has a long-standing focus on the politics of migration. He is currently a postdoctoral researcher affiliated with the Centre for Migration and Refugee Studies at the American University, Cairo, and the Centre d'Etudes et de Documentation Economiques, Juridiques et Sociales, Cairo, with research support from the Swiss National Fund. In 2015, he completed a Ph.D. in research architecture at Goldsmiths, University of London, where he continues to be affiliated as a research fellow. His writing has appeared in the journals *Global Media and Communication* and *Philosophy of Photography*. Together with Lorenzo Pezzani, he has been working since 2011 on Forensic Oceanography, a project that critically investigates the militarized border regime and the politics of migration in the Mediterranean Sea, and cofounded the WatchTheMed project. Their collaborative work has been published in several edited volumes as well as in the journals *Cultural Studies*, *Postcolonial Studies*, and the *Revue Européenne des Migrations Internationales*.

———

CLARA LECADET is an associate researcher in the Urban Anthropology Laboratory, École des Hautes Études en Sciences Sociales (EHESS), Paris. In 2013–2014, she was a postdoctoral fellow for the research program Global Mobility and Migration Governance (MOBGLOB) at EHESS. Her research focuses on the emergence of expelled migrants' protest movements in Mali and other African countries, and on the various forms of organization used by expelled migrants during the post-expulsion period. With Michel Agier she coedited *Un monde de camps* (2014) and is the author of the book *Le manifeste des expulsés: Errance, survie et politique au Mali* (2016).

———

SOUAD OSSEIRAN is a Ph.D. candidate in the Department of Anthropology at Goldsmiths, University of London. Her doctoral dissertation is titled "Migration, Waiting, and Uncertainty at the Borders of Europe: Syrian Migrants and Refugees in Istanbul." In her ethnography, she explores the presence of Syrian migrants/refugees in Istanbul, the legal framework underlying their presence, and the ways they experience temporality.

———

LORENZO PEZZANI is an architect and a Lecturer in the Centre for Research Architecture, at Goldsmiths, University of London, where he currently convenes the M.A. stream in Forensic Architecture, and where he obtained his Ph.D. in 2015. He has previously taught at the Bartlett School of Architecture, University College London, and held a postdoctoral fellowship in the School of Law at the University of Kent. His work deals with the spatial politics and visual cultures of migration, human rights, and media, with a particular focus on the geography of the ocean. He has published in the journals *New Geographies* and *Harvard Design Magazine*. Together with Charles Heller, he has been working since 2011 on Forensic Oceanography, a project that critically investigates the militarized border regime and the politics of migration in the Mediterranean Sea, and cofounded the WatchTheMed project. Their collaborative work has been published in several edited volumes as well as in the journals *Cultural Studies*, *Postcolonial Studies*, and the *Revue Européenne des Migrations Internationales*.

———

FIORENZA PICOZZA is a Ph.D. student in the Department of Geography at King's College London. Her thesis is provisionally entitled "Europe's Geographies of Asylum: Mobilities, Subjectivities and Solidarities within and against the Asylum Regime." She holds an M.A. in Migration and Diaspora Studies from the School of Oriental and African Studies (SOAS), University of London, and a B.A. in philosophy from the University of Rome–La Sapienza. She has also worked in education projects with migrants and refugees in Rome.

———

STEPHAN SCHEEL is a postdoctoral researcher on the project Peopling Europe: How Data Make a People (ARITHMUS) in the Department of Sociology of Goldsmiths, University of London. He defended his doctoral thesis in 2014 in the Department of

Political and International Studies at the Open University (UK). His book *Autonomy of Migration? On the Appropriation of Mobility within Biometric Border Regimes* is forthcoming. Another research interest concerns how humanitarian regimes intersect with security practices. He has published in the journals *Cultural Studies, Millennium, Postcolonial Studies*, and the *Journal of Ethnic and Migration Studies*. He is also a member of the Network for Critical Border and Migration Studies (Kritnet; www.kritnet.org).

———

MAURICE STIERL most recently held an appointment as Visiting Assistant Professor in Comparative Border Studies at the University of California, Davis. Previously, he was an Early Career Fellow at the Institute of Advanced Study at the University of Warwick, where he received his Ph.D. from the Department of Politics and International Studies. His research focuses on migration and border struggles in contemporary Europe and North Africa. He has published in the journals *Citizenship Studies, Globalizations, Movements, International Migration Review, Antipode*, and *Global Society*. He is a coeditor of the journals *Citizenship Studies* and *Movements*. He is also a member of the research and activist collectives WatchTheMed, Kritnet, MobLab, and Authority & Political Technologies.

———

LAIA SOTO BERMANT is a postdoctoral fellow in the Department of Social Research at the University of Helsinki, where she is working on borders, trade, and transit in the Mediterranean. Previously, she has been a lecturer in social anthropology at the University of Bournemouth (2014–15); a research associate in the Department of Geography at the University of Loughborough (2014); a postdoctoral research associate in Comparative Border Studies at Arizona State University (2013–14), where she continues to be affiliated as a visiting scholar; and a postdoctoral associate at the University of Oxford (2012/13). She received a Ph.D. from the Institute of Social and Cultural Anthropology at the University of Oxford in 2012. She has conducted fieldwork in Spain and Morocco since 2008, and has a long-standing interest in the historical and contemporary interrelationship between the northern and southern shores of the Mediterranean. She has published in the *Journal of North African Studies* and *Powision: Neue Räume für Politik,* and is completing a book manuscript titled *Beyond the Fence: Anatomy of a Border Enclave.*

———

MARTINA TAZZIOLI is a Lecturer in the Department of Geography at the University of Swansea. She previously held postdoctoral research positions in the Mediterranean Sociology Laboratory (LAMES/LabexMed) at the University of Aix–Marseille and the University of Oulu (Finland). She received her Ph.D. in politics from Goldsmiths, University of London. She is the author of *Spaces of Governmentality: Autonomous Migration and the Arab Uprisings* (2014), coauthor of *Tunisia as a Revolutionized Space of Migration* (2016), coeditor of *Spaces in Migration: Postcards of a Revolution* (2013), and coeditor of *Foucault and the History of Our Present* (2015). With Nicholas De Genova, she coordinated and coedited the collaborative writing project involving 15 co-authors (including several of the contributors to this volume), on "Europe/Crisis: New Keywords of 'the Crisis' in and of 'Europe,'" published by *Near Futures Online* (2016). She is also part of the editorial board of the journal *Materialifoucaultiani* (www.materialifoucaultiani.org).

INDEX

Aalberts, Tanja E., 74, 117n21
abandonment, 4, 28, 167–68, 170, 172, 175–76, 179, 181, 183, 238. *See also* abjection; Choucha camp (Tunisia-Libya border)
abjection, 142, 175, 184n4, 214, 240, 264, 269–70, 278, 281; and deportation, 142
Aboubacar, Razak, 152
Aegean Sea, 16, 33n4, 35n16. *See also* Mediterranean Sea
Aeneid (Virgil), 132
Afghanistan, 18, 35n19, 84, 235, 238, 239, 247, 251, 254n10
Afghans, 30, 35n19, 153, 216, 235–51, 253n4, 254n10; British and French collaboration around deportations of, 153
Africa, 12, 18, 26, 28, 33n4, 41, 43, 61n5, 69–74, 83, 85, 88, 129, 133–36, 138, 139n2, 141–64, 269. *See also* Ceuta (Spain); Canary Islands (Spain); Melilla (Spain); North Africa; West Africa
Africans, 20, 22, 28, 41, 43, 64, 73, 77, 81, 85–88, 90, 120–22, 126, 133, 135, 141–64, 167, 175, 191, 192, 226, 255, 259, 263, 266–67, 275
Agamben, Giorgio, 171. *See also* Exception (governmental logic of)
agency, 16, 49, 97, 236, 266; critique of concept of, 39, 50–51, 53, 56, 60. *See also* appropriation; autonomy of migration; subjectivity
Agier, Michel, 66

agriculture, 30, 131, 255–82
airports: as borders, 105, 129, 198, 206, 218; in deportations, 143, 146, 151
Aksaray (Istanbul neighborhood), 196, 197, 201
Algeria, 77, 87, 122, 124, 127, 139n2, 143, 155–56, 159, 182–83; deportations from Tamanrasset into Mali, 155–56
Algerians, 135, 246
Alioua, Mehdi, 105
alter-globalization movement, 162
Al-Wardia (detention center in Tunis), 182–83
Amnesty International, 68
Amsterdam, Treaty of (1997), 34n13
Andrijasevic, Rutvica, 213
antiracism, 61n3, 162. *See also* racism; solidarity movements
Appel, Hannah, 138
appropriation: of mobility, 17, 25–26, 37–63, 97; of space, 18, 98, 115, 279; of resources, 63n16. *See also* agency, critique of concept of; resistance, critique of concept of; subjectivity
Arab countries, 43
Arabs, 15–16, 43
Arab uprisings, 96, 108
Aradau, Claudia, 181
Ardener, Edwin, 269
Asad, Talal, 1
Asia, 24, 41, 61n5
Asians, 41

camps (continued)
(Tunisia-Libya border); detention;
Gran Ghettò (migrant farmworkers
camp, Italy); hosting centers (for
migrants/refugees); "Jungle, The"
(Calais, France)
Canary Islands (Spain), 70–76, 82–85, 88,
139n8
Cape Verde, 73, 76
capitalism, 5, 21, 30, 35n18, 89, 98, 125,
136–38, 149, 188, 214, 243, 256, 259–61,
264, 266, 268, 272–74, 279–80; and
urban space, 273. See also crisis
(capitalist/economic/financial); labor;
neoliberalism
Capitanata Plain (Puglia, Italy), 30, 255–82
capo. See gang-masters (in agricultural
labor)
"Capo Free, Ghetto Off" (resolution of
the regional government of Puglia,
Italy), 268–69, 282n11
capture, apparatus of, 26, 28, 55, 60, 63n14,
174, 178, 180, 225
caravans, as cross-border form of protest
mobilization, 23, 163
Carr, Matthew, 33n6
Cassarino, Jean-Pierre, 118n24
Castro, Américo, 133, 140n11
Center for the Temporary Stay of Migrants
(CETI) (Melilla, Spain), 121–22.
See also camps (for migrants/refugees);
detention; reception
Centre for Migration, Information, and
Management (CIGEM) (Bamako,
Mali), 158–61
Ceuta (Spain), 65, 69, 71, 76–77, 79, 85–87,
120, 124, 127, 128, 137, 138n1, 139n8, 143,
149, 152, 159. See also Melilla (Spain)
Chakrabarty, Dipesh, 179
Channel Tunnel, 10, 248
Charlie Hebdo (French satirical
magazine), 16, 35n17
Choucha camp (Tunisia-Libya border),
28, 165–84

Christianity, 12, 128, 131–33, 135–36,
139n10, 227
Christmas Island (Australia), 137
CIMADE (Comité inter-mouvements
auprès des évacués) (NGO), 159
circulation, 41, 97, 102, 163, 241, 243, 247.
See also mobility (human)
cities. See urban space
citizenship, 14, 28, 31, 58, 132, 138, 145,
152, 157–58, 164, 233, 235, 236, 241, 253,
254n7, 266, 274, 284–89, 292, 294–97,
298n3; and the deported, 157; and diaspora, 157–58; "failed," 298n3; rejected,
164; in Turkey, 191–92. See also citizenship (EU)
citizenship (EU), 19, 23, 90, 140n12, 143,
236, 240, 261. See also free mobility (in
Schengen area)
clandestine migration, 37, 43–44, 54, 57,
61n1, 96, 104–5, 110, 114, 115n1, 117n17,
128, 154, 160, 213, 252. See also illegality
(migrant); illegalization (of migrants/
refugees); imperceptibility; invisibility
Cold War, 18–19, 89
Collettivo RicercAzione, 276
Cologne (Germany), 15–17
colonialism, 18, 24, 35n18, 98–99, 116n9,
127, 132–33, 135, 138, 147, 149–50,
226, 256, 267–69, 282n9. See also
postcoloniality
Common European Asylum System,
253n2. See also asylum; Dublin
Regulation
commons, the, 58, 98, 274; practices of
commoning, 272, 281. See also mobile
commons (concept of)
communitization (EEC/EU), 143, 153.
See also Europeanization; harmonization
compliance, 12, 57, 113, 177, 268
complicity, 13, 52, 110–11, 147, 149, 155,
164, 241, 285, 296
confinement, vii, 169, 221, 225–26, 244;
self-, 225–26. See also detention
Congo, 155

135; and urbanity, 13, 131–32. *See also* Europeanization; European Question; Orientalism; race; whiteness

European Parliament, 140n13, 142, 153, 160. *See also* European Union (EU)

European Question, 1, 23–24, 89–90, 120

European studies, 22, 24, 32

European Union (EU), 3, 5, 12, 14, 15, 22–27, 29, 30, 34nn12–13, 34n15, 35n16, 35n19, 37–39, 41–42, 46, 49, 61n1, 62n11, 62–63n12, 64–68, 70, 73, 76–79, 85, 86, 88–91, 95, 103, 105–9, 113, 114, 116n13, 116n15, 118n24, 120, 124–25, 128–29, 134–38, 139n6, 140nn12–13, 142–46, 149–50, 153–55, 157–61, 167, 177, 178, 185–208, 208nn2–3, 215–17, 220, 222, 225–28, 231n3, 231n7, 234–36, 240–43, 259, 267, 287–89; British exit from, 22; as experiment, 24. *See also* citizenship (EU)

Euro-skepticism, 135

EUROSUR (EU external border surveillance system), 77–78

Eurotunnel, 10, 248

EU-Turkey deal (March 18, 2016), 35n16, 62–63n12, 67, 208n3, 209n8

everyday life, 31, 172, 180, 224, 233, 236, 251, 274

Evros River (border of Bulgaria, Greece, and Turkey), 31, 198, 219, 221

Exarcheia (Athens neighborhood), 217

exception (governmental logic of), 9, 34n11, 69, 102, 129, 137, 170–74, 268

excess (concept of), 29–30, 38, 49, 143, 179, 182, 210–31, 253, 270

exclusion, 11, 110, 113, 129, 132, 142, 143, 227–28, 240, 260–62, 269, 275, 278; and asylum, 171, 181–82; and Europeanness, 120, 135, 138; and humanitarianism, 173. *See also* differential inclusion (concept of); illegality (migrant); illegalization (of migrants/refugees); subordinate inclusion (concept of)

"expedited removals," 122–24

expelled migrants, 28, 141–64. *See also* deportation; deportees

expulsion. *See* deportation

externalization (of borders), 12, 21, 24, 32, 33n2, 34n15, 73, 88, 91, 104–5, 118n24, 124–25, 143, 153, 167, 177–78, 189–90, 215, 229, 267; and "transit," 190. *See also* bordering; "transit"

Eyezo'o, Oscar, 152

Facebook, 123, 135, 194. *See also* mobile commons (concept of)

family reunification, 48–49, 51, 52, 161, 195–96, 200–201, 204, 212, 218, 221–22; and asylum, 233

fascists: in Greece, 225; in Italy, 244. *See also* racists

fascist states, 285

Fassin, Didier, 69, 92n7, 240, 244

fingerprinting, 39–40, 50, 53, 62nn9–10, 181, 187, 199, 204–7, 219, 237–38, 242, 247, 253n2, 254n11; as fixation of relation to a particular state, 204; as infiltration of borders into the body, 242. *See also* biometrics; EURODAC

Fischer-Lescano, Andreas, 101

Foggia (Italy), 257, 271

"Fortress Europe" (discourse of), 61n3, 267

Forum for a Different Mali (FORAM), 154

Foucault, Michel, 29, 41, 60, 63n14, 63n16, 94n29, 102, 108, 117–18n23, 211–12, 222–27, 229–30, 295; on biopolitics, 108, 117–18n23; on circulation, 41, 102; in *Discipline and Punish*, 295; in "Lives of Infamous Men," 29, 211–12, 222–27, 229–30. *See also* governmentality

France, 10–11, 14, 46, 69, 91, 105, 112, 118n28, 127, 139n7, 147–48, 150, 153, 155, 157, 160–61, 163, 190, 196, 201–4, 216, 240, 246–47, 254n13, 285; as virtual detention center, 202. *See also* Calais (France)

freedom, securitized, 31, 283–98

freedom of movement, 5, 6, 17, 24, 57, 113, 140n12, 152, 155, 163, 171, 213, 273

freedom of the seas (concept of), 99, 102

free mobility (in Schengen area), 14, 19, 34n12, 153, 200, 236, 241, 247. *See also* freedom of movement; Schengen agreement; Schengen area

Freire, Paulo, 278

Friedrich, Hans-Peter (German Interior Minister), 216

Frontex (European border management agency), 38, 71, 73, 76–79, 91, 105–6, 154, 216

Gaddafi, Muammar (Libyan dictator), 88, 108, 112

Gammeltoft-Hansen, Thomas, 74, 117n21

gang-masters (agricultural labor), 259, 262–64, 272, 277; as extensification of supervision, 263–64; and race, 263

Garelli, Glenda, 68, 236

gender, 15–16, 130, 132, 141, 190, 195, 200, 220, 228, 236, 250–51, 259, 262, 264–65, 281n7, 284, 292, 294

geopolitics, 22, 98, 101, 108, 167, 256

geopower (concept of), 97, 105, 107

Germany, 11–13, 16, 23, 33n6, 35n16, 134, 139n7, 140n12, 151, 158, 195, 197–201, 206, 216, 218–22, 226–27, 237–39, 246, 254nn9–10, 254n12, 285

ghettos (of deportees, in Tinzawa- ten, Mali), 155. *See also* camps (for migrants/refugees); Gran Ghettò (migrant farmworkers camp, Italy)

Gibraltar, Strait of, 31, 76, 80–83, 87–88

Giordano, Cristiana, 239

global border regime, 6, 88, 106; as global apartheid, 241

Goldberg, David Theo, 226–27

Golden Dawn (Greek fascist movement), 225

Gourougou Mountain (Morocco), 121–22, 124, 126, 138. *See also* Melilla (Spain)

governmentality, 9, 24, 33n5, 34n11, 97, 104, 108, 113, 114, 169, 174, 213, 242. *See also* border regime (concept of); sovereignty

Gramsci, Antonio, 254n14

Gran Ghettò (migrant farmworkers camp, Italy), 30, 255–82; as affront to state sovereignty, 268–70

Great Britain. *See* United Kingdom

Greece, 2–3, 11–12, 29, 33n4, 35n16, 63n12, 65, 71, 79, 93n11, 134, 185, 190, 192, 196–99, 202, 204, 206, 208n3, 208n5, 210–12, 215–30, 231n7, 236–38, 253–54n5, 254n12, 267; ancient, 132

Greek Council for Refugees, 217, 218

Gregory, Derek, 18

"grey labour" (concept of), 261

Grosz, Elisabeth, 97

Grotius, Hugo, 99

Guardia Civil (Civil Guard, Spain), 70–71, 73, 76–78, 81–83, 85–87, 91, 93n12, 93n23, 122–23, 139n5

"guest" (as legal status, in Turkey), 188. *See also* temporary protection

guestworker programs, 104, 134, 139n7

Gypsy. *See* Roma

Hage, Ghassan, 195, 252

Hamburg (Germany), 247–48; refugees of Lampedusa in, 170

Hardt, Michael, 213

harmonization, 153, 207, 242, 288. *See also* communitization; Europeanization

Harvey, David, 131

Hera (Frontex maritime patrol mission). *See* Joint Operation Hera (Frontex maritime patrol mission)

Hess, Sabine, 190, 202

Heyman, Josiah, 72

Hirsi (legal case), 76, 79, 117n19

Holland. *See* Netherlands

hosting centers (for migrants/refugees), 121–22, 174–78, 180, 181, 184n9, 238–39, 243–44, 246, 248, 250; at Medenine (Tunisia), 174–78, 184n9; at Melilla

immigration/asylum law; international law; maritime law

"left-to-die boat" case, 95–119. *See also* boats ("migrant"); deaths (migrant/refugee); shipwrecks (border-crossing)

liberal democracy, 23, 31, 90, 102, 116n15, 150–51, 157, 177, 178, 283–98

Libya, 7, 18, 28, 31, 33n4, 35n16, 35n18, 66, 76, 79, 88, 96, 107–9, 111, 117n16, 118–19n28, 143, 156, 159, 165–66; refugees from (at Choucha camp, Tunisia), 165–84. *See also* Lampedusa (Italy); "left-to-die boat" case

Liechtenstein, 234

Lipothy, Robert Alain, 152

London (city), 30–31, 248–50, 286, 291

London (as metonym for UK government), 68

Macedonia (Republic of), 11, 35n19

Madrid (city), 73, 78, 91

Madrid (as metonym for Spanish government), 76, 86

"Mafia Capitale" scandal (Italy), 244

Maghrebi (as racial category), 81

Mali, 18, 28, 31, 139n5, 141–64

Malian Expelled Migrants Association (Association Malienne des Expulsés, AME), 28, 141–64

Malians, 139n5, 141–64

Malmström, Cecilia (EU Home Affairs commissioner), 77–78

Malta, 7, 11–12, 65–66, 75, 107, 112, 117n21, 118–19n28. *See also* Lampedusa (Italy); "left-to-die boat" case

March of Hope (migrant/refugee mobilization, Budapest), 11–12

Mare Clausum (book by John Selden, 1635), 99

Mare Liberum (book by Hugo Grotius, 1609), 99

Mare Liberum (international legal concept of the freedom of the high seas), 74, 99. *See also* maritime law

Mare Nostrum (operation of Italian Navy), 28, 64, 67–68, 76, 79, 82, 87–88, 94n27, 174, 181. *See also* Lampedusa (Italy); Mediterranean Sea; rescue

Mariko, Oumar (Malian left-wing politician), 149

maritime borders, 2, 7, 24, 33n2, 66, 69, 71, 78, 79, 87, 89, 92, 93n11, 93n23, 95–115, 216. *See also* Aegean Sea; Mediterranean Sea

maritime law, 98–107. *See also* international law

Maritime Search and Rescue (SAR), International Convention on, 101. *See also* search and rescue zones (SAR)

Martin, Trayvon, 293

Marx, Karl, 259, 282n8

Massey, Doreen, 194

Mauritania, 73, 76, 79, 83, 143, 155–56

Mbembe, Achille, 269, 270–71, 273

McKeown, Adam, 242

Médecins du Monde (NGO), 159

Medenine (Tunisia), 166, 170, 174–78; 184n9

Medico International (NGO), 159

Mediterranean Sea, 1–4, 7, 26–27, 33n2, 33n4, 34n8, 38, 44, 63n12, 64, 68, 75–76, 78, 84–86, 88, 95–115, 116n10, 118–19n28, 120, 131–33, 143, 172, 174, 175, 181, 216, 227, 265, 267; and human trafficking, 7; and Mare Nostrum, 28, 64. *See also* Aegean Sea; boats ("migrant"); deaths (migrant/refugee); rescue; shipwrecks (border-crossing); violence

Melilla (Spain), 26–27, 64–65, 68–71, 79, 85–86, 92n2, 120–38, 138n1, 139n3, 139n6, 139n8, 143, 149, 152, 159; violence at border, 64, 68, 121, 149. *See also* Ceuta (Spain)

Mérimée, Prosper, 132

Merkel, Angela (German Chancellor), 35n16

methodological nationalism, 241

politics of recognition, 179

Portugal, 135, 190, 191

postcoloniality, 18, 21, 23–24, 89, 104, 147, 148–50, 226, 256, 267–68; and deportation, 147, 155; and ghettos, 266–67. *See also* colonialism; "European" Question; race; racism

poverty, 9, 15, 20, 44, 47, 86, 88, 128, 134, 139n3, 149, 220, 239, 243, 249–50, 272, 293, 296, 298n3

Povinelli, Elizabeth, 179

precarity, 4, 16, 21, 59, 106, 202, 221, 225–28, 230, 237, 242–48, 261, 274–75

presence, politics of, 6, 167, 178–79, 182, 268

privatization (of border control), 5, 40, 117n21, 124–25, 158, 238, 244, 248–49. *See also* neoliberalism; outsourcing (of border control)

profiling: in assessment of asylum claims, 173; in assessment of visa applications, 45–49, 53, 57–58, 62n7, 67; racial, 217, 226, 289. *See also* bureaucracy, and discretion; discretionary power (bureaucratic)

prostitution. *See* sex work

protection (of migrants/refugees), 8, 9, 17, 72, 149, 153–55, 168–70, 173, 175, 177, 178, 182, 187–88, 196, 201, 218, 234, 236–37, 240, 243, 249, 271, 275

Puglia (Italy), 30, 255–82

pushbacks, 26, 64, 76, 79, 85, 92n2, 123–24, 253n5. *See also* deportation; *Hirsi* (legal case)

Qamishli (Syria), 195, 197, 200–201

race, 1, 14–16, 20–24, 81, 86, 92, 122, 126, 132–33, 137, 211–12, 226–27, 229–30, 242, 256, 263, 266–68, 275, 287–89, 293, 296, 297–98n3; and labor organization, 263; and migrant/refugee deaths, 21–22; and perceptibility, 221–22, 226; and "purity of blood,"

133, 139n10. *See also* racism; whiteness; white supremacism

racial profiling, 217, 226, 289. *See also* racism

racism, 4, 15, 16, 22, 23, 88, 135, 190, 217, 260, 275, 293; anti-Muslim, 14–17, 23, 35n17, 132. *See also* antiracism; persecution; race; whiteness; white supremacism

racists, 4, 15–16, 23, 217, 225. *See also* racism

raids (immigration), 139n2, 250, 283, 297. *See also* Xenios Zeus (Greek police operation)

railway stations, 11, 180, 181, 238; in Budapest, 11; in Rome, 238

Rancière, Jacques, 157; conception of the aesthetic as partition of the sensible, 105, 110

rape, 15–17, 219, 222, 228

Ras Jadir (Tunisian border post), 165–66, 176, 178

readmission agreements, 69, 76, 139n2, 147, 153–56, 160, 189, 216; and Dublin Regulation, 242; EU-Turkey, 216; as "migration clause" in economic partnerships, 154; and "transit" countries, 189–90. *See also* deportation; Dublin Regulation; EU-Turkey deal; return (agreements/directives/policy)

rebordering, 11–13, 134, 208n2, 214, 216, 288, 292. *See also* bordering

reception, 14, 28, 66, 69, 77, 82, 146, 159, 164, 167, 173, 184n10, 199, 233, 236, 238, 242, 244–45, 249, 251. *See also* detention; hosting centers (for migrants/refugees); "refugee management" (discourse of)

recognition, politics of, 179

Reconquista (in Spain), 133, 135

Red Crescent/Croissant Rouge, 83, 174, 177

Red Cross, 66, 69, 72, 81–84, 90, 176, 180

refugee (as category), 9. *See also* asylum-seeker (as category); mobility (human), governmental categories of